PELICAN BOOKS

A SOCIAL HISTORY OF ENGLAND

Asa Briggs was born in 1921 in Keighley, Yorkshire. He was educated at Sidney Sussex College, Cambridge, and in 1945 he became a Fellow of Worcester College, Oxford. He has been Provost there since 1976. From 1966 to 1976 he was Vice-Chancellor of the University of Sussex.

He has written many articles and books on nineteenth- and twentieth-century history, including *Victorian Cities*, *Victorian People*, *The Age of Improvement* and four volumes of *The History of Broadcasting in the United Kingdom*. He also wrote the introduction to the latest edition of Trevelyan's *English Social History*. He has been President of the English Social History Society since its foundation, and from 1976 to 1986 was Chairman of the Heritage Education Group.

Asa Briggs is married and has four children. He was made a Life Peer in 1976.

D0875002

A
SOCIAL HISTORY
OF ENGLAND

ASA BRIGGS

SECOND EDITION

PENGUIN BOOKS

ACKNOWLEDGEMENTS

The draft of the first edition of this book was read by my colleagues Professor Barry Supple and James Campbell. The fact that it was completed within a reasonable time owed much to the meticulous labours of my editor, Vicky Hayward. In the process, however, it was cut, often drastically. This completely rewritten new edition restores some of the cuts, introduces new material and includes a selective reading list.

I am grateful to many readers of the first edition who wrote to me with queries and comments, to Margaret Stevens and Carol Freeland for the retyping, and, above all, to my friend Dr B. Mellor for reading the new proofs.

PENGUIN BOOKS

Published by the Penguin Group
27 Wrights Lane, London w8 5tz, England
Viking Penguin Inc., 40 West 23rd Street, New York, New York 10010, USA
Penguin Books Australia Ltd, Ringwood, Victoria, Australia
Penguin Books Canada Ltd, 2801 John Street, Markham, Ontario, Canada l3r 1b4
Penguin Books (NZ) Ltd, 182–190 Wairau Road, Auckland 10, New Zealand

Penguin Books Ltd, Registered Offices: Harmondsworth, Middlesex, England

First published in Great Britain by Weidenfeld & Nicolson 1983
First published in the United States of America by The Viking Press 1984
Published in Penguin Books 1985
Second edition published in Pelican Books 1987
3 5 7 9 10 8 6 4 2

Filmset in Bembo (Linotron 202) by
Rowland Phototypesetting Ltd,
Bury St Edmunds, Suffolk
Made and printed in Great Britain by
Richard Clay Ltd, Bungay, Suffolk

CONTENTS

LIST OF MAPS AND FIGURES

MAPS

FIGURES

PREFACE

No nation has carried its whole past so completely into the present. With us historical associations are not matters of rhetorical reference on great occasions; but they surround the Englishman in everything that he does, and affect his conception of rights and duties on which national life is built.

Mandell Creighton, *The English National Character*, 1896

A people without history
Is not redeemed from time, for history is a pattern
Of timeless moments. So, while the light falls
On a winter's afternoon, in a secluded chapel
History is now and England.

T. S. Eliot, *Four Quartets*, 1943

The English Character is not only stable and uniform, but various and heterogeneous; it is at once obvious and elusive, and every generalization must be not so much qualified as confounded.

Henry Steele Commager, *Britain through American Eyes*, 1948

OF THE many kinds of history, social history was often thought of in the past as more trivial than constitutional, political or military history. They dealt with great events; it dealt with everyday things. And even when economic history was taken into the reckoning and social history was bracketed with it, as it usually has been, the economic was felt to come first. Ways of life were considered less 'fundamental' than standards of living.

In recent years, however, all this has changed. Social history has now become a favourite kind of history, and as its range and methods have expanded, it has attracted more and more serious study. There are important monographs, some of them highly sophisticated, dealing with almost every period and almost every problem. Furthermore, the subject has come to attract theoreticians, many of whom use concepts and techniques derived from current sociological analysis. There are dangers in the new approach just as there were weaknesses in the old. In particular, it sometimes concentrates more on abstractions than on people. The time is ripe, nonetheless, for a preliminary attempt at a synthesis covering the centuries, difficult though the task may be.

There is particular difficulty when the task is undertaken by a single historian working on his own. First, he is confronted with such a massive volume of evidence, verbal and visual, that it is impossible for him to consider more than a minute fraction of it. Second, when he turns, as he must, to what other historians, not least social historians, have written, there are innumerable gaps. The guidance which such historians provide for him is, therefore, strictly limited. Third, since the techniques of historical analysis have become increasingly varied and sophisticated, he will be in a position to employ only a limited number of them with the necessary skills. At the same time, he has advantages over a group of historians tackling the separate periods in which they are specialists and presenting their individual chapters as a synthesis. He can be more consistent in his judgements and more able to point to continuities and discontinuities in the story. Provided that he takes his readers into his confidence by pointing to what is unknown as well as to what is known, he can serve as an honest and reliable guide.

The need for a synthetic history has increased rather than diminished just because the study of history in schools and universities has changed. It rarely concerns itself now with 'coverage'. Whole periods are left out and more attention is paid in teaching to the techniques and uses of history than to its content. Fortunately, adults studying history, particularly local history or family history, do not choose to limit their curiosity; and for this and other reasons general readers, if not specialist historians, continue to demand history as story or as synthesis.

They set an example, though it should be obvious to school and university historians that however much they may choose to specialize, they will carry with them, like general readers, some version, however patchy and in places obscure, of human history 'as a whole' and of the history of England in particular. For equally obvious reasons it is desirable that this version should be less murky than it often is.

There can, of course, be no single definitive social history of England, whether written by several hands or one. History thrives on argument and social history, which for me, as for most social historians, is concerned with processes more than with events, is often difficult to chart, let alone to interpret or to explain. Moreover, the argument, like the processes themselves, looks different in the light not only of changing contemporary scholarship but of changing contemporary political, social and economic circumstances. This volume then, is *a* social history of England written by one particular social historian in one particular place at one particular point in time. It is the product of years of both study and talk, going back beyond both my teaching years and my undergraduate days in Cambridge to my Yorkshire upbringing in an industrial town on the edge of the moors, as distinctive an environment as a seaport, a cathedral city or a Suffolk village.

I owe an immense debt, of course, to many other historians, English and non-English, some of whose approaches and conclusions contrast sharply with my own; and their work is mentioned in the brief bibliographical notes to each chapter which, like my history itself, are necessarily selective. For me, as for a new generation of social historians represented in those notes, social history is neither peripheral nor trivial. It is the history of society, a term which itself requires examination. It is concerned both with 'structures' and with processes of change. Nothing is irrelevant to it, nor can it dispense with any evidence, even the most ephemeral. Although there is an obvious necessity to relate it to economic and demographic history, both of which are concerned with human subsistence, it cannot ignore cultural history, which reveals how a society expresses itself in arts, crafts, folklore and religion. Nor can it ignore geography, to which I hope to turn in more detail later in a complementary volume to this one.

As for the political element in social history, which in my view should never be left out, it is important that it should be comprehensive in coverage. While it is part of the appeal of social history that it illuminates the experience of people who left no name behind them and who were often the victims of the power systems of their day, it cannot forget people of power. It must turn to the court and to the cabinet, to the party meeting and to the business – or trade union – conference as much as to the field or the furnace. It must take account of the drawing-room as much as the kitchen or the garage or the bedroom. It must reveal not only how different groups in society considered themselves but how they were related to other groups in fact and in their own minds. It is the relationships which are crucial.

The social history of England is fascinating both in itself and because it has been felt to be directly relevant also – either as model or, more recently, as warning – to the history of other societies, even those with a different cultural heritage. There are, in fact, no easy lessons to be derived from it, no commanding theses. In particular, it is a mistake to see everything leading inexorably – either triumphantly or depressingly – towards the present. We can usefully search for tendencies and lines of direction, but we must often be content to take the past on its own terms, and to note foregone options as well as realized choices. There is comedy in the story and there is tragedy.

Six features of my own approach should be identified from the start. First, I try to focus on experience, the experience of individuals and of groups, shared or contrasting, rather than on concepts, although these must be part of the scaffolding. Second, and because of such focusing, I am as much drawn to the study of language, literature, art and music as to the social sciences, although I attach importance to both. Third, I do not view the scene exclusively from London: I have made much use of the growing volume of local and regional history, which I shall explore more fully and systematically in my complementary volume. Fourth, I am concerned with England, not with Scotland, Wales or Ireland, each of which has its own distinctive social and cultural history. Fifth, I do not hesitate to make cross-references through time: it is always interesting to examine what one age (or one generation) thinks of another. Sometimes it is through a distant mirror that we can most clearly see significant features of our own society and culture. Sixth, I maintain throughout that social historians must be explorers who should never stay in their studies: they must use their eyes and feet as much as their brains, watching what goes on in fields and gardens, in streets and shops. We learn through things as well as through ideas, and through reminiscences as well as through documents – or statistics. As the appeal of social history has increased in recent years, it has been enriched, therefore, by a deeper concern for visual and oral material.

The illustrations in the first edition of this book were an integral part of the exposition, and they included maps, prints, paintings and photographs. Although they are not incorporated in this revised edition, the interested reader is recommended to go back to the first edition to decide for himself how significant they are not as illustrations but as evidence. G. M. Trevelyan was not involved in the choice of the illustrations for the illustrated version of his *English Social History* which appeared in 1941 and for which I wrote a new introduction. I was involved directly in the choice of all of mine. Our two versions of English social history have been compared. My own background and many of my conclusions are as different from those of Trevelyan as is my approach, and I am separated from him by more than a generation. Yet I share his feeling for the poetry in the story. I also share his confident affirmation that as we attempt to reconstruct 'the whole fabric of each passing age', we get to know 'more in some respects than the dweller in the past himself knew about the conditions that enveloped and controlled his life'.

Asa Briggs

Worcester College, Oxford, March 1986

I am redye to revoke my sayenge, if any-thynge have passed my mouthe for want of lernynge and to submytte myselfe to correction, and my boke to reformatyon.

John Fitzherbert, *Boke of Husbandry*, 1534

1

UNWRITTEN HISTORY

Antiquities are history defaced, or some remnants of history which casually escaped the shipwreck of time.

Francis Bacon, *The Advancement of Learning*, 1605

Prehistory deals with fundamentals. It makes the child think about what really are fundamental necessities of life, and shows the ancient origin of familiar things.

D. P. Dobson, *The Teaching of Prehistory in Schools*, 1928

The traditional view of prehistory is now contradicted at every point.

Colin Renfrew, *Before Civilization*, 1973

ENGLAND is a small country – its area is only a sixtieth of that of the United States – yet it is the centre of an old society. When the American colonists declared their independence in 1776 they were proud of the newness of their continent. For most of the English, by contrast, age is an asset, not a liability; time at its best can be immemorial.

There are as many varieties of setting in the English countryside as there are layers of history in English society. The landscape reflects the complex geology and varied weather of the island. Yet it reflects much else besides. Some of the wildest twentieth-century landscapes, like the bleak heathland of Dorset, were cultivated very early in English history. 'England's green and pleasant land', as the eighteenth-century English poet William Blake called it, is as much the product of history as its 'dark satanic

mills'. The seashore has changed too, although the presence of the
sea and the nearness of all English places, however remote, to it
have been perpetually significant in English history, as significant
as mountains or deserts in other parts of the world. Nature in the
form of hill or valley, lake or fen, copse or forest, has often
consoled or inspired the English when events have numbed or
shocked, and the fear that nature may be threatened can still be
strong. 'This is our own, our native land.'

Yet it is at least as much the achievements – and, more recently,
the problems – of Englishmen as the delights of nature which
invite exploration of the island in the late twentieth century.
Contemporary explorers may be just as interested in industrial
archaeology, parliamentary democracy or the Law Courts as in
Windermere or Land's End. And if there is no need to choose too
firmly between them, it is because nature and culture – the latter a
word derived from the land – are inextricably entangled in Britain
as a whole.

The fact also that British achievements and problems are
themselves historically entangled with those of other developing
societies and cultures, some of them far across the oceans, encour-
ages large numbers of non-English explorers who might otherwise have stayed at home or nearer home to visit England. For
them, as indeed for Englishmen themselves, exploration without
explanation is not enough. Even if there are no easy answers, the
contemporary explorer will at least want to pose questions. The
two most obvious are, 'Why have the English done what they
have done?' and 'How and why have they become what they now
are?'

The historian himself will have to explore before he sets out to
explain, using every kind of evidence, visual, oral, written and
non-written, as grist for his mill. And if he wishes to explain the
present he will often have to go very far back in time. It was a
French rather than an English social historian, the great Marc
Bloch, who wrote that 'a society that could be completely
moulded by its immediate preceding period would have to have a
structure so malleable as to be virtually invertebrate.' Trevelyan,
whose *English Social History* was one of the great popular
successes of the 1940s, went back in his book no further than

'Chaucer's England', when 'England was beginning to emerge as a distinct nation, and when the English language, which in itself reflects so much social history, was beginning to come into its own.' There are reasons, however, for going much further back. Very early history focuses attention on man and nature, bones and rocks, island and mainland, geography and geology. It deals with what a 1928 handbook for prehistory teachers called 'fundamentals'. In this handbook less emphasis was placed on the limitations of the available evidence than on the centrality of the questions it posed; and it gave a different and more engaging reason why children should study prehistory. Since they were 'primitive beings' themselves, 'primitive occupations' would appeal to them.

Time scales have changed dramatically since the early nineteenth century. The biggest changes in our interpretations of the distant past, however, have taken place within the last twenty years as new schemes of dating, new discoveries of material remains and new assessments of available, usually uneven, evidence have come so fast that earlier surveys have been rapidly outdated. It is through our late-twentieth-century sense of time and space, so different from that of previous centuries in that it is governed by science, that we now step backwards and reach out to our most remote ancestors. This does not mean that we should ignore the journeys of past explorers of history when we make our own journeys through time, for the social historian learns much about social history both from myth and folklore and from out-of-date and discarded explanations. Nor does it mean that as we journey ourselves, seeking 'a reasoned history of man', all wonder will disappear. We soon appreciate, indeed, that a journey into the past has even more mystery about it than a journey into strange continents. There remains so much that we cannot explain. Stonehenge, for example, recently re-explored and redated, is still an enigma.

The explorers of the eighteenth and nineteenth centuries were the first to lengthen the time span of natural and human history and to seek to order it more systematically. Proud of their unprecedented material progress, they were willing, often through heated debate, to abandon old ways of thinking. They reflected with wonder on the fact that lumps of coal, for them a source of wealth and power, derived from great carboniferous forests which had flourished in the island millions of years before; indeed, it was an earlier member of the Trevelyan family who discovered twenty upright trees buried deep in a coalfield on the Northumbrian coast. The excavations necessary for the construction of railways and sewers led to other striking discoveries.

The Victorians noted also, with awe as well as with wonder, how lost animals, among them giant reptiles and elephantine mammals, models of which were displayed in the new Natural History Museum opened in 1881, had once roamed the island. They spent hours collecting and classifying flints, not always sure whether or not they were products of nature or human tools. They knew nothing of such scientific methodologies as pollen or bone analysis and radiocarbon dating, but in their absence they methodically divided prehistoric time into ordered periods, based on the objects that had survived, which they assembled in cabinets in their homes and displayed in their museums. This was an age of amateur enthusiasm for archaeology, although there were always more excursionists observing what was happening, or would-be buyers searching trade catalogues, than there were diggers in the field.

Geological periodization provided a guide to the classification of human history. Britain is a natural museum of geologists, who, in this context, like historians in others, must take the whole island and not just England as their unit of study. Victorian geologists found examples of rocks laid down in each of the great periods in the history of the earth, and they gave native British names to two of the four grand divisions of time which they called 'eras'. Thus, there was a Cambrian period, which took its name from Cambria (Wales), lasting about 100 million years, and a shorter and earlier Devonian period, initially an age of ferns and fishes, which lasted for about sixty million years. There were also Ordovician and Silurian periods: these less homely labels derived from the names of 'ancient British tribes'.

The labels tell us as much or more about the social and intellectual history of the nineteenth century than they do about the making of the earth itself. There were two points in the mysterious story, both of them involving contrasts, which seemed particularly striking then. While the physical making of the island had been achieved only through cosmic violence and a consequent total transformation of the environment, human history had been more peaceful and continuous. The very same Victorians who revolutionized geology and biology were proud of this relative absence of revolutions in English history, little imagining that some late-twentieth-century social historians would argue that England had suffered through their seldom having taken place.

The second point also contained a paradox. While it seemed to the Victorians that the personality of Britain was determined by its island status, it was now revealed that human history began at a time when Britain had been not an offshore island but part of a bigger landmass. In the most distant times, which had lasted until a post-glacial period about 10,000 years ago, bands of hunters had followed their game across the unsubmerged areas of the continental shelf to the grasslands of what is now England. The final separation, indeed, less than 9,000 years ago, was not 'very old'. It seemed strange that the natural links that had once existed between England and the outside world had been even more intricate than the multiple economic, social and cultural links of the busy nineteenth century when the modes of human communication had been transformed.

It was not easy, therefore, in the nineteenth century – nor, indeed, is it easy today – to pass serenely from the history of the earth to the history of men and women, for while, as one nineteenth-century writer put it, 'the only trustworthy annals of primitive humanity are written in the Book of Nature', the Book turned out to be neither easily accessible nor completely trustworthy. The so-called Piltdown skull, 'discovered' in Sussex in 1912, was claimed as a unique English proof of the infancy of man's development, but it turned out to be a fraud. Likewise, fanciful visual reconstructions of past modes of life, like those of the Glastonbury lake village in Somerset 'discovered' in 1888, contained an obvious element of caricature. The interpretation of the Book of Nature has been transformed only by spectacular advances in recent research, some of them centred in the laboratory. Quantitative analysis has become far more sophisticated: bones are studied not only to trace origins but also to reveal diseases; insect remains are analysed; and the explorer of the Somerset levels near Glastonbury now collects from the peat ancient pollen as well as flints. New attempts are being made to explain the sequence of change.

Before the development of the new scientific archaeology, the main key to the understanding of early Britain seemed a different one: a fuller understanding of other peoples, past and present. 'Archaeology is merely the past tense of anthropology,' wrote O. G. S. Crawford, founder in 1925 of the periodical *Antiquity* and himself a pioneer of new techniques of air photography applied to archaeology. Much of the anthropology was evolutionist and had nineteenth-century origins. There were, it was claimed, common evolutionary sequences to be traced in quite different parts of the world, beginning with hunters and progressing through food gatherers, farmers, metal workers and 'priests': in consequence, group 'mentalities' could be probed as well as material cultures. In a well-known series of prehistory books that were used in schools before the Second World War, Peake and Fleure introduced a whole gallery of 'types', identifiable in different places and through the 'corridors of time'. The first volume, published in 1927, was called *Apes and Men*, the second volume *Hunters and Artists* (there were very early animal paintings of exceptional interest in prehistoric caves), the third volume *Peasants and Potters* (the evidence of pottery was of such crucial importance to archaeologists that pots often mattered more than people) and the fourth, and final, volume *Priests and Kings* (social structures, it was maintained, required both religion and leadership, swords of the spirit and real swords that could be put to the test).

While geologists and archaeologists were lengthening the time span, therefore, they were contracting space: all mankind was deemed to be one in fundamentals, and the earliest social history of England, now seen simply as a particular example, could be worked out, at least partially, by processes of induction and deduction. When Early/Middle Neolithic female figures and phallic objects were found at Grimes Graves in Norfolk, for example, they could be, and were, related to a world-wide phenomenon, worship of the goddess of the earth.

Nonetheless, the nineteenth-century naming of the periods of human history, starting with the Stone Ages – Palaeolithic, Mesolithic and Neolithic – and running into written history through the Bronze and Iron Ages (the advent of metals was given special significance in the story) was related more to the materials men used and fashioned than to their values. It is no coincidence that the term prehistory was first used in England in 1851, the year when the Great Exhibition was displayed in the Crystal Palace. If the products of all nations in the nineteenth century could be assembled in witness of material progress, would it not be possible to periodize progress through the collection and display of the products of each of the different stages of man's past? Already, by 1851, Stone, Bronze and Iron Age periodization had made its way into England and, despite critical comments at the time that history could not be 'treated as a physical science and its objects arranged in genera and species', the classification had come to stay.

Eventually, in the course of decades of excavation, collection and research, all kinds of refinements were introduced into the classification, and the dangers of drawing too rigid boundaries between one period and another after the retreat of the ice 14,000 years ago were increasingly emphasized. Yet the framework persisted. Moreover, just as the labels attached to geological periods reflected British influence, the labels attached to geological collections reflected continental influence. The caves of Aurignac, for example, with their fascinating primitive art, gave their name to 'Aurignacian', to which British evidence from Creswell Crags in Derbyshire (one cave there bore the far later mythical name Robin Hood's Cave and another Mother Grundy's Parlour) was related. The quest for uniformities and links was relentless.

To account for English cultural affinities with Europe, archaeologists fell back on what has been called 'the invasion hypothesis'. Given that, at least as far as archaeologists were concerned, the dynamic of social history was either the movement

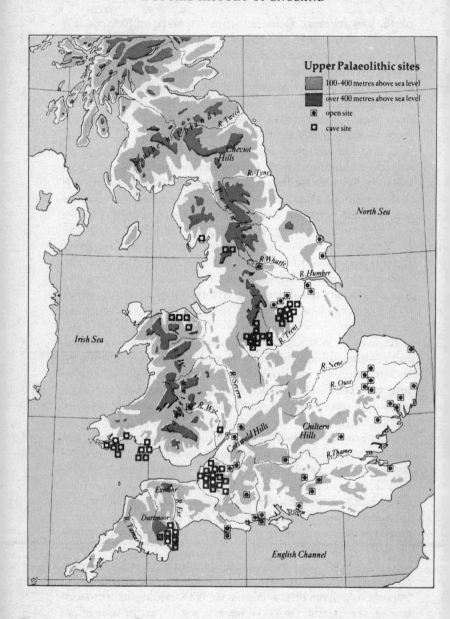

Upper Palaeolithic sites

of peoples (migration) or the transfer of arts and techniques (culture contact), and given also that Britain was an island, the dynamic of its early history had to be migration. The process had begun with the greatest of all early environmental transformations attributed to 'mankind', the coming of agriculture, which archaeologists traced back to a centre of origin in the Near East, from which domesticated wheat and barley, along with domesticated animals, had spread westward and northward. Since the wild ancestors of both the domestic crops and the domestic animals of Neolithic Britain were not native to the country, there had to be 'invasion' at the start. European barbarism was 'irradiated', as Gordon Childe put it, by 'Oriental civilization'; and while Britain was at the periphery of the process, it was nevertheless an inviting periphery for outsiders because of its estuaries and peninsulas. Childe, who did much to popularize the concept of prehistoric 'cultures', stressed that throughout prehistory the stage was occupied not by individual actors but by peoples, and that the drama lay in their 'differentiation, wanderings and interactions'. He was writing in this vein as a social historian, and his book *Prehistoric Communities of the British Isles* was published one year before Trevelyan's *English Social History*. Later in his life, Childe maintained also that prehistorians seek to distil from archaeological remains 'a pre-literate substitute for conventional politico-military history, with cultures instead of statesmen as actors and migrations in place of battles'.

Such a diffusionist approach, once so exciting, now seems restricted, although the notion of a culture (people plus an assembly of artefacts plus 'mentalities') survives as strongly as ever. There is a danger in concentrating too heavily on migrations across space. As more and more material from Britain has been studied systematically, site by site and region by region, more emphasis has, rightly, been placed on local adaptation to environment and, after the first settlements, on parallel development. In addition, Childe's phrase 'in place of battles' seems misleading. In telling the story of prehistoric times, it is no more possible to leave out the history of fighting than it is for the modern social historian to leave out politics, as Trevelyan tried to do. The novelist John

Fowles has perceptively suggested that 'if the best Stone Age tools are for handling wood and stone, the best Bronze Age ones are for killing or subjugating other human beings', and although his observation can be challenged, there can be no dispute about the existence of ancient violence. The skeleton of a grown man with a leaf-shaped flint arrowhead in his side has been found in a long burial mound south-west of Salisbury, Wiltshire, and one of the score of people interred in a long-chambered tomb at Wychwood forest on the edge of the Cotswolds was killed by an arrow that penetrated his right side from below, embedding itself in his backbone. The social history of any period has to be both comprehensive as well as sensitive, taking full account of prestige and power.

The 'dating revolution' of the last twenty years has forced re-examination of space as well as of time. Thus, while the conception of a Neolithic age has been pushed further back, the outer islands of Britain, including those in the far north, now play a more important part in archaeologists' work. In England itself familiar places like Stonehenge have taken on a new meaning: it has been shown that Stonehenge I was already old and that Stonehenge II had been built when the Abraham of the Old Testament was alive. The megaliths in western European countries, including those in southern England, were not grouped together as megaliths until the nineteenth century, but they are now known to be older than Mycenae in Greece. Stone circles are scattered throughout the British Isles. So are standing stones.

Many different sciences have contributed not only to a new chronology but also to a new interpretation of unwritten history, for as dates change in the aftermath of radiocarbon redating (which won Willard Libby a Nobel Prize in 1954), inevitably new questions emerge. While much guesswork is eliminated, there is greater scope for inference. Some archaeologists have tried to set limits to the latter: archaeologists, they suggest, should ask and answer only a limited range of questions determined by the data. Nonetheless, generalization, however difficult and even controversial, is being attempted, as six fundamental features of prehistoric society invite systematic study: subsistence, technology, social organization, trade and communication, culture and demography (the analysis of population).

The six features are obviously interdependent, as they are in later societies. Thus, subsistence clearly influenced population and vice versa. Likewise, technology and social organization influenced one another: technology affected farming methods – and, therefore subsistence – and social organization was clearly related both to trade and communication and to culture. It is possible to identify these features and point to relationships between them in the form of models even when empirical data is fragmentary and impossible to aggregate satisfactorily. There is usually room for detective work, and some of the pictures of society that we can now paint are far more convincing, if still sketchy and tentative, than the old faded illustrations of paleolithic camps and lake villages.

Subsistence is of fundamental importance in any society and archaeologists chase every scrap of evidence concerning the quest for food in prehistoric times. The Neolithic shift from dependence on hunting to the development of agriculture with cereal crops and domestic animals did not mean the end of hunting. Nor did settlement mean security. It meant, however, that food had to be stored, that boundaries had to be marked and that ancestry mattered. Intensive studies of the use of land and of coastal resources point to a complicated chronology, related to population and social organization, with some areas passing out of use through exhaustion and other areas being brought into cultivation. Within a narrower focus, great ingenuity has been shown recently in reconstructing diets, which included fish as well as meat and vegetables. Different sites have revealed different patterns of remains, suggesting that there was a ranking order.

One major question linked to subsistence, which arises also in relation to later societies, concerns what was left over by way of food after immediate needs were met – the so-called agricultural surplus. Was it the result of 'windfalls' or was it purposefully built up? It would have been impossible to build Stonehenge without a remarkable diversion from food-gathering pursuits, since a single stone of around thirty-five tons would have required 600 or 700 men, all tugging on hide ropes, to shift it. The same kind of calculations have been made in relation to megaliths in Cumbria, a part of the country where for centuries there were to be geographic obstacles both to effective subsistence farming and to easy communications. How was the diversion achieved?

Technological processes of every kind, including stone moving, can be deduced from a study of the tools and materials used for particular constructions. In particular, it was possible to do things with bronze that could not be done with flint, and with iron that could not be done with brass, and bearing this in mind periodization in terms of the sequence of Stone, Bronze and Iron Ages remains helpful. It must be recognized, however, first, that these materials could be – and were – complementary and, second, that since wood and leather have not normally survived, they are omitted from the list.

The links between technology and social organization always involve considerable speculation. Nonetheless, it is plausible to suggest, given the marked increase in the number of burial mounds in Wessex 4,000 years ago (mounds for single rather than communal burials) and the rich Early Bronze Age finds there, that populations had increased and that rank had begun to count for more than it had done previously in society. And thus we begin to reconstruct the whole fabric of the past, as Colin Renfrew has done. He has noted, for example, a diminished emphasis on the mobilization of manpower for public works and much more emphasis on the person, wealth and prestige of the chief and subchiefs. There were many signs of conspicuous consumption. An addendum is necessary. In dealing with social organization, much of the evidence relates to ways of death, or at least of burial, rather than to ways of life.

The study of the role of culture as a set of symbols, ultimately conveyed through 'art' and 'religion', often through material artefacts, has much concerned anthropologists and archaeologists. Subsistence never seems to have been all. Specifically English evidence is fragmentary, however, when compared with what has survived further east. There is little Palaeolithic art, although a horse engraving has been found on a rib fragment from Creswell Crags and a fish design has been traced on an ivory point from another Derbyshire cave. There are also small phallic objects of a later period which point to links between culture and fertility. The paucity of evidence has not inhibited the further generalization that there was a huge transformation in religious attitudes: looking down into the earth gave way to looking up into the sky.

Tracing the way in which material objects were moved from place to place often involves as much speculation as the diffusion of religious attitudes and rituals. Yet some of the evidence is reassuringly concrete. We can note in some detail patterns of movement of pottery, for example, and we have been able to trace back to early times both wooden trackways, which served as an element in land communication, and some survivals of communication by water. Clearly, trade and communication had become relatively sophisticated by the time of the Roman invasion, and, in fact, the Romans and Greeks had known of Cornwall as a source of precious metals long before that. We also know of changes of fashion: the switch from buttons to pins for fastening garments 2,500 years ago may be compared with the switch from buckles to shoestrings two centuries ago.

Demography, one of the most challenging areas of study for the social historian – if only because demographic data was collected for its own sake so late in history (there was no national census in England until 1801) – remains a problematic subject for these distant centuries. Yet all social history must rest on demography and economics; significantly, it was a far-reaching discussion of population growth in the eighteenth century before adequate data began to be collected that first pointed to the six fundamental features of a society and culture outlined here in relation to prehistoric society. They form not a sequence, but a circle.

As far as prehistory is concerned, until recently historians tried to do little more than exercise ingenuity in making estimates of the number of people on particular sites and their age and sex balance, or in suggesting how population pressures changed from time to time and whether or not the people in question were newcomers. The last issue remains important. However much we tire of invasion hypotheses, we know that there were many genuine newcomers in prehistoric times, the last of them 'Belgic' invaders from across the Channel who arrived less than a hundred years before Julius Caesar. It is possible perhaps to go further now, however, for estimates of population have changed as much as notions of time and space have done during the last twenty-five years, and our curiosity has increased accordingly. Simulation exercises have been carried out to re-enact how people actually lived on the foods available and how healthy they were. More revealing still has been the application of knowledge derived from later population and subsistence patterns to prehistoric times. Ambitious attempts have been made to construct local and British population aggregates. Thus, it has been suggested that in Upper Palaeolithic times there were between 250 and 5,000 people, that at the peak of the age of the hunters there were between 3,000 and 20,000 people (probably with considerable ups and downs of population), that in Neolithic times the population numbered between 10,000 and 40,000, in the Bronze Age between 20,000 and 100,000 and in the Iron Age between 50,00 and 500,000.

Fascinating though such estimates are and stimulating though it is to ponder on the six features of a society and culture as they then presented themselves, it remains more rewarding to return to ways of life on specific individual sites. The present-day explorer may start at Heathrow Airport, fifteen miles from London, where thousands of visitors from abroad arrive and depart every day. Archaeological evidence of ancient occupation 2,400 years ago was unearthed when work was being carried out on the airport runways during the 1950s; and it has subsequently been established that the airport is built on the site of an Iron Age settlement, which included a shrine. The people who lived and worshipped there were the kind of people whom the Romans encountered when they arrived in the island nearly 500 years later. It should be remembered, however, that these were not the first islanders. 'Who the first inhabitants of Britain were,' wrote the Roman historian Tacitus, 'whether natives or immigrants, remains obscure,' adding, somewhat patronizingly, that 'one must remember that we are dealing with barbarians'.

It is a short journey in space, but a long one in time, from Heathrow to Swanscombe, Kent, on the south side of the River Thames, twenty miles from London, where skull fragments were found in 1935; they date back to the Hoxnian interglacial period which is believed to have ended 250,000 years ago. The excavations at Swanscombe revealed hand-axes, knapped flints and butchered animal bones. At Kent's Cavern near Torquay excavations have revealed a Middle Palaeolithic 'hunters' base camp which was occupied until about 14,000 years ago; the rich remains found there include woolly mammoth and rhinoceros bones, as well as traces of the wolf, the hyena, the bear and, interestingly, given its later significance in English social history, the horse. Pollen analysis has suggested that grasses and herbs, willow, juniper and occasional pine, oak and lime trees were all growing; the artefacts include spearheads, blades and bone pins.

The early hunters did not necessarily live in caves, but they did make effective use of local materials, including bone. Thus, at Star Carr, a well-placed later hunters' site near Scarborough in Yorkshire that is no longer visible, almost all the materials found at the site could have been obtained within an hour's walk of the encampment, with the exception of iron pyrites, probably used for striking a light from flint: these are close in appearance to specimens from south Yorkshire coalfields. The importance of fire and heat in the hunters' world is obvious.

The world of Neolithic man had different horizons from that of the hunters. Coming from across the North Sea 6,000 years ago, Neolithic men and women cleared scrub and recently grown forest, made pastures for their animals and grew their own crops. They probably arrived in skin boats and, once settled, built small roughly rectangular dwellings, used light ploughs, mined flints and baked pottery. Such activities involved a new balance between instinct and experience and put a new premium on work: axes were in such demand that archaeologists even speak of stone-axe 'factories'. The Neolithic people were small in stature, seldom more than 5·5 feet tall, although they were capable of hard physical labour. We know little in detail of the processes whereby they settled in groups larger than individual families, nor do we know much about daily life in their families. What we do know is that they left behind them enduring monuments.

These mean more to twentieth-century scientists than they have meant to any previous generation. We now know from the monuments that the Neolithic story starts with cultures brought in by newcomers, the first of them identifiable in terms of a number of distinctive features: causewayed enclosures with embankments, houses with hearths, flint mines and long barrows (burial chambers usually over 100 feet in length). Windmill Hill, an early Neolithic causewayed camp in Wiltshire, is only 1·5 miles from a great stone circle at Avebury; and the other visible remains in a relatively small surrounding area – Stonehenge is only eleven miles distant – are so rich that G. M. Young, the twentieth-century cultural historian, was led to claim that the brooding sense of the distant past was stronger in this area than anywhere else in England. To create Silbury Hill, the biggest man-made prehistoric mound in Europe, twelve million cubic feet of chalk had to be moved. Young called historians 'the high priests of continuity' and a journey across the Wiltshire Downs along the Ridgeway (an ancient road crossed by the modern M4 motorway) 'a walk in the footsteps of three hundred generations'.

What makes this part of Wiltshire fascinating to the social historian is not just the sense of the very distant English past, but an equally strong sense that nature itself is a character in the story. Yet the loneliness of the scene today should not mislead. In Neolithic times, and in later phases of the Iron Ages, this was some of the most densely populated land in the country, as also were the Cotswolds, the Derbyshire hills and the Yorkshire wolds, all limestone areas with light soil, which could be more easily farmed with the tools of the period than the deeper, richer soils to be found in the river valleys.

There are so many layers of history in Wiltshire that the works of different generations have become confused. We now know that there were at least five stages in the construction of Stonehenge, the great ruin on Salisbury Plain sixty miles from Heathrow, the final stage of which was as long after the first as we are from the misty seventh century. We know, too, that the first builders of Stonehenge began their work not less than 1,800 years before the arrival of the Romans. They seem to have been determined that their monument should last: as the American novelist Henry James observed, 'it stands as lonely in history as it does on the great plain'.

There can be no doubt that different interpretations of Stonehenge by different generations, including our own, reveal almost as much about English social history as the monument itself does about the work of the successive generations of builders. In the twelfth century the chronicler Geoffrey of Monmouth placed the building of Stonehenge only seven centuries earlier, which would make it contemporary to Wansdyke, a huge fortified ditch originally fifty miles long. In the seventeenth century Stonehenge came to be associated with the Druids, the 'priesthood' whom the Romans encountered, while in the twentieth century it has come to be associated not only with scientists and computers but with hippies and policemen. In between, a different perspective was offered by William Stukeley, the pioneer eighteenth-century enthusiast for archaeology, who observed that its contemplation afforded 'the highest pleasure imaginable to a regular mind'.

The continuing puzzles of Stonehenge, like those of other monuments, including Silbury Hill and Durrington Walls, lie less in the vast amount of organized labour which went into its construction – eighty much prized blue stones appear to have been carried, mainly by water, a distance of 135 miles from Pembrokeshire in Wales – than in the uses to which the structure was put. Stonehenge I was built somewhere between 5,000 and 4,500 years ago; it has astronomical as well as archaeological interest. So also does Stonehenge II, as both Alexander Thom, who called the monument 'megalithic geometry in standing stones', and G. S. Hawkins, who wrote *Stonehenge Decoded*, have suggested in their detailed studies of its arrangement and orientation: the measurement of time and projection of the seasons were obviously of practical interest to its builders and users. Stonehenge II was the work of the so-called 'Beaker people' from the Rhine basin, the last major incursion of people to settle in England for over a millennium. They have been named after their well-made beaker-shaped pots with rich, reddish-brown surfaces, but they had other outstanding characteristics: they buried their dead singly in round barrows although they also practised cremation and employed metals. They probably mixed with, rather than subjugated, the existing population, and doubt has recently been cast on the extent to which they were innovators with a distinct culture.

Stonehenge III, the structure of which was substantially modified as sarsen (natural sandstone) stones were brought in from Marlborough, has been associated with the later so-called 'aristocratic' Wessex culture. Burials then were more rich and elaborate, and the burial barrows were often clustered together in cemeteries. Many interesting objects of copper, gold and the alloy bronze have survived from this period, as well as beads of faience, a blue vitreous paste, found in women's graves. (It has even been suggested that the richness of the women's graves might imply an improvement in their status after the Beaker period.) To what extent these relics genuinely represent the fullness of the culture has been a matter of argument; so also has the extent to which they imply dependence on improved technology (lathes) and increased trade. It has been argued instead that economic gains are based on a far more highly developed pastoral agriculture. A recent excavator of Stonehenge, R. J. C. Atkinson, claims that we now have evidence 'for the concentration of political power, for a time at least, in the hands of a single man, who alone could create and maintain the conditions necessary' for an undertaking on the scale of Stonehenge.

What political power meant in such a context is entirely a matter of conjecture; indeed, we might substitute for 'political' either 'coercive' or 'religious'. One point that seems clear is that there was in this period a greater specialization in society than ever before as metals were mined, mixed, fashioned and distributed. But beyond that there is more that is not clear, for there is as much mystery in the abandonment of major work on, and maintenance of, Stonehenge and other great stone circles as there used to be surrounding their construction.

The label Late Bronze Age is completely inadequate to cover the period before the Iron Age, or Ages, which began in the millennium before the Romans came. Although the changing use of bronze itself in ornaments and weapons can be traced from plentiful bronze hoards, it is not clear how much social change was associated with bronze in its different phases – in settlement patterns for example, or in the appearance of the landscape. That there was change has been emphasized recently. Good farm land was prized, and there were complex patterns of movement. What we know is severely limited, however, because of the accidents of survival. Archaeological exploration of the distinctive and continuous Deverel-Rimbury culture in Dorset, which flourished 1,400 to 1,000 years ago, reveals that hoeing irregular plots had given way to ploughing square 'Celtic fields' before the Iron Age and that there were 'cattle ranches' and 'storage pits'. Far away in the north of England, roofed round houses were being built with central posts, and in the east there is evidence from the Fens district of hitherto marginal land being farmed. Eight centuries before the Roman invasion, trade between England and the continent seems to have been increasing, but two centuries later it had contracted again. There seems also to have been more violence in society, possibly brought about by pressure on land generated by an increasing population and by climatic change. In weaponry the double-edged heavy Bronze Age sword displaced the older rapier: it was designed for slashing as well as for stabbing. Not surprisingly, bronze shields were in evidence too, and horse-gear could be elaborate with bridle bits and terret rings. There were also hill forts.

Iron weapons – and implements – were being produced in England less than 3,000 years ago, 600 years before the Roman invasion. Some were handsomely decorated. They suggest a society in which fighting was common. Iron technology, introduced from continental Europe, was at least equal in development to that of the Greeks and Romans, and although there is continuing argument about whether or not it was 'imposed' on previous inhabitants by migrants from outside the island, it seems clear that society was more fragmented. There are certainly important archaeological finds in the east of Yorkshire revealing direct foreign influence half a millennium before the Romans. In the north and west of England pastoral peoples seem to have favoured enclosed homesteads, in the Midlands and east open village settlements. In the south, however, the strongly fortified hill fort was a characteristic Iron Age feature. There were at least 3,000 of them, of all sizes, some of which, like the most famous, Maiden Castle in Dorset, were superimposed on older structures.

Neolithic farmers had built a causewayed camp at Maiden Castle centuries before, and in the Iron Age it was radically improved with an additional ditch and heightened ramparts; the height of the main sloping rampart, from the top of the walls to the bottom of the ditch, was now eighty-three feet. (This was the age of the sling as well as of the iron sword.) The interiors of some of the bigger forts, it has been suggested, now took on the appearance of towns: they were certainly planned with roadways, round houses and pits for storing corn, and they could be very densely built up. It was during these years that horses were beginning to stand out among the animals, and the White Horse at Uffington, on the chalk hillside close to the Ridgeway, putative ancestor of many later white horses on the hills (most of them produced during the last 200 years), may belong to this period; certainly, horses appear on Iron Age buckets and coins – the real horses of the period were slender-limbed, measuring 11·5 to 12·5 hands and were used to draw chariots which were eventually to have spoked, iron-tyred wheels. Oxen drew the plough and there was cross-ploughing to break up the soil. Iron axes were used to clear woodland. The religion of the period and its free-flowing curvilinear art were associated with sacred places beside streams and woods, and the economy was far more complex than that of previous periods. There was an increasing production of coins.

The nearer we get in time to the Roman invasion, the more archaeological evidence we have at our disposal, although it is still patchy and incomplete. It reveals the existence of tribal units bigger than the family, each with their own identity. Among them were the Trinovantes living north-east of the Thames, the Durotriges and the Dumnonii in the south-west, and the Brigantes, who held much of the Pennines and the adjacent plain in the north of England. We can trace in several areas the distribution both of single homesteads and of nucleated settlements, and we can survey Iron Age agriculture in which arable farming (with wheat and barley as the main crops) and pastoral, mainly sheep, farming were closely linked in varied and efficient cultivation patterns that depended on animal breeding, manuring and careful conservation of seed corn.

Technology in general was more varied than in previous periods. Pottery was produced by the fast-turning wheel introduced in the century before the Romans came, and there was a distinction between the coarse and better quality ware; textile spinning was assisted by bone, pottery or stone spindle whorls, as in previous periods, and weaving was now carried out on upright looms with clay weights and bone combs; iron, the metal which was to give its name to the age, was probably smelted in bowl furnaces. This was an age when the number of luxury items increased to meet the demands of a society in which consumption seems to have been socially stratified. Mediterranean wines were being imported, and with them went frequently ornate drinking vessels. There were highly decorated brooches, too, and tombs might contain mirrors as well as weapons.

But unwritten history remains full of mystery. How many newcomers were there, and when did they arrive? Did innovation depend on immigration? How did development in the south of England, particularly the south-east, the area best known to the Romans, relate to development further inland and in the north? Why were the first coins to be minted all gold coins, unsuitable for the ordinary purpose of exchange? Were they for tribute or for some other purpose? What part did women play in the economy? How were children brought up?

Written history begins with the society encountered by the Romans, which, together with the characteristic square-ploughed fields associated with that culture, was later described as Celtic. In fact, there is no ancient source to link the term 'Celtic' in any special way with England: it was only in the sixteenth and seventeenth centuries that scholars deduced that Gaelic and Welsh were derived from the language of the ancient Celts who had once inhabited England as well as Scotland, Wales and Ireland.

In one part of England, Cornwall, a Celtic language was still being spoken at that time, and then, as now, the names of many rivers and streams elsewhere in the country were Celtic: Aire, Avon, Dee and Derwent, Mersey, Severn and Thames. Leeds is the biggest modern provincial city with a Celtic name, and places like Thanet, Wight (in the Isle of Wight) and Craven, the beautiful fell country in Yorkshire, are also Celtic in origin. Nature and language moved closely together in unwritten history, and the link has survived.

What is surprising is that while we can produce a Celtic map of England, very few other Celtic words from that distant period have entered the language and stayed with us through the centuries, the best known of the few being the word 'ass' and the word 'combe', a small valley, which belongs more to the map than to the vocabulary. Far more Celtic words came into the language later, indirectly, through the French and Irish languages. There is, nonetheless, an old Celtic strain in the English inheritance which has been acknowledged by some writers. As A. L. Rowse, one of our best-known twentieth-century historians – himself from Cornwall – has most eloquently put it, 'Nineteenth-century historians were apt to regard us as Anglo-Saxon folk. In fact we are really an Anglo-Celtic people.'

2

INVASION, RESISTANCE,
SETTLEMENT AND CONQUEST

But the Romans came with a heavy hand,
And bridged and roaded and ruled the land,
And the Romans left and the Danes blew in –
And that's where your history-books begin.
                    Rudyard Kipling, *The River's Tale*, 1911

I should like to get a clear picture of the movements of people
spreading over the top of each other and getting continually mixed
up, but each still keeping something that it had from the beginning. One thinks with horror of the inconceivable suffering of
humanity at that time. Don't you think that an account which
disregarded individuals and told of the march of peoples, a short
staccato account, would paint a terrible picture but one from
which much could be learnt?
                    Alexis de Tocqueville, *Reflections on English History*, 1828

The Norman Conquest was a Good Thing, as from this time
onwards England stopped being conquered and thus was able to
become top nation.
                    W. C. Sellars and R. J. Yeatman, *1066 and All That*, 1930

THE ROMANS were the first invaders of Britain to document
their invasion. They had long known Britain as a remote
land beyond the ocean, they were aware that it was roughly
triangular in shape, and they knew also that there were contacts
between the peoples on either side of the Channel. After Julius
Caesar had conquered Gaul and received the submission of its

major tribes, it was tempting for him to think of an expedition to
Britain, if only for reasons of personal ambition and glory. He
carried out two expeditions, neither of which led to immediate
Roman settlement. Nothing was gained by the first except reconnaissance; the second was more successful, but brief. Gaul had
been conquered in only two seasons of campaigning, but no
Roman general was to land in Britain again for ninety-seven
years. No traces were left. Shakespeare was to recall centuries
later in *Cymbeline* that Caesar in 'a kind of conquest'

> was carried
> From off our coast, twice beaten and his shipping –
> Poor ignorant baubles! – on our terrible seas,
> Like egg-shells moved upon their surges . . .

There is a two-fold significance in the precise dates of Caesar's
invasions, 55 and 54 BC. First, English history thereafter is no
longer completely unwritten history. The Romans had a literature of their own, and Caesar himself was a writer as well as a
general, anxious to set down an account of what he had done.
From this time onwards, historians have access to a new kind of
evidence about England, although for the whole Roman period it
is episodic and patchy and we cannot reconstruct society on the
basis of it. We have to infer much from the evidence from other
parts of the Roman Empire. Second, the dates 55 and 54 BC
belong to a calendar which is itself new to the story. Precise dates
are less significant to social historians than the charting of longer-
term social processes, and the fact that Caesar's expeditions took
place half a century before Christ is of less significance to them
than the fact that the Celtic people of the Iron Ages, who were to
remain the majority of the population throughout centuries of
Roman occupation, were changing their habits both before
Caesar came and in the century between his expeditions and the
arrival of Claudius in AD 43. Nonetheless, the BC and AD chronology is important because it indicates that, through Rome,
England was first drawn into a Christian orbit, a point of major
importance in subsequent social and cultural, as well as political,
history. The Christian calendar itself was devised only in the sixth
century, after the Romans had withdrawn: it was a by-product of

arguments about the timing of Easter and it took the place of genealogical dating through lists of the dates of kings only in the seventh century. Yet before there was a Christian chronology there was a Christian history. The oldest indigenous British historical text was written in Latin by a monk, Gildas, in the mid-sixth century.

What did the Celts and their island seem like to Caesar and his contemporaries? Theirs was the first outsiders' view, which may be compared with colonists' views of the Polynesian 'noble savage' or American 'Red Indian' centuries later. First, the island, they noted, had many physical assets: as an outsider from Italy was to remark in the sixteenth century, 'Nature has endowed it with beauty and great bounty.' Second, the people who lived in it were, as the historian Tacitus put it, 'barbarians'. Third, they were disunited. The island was not one, and there were 'warring factions', even in the distinct parts of it. In the few pages which Edward Gibbon devoted to the island in his *Decline and Fall of the Roman Empire* (1776–88) he balanced his phrases, as always, when he wrote of Celtic Britain that 'the proximity of its situation to the coast of Gaul' invited Roman armies and 'the doubtful intelligence of a pearl fishery attracted their avarice'. As for the Celts, whom he also called 'barbarians', they showed 'valour without conduct and the love of freedom without the spirit of union'.

For Strabo, the Roman geographer and historian, who was a boy when Caesar landed, 'the greater part of the island' was 'level and wooded', but there were many 'hilly tracts'. This obvious contrast between upland and lowland was to fascinate many subsequent geographers and to point later to geographical interpretations of British history. These have subsequently been considerably qualified, but in the most general terms – and subject to local variations – the wetter upland, or highland, pastoral zone in the west was to have a different history from the drier arable lowland zone in the east. The island, Strabo went on, produced corn – one of the early tribal coins bore the design of an ear of barley – cattle, gold, silver, iron, tin, hides, slaves and 'dogs useful for hunting'. Tacitus, born a century after Caesar's invasion, took this inventory for granted, but added that the island's northern shores were 'beaten by a wild and open sea'.

These northern shores were never to become the boundary of the Roman Empire: like Ireland, they remained beyond it to the end, a fact of cardinal importance in later English history. The Romans never conquered the whole island: there were large numbers of Celts who remained outside the bounds.

For Caesar, who knew the north of the island only by repute, 'by far the most civilized inhabitants' lived in the maritime districts of Kent, where he landed. They were certainly most like the people he had already conquered in Gaul and there were many contacts between them. The inhabitants of other areas were to retain a separate identity. 'Most of the tribes in the interior', he believed, did not grow corn, but 'lived on milk and meat' and wore skins. It was their fearful appearance in battle which most impressed him. They carried long Celtic swords and wore no body armour. 'All the Britons dye their bodies with woad,' he explained, 'which produces a blue colour . . . They wear their hair long and shave the whole of their bodies except the head and the upper lip.'

The awkward term tribe (Latin *tribus*) used by Caesar has misleading modern associations. It has been related to the Celtic *tref*, or *treb*, populations who had cleared and worked ground and who were ruled by a king (or queen). More than twelve tribes have been identified for England at the time of the Roman conquest, some of which, like the Atrebates, had a tribal centre – theirs was at Calleva (known to us as Silchester, Berkshire) – and others of which, like the Dumnonii in Devon and Cornwall, did not. Camulodunum (Colchester), which was to become the first Roman capital, was the capital of the Trinovantes. Written evidence about customs and institutions is scanty. Within each tribe there was at one end of the social spectrum an 'aristocracy', which might be separated from the daily routines of agriculture, and at the other, slaves. There were also – and this particularly interested Caesar – the Druids, a 'priesthood' of wise men or soothsayers who, beside teaching the young, might be called upon to judge in disputes between adults. They thus had a public role and received dues in money and kind. Caesar believed that they originated in Britain and that they had shrines in the country in 'groves of oak', where the moon as well as the trees (and the

Tribes in Roman Britain

100–400 metres above sea level

over 400 metres above sea level

occasional mistletoe on them) played a part in their rites. The moon dictated *their* calendar, and their time unit, the fortnight, still survives. The Romans disliked what they heard of the bloodthirstiness of the Druid religion, but before the advent of Christianity their gods very quickly became confused with those of the Romans.

Caesar was the first writer to describe women as well as men, claiming that wives were 'shared between groups of ten or twelve men, especially fathers and sons'. The Romans also met tribal armies led by women, some of them, like Boadicea, memorable enough to stand out as individuals though subject to many subsequent reinterpretations. We know that many Celtic women were eventually to marry soldiers in the Roman armies, but, tantalizingly, we do not know a great deal about Celtic family patterns or population. As far as the latter is concerned, historical demographers offer a range of ingenious estimates similar to those for prehistoric peoples, based on agricultural capacity and likely density of settlement. The peak figure for Roman Britain, which was once set as low as 500,000 to one million, has more recently been calculated as four to six million, a far higher total than most of the estimates for England after the Norman Conquest in 1066 or for the England of Henry III.

During the century between Caesar's expeditions and the successful invasion by Claudius in AD 43 the habits of the Celtic people continued to change and the links between some of the British tribes and the Romans were strengthened. Trade with the Roman world, including the export of slaves from Britain and import of wine from the south, had also increased. Yet when Claudius mounted his invasion, his army was reluctant to sail into a land of mystery beyond the limits of the world. 'Men coming from these remote regions,' Tacitus was to write, 'told strange stories – of hurricanes, unknown birds, sea monsters, and shapes half-human and half-animal.'

Claudius's victory won him a proud inscription on his triumphal arch in Rome: 'He was the first to subject the barbarian peoples beyond the Ocean to the power of the Roman state.' Roman poets eagerly took up the same imperial theme. 'Forget not, Roman,' Virgil exclaimed in lines which were to appeal centuries later to British imperialists, 'that it is your special genius to rule the peoples, to impose the ways of peace, to spare the defeated, and to crush those proud men who will not submit.' Whatever their economic or political motives, the Romans made much of their mission to 'civilize', or, as Tacitus put it, 'to induce a people hitherto scattered, uncivilized and therefore prone to fight, to grow pleasurably broken in to peace and ease'.

What actually happened during the civilizing process and an occupation of four centuries, inevitably with many changes within them, was far more complicated than Tacitus suggested, particularly after the advent of Christianity in the second century. Already by the fourth century there had been one Christian soldier martyr in England, Alban; and within two years of Constantine's recognition as Augustus of all the West in 312 – he had been hailed as Emperor six years earlier by Roman soldiers at York – three bishops from Britain were to appear at the Church Council of Arles. It was after this that a woman who was buried in style at York carried with her earrings, a mirror, a glass jug and a piece of bone pierced with the Christian motto, 'Sister, hail! May you live in God!' Christians ceased to be persecuted in Britain several decades before Constantine became a Christian, but there seem to have been few of them even after his conversion. Christianity seems to have been most practised by a small but influential group of 'civilized' aristocrats, and a strong indigenous pagan element still persisted. No large Roman church structures have been identified; the largest of them, at Silchester, holds no more than sixty people. Doubtless other buildings were used for Christian worship; in 1975 a remarkable collection of Christian liturgical vessels, the earliest surviving church plate from the whole Roman Empire, was discovered in Cambridgeshire at Water Newton (Durobrivae) in the highly populated Nene valley. The earliest known portrait of Christ in Britain was found in a villa at Hinton St Mary in Dorset. Such limited survivals do not suggest the existence of a widespread Romano-British ecclesiastical art. A flourishing Celtic Christian culture did, however, exist in Ireland in the time of Patrick (the son of an English landowner who had first been to Ireland as the captive of slave-traders), and Celtic Christians brought both the Christian message and the

inspiration of the Celtic Christian culture over to western
England in the fifth century.

Because there was more effective communication both inside
the country and with other parts of the Empire, the civilizing
process was usually associated as much with travel and trade as
with ideas and beliefs. The great Roman roads, designed for
military purposes in 'flexible lines of straight pieces', carried not
only troops but also goods and, equally important, information.
There were post and relay stations from eight to fifteen miles
apart, sometimes with facilities for changing horses and taking
hot baths. The road plan was systematized, with three main arms
that radiated from London – to York and the north, to Chester
and Carlisle, and to Gloucester, Wales and the south-west. Roads
were one of the most remarkable Roman achievements, as the
Romans themselves recognized: an inscription in remote
Swaledale in Yorkshire reads simply 'to the god who first thought
of roads and paths'. The writer might have added waterways, for
river traffic was supplemented by canals, and there were sturdy
Roman bridges, docks and aqueducts. The Car Dyke, a series of
canals which drained part of the Fens, linked the River Cam at the
Waterbeach near Cambridge and Lincoln, which was also
connected with the Trent, the Humber and the Ouse.

Roman rule imposed financial and political burdens on the
population in cash and kind, but at the same time it was capable of
appealing both to the desire to serve and to the profit motive.
Taxation, regularly reviewed, was high, and the costs of the
army, which provided a substantial indirect employment to serve
its wants, were met by the British people. There were as many as
60,000 soldiers in the army, a far larger force than medieval kings
could have maintained, and·it required the produce of 100,000
acres to support it. When Britons joined the army, as with other
'barbarians' from across the Channel and the North Sea, their
loyalty to the Emperor carried with it incentives and privileges.
After twenty-five years' service there were gratuities and grants
of full citizenship. At another level, since there was a relatively
small number of paid Roman officials residing in Great Britain, as
in British India centuries later, it was in the interests of the
governor – or governors after Britain was divided into provinces,

Roman Britain

- 100–400 metres above sea level
- over 400 metres above sea level
- marshland
- lowland forest
- ● Municipium
- ○ town
- ▣ legionary fortress
- ▲ fort
- ━━ road
- ■ other site referred to in text

Firth of Forth

Antonine Wall

Firth of Clyde

Hadrian's Wall

Luguvalium (Carlisle)

Solway Firth

Arbeia (South Shields)

Isle of Man (not occupied by Romans)

Cataractonium (Catterick)

R. Ouse

Irish Sea

Isurium Brigantum (Aldborough)

Eburacum (York)

R. Humber

North Sea

Lindum (Lincoln)

Deva (Chester)

Foss Dyke

The Wash

Branodunum (Brancaster)

Viroconium Cornoviorum (Wroxeter)

R. Severn

R. Trent

Ratae Coritanorum (Leicester)

Durobrivae (Water Newton)

Venta Icenorum (Caistor)

Durolipons (Castrum)

Salinae (Droitwich)

Durobrivae

Magnis (Kenchester)

Abonium (Weston)

Glevum (Gloucester)

Corinium Dobunnorum (Cirencester)

Verulamium (St. Albans)

Camulodunum (Colchester)

Isca (Caerleon)

Woodchester

Durobrivae (Rochester)

Venta Silurum (Caerwent)

Aquae Sulis (Bath)

Calleva Atrebatum (Silchester)

Londinium (London) R. Thames

Durovernum (Canterbury)

Venta Belgarum (Winchester)

Hinton St. Mary

Clausentum (Bitterne)

New Forest

Regnum (Chichester)

Romney Marsh

Isca Dumnoniorum (Exeter)

Durovaria (Dorchester)

Purbeck

Fishbourne

Portus Adurni (Portchester)

English Channel

two in AD 197, four in AD 284 and five in AD 369 – and the fiscal procurator to turn for support in the governing process to the *curiales*, better-off élites (as they have been called), in the towns. Reliance on these was an economic arrangement for the Romans, and it favoured socially those who took office. There was an element of corruption both in the system of supplies and in the farming out of taxes to individual bidders. At the same time, within an imposed centralized system the main units of local administration corresponded significantly to older divisions, just as tribal divisions were to persist centuries later in the colonies of the British Empire.

As for profit, the establishment of a money economy was an essential feature of Roman Britain, even though this was a limited economy which rested on subsistence agriculture and left an important place for the exchange of gifts and favours. Most of the coinage was imported from Italy and Gaul – and there were frequent debasements – but official mints were set up in Britain itself at various times. The money flow was uneven and at certain times there was considerable inflation, particularly in the early fourth century. There also seems to have been an interest in retaining 'sound' silver currency when debased coins were introduced.

The circulation of small coins has been taken as a sign of vigorous local trade and numismatic evidence has been employed also to point to wider patterns of trade. Money was used from the beginning of Roman control to buy food – some imported, much home produced – including salt (some from Droitwich, some from the Lower Rhine), beer (a prized local product), wine, pottery, furnishings and jewellery, not to mention oysters, which, it has been claimed, were prized, with or without pearls, as much in Rome as in England. More distant connections still are suggested by the tombstone of the wife of a merchant of Palmyra at South Shields in Northumberland. Merchants had their guilds, and even before the end of the first century there was a *collegium* of metal craftsmen at Chichester. Similar craftsmen flourished in other towns until the end of Roman control. Mineral wealth was exploited too in widely scattered places.

The changing fortunes of the pottery industry reveal the

complexity of the civilizing process and all that went with it. The relationship between sales of pottery made at home and imported pottery has been studied in detail by archaeologists and it is clear that throughout the Roman period there were both imports and exports, sometimes substantial, tied in with changes in demand and taste. Earlier Iron Age traditions of production persisted during the first years of Roman rule (in Dorset, for example), but there were huge imports. Meanwhile, the demand for pottery by the army led to the creation of workshops under military supervision. New civilian workshops soon followed, with Durobrivae becoming a specialized centre of large-scale production. There were also large numbers of small potters in the New Forest offering less elaborate wares, so that whenever there were no military or political interruptions to trade and production, there was ample competition and choice. Potters' stalls and shops have been excavated in several Roman towns.

The civilizing process did not affect all people equally, of course, however desirous they may have been to benefit from it, and many people – and districts – were left outside it altogether. There was unevenness of development. Nor did the civilizing process narrow the gap between the haves and have-nots. 'Rufus, son of Callisunus,' we read on a writing tablet found in the River Walbrook in London, 'greetings to Epillicus and all his fellows. I believe you know I am well. Do look after everything carefully. See that you turn the slave girl into cash.' Ninety-seven burials at a villa near Marlow have suggested that there was an 'industry' there, perhaps textiles, employing young female slaves; at the end of the Roman Empire there were large numbers of slaves in Kent, as there were also in the far west.

History from below is often more forbidding than history from above. In the first Roman campaigns, for example, defenders of Maiden Castle against a young Roman commander Vespasian, who was later to become Emperor, were slaughtered *en masse* and buried in a cemetery at the east gate. In AD 59–60 there was a revolt in eastern England led by Boadicea, the warrior queen typically portrayed in her chariot; according to one obviously exaggerated estimate, as many as 80,000 rebels were killed near Verulamium (modern St Albans, Hertfordshire). Previously, she had devastated Colchester and St Albans itself. The conquest of the north of England in AD 78 under the governorship of Agricola involved the overthrow but not the final destruction of tribal power.

During the next centuries, there was relative peace. The greatest surviving Roman landmark, therefore, is a defensive wall, Hadrian's Wall, begun in AD 122 after the Britons, in the words of Hadrian's biographer, 'could no longer be held under Roman control'. It took six years to build, was nearly eighty Roman miles long (a Roman mile was 1,620 yards) and stretched almost from sea to sea. Magnificent though it now seems, its building was greatly resented, and there was hostility from the local population on both sides of it. Turrets served as observation points sufficiently high to protect the sentries from attack. Hadrian's successor built a much shorter Antonine Wall, a barrier of turf further north above the present boundaries between England and Scotland, which is less than half the length of Hadrian's Wall, but this last of the imperial linear frontiers had only a brief history. Not only were the Picts never overcome but there were to be further uprisings among the Brigantes. The years from AD 213 to AD 342 have been described as 'years of peace', but there was a continual threat from the sea as well as from the land, first from pirates and later from would-be Saxon settlers; and in the third century powerful forts were constructed on the coast from Brancaster in the north to Portchester in the west. The long coastline was always vulnerable to attack.

It was for such reasons that only a part of Britain was densely populated and that secure towns could be developed, as in other areas of the Roman Empire. Most Roman towns were not by the sea. Some, like Durovernum (Canterbury) or Calleva (Silchester), were on old sites while others were on fresh sites not very far away from old ones; a typical prehistoric gully bounding a hut site was found at Canterbury in 1946 and Dorchester (Durniovarium) was only a few miles away from Maiden Castle. From the start, however, the Romans endowed their bigger towns with a social and cultural significance that was new to England, arranging them in a formal grid pattern, with straight lines and rectangles. Like the straight

Roman roads, Roman towns defied all the favourite curves of the Celts. In the twentieth century Lewis Mumford, historian of cities throughout the ages, was to generalize scathingly about Roman towns as 'forum, vomitarium and bath', but he left out the temple and the amphitheatre. In fact, for most civilized Romans, urban buildings mattered less than the citizens of a town: 'the pleasantest, yes and the most profitable side of city life is society and intercourse.'

Roman towns can be divided into categories. Whether near to old sites or not, they usually were or had begun as garrison centres like Luguvalium (Carlisle) and Catarectonium (Catterick), the latter still a military camp in the twentieth century. Some of them became *coloniae*. The first of them, Camulodunum, established as such after the first legionaries stationed there had moved to Gloucester, was erected as early as AD 49. Glevum (Gloucester) and Lindum (Lincoln) followed later in the first century. Each *colonia* had its *ordo* or council, modelled on the Roman Senate and elected by citizens who had the right age and property qualifications. It chose two pairs of magistrates annually, one pair responsible mainly for the maintenance of public buildings and amenities. One town in Roman Britain, Verulamium, was probably designated a *municipium* or charted city, the citizens of which had a limited form of Roman citizenship.

During the long Roman occupation, each town, big or small, had its own history. What buildings have survived or have been excavated is largely a matter of accident, yet patterns of development can be traced. The building of a wall and impressive gateways was deemed important symbolically as well as in terms of defence. So too was the shift from timber to stone. The commonest form of urban house was the strip house: a long narrow building fronting the street in 'parades' with a gable end. There seem to have been no large multi-storey apartments as there were in Italy. Public buildings were erected at different times as towns grew in size and in wealth, and private housing, with painted walls outside and inside, could reflect this growth. Some towns had an aqueduct; all seem to have had baths and public lavatories. Some had a market hall (*macellum*) as well as a *forum*, which served as a meeting place as well as a market-place; all seem to have had shops. The basilica on one side of the forum was the largest covered meeting hall. The temple in pre-Christian times and the amphitheatre, elliptical in shape, were common features of urban life. We know little of the balance between public and private, though there were some houses enclosed in gardens. In pre-Christian times each house had its shrine to the household gods, the *lares*.

Plagues and fires were major regular hazards both to private and public buildings, as they were to be for generations to come. Thus, when the forum at Viroconium (Wroxeter), the site of which now consists entirely of ploughed fields, was destroyed by fire at the end of the third century (it was the second great fire in the history of the city), it was not rebuilt. The impressive baths continued in use, however, and were reconstructed later; there was further work on them even at the beginning of the fifth century.

At Verulamium, as at Durovernum, the building of a theatre in the mid second century must have been a major event: it provided more seating accommodation than any hall in modern St Albans, which now has 50,000 inhabitants. A great fire there in AD 155 had destroyed many buildings. Yet the range of civic amenities increased, and the theatre was extended as late as *c.* AD 300, when races, 'beast shows' and gladiatorial contests were popular, not least, perhaps, because admission was free. Later in the second half of the century it went out of use. Verulamium also had a stone market-building with two rows of nine shops and a courtyard.

Eboracum (York), where walls, burial grounds and religious relics can still be seen, became the provincial capital of Britannia Inferior, with its own governor, after Britain had been divided into two provinces (Britannia Superior was so called because it was nearer to Rome). Two Roman emperors died there, the first, Septimus Severus, in AD 211, the second, Constantine, in AD 306. The importance of Eboracum is attested by its magnificent fortress, completed around AD 300 and said to be the best of its kind in the Empire. From before that date a reredos showing Mithras in the act of slaying a bull has survived. The slaughter was the main feature of pre-Christian Roman religion which had

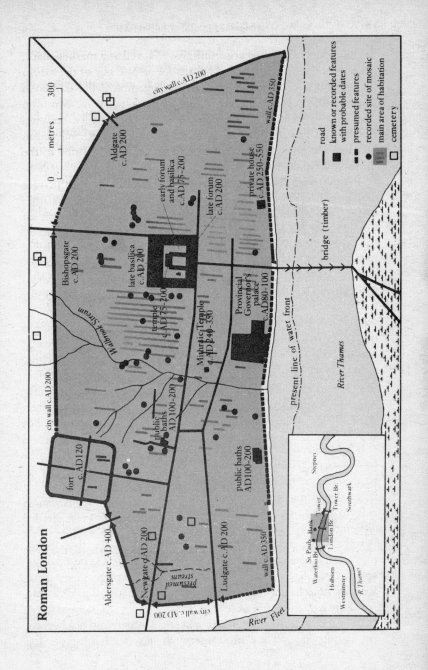

Roman London

city wall c. AD 200

Aldersgate c. AD 400

Newgate c. AD 200

Ludgate c. AD 200

wall c. AD 350

presumed stream

River Fleet

city wall c. AD 200

fort c. AD 120

public baths AD 100–200

public baths AD 100–200

Mithraic Temple c. AD 240–350

Provincial Governor's palace c. AD 80–100

temple c. AD 75–200

late basilica c. AD 200

Bishopsgate c. AD 200

Walbrook Stream

early forum and basilica c. AD 75–200

late forum c. AD 200

Aldgate c. AD 200

private house c. AD 250–550

city wall c. AD 200

wall c. AD 350

Present line of water front

bridge (timber)

River Thames

metres
0   300

road

known or recorded features with probable dates

presumed features

recorded site of mosaic

main area of habitation

cemetery

Westminster   Holborn   St. Pauls   Bank   Stepney
Waterloo Br.   London Br.   Tower   Tower Br.   Southwark
R. Thames

strong appeal for soldiers. Another deity popular among pre-Christian soldiers for less mystical reasons was Fortuna, the goddess of fortune; in different guises she figures in all periods of social history.

Londinium had to await twentieth-century bombing for its Roman riches to be revealed. The Thames was important before the Romans came, but Londinium itself was a Roman development on an exceptionally favourable site. There was an early Roman military camp there, but the town grew through commerce rather than through war. When a magnificent forum was laid down there before the end of the first century, an even older building and piazza had to disappear, and there was a succession of massive timber wharves, warehouses and a bridged pier. Londinium was directly linked to the trade of continental Europe. It also became a financial and administrative headquarters, and in the early third century it began to acquire its walls. Its population may have risen to about 30,000, and its area grew to 330 acres, over twice the size of Roman Paris. The stone for its public buildings was brought from many parts of the country: Northamptonshire, for example, and Purbeck in Dorset, together with Aquae Sulis (Bath), itself a small Roman town where stone buildings were constructed around curative hot springs early during the Roman occupation. The bath in Aquae Sulis underwent many changes before becoming disused by the end of the fourth century.

It has been suggested that the importance the Romans attached to their towns, which were, in fact, 'parasites on the country', led to an anti-urban bias in English thinking that has persisted ever since: the poor as well as the rich continued to prefer the countryside to the town. Such continuities are impossible to prove, although R. G. Collingwood, who propounded the thesis, believed also – and perhaps with more justification – that 'the dreary mediocrity of Roman provincial art' stifled the Celtic creative spirit. In reality, town and country were interdependent. Few Roman villas in the countryside were more than half a day's ride from a town, and there were apparently very few of them in some of the rural western areas. Moreover, the Romans did not neglect the countryside. They brought much new land into use: for example, in Kent and Essex and in the eastern Fens, parts of which were drained and reclaimed. There were also large numbers of nucleated settlements, villages as well as hamlets. In the Nene valley in the south Midlands alone 434 of them had been identified by 1972, fourteen times as many as had been identified in 1930. Many farmers seem to have preferred keeping cattle and pigs to sheep.

The earliest of the 600 known Roman villas, some of them built before the end of the first century, were located close to the sea, in Kent and Sussex. Some were comparatively unsophisticated bungalows of six to ten rooms; others were enlarged or improved as the years went by, with the addition of, for example, baths and accommodation for estate workers. Around towns like Verulamium and Corinium (Cirencester) there was large-scale villa development. One villa near Winchcombe in Gloucestershire was made of Cotswold stone cut into small blocks and was roofed with local Stonesfield slates. Another one in Gloucestershire, Woodchester, was as large as many eighteenth-century country houses.

The best-known villa of all, Fishbourne, near Chichester in Sussex, was discovered in 1960 and has rightly been described as a palace. In the second half of the first century the timber house there was replaced by a substantial house in stone, and the Flavian Palace constructed between AD 75 and AD 80 featured an imposing entrance hall 105 feet long and 60 feet wide and a magnificent audience chamber which has been compared with that in the Palace of Domitian on the Palatine Hill in Rome. There was nothing 'drearily mediocre' about this highly sophisticated edifice which drew on the services of immigrant craftsmen and may have been occupied by Cogidubnus, a client Celtic king who was also a Roman citizen.

Smaller objects found at Fishbourne make it possible to re-capture aspects of everyday Roman life, or at least that of the well-off. The absence of brooches amongst the objects suggests that togas and not Celtic garments, which had to be fastened together, were the form of dress; leather shoes were worn. Textile fabrics have disappeared, but there is evidence of the use of cosmetics. And a gold earring and other rings point to the privileges of rank. In the kitchen are pottery jars, which may have contained honey, the only sweetener of the time, and a jar of lentils, all that has survived from a vegetable larder that probably once contained imported figs and poppy seeds, cabbage, lettuce, peas, beans and root crops (but no potatoes, of course, for they were to come to England many centuries later). Professor Barry Cunliffe, who has catalogued the objects, has drawn attention also to small pebbles for counting, and although there are no written records from Fishbourne, ink wells survive, as do a bronze stylus case and styli for writing on wax tablets. Such artefacts survive from many other Roman towns.

Parts of Fishbourne were destroyed by fire during a time of unrest towards the end of the second century, and the construction of coastline fortifications is evidence of a threat to order elsewhere during the early third century. Yet it is a measure of the extent of regional differences that during this same period the Vale of York was enjoying the full benefits of the *pax Romana* for the first time. Farms there were prospering and the first stone buildings began to appear.

It was during the early fourth century, which has been described as the golden age of Roman Britain, that some of the greatest Roman villas were built or extended by landed proprietors who were prepared to spend money lavishly. There was a favourable balance of trade, and exports included woollens as well as corn. Important legal changes at the end of the second and beginning of the third centuries, which probably reflected antecedent social change, had broadened citizenship. They had not, however, reduced social inequalities. Although in 197 serving soldiers were allowed to live with their wives, and fifteen years after that Roman citizenship was granted to all free inhabitants of the Empire, there was an increase later in the number of *equites*, 'equestrians' (the term derives from *equus*, a horse), people enjoying the privileges of the highest Roman rank. The *equites* were people able to pass on to their sons as of right a place in the *ordo equester*; these were the spenders. The order went with the law.

As the integrity of the Roman Empire was challenged, the situation favoured not only the lawless, but the rich and the ambitious; and Britain, described by the monk Gildas as 'a stiff-necked and stubborn island', was not alone among the western provinces in displaying what has been called a remark-able 'propensity to produce usurpers'. When the rebel naval commander, Carausius, took possession of Britain following earlier disorders and declared himself Emperor in 286, using sea power to support him, his rule may have been welcomed by people in Britain, who felt that the island on the periphery could be more peaceful than the Empire as a whole: his coins bore the inscription *Genius Britanniae*. Roman authority was soon restored, however, even in the north, as it was to be restored again, this time precariously by Magnus Maximus, after a further rebellion in 383. There was also, in 367, a brief, but alarming and unprecedented barbarian coalition that included Franks and Sax-ons from across the North Sea as well as Picts and Scots, during which one of the highest imperial military officials was killed. It required the intervention of an able commander, Theodosius, father of the emperor of the same name, to discipline the Roman troops and pacify the island. Yet there was little he could do to guarantee the security of the long, always vulnerable coastline. No coins were minted in Britain after 326 and imports of coins minted in Rome fell in the late fourth century.

It was during the reign of Honorius (395–423), 'the weakest of all Roman emperors', that the situation in Britain was irretriev-ably transformed. By 401, Roman troops were being withdrawn from Britain for the defence of Italy against Alaric's Goths; and over the next decade, during which troops in Britain proclaimed no fewer than three usurpers, the import of coins from Rome came to an end, Roman control of western Europe broke down and Alaric sacked Rome itself. Britons were now left to look after their own interests, and Honorius was free from illusions when he wrote not to Roman officials but to the *curiales* in 410 telling them to undertake their own defence. We know from the biographer of St Germanus of Auxerre, who visited Britain four decades later, that by the middle of the fifth century all direct links between Britain and Rome had long since been broken. We know little, however, of who held power.

The biographer of St Germanus, who had come to Britain to preach to Christians attracted by the heresy of Pelagius, Britain's first (or first remembered) heretic, and who met the *curiales* and prayed at the tomb of St Alban in Verulamium, recorded raids by Saxons from Germany and Picts from north of Hadrian's Wall during his visit. There was nothing new about such raids. The best evidence of them, and of early Saxon settlement, is archaeological. We know more about things than about events, even though they are often difficult to interpret.

The years between 410 and 600, during which Roman control ended and the Saxons settled throughout eastern England, have been described as 'lost centuries' and it is impossible at our distance to judge where history ends and myth begins. There has been as much argument as to who Vortigern, the 'proud tyrant' who, it was claimed, summoned the Saxons in, really was as there has been about the role of Arthur, the reputed hero of the resistance to the Saxon invaders. We do know of their defeat, however, in at least one great battle, Mount Badon, *c.* 520, which temporarily checked their move westwards. The appeal of the Arthurian legend, of a 'once and future king' as Sir Thomas Malory described him in his fifteenth-century *Morte d'Arthur*, has lasted to our own day, and in the nineteenth century a symbolic Camelot was created by Tennyson's *Idylls of the King*.

Latin culture did not collapse all at once, nor the Christianity which came to enshrine it. Yet, in the face of successive invasions from across the North Sea, society was severely strained. The Roman roads were not maintained; the towns languished and their internal order broke down, although not everywhere at the same time; villas were abandoned, although not necessarily all work on their estates; industries, like the iron industry of the Weald, which had sustained Roman fleets, collapsed, although again not necessarily all at once; and there was no longer a money economy, although coins might be prized as ornaments when they had ceased to be a medium of exchange or a unit of account. Nearly all the issues that concern the social historian of the fifth and sixth centuries centre on the extent of these continuities and discontinuities. German historians in the nineteenth century who were seeking the origins of 'medieval civilization' believed that in the fifth century there was a *caesur*, a sharp and clean cut, which allowed them tidily to sum up the Roman Empire, from Caesar to *caesur.* More recently, however, there has been a search for social continuities, particularly in the English countryside. It has been noted that when villas were abandoned, there was sometimes a retreat to old prehistoric hill-top sites, like South Cadbury in Somerset, and that some Saxon place names ending in 'ham' were near to Roman roads or villas. Recent excavations in London have shown that it remained an important trading centre. A water pipe was laid down at Verulamium in the mid or even late fifth century.

The end of Roman control brought with it very different patterns of life, although it is difficult to identify patterns of authority. They varied from one part of the country to another. The Saxons used knives and spears and made metal ornaments, including brooches and beads, although they did not build in stone or use the potter's wheel until the seventh century. By then authority was clearly in the hands of 'kings', documented by Church chroniclers, and the rural resources of England seem to have been almost as fully exploited by a relatively mobile population as they were to be in the eleventh century. Light sandy soils tended to be rejected, however, and marshlands went undrained. The most common cereals were barley, oats and wheat, although no ploughs and only a few ploughshares have survived.

Housing was simple, and most of the Saxons lived in very small houses with sunken floors. If Mucking in Essex, a commanding site over a bend in the Thames estuary, is typical, there were no street lines. Yet there were boundary ditches at West Stow in Suffolk. As settlement became more permanent and authority established, impressive royal sites were developed, as at Yeavering in Northumbria and Cheddar in Wessex. Great mead halls, high ceilinged and made of wood, with walls hung with shields and tapestries – so different from tiny cottages with sunken floors – were at the centre of royal life and the 'joys of the hall', with noisy junketing at festival times and in celebration of great events. Ornamental drinking horns figure prominently in Saxon wills, valuable for the interpretation of later Saxon history, as do silver cups and tapestries. Within the hall minstrels would often be in attendance with their harps – 'singers of men', who, like Christian missionaries, were often 'destined to wander through many lands'.

A great Saxon oral tradition first expressed in the sagas reveals something of early Saxon culture: in the beginning were the gods – Woden and Thor – to whom the names of the days of the week are a continuing testimony. The poem *Beowulf*, of uncertain date, *c.* 675–875, tells us of evil monsters descending 'from crags of mist across the moor', of nature's beauty and power, of the ties of kinship, of ring-givers, of royal deeds of fearless valour, and of treachery and feud. Another poet was to note how 'each of us must experience an end to life in this world' and to add 'let him who can achieve glory before he die'. Nonetheless, poets knew that epidemics and famine often came in the aftermath of fighting and they tell us also of the bands of men who travelled in wooden ships across 'the tempest and terrible toil of the deep' and of the land, the source through toil of a new livelihood.

English land had to be worked in English weather. It was farmed laboriously and passed down from one generation to another through different inheritance customs. Historians are ignorant of the origins of the common-field system, which was to dominate medieval agriculture, although most evidence of land worked in strips in great open fields and of cooperation between neighbours comes from later Saxon England. It has been suggested that the oldest element of the common-field system was the right of common grazing on pasture and waste land. Some farmers were pastoralists, and while cattle were most prized, sheep provided milk, meat and wool. Pigs were ubiquitous, but there were few goat herds. Arable farming – mainly of wheat and barley – itself depended on animals, not only for power but for fertilization. Heavy ploughing did not become common until the tenth century.

While settlement continued, there were ebbs and flows of power between one part of the country and another as different 'kingdoms', some of them British, battled with each other in contests for supremacy which the seventeenth-century poet John Milton was to call the 'wars of kites and crows'. Yet he knew nothing of Saxon treasure. The wealth, power and trading contacts of some of the kingly contestants were revealed in 1939 when a seventh-century East Anglian king's grave was discovered at Sutton Hoo, near Woodbridge in Suffolk. All that remained of the boat in which the king was buried at sea were marks of decayed wood in the sand, but the treasure which went with him included a great silver dish from Byzantium, a jewelled Rhenish sword, an even more elaborate shield with bird and dragon figures, a magnificent helmet, cloisonné shoulder straps, flamboyant polychrome jewellery, coins (before they had come back into general use) and a unique whetstone sceptre.

Christianity did nothing to change the basic economics and demography of Saxon England: individual lives were short, and personal bonds mattered more than abstract argument. The meaning of conversion depended on status and experience. When it was conversion from above, it did not quickly destroy old habits. Kings themselves could abjure their faith, and long after Christianity was taken for granted they could behave in old ways in their marriage and burial arrangements. It is clear, too, that conversion never dispelled belief in 'magic'; it could even lend it new dimensions. Magical wells could become Christian shrines; old oaths, which now might be taken on holy relics or the Bible, and potions drunk out of church bells were believed to be especially efficacious.

The first Saxon king about whom much is known is Aethelbert of Kent, who married a Christian princess and himself converted to Christianity. He was one of many kings, however, some of whom were rich and strong, but only one of whom had widely recognized general authority as *bretwalda* (a 'wide ruler' or 'over-lord'). Sussex and Wessex figure in lists of *bretwaldas* before Aethelbert, East Anglia comes in rather later, and Northumbria later still in the seventh century with Edwin, Oswald and Oswy. Each Saxon king traced his ancestry back to the gods, either Woden or Saxneat. Pedigrees mattered. One king of East Anglia felt it expedient to include Caesar among his ancestors, and Romulus and Remus figure on East Anglian coins. In Christian times Adam too could be added to the list.

Aethelbert's conversion to Christianity came at a time when Kent was a rich kingdom, the importance of which was recognized by Gregory I, the Pope, who sent St Augustine to

Canterbury at the head of forty missionaries. Equal importance was attached to the conversion of Edwin in Northumbria, and although his immediate successor (like Aethelbert's successor, Eadbald) apostatized, Northumbria – and the island of Lindisfarne in particular – very soon became a centre of Christian light and learning. In 664 at Whitby on the Yorkshire coast an important religious synod resolved sharply contested differences about the date of Easter (a name derived from a pagan goddess) between Celtic Christians, whose Christian activity had preceded the Saxon conversion and who had developed their own forms of monastic organization, and Roman Christians, who looked directly to the Pope. The decision went in favour of the latter. Thereafter, before there was one kingdom there was to be one church. And five years after Whitby an outstanding new 'pastor of flocks', Theodore of Tarsus, Archbishop of Canterbury from 669–90, who arrived in England from Asia Minor, a refugee from Arab invaders, did much to create and consolidate its diocesan structure.

Penda, the pagan king of Mercia (the middle kingdom), who is said to have given his name to the penny, had been defeated in 655 by Oswy, king of Northumbria, but soon afterwards Mercia enjoyed a period of supremacy (670–796) with a royal centre at Tamworth and authority over people as different as the hill-folk of the Peak District, Shropshire and the Chilterns and the plains-dwellers of Lindsey and the Fens. Indeed, Wulfhere, the Mercian king who broke Northumbrian supremacy, was even in a position to sell the bishopric of London, dispose of the Isle of Wight and control Hastings in Sussex. A later Mercian king, Offa (757–96), was described in his time as '*Rex Anglorum*'. Later chroniclers claimed that he founded St Albans Abbey and a short-lived archbishopric, with its centre not at Canterbury but at Lichfield. He certainly has a special place in the social history of England. The distribution of his coins suggests widespread, if small-scale, trade, and one gold coin, his dinar, suggests that it extended even beyond Europe to the distant Caliphate. Offa is also known for his great dyke, over seventy miles in length, which provided a line of defence against the Celts, often through mountainous country from the Irish Sea to the Bristol Channel. It involved conscious diversion of labour and wealth and has been called the greatest public work of the Saxon age.

While the power of kings was apparent both in their trading contacts and in their works, the power of bishops was obvious too in the eighth century. Their dioceses, based on kingdoms or sub-kingdoms, had their own order and rules. A gallery of Saxon saints figures prominently in the great history concluded in 731 by the Venerable Bede, who spent most of his life in the twin monastery of Monkwearmouth and Jarrow in Northumbria, one of a number of large and rich monasteries. Bede was a great historian, unwilling to use his powerful imagination to fill in gaps in the available historical evidence ('it is said that' was one of his favourite prefixes). Like many of his contemporaries, he was fascinated by surviving prehistoric remains, which were thought to be the work of 'cunning giants'. He was not, however, writing 'simple ecclesiastical history', the title of his book, but a species of hagiography, in which the English people are sometimes described in the same terms St Paul used about the people of Israel.

The eighth century was a peaceful period of cultural vitality, particularly impressive in the 'age of Alcuin', as it has been called. Alcuin of York (c. 735–804) was educated in the cathedral school there, but spent much of his life in Charlemagne's Europe. He was a prolific letter writer as well as a theologian, and his letters (very few of them in English) covered an immense range of subjects from law and chant to natural history and astronomy. His was also the age of the superbly illuminated gospels, the famous crosses at Bewcastle and Ruthwell and the first royal charters (not from Northumbria but from Kent and Sussex). Meanwhile, in the south, the first codes of laws had been drafted: one of the first, that of Ine of Wessex dates back to the late sixth century, and the power of his kingdom, which under Alfred in the ninth century was to be the eventual winner in the contests for kingly supremacy, began to increase. We know most about Saxon society from its codes of law, and they can be suspected, as historians have pointed out, of revealing more about society as it should have been than as it actually was. There is no doubt, however, about the appeal of surviving cultural evidence. The Lindisfarne Gospels, written and illuminated in the half century before Alcuin, are only one magnificent example. Saxon script was in marked contrast to Roman inscription.

All the many signs of cultural renaissance were overshadowed, however, by 'dire portents' which began to appear over Northumbria in the late eighth century: 'immense whirlwinds . . . flashes of lightning . . . and fiery dragons . . . flying in the air'. The Viking raids had begun. The earliest raids were the work not of the Norsemen we know as Danes but of the Norwegians. Their immediate consequences were beyond dispute: material loss, humiliation for men and women (rape figures in the accounts as well as murder), a threat to precariously established 'civilization' (already of a very different kind from Roman civilization) and, following the first raids on the north of England, a geographical switch in power from north to south that was not to shift back until the industrial revolution of the eighteenth and early nineteenth centuries. Lindisfarne was sacked in 793, York was taken, 'the sanctuaries of God' were desecrated, 'the bodies of the saints trampled on like dung in the street'. No fewer than three bishoprics disappeared.

It has been pointed out recently that since many accounts of Viking attacks were written by monks or priests – they wrote little or nothing about themselves – the violence of their assaults, particularly on churches and holy places, may well have been exaggerated. Yet while it was in part the paganism of the Vikings which led them to assume the character of a scourge – they were even described as the anti-Christ – the exceptional violence of their raids is difficult to dispute. They themselves were silent about their hopes and fears. At first, they may have cared more for loot than for land, but, unlike the first Saxon invaders, they were interested also in trade. Their land hunger was noted by King Alfred, who was told by a Viking guest how the lands from which he came in the north of Europe were 'very long and very narrow', and that all that could either be pastured or ploughed lay by the sea, 'though it is in some parts very rocky'. The guest, Alfred noted, was 'one of the first men in that country, yet he had not more than twenty horned cattle, twenty sheep and twenty swine, and the little that he ploughed he ploughed with horses'.

It is the Danes, drawn to lowland England, who have passed

The Anglo-Saxons and the Danes

Scandinavian settlement by 876

Danelaw

■ Five Boroughs

KENT early shire

Kingdom of Picts and Scots

Lothian

NORTHUMBRIA

STRATHCLYDE

Galloway

Carlisle

Durham

Lindisfarne I.

Bernicia

R. Ouse

YORK

York

Isle of Man

Irish Sea

North Sea

DANISH MERCIA

Chester

Gwynned

R. Trent

Lincoln

Stafford

Derby

Nottingham

Powys

Shrewsbury

Tamworth

Leicester

Stamford

NORFOLK

Thetford

Bridgnorth

R. Severn

Warwick

R. Nen

SUFFOLK

Worcester

Northampton

Ely

Cambridge

Offa's Dyke

MERCIA

Bedford

EAST ANGLIA

Brecknock

Dyfed

Gwent

Gloucester

Buckingham

Colchester

Witham

Glamorgan

Ashdown

Oxford

Maldon

ESSEX

R. Wye

Wantage

London

BERKSHIRE

R. Thames

Sheppey

Chippenham

SURREY

Canterbury

Wedmore

KENT

SOMERSET

Glastonbury

Winchester

X

Appledore

Dover

Pilton

Wilton

HAMPSHIRE

SUSSEX

Exeter

DORSET

Chichester

Lewes

Hastings

Lydford

Wareham

Southampton

WEST WALES

Wight

English Channel

into English history. They came in different kinds of ships to meet different needs, all requiring remarkable skills to handle them, many carrying large numbers of armed men and, sometimes, horses. They continued to fight after they began to settle in the north and the east, and soon conquered Northumbria, Mercia and East Anglia, thus breaking down the old if loose divisions of the Saxon kingdoms. Alfred, who became King of Wessex in 849, was the first king able to withstand them after they had sent a great army in 865. 'With a small company he moved into inaccessible places . . . and continued fighting against the Viking host.' Having fought them to a standstill, he thereby established the power of a West Saxon dynasty which was to last for nearly 200 years, and a reputation as a hero that was to appeal even longer: later generations were to bracket his name with that of Arthur. Yet at the time not all Englishmen thought of him as a supreme leader.

Alfred's achievements were beyond doubt, and most of them had social implications. He was one of the few kings in any age to write books. He designed candles marked to tell the time. His is the first surviving code of law in its original form. By building ships, by reconstructing his army or *fyrd*, by erecting fortified towns or *burghs* (some of them on or near the sites of Iron Age or Roman forts), and by defining boundaries, one of which ran for fifty miles along the old Roman road, Watling Street, Alfred ensured that the Danes were contained in a huge region of their own, which in the eleventh century became known as Danelaw. The imposition of Danish law in large parts of this region did not mean, however, that the whole area was colonized by Danes: their main settlements were in Leicestershire, Lincolnshire, Nottinghamshire and Yorkshire.

An important element in Viking activities was the extortion of payments of treasure from the Saxons: from 991 (under King Ethelred) such payments were made at frequent intervals, and for long they achieved their immediate object, so that Alfred's successors, from whichever part of England they came, benefited from years of peace. Indeed, the greatest of them, Ethelred's father, Edgar, who died in 975, had already earned the title the 'Peaceable'. He was crowned at Bath in 973 as King of all

England, and when he held court at Chester in the north, eight lesser kings rowed him up the Dee. He had been crowned by a saintly monk, Dunstan, who was born near Glastonbury, related to the royal family and was later to become Archbishop of Canterbury. Edgar himself was deeply devoted to a monastic ideal that gripped many of his contemporaries, women as well as men, after a period when the first monasteries had declined. He is known for his coins, however, as well as for his prayers: one of them showed the Hand of Providence emerging from a cloud.

On Edgar's death, further internal 'strife threw the kingdom into turmoil, shire against shire', and a further series of Viking raids culminated in the taking over of the whole country by the Danish King Cnut (1017–35). The fact that in 1012 the Danegeld, a term not used at the time, had begun to be collected on a regular basis as an organized land tax had not saved the Saxons; and the tax continued to be levied on a regular basis on into the twelfth century long after Cnut's conquest. It was calculated, like earlier Saxon taxes (and claims on military service), on the basis of the hide as a land unit. Church taxes took the form of tithes (a tenth of income in cash or kind) with additional payments at particular times of the year, beginning with 'plough alms'.

Measurement obviously mattered increasingly to Saxons and Danes alike – to rulers and ruled – by the eleventh century. Although units like the hide were not uniform in all parts of England, all Englishmen were made to know very early in their history precisely what taxes meant. Thus in 1041 King Harthacnut ordered the whole of Worcestershire to be punished because two of his thanes had been murdered in Worcester Cathedral when they were collecting taxes.

Hides were thought of imprecisely at first as the amounts of land necessary to support one labourer's family. By the eleventh century these were far bigger land units as well, for already England had been divided into shires, also unequal in size and wealth, later to be called counties; some were ancient kingdoms, like Kent. In late Saxon England each shire had a court which met twice a year and was presided over by the king's representative, the shire-reeve (sheriff), and the shires in their turn were divided into hundreds (or in the lands of the Danes, wapentakes), again unequal in size and each with its own court; this was the court most used by the rural population who lived in villages.

The urban population remained small, although there had been trading centres in each of the major Saxon kingdoms from the seventh century onwards, some of them relatively large, like Southampton (seventy-two acres). Not far away, Winchester, refounded in the ninth century, may have had 10,000 inhabitants. There were a number of primary centres inland such as Banbury and Melton Mowbray in the Midlands and Maidstone in Kent, where there were links with older settlements, both Roman and pre-Roman. York had at least 8,000 and Norwich and Lincoln 5,000 inhabitants. At the far end of the scale, London, which had been described by Bede as an 'emporium' for people coming by sea as well as by land and which was already capital of a religious see, may have had more than 12,000 inhabitants by the eleventh century. It had twenty 'moneyers' simultaneously minting coins in 1042.

In all the larger towns there was an interest in mercantile contacts which had nothing to do with older ties to kinsmen; in finance, which meant making money as well as coining it; and in order, which could only be deemed secure if there were conditions of internal and external peace.

Danish kings, like Saxon kings, thought of themselves as unifiers and as lawgivers, and Cnut's 'dooms' or laws were the most advanced in Europe. There was an obvious irony here: the word 'law', which implies the very reverse of arbitrary violence, is a Danish word by origin, as the great historian Maitland pointed out, so that 'if we can today distinguish between *law* and *right*, we are debtors to the Danes'. Kings were expounding the law, not inventing it; and the oldest law was the best. By the tenth century the laws reveal a carefully defined hierarchy, although a man's position in society was determined not only by the law but also by custom and titles, which differed from one part of the country to another. Kindred was still the basis of status, and freedom itself was divisible. At the base were the completely unfree, the slaves, some of them descendants of pre-Saxon peoples, some victims of individual or family misfortune. Above them were large numbers of half-free people, cottagers who were closely tied in their work and obligation to their lord's will; they were not paid, nor did they pay rent, and the Normans were to call them villeins. At the top were magnates, warriors or descendents of warriors. The bond between man and lord, expressed in different ways, was paramount, and men without lords were outside the basic social structures, unless they were lords themselves. As lesser men came to depend more on their lords than on their kinsmen, the fact of lordship came to be given greater prominence than the fact of kinship. Thus, the ninth-century laws of Alfred had laid down that 'a man may fight on behalf of his lord if the lord is being attacked without incurring a vendetta' and, furthermore, that 'a man may fight on behalf of his born kinsman, if he is being wrongly attacked, except against his lord; that we do not allow'.

A tenth-century monk, Aelfric, Abbot of Eynsham, an early master of English prose, simplified the reality of the social structure when he explained that the throne stood upon 'three supports': *laboratores, oratores,* and *bellatores*.

Laboratores are they who provide us with sustenance, ploughmen and husbandmen devoted to that alone.

Oratores are they who intercede for us to God and promote Christianity among Christian peoples in the service of God, as spiritual toil devoted to that alone for the benefit of us all.

Bellatores are they who guard our boroughs and also our land, fighting with weapons against the oncoming army.

This threefold division, inadequate and incomplete though it was – and it became increasingly so – was to be taken for granted for centuries. So too was the lack of freedom at the base. Aelfric's ploughman ended his complaint with the simple words, 'It is very hard work because I am not free.' Aelfric also gave a vivid description of what the ploughman had to do.

I work very hard. I go out at dawn and I drive the oxen in the field and yoke them to the plough. However stark the winter is, I dare not stay at home, for fear of my lord. I have to yoke the oxen and fasten the share and coulter to the plough, and every day I have to plough a full acre or more. I have a boy who drives the oxen with a goad, and even now he is hoarse from cold and shouting. I fill the ox-bins with hay and water and I clear out the dung.

Such a capacity for empathy introduces a new kind of evidence into English social history, something very different from classification.

Later generations were to simplify these structures in a different way from Aelfric, distinguishing simply between *eorls*, men with authority, and *ceorls* (churls), the simple: the rhyming was irresistible. In fact, there were as many divisions among the *ceorls* as there were among the *eorls* or *thegas* (thanes), men who had originally been the king's companions (*gesiths*). In the eleventh century some *ceorls* moved upwards, but more moved downwards, augmenting the ranks of the half-free. Many of them passed on their land as husbandmen from one generation to another, but in Kent, from the start a kingdom with a difference, it was divided into portions. Moreover, the proportions and status of people in different social groups varied from one part of the country to another. Some *ceorls* could be slave-owners in Kent, but in Wessex, even if they were rich their wealth could not secure them the highest social status unless they owned the land. The average landholding of a *ceorl*, however, was small.

There was no pretence at equality. Stag-hunting, fox-hunting and hawking were reserved for the lords, who did not work with their hands; and some parish priests were treated as household servants by lords who had themselves set up the parish churches. If families which owned an abbey had no eligible candidate to be abbot, the right of promotion could be sold and bought. Nonetheless, through Church poverty there could be avenues of individual mobility. Kings might deliberately prefer priests as their advisers to the kinsmen of great families. Women occupied a formal place within this social system, as they did in the system of work. They cleaned and cooked, but they also milked goats and ewes, sheared sheep and made clothes. They had figured in the earliest law code, that of Aethelbert of Kent (*c.* 600), when widows' compensation was specified carefully but cryptically: 'if a woman bear a living child, she shall have half the goods left by her husband if he dies first.' In many ways women were highly privileged in this period compared to later centuries: they could not be compelled to marry a man they disliked; divorce was easy; in the higher ranks of society they could own land and other property, receive gifts of marriage, including furniture and houses, and make wills; there are even instances of women disinheriting their sons.

The last successful invaders of England, the Normans, who came in 1066, were to introduce new features into the social structure. Yet they were of Viking stock, and their adoption of French had only recently been completed. Moreover, the Norman invasion itself was immediately preceded by a Scandinavian invasion: the last Saxon king, Harold II (1066), had been victorious in a bloody battle against the Norwegian leader Harold Hardrada near Stamford Bridge in Yorkshire immediately before he was defeated by the Normans near Hastings.

The Norman victory has been seen by a historian of medieval technology as a triumph of the military methods of the eleventh century over those of the seventh: Harold fought without cavalry, with a few archers and with a shield wall; William the Conqueror had employed shoed and stirruped horses and bowmen. This was certainly not the contemporary interpretation; the feeling of guilt and divine retribution was strong. The biographer of a supporter of William I, Bishop Wulfstan, was to write angrily, for example:

> Such was the feebleness of the wretched people that after the first battle they never attempted to rise up for liberty behind a common shield. It was as though with Harold had fallen also the whole strength of the country.

The long-term consequences of the Norman invasion have been much debated. Some historians have opted retrospectively for the benefits derived from the arrival of the 'constructive' Normans, drawn from Europe's mainland and facing south rather than north. Other historians have extolled the 'free' Saxons, struggling against what proved to be a 'Norman yoke'. Most historians have emphasized the continuities, following the example of William, who promised to respect and maintain ancient customs. He had crossed the sea to become king, not unjustly by force of arms alone, but, he claimed, 'in defence of right', promised the crown by Edward the Confessor (1042–66).

The Normans were to prove effective colonizers, endowed with a 'habit of authority', but critical voices were never entirely silenced, and a myth was sustained that there had been a golden age before they arrived. Even in Mrs Markham's highly popular *History of England*, published in 1823, two children who have been reading about Saxon England are reminded by their mother, 'As the Saxons continued in the country after the Conquest, and were much more numerous than the Norman settlers, we are still almost all of us chiefly of Saxon descent; and our language and many of our habits and customs sufficiently declare our origin.'

3

DEPENDENCE,
EXPANSION AND CULTURE

Norman saw on English oak
On English neck a Norman yoke;
Norman spoon in English dish,
And England ruled as Normans wish:
Blithe world to England never will be more
Till England's rid of all the four.

Wamba in Sir Walter Scott, *Ivanhoe*, 1820

What concern is it of monks – men who have resolved to flee the world – what does it matter to them who serves in the world, or under what name? Is not every man born to labour as a bird in flight?

St Anselm, *Letter to Two Monks*, 1081

Servitude is ordained by God, either because of the sins of those who become serfs, or as a trial, in order that those who are thus humbled may be made better.

Twelfth-century theological fragment

WHEN Domesday Book, an invaluable although incomplete survey of England's land and people, was meticulously but speedily drawn up, hundred by hundred, in 1086, it recorded the manifold activity of an old society which was still evolving and not the arrival of dramatic social change. On the eve of the Domesday survey a contemporary commentator noted how William I 'had deep speech with his wise men about this land, how it was peopled and by what sort of men'.

Nevertheless, the Norman Conquest did have immediate social, political and cultural implications. The old English thegnhood lost its land and, therefore, its influence, and a new, tough and resilient foreign aristocracy acquired power. By 1100 there were 500 Norman castles, symbols of power, scattered throughout the English countryside at strategic points – among them Windsor Castle, scanning the Thames Valley – but built according to no general strategic plan. There was a break in the Church too. Saxon bishops were either deposed or replaced by Normans after their death, and the organization of the Church, both monasteries and cathedrals, was reshaped. There was an abbey near Hastings, where the invasion battle had been won.

William's 'wise men' were a more broadly based group than his warriors. They included the kind of churchmen, unhampered by family ties, who were to serve all the Norman kings as royal ministers and clerks. During the eleventh and twelfth centuries they were to develop an apparatus of government of exceptional effectiveness, particularly remarkable, it has been claimed, for its 'rationality'. Indeed, continental historians have contrasted the monarchical centralization and political coherence of eleventh- and twelfth-century England with the 'extreme fragmentation of authority' in France.

England was also drawn at once into close cultural links with the other side of the Channel. Lanfranc, for example, the new Archbishop of Canterbury in 1070, was a former prior of Bec and Abbot of Caen; he was also a former teacher of the Pope. And many monks followed in his wake. At first, they were Benedictine 'black monks', who came from the great reformed abbeys in Normandy and went on to establish themselves in English towns, many of them cathedral sees; there were already thirty-five Benedictine monasteries when the Normans arrived. Half a century later, the Cistercian 'white monks' arrived. Unlike the Benedictines, they founded their monasteries – and these were soon numerous – in secluded places far from centres of population. Rievaulx, Fountains and Byland Abbeys, for example, were built by them within a century of the conquest. The years from 1070 to 1216 have been described as 'the monastic period of English spirituality', but while monks were living a life apart, new Norman barons were helping in the process of ecclesiastical reorganization.

There was a language gap between the local population and the new landowners, both Churchmen and aristocracy. Latin was a language of mysteries; Norman French was now the language of law and authority, and the first 'loan words' into English included castle and prison, cardinal and prior. Inflected English, spoken differently in the various regions of the country, a legacy of earlier settlement patterns, remained the language of the people. It was not displaced, and the *Anglo Saxon Chronicle* was continued for nearly half a century after the Conquest. The novelist Sir Walter Scott was to point out centuries later that in Norman times 'Old Alderman Ox continues to hold his Saxon epithet while he is under the charge of serfs and bondsmen, but becomes Beef, a fiery French gallant, when he arrives before the worshipful jaws that are to consume him.' Yet precisely because English was neither spoken by the colonists nor taught in the schools, it developed as a particularly rich language, taking time to move up the social scale.

For contemporary evidence about the effect of the Norman Conquest on Anglo-Saxon society that is free from later medieval or modern glosses, Domesday Book, the name current later and suggesting the last judgement, provides unique information concerning the distribution of land, the key to order and to power, and in its celebrated pages we become aware of continuities rather than changes. It was of immediate practical use as well as 'an inestimable boon to a learned posterity'.

Norman society rested on 'lordship', secular and spiritual, and the king, wise or foolish, was the lord of lords, with only the Lord in Heaven and the saints above him. Abbot Walter of Evesham claimed that the Norman victory in 1066 had demonstrated the inadequacy of prayers addressed to the old English saints. William I, pressing for continuity and consent, developed the custom of wearing his crown in three of the important towns of Southern England on the greatest feast days of the Church. In the North of England, however, he was to reveal his power in different fashion: there he laid waste to vast stretches of Yorkshire.

Because the crown was his by conquest, William I was able to acquire a huge royal demesne for himself, in size double that of

Edward the Confessor. All land belonged to the crown and all the great landholders to whom William directly parcelled out land were his tenants-in-chief. There were 170 of them, and they held their land at his gift and in return for specified services. There were no absolute freeholds, secular or ecclesiastical, and the tenants-in-chief held their own demesnes, parcelling out land to their own tenants. They also required knightly service from them. During William's reign, they were owed service by at least 4,000 knights, who were distinguishable as a social group from their lords. The two groups have sometimes been lumped together as 'powerful men', as opposed to 'poor men', both by historians and in medieval schemes of classification, but neither group was homogeneous. Each included great and small.

Historians have introduced into their interpretation of Norman (and other European) lordships the term 'feudalism', first employed during the seventeenth century by lawyers. It may be set alongside 'capitalism' and 'imperialism', other 'isms' which have acquired an extended use in relation to all societies and which invite comparisons between them at different periods of time and at different 'stages' of development. Since Marx first discussed 'the transition from feudalism to capitalism' as one of these 'stages', much has been written about feudalism by social and political historians. They have emphasized that feudalism was neither a static nor a uniform system, and they have used the term in both a broad and a narrow sense. Narrowly, it has been related to military (knightly) service as a condition of tenure of land. Broadly, it has been related to the tenure of the land itself, obligation and dependence, as expressed in the concept of vassalage. The first relationship focuses on warfare in an age of violence, the second on the use as well as on the tenure of land in an age when possession of land was the key to society.

Both interpretations have their point. Between the Norman Conquest and the Black Death of 1348 there was only one period of domestic peace in England lasting more than thirty years, and for much of the time Englishmen were involved in wars across the Channel. There was little new immigration into England and Normandy was lost in 1204, but a new and bigger English stake in France was secured when Henry II (1154–89), who had married

Eleanor of Aquitaine in 1152, founded the Angevin Empire. The military service and dues owed to the crown therefore mattered profoundly throughout the period. They were particularly important in the first years after the Norman Conquest, both when the king was in command, as William I or Henry I (1100–35) were, and when there was baronial anarchy, as there was under Stephen (1135–54).

Permission to build a castle, a licence to crenellate, had to be secured from the king, and the king had the right to garrison men there in case of need. Yet in an age when rivalry between tenants-in-chief was endemic, 'adulterine castles' were built which had no royal warrant. It was then that the chronicler William of Malmesbury, writing from the vantage point of a monastery, claimed, not without irony, that many castles nominally 'defending their neighbourhoods' were 'more probably speaking, laying them to waste': 'the garrisons drove off from the fields both sheep and cattle, nor did they abstain from churches or church yards.' It was a sign of the effective power of Henry II, Stephen's great successor, who reconstructed law and government, that while he destroyed large numbers of adulterine castles, he built only one completely new castle himself. It was at Orford in Suffolk and it had a magnificent polygonal keep.

By making justice available to all freemen Henry II laid the foundations of the common law which derived from older customary law but was capable of evolution through judgements reached in particular cases. The criminal law was tightened up and more severely enforced in the interest of order. English feudalism did not involve, therefore, a general fragmentation of public authority. Nor did it involve freedom from taxation. For Henry II's treasurer, Richard Fitzneale, Domesday Book remained 'the inseparable companion in the Treasury of the royal seal'. Royal revenues were carefully accounted and new administrative procedures introduced even before the Exchequer moved to Westminster under John (1199–1216), Henry's youngest son. It was under John that Normandy was lost in war by the English crown.

In the redistribution of land that had taken place immediately after the Norman Conquest, bishops and abbots had received 26 per cent, and lay barons 49 per cent, of the land. The powerful men, given huge estates or fiefs, included William's half-brother, one of only four earls left in the kingdom by the time of Domesday, and Roger de Montgomery, another earl, who received large estates in counties as widely separated as Sussex and Shropshire. Two other substantial beneficiaries were William Fitz Osbern, who had fought with William the Conqueror at Hastings and was now given a new base at Winchester, the old capital of Wessex, and William de Warenne, who had also fought at Hastings and subsequently acquired huge and widely scattered estates. Both de Warenne and Fitz Osbern retained lands and influence in Normandy as well as England after 1066; they were effectively Norman barons who became Anglo-Norman only later. If their estates were to be developed effectively, there had to be delegation and inevitably, therefore, many of their manors were quickly farmed out to others.

The fortunes of the first families diverged considerably in the eleventh, twelfth and thirteenth centuries. The loss of Normandy broke many family links. Those of the Fitz Osberns, for example, went rapidly down, while those of the de Warennes stayed up. By the end of the twelfth century many of the leading Domesday families had already disappeared. In each generation too new families regularly emerged, often 'raised from the dust' by royal favour; they consolidated their position by the right marriages to the right heiresses at the right time. The wheel of fortune continued to turn. The Lisles, for example, benefited greatly from a series of successful marriages that led from knighthood to nobility, while the Peverels suffered from a succession of daughters as heiresses. Conscious family strategy became a necessary means to the hereditary transmission of estates, for, if it failed, land reverted to the crown through escheat. Nonetheless, while only thirty-six of the English tenancies-in-chief, or baronies, remained within the same male line for the period from 1066 to 1327 and many men of knightly rank gained at the expense of great landlords, the gap between the many and the few remained as wide as ever.

English radicals in succeeding centuries were to complain, therefore, not only of a loss of native freedom in 1066, but of a continuing 'rain of locusts' generation by generation: Tom Paine, the eighteenth-century radical inspired by the French Revolution, was to suggest that, despite Magna Carta, 'the country is yet disfigured with the marks' of Norman-imposed authority. A diametrically opposed view was expressed a century later by Sir John Fortescue, historian of the British army. England had passed, he observed of the country after 1066, 'to her great good fortune, under the sway of a race that could teach her to obey'; and he saw the strengthening of lineage as a strengthening of the nation. Such sharply contrasting verdicts reflect significant differences in Englishmen's approach to the whole shape of English social history. Radicals were to condemn privilege and, with Church as well as State in mind, to welcome dissent; conservatives were to praise deference and to defend obedience. In time, of course, all these qualities were deemed to be distinctively 'English', as was consensus, so that incompatibilities could conveniently be treated as complementarities.

In fact, lords themselves, big or small, cultivated only one-third to two-fifths of the arable land in use. The rest outside their demesnes, which they reserved for their own use, was cultivated by various kinds of 'peasants' although this was a controversial term not in use at the time. The contemporary terms were *villani*, villeins (41 per cent of the total group, holding 45 per cent of the land); *bordarii*, cottagers or small householders (32 per cent of the total group, holding 5 per cent of the land); *liberi homines*, free men (14 per cent of the total group, holding 20 per cent of the land) and *servi*, serfs (10 per cent of the total group with no land at all). Work on the lord's demesne itself was a feudal obligation; it varied in scale and scope from one part of the country to another.

Taking the country as a whole there was a great variety of changing status relationships. Nor did the initial proportions of the different social groups hold; there is evidence, for example, that the number of *servi* fell even between 1066 and 1086, when the Domesday Book was commissioned. The basic distinction between free and unfree, which was tersely expressed in a lawyer's dictum of the twelfth century that 'all men are either free or serfs', as simple as a modern economist's dictum that all men are rich or poor, did not save society from continuing argument or litigation. There were always many intermediate status grades, some surviving from Saxon England, and great regional variations, all with their own history. There were, for example, significant differences between Sussex and Kent, where gavelkind, the inheritance system under which land was divided between heirs, was perpetuated and seemed to go with freedom. In the old northern Danelaw, too, free tenants were sometimes a majority of the village population. During the second half of the twelfth century social grades were more sharply defined as the legal system took shape. In the process, however, dependence also was more clearly articulated.

Complexities were accentuated by the fact that rural England was divided into both villages (or hamlets) and manors, the latter basic economic units like factories of modern times, and that they did not necessarily share the same boundaries. A village might be divided between two or more manors, and a lord might hold manors in several villages. Such differences sprang from the fact that while a manor was a piece of landed property held by a lord and managed, at least in the first instance, from a single centre, the village was a community of people living side by side, with or without a lord in residence. Two adjacent manors might be quite different in their organization and customs, therefore, just as two adjacent villages might be quite different in their size, appearance, social composition and wealth. Manorial records are an invaluable historical source.

Leicestershire, where W. G. Hoskins has traced the history of the village of Wigston Magna through the centuries, provides good examples of these complexities. In Wigston there was an absentee landlord and nearly half the land in the village, which had grown in size and numbers under the Danelaw, was owned – a term which was beginning to count for more by the thirteenth century – by smaller landlords 'of free condition'. But other Leicestershire villages were in a quite different position, dominated by particular families over a long period of time. And even in manors like these, where there was an active landlord in residence, the service in kind required of the bondsmen could vary substantially, the heaviest services tending to be demanded on the estates that were of largest or of oldest formation. It is impossible to generalize, however, and the heaviest labour obligation, 'weekwork' (regular work for the lord on his land), was required in some villages and not in others.

One of the most important general points about the Domesday pattern, much of which was to change drastically between the eleventh and the end of the thirteenth century, was that nine out of ten people still lived in completely rural communities. The remaining people were not necessarily 'urban' dwellers. Only one out of twenty-five people lived in the ten towns with over 2,000 residents – they included York, Norwich, Lincoln, Stamford and Leicester – and nearly half of this group lived in London. The rest lived in centres where farming prevailed, but where other occupations were represented; a bishop, for example, might work in such a centre, or a sheriff, the royal official in the shire on whom the king initially depended. There could also be craftsmen, among them masons, potters, weavers and tanners. Rural craftsmen included potters in Wiltshire, smiths in several counties, and ironworkers in Devon and the West Riding of Yorkshire. Some occupations were clearly not represented in the returns: only one carpenter was mentioned in the whole of the countryside (in Herefordshire), and in a country where much fish was eaten, there were far too few fishermen in the count to have satisfied their fellow countrymen except by a miracle.

Population as a whole was unevenly distributed at Domesday. The north was particularly thinly settled and the east densely populated, but even in counties like Warwickshire, where there were substantial populations, some woodland areas were sparsely peopled. There was already relatively dense settlement in the prime arable areas of the country like Norfolk, Suffolk and Leicestershire. Modern estimates of England's total population, extrapolated from Domesday patterns, vary between one and three million. The extent of such variations reflects the disagreement among experts concerning the multiplier that should be used to convert entries in Domesday Book, which is a list of tenants-in-chief and their dependents of every degree, into a comprehensive register.

Domesday Book was designed for fiscal purposes, to protect and to increase the king's revenue, and it carefully catalogued circuit by circuit the amount of arable land in the areas it covered. Indeed, one chronicler complained that it was 'shame to tell, though he [William] thought it no shame to do, there was not even an ox or a cow or a pig left that was not set down in writing'. It remained a formidable working record. Perhaps the most surprising fact for the modern reader is that as much as 93 per cent of the land under the plough in 1914 was already being tilled in 1086. Daily life in the fields was going on as before, although the increased use of heavy ploughs made it easier to reclaim land and to extend cultivation. Unlike the Anglo-Saxons and the Danes, the Normans were not drawn to England by a desire to farm land and their arrival brought no changes in farming practices, except, perhaps, for the laying down of vineyards. The fields were dug in the autumn, harrowed in winter and sown in spring, but the busiest time of the year was the late-summer harvest. Every year much of the land was left fallow. If too much land was cultivated, the number of livestock maintained would fall. By the thirteenth century, however, after protracted expansion of the area of land under cultivation, careful attention, well documented, was being paid to the economics of farming. By contrast, Domesday does not give details of landscapes, communications or the yield of crops – omissions that are now a matter of regret.

The full implications of the social, political and cultural changes following the Norman Conquest took time to work themselves out, and the patterns of change over the next three centuries were intricate. Nor did all the changes point in the same direction. Constitutional historians have focused on various areas: first, the development of strong royal government, which made for what was then in the European context a relatively efficient state; second, the emergence of English common law, moving, unlike the Roman law in use in other countries, from precedent to precedent; third, the sometimes stormy relationship between the king and the barons; and, fourth, the making of Parliament. Economic historians have focused on a striking growth in population with short-term set-backs which may have raised it at its peak well above four million; on an expansion of cultivation, often by small men without power, towards and into poorer marginal lands; and on the development, marked from the twelfth century onwards, of trade, commerce and urbanization. It is an open question as to whether population growth by itself accounted for 'agrarian crisis' in the thirteenth century.

Both constitutional and economic themes have their social dimensions. Thus the presence in Parliament in the reign of Edward I (1272–1307) not only of lords, bishops and great abbots but also of a 'commons' demonstrated the growing wealth of townsmen and knights of the shire and their growing consequence in the local communities which they represented, while the fact that townsmen and knights sat together encouraged the merchants and feudal elements, divided in many political societies, to think of their common interests. Parliament was a new device before it became an established institution. It was a device to secure consent, particularly to collect taxes, but inevitably it involved processes of bargaining.

The levying of taxation was regarded as 'the hardest task which the king and his advisors could undergo'. One of the most interesting books written in the reign of Henry II is Richard Fitzneale's *Dialogue of the Exchequer*, completed around 1179, in which the author described the working of the king's Exchequer, complete with its abacus, the computer of the age brought in from the distant Arab world. Fitzneale stated categorically that the 'state of the realm' depended on the wealth of the king. The king's subjects might look at the matter differently. Taxation, particularly for war, was the hardest burden imposed upon them.

It was largely because of disputes about taxation – pressure on the pocket (though there were no pockets in men's clothes at this time) is more quickly felt than pressure on the mind – that John was forced by his barons in 1215 to seal Magna Carta, which linked taxation with consent. Already it was possible through 'scutage' payments to substitute cash for military service, and this could be a mutually acceptable device. John had added extra charges to marriage and wardship dues, however, and these were inevitably one-sided. Harassed as most kings were – and were to be – by the demands of war, he had extorted maximum feudal payments, thereby irritating many of his most powerful subjects, who had many valuable privileges of their own *vis-à-vis* those dependent on themselves. He had extended further more novel taxes on incomes (thirtieths, sevenths and even fourths). Opposition was inevitable and Magna Carta was a rather hastily drafted document dealing essentially with the privileges claimed by Norman barons. Nonetheless, over the years, while tax systems were to change, it was to become part of the English constitutional inheritance, because the claims for privileges set out in its clauses could in time be translated into a universal language of freedom and justice.

Later medieval kings were to rely increasingly not only on feudal dues but on what were in effect general property taxes levied on people in towns as well as people in the country, and, from the reign of Edward I (1272–1307) on, levies on trade and customs duties. Once again there was a link between economics and politics, since in order to secure necessary assent the king was forced to turn increasingly to 'parliaments'. As early as the 1240s, chroniclers wrote of 'most general' or 'great' parliaments to which prelates, earls and barons were summoned by the king's sealed writ, and in 1265 the 'commons' began to be summoned to some of them too. They attended only one in eight parliaments before 1284, but one in three in the later years of Edward I's reign. From Edward I's reign onwards kings were able to tax the clergy without the Pope's permission and to share in the levies imposed upon the clergy by the Pope.

Alongside changes in taxation and the making of Parliament it is possible to trace the gradual development in the twelfth and thirteenth centuries of a more complex society and a richer culture with far more organized institutions than there had been in 1066. When John of Salisbury, perhaps the most learned classical writer of medieval times, produced his *Policraticus*, a map of society, in 1159, he still did not include alongside the *bellatores*, *oratores* and *laboratores* (the three orders Aelfric had defined in the tenth century as 'they who guard our boroughs and also our land', 'they who intercede for us to God', and 'they who provide us with sustenance') either townsmen, who were increasing in numbers and wealth, or administrators and courtiers, not a professional civil service, who were growing in importance as the king looked for wise counsel and as new institutions of government and administration developed. But these changes had become clear by the end of the thirteenth century. We can then identify, at least in the largest towns, a complex urban social structure with marked inequalities of income, dress, status and power. The ways of the merchant, uncategorized in surveys of society, diverged sharply from the ways of the *oratores* and the *bellatores*, although the former might develop substantial mercantile enterprises of their own and the latter were prepared to send their children to the city. There were also a growing number of literate laymen, although the *laboratores* and the *bellatores*, many of whom were now speaking English, remained largely illiterate throughout this period.

John of Salisbury also failed to note the inadequacy of the designation *oratores*. They now fell into quite different groups (indeed, there could be conflict between different orders of monks who stressed different values and who assumed different roles in society) and they included teachers (the Church had a monopoly of education), administrators and scholars, prophets and philosophers, artists and musicians. (Descants were introduced in the twelfth century, ornamental variations above the plainsong which had been sung for centuries.) This was a period of intellectual as well as artistic renaissance; the scholars employed Latin as their language and were now passing far beyond literacy into realms of intricate analysis and speculation. New learning about the ancients arrived from the Arab world, and soon English philosophers would read Thomas Aquinas, born in 1225, who looked back to Aristotle as he set out to harmonize faith and reason. The scholars were creating new institutions of their own – universities, where they could meet together, learn and dispute.

The story of Oxford illustrates the sequence of development. The Normans had begun with a castle there in 1071. Forty years later they built a priory, and soon afterwards a hospital and a nunnery. (Near by was a hunting-lodge at Woodstock.) The town acquired a charter in 1155 and a common seal in 1191. Scholars were lecturing in the town by the late twelfth century and a small community of students was also beginning to be built up; in 1209 a number of them moved east to Cambridge. The impulse to congregate students as well as scholars quickened following the arrival of representatives of the new thirteenth-century religious orders, Dominicans first, Franciscan friars second, and by the end of the century the older orders of monks, the Benedictines and the Cistercians, had also established institutions in the town. Tales of miracles abounded, and there was a cult of relics. Yet one notable thirteenth-century Franciscan scholar in medieval Oxford, Roger Bacon, described mathematics as the only discipline by which truth could be established without fear of error, and he looked outside his time to envisage a future which included spectacles, submarines and flying machines.

Meanwhile, the *bellatores* also developed their own culture. When William the Conqueror dubbed his son a knight at Whitsuntide 1086, the year Domesday Book was commissioned, it was in a far simpler ceremony than those of the thirteenth century, which included purification, confession and communion. By the latter date the *bellatores* were drawn to elaborate codes of honour (a word of Norman–French origin) that focused on loyalty and prowess, a combination of strength, daring, courage and skill and on armoured display. The codes of chivalry were aristocratic, crossed geographical and dynastic divides, contained a religious element, were nourished by romance and even by fantasy, and in time were to seem 'four parts in five illusion', but they belonged unmistakably, like the tournament, to the pattern of the age. 'What is the function of orderly knighthood?' John of Salisbury asked, giving as his answer 'to protect the Church, to fight against treachery, to reverence the priesthood, to fend off injustice from the poor, to make peace in your own province, to shed blood for your brethren, and, if needs must, to lay down your own life'. Only a few people could share such an ideal. Even fewer could follow it. Yet the ideal was a necessary feature of the culture; it influenced the way in which privileged children were brought up.

The *bellatores* did not fight only in Europe. Some of them also sought through crusades, the first of which was organized in 1095, to 'reconquer and redeem' parts of the Arab world; and two English kings, Richard I, Coeur de Lion (1157–99), son of Henry II and older brother of John, and Edward I went on crusades, the first in 1190, the second in 1270. Neither the realities of war, nor the ribaldry that went with it, easily fitted the codes of chivalry. The crusades themselves were at times as barbarous as – and far more calculated in their barbarity than – the Viking raids had been, while war in France always involved plunder and often treachery. Ravaging lands and burning villages counted for more than set battles. Of England itself, Peter of Blois, writing in Henry II's reign soon after the murder of Archbishop Thomas Becket in 1170 by four knights at the altar of his own cathedral at Canterbury, observed that 'in these days of ours the order of chivalry is mere disorder. For he is accounted stoutest and most illustrious among knights whose mouth is defiled with the most filthy language, whose oaths are most abominable, and who most despises good.'

If some changes in culture, including literature and art, seem to have been superimposed on a rough society, others, including architecture, obviously reflected social change. Castles, cathedrals and towns looked different at the end of the thirteenth century from how they had looked in 1086. The first castles had been of a 'motte and bailey' type, the motte being a mound at the centre of the castle, either a natural hilly feature or earth thrown up during the course of digging a deep circular ditch, and the bailey an open space at the base encircled by a ditch. The later castles were deliberately imposing with stone towers and keeps. They could look, and sometimes still do, like magic castles in a romance. It must have been a new and exciting experience for people to see castles change or to take part in the work of changing them. At Norwich, for example, workmen in the reign of Henry I replaced a timber castle with a great stone edifice and a novel rectangular keep, and more than a century later Simon de Montfort built elaborate water defences at Kenilworth.

There was even more visual change to see in cathedral towns for, like Stonehenge before them, most English cathedrals belong to different dates. At Durham, work on the cathedral on the hill began in 1093; it proceeded fast and the cathedral was consecrated forty years later. The powerful columns and magnificent nave carry a continuing sense of Norman energy and the will to dominate. Far to the south, the cathedral of Rochester was rebuilt by its bishop, Gundulf, the great builder of castles and architect of the White Tower in London. Cathedral building, like the construction of castles, was seldom a single, consecutive process, and only Salisbury, built between 1220 and 1266 (except for its fine fourteenth-century steeple) was constructed in this way. Most English medieval cathedrals belong to a number of different periods, with significant differences in architecture between one period and another. Thus, between 1170 and 1200, rounded Norman arches gave way to pointed Gothic architecture, with a remarkable burst of further elaboration in 'decorated styles' imported from France and popular between 1250 and 1330. (The ribbed vaulting in the choir of Ely Cathedral is a good example.) Later generations, particularly those guided by Pugin and John Ruskin in the nineteenth century, were to claim not only that Gothic was the supreme architecture, but also that the men who created it had belonged to an organic society and culture, the secrets of which had been lost or deliberately destroyed following the rise of trade and industry. The same view was shared fifty years later by the American writer Henry Adams, who compared the inspiration provided by the thirteenth-century cult of the Virgin with that of the twentieth-century cult of the dynamo.

This was a society where the rites of the Church, a universal Church, encompassed all the main events in the local life of the individual and the family. Birth, marriage and death all had their rituals. Whatever messages the villager or townsman, simple or relatively sophisticated, might receive about history or beauty, morality or eternity, came through the Church and at a local level: the parish priest as shepherd was the intermediary between the villagers, his sheep, and their Maker. And the boundaries between the religious and the secular were always blurred. It was through the building itself as much as the services that took place inside it that the Church exercised such a pervasive influence; it spoke through its images – stained glass windows, wall paintings, stone statues and carved fonts (in Edward I's reign some of these were eight-sided with carvings on each side) – and through its monumental brasses, which date back to before 1300. It spoke also through its graveyards, shrines, monuments and crosses. Inside the church communication by word mattered less than communication by eye: there are no pulpits in England which can be ascribed to an earlier date than 1340. Preaching outside the church by friars, God's minstrels, was a different matter and their sermons were deliberately homely in their themes and images.

Religious ritual gained its significance from the fact that confession and penance were a necessary part of the pattern. It would be a mistake, therefore, to consider the Church as a 'kindly mother waiting for the coming of her children', for it enforced its claims as vigorously as it organized its festivals. It had a monitorial function too. As a poem in 1303, entitled *Handlyng Synne*, warned:

> Karolles, wrestlyinges, or somour games,
> Who so ever haunteth any swyche shames
> Yn cherche, other yn chercheyerde
> Of sacrylage, he may be a ferde.

The sheep had their mastiffs as well as their shepherds.

There may have been as many as 40,000 ordained priests during the thirteenth century, a sizeable group recruited from all sections of society including the poorest. While inside church they might 'recite the words of others without knowing in the least what they mean, like parrots and magpies', as Roger Bacon once put it from the vantage point of Oxford; outside church they often had children, got drunk or went poaching, although they were increasingly warned not to do these things and to set a good example. When John Peckham, the Franciscan Archbishop of Canterbury of Bacon's own day, himself the son of a farmer, carried out visitations to try to discover exactly what was going on in all the parishes under his care, he even found it necessary to prescribe that priests' children should not succeed to their fathers' benefices.

The parish church came to handle sin as actively as it fostered virtue. Lay proprietors of church benefices (endowments) often conceived of them as a piece of property. The Church continued to benefit from lay giving until the Statutes of Mortmain of 1279 and 1290 forbade all men to give or bequeath land to the 'dead hand' of a religious body without a royal licence. The religious orders, which controlled a quarter of the parish churches of England in 1200, were also jealous of their rights; indeed, the history of land use was influenced by bishops and abbots as much as by lay lords, and here religious and secular interests become indistinct. The Franciscan Friars, who preached poverty, themselves benefited from lay giving.

The boundaries between the religious and the superstitious, between the Christian and the pagan, were equally indistinct. Why, for instance, did provincial constitutions drawn up in 1236 lay down that 'fonts are to be kept closed by locks because of witchcraft'? Images were often believed to have magical efficacy, and the Lateran Council in distant Rome ruled that the elements of the Eucharist and the holy oil should always be kept under lock and key. The parish church was a familiar feature of the rural landscape, but its teaching was still mingled with old beliefs and adapted to the felt needs of everyday life.

There is considerable disagreement among historians about the basic question of the standard of living of the majority of the population – Aelfric's *laboratores* – by the end of the thirteenth century. By that time population had probably more than doubled since Domesday, from around one and a quarter million to over four million, and this was bound to have far-reaching effects. For some historians, most Englishmen at that time were struggling to exist on inadequate smallholdings. For others, England was essentially a prosperous country except in certain crisis years. While there is agreement that there was an expansion of trade during the twelfth and thirteenth centuries, some historians suggest that the chief explanation is that people were being pushed out of an over-populated countryside. Indeed, it has been argued that, at the end of the period, it was the poverty of villagers which encouraged the important new economic development, the growth of the worsted trade.

There is no doubt that the scarcity of good land led to a significant further expansion of cultivation during the twelfth and thirteenth centuries into less favourable lands: woodland, moorland, fenland and marshland. The 'wastes' of Dartmoor, for example, were cultivated; terraced hillsides, once thought to be prehistoric, were farmed at Mere in Wiltshire and in Dorset; the monks of Battle Abbey in Sussex constructed successive seawalls to reclaim the marshes. By the late thirteenth century a bigger area was cultivated than at any period before the wars of the twentieth century. Development was, as always, uneven and locally determined, but expansion of cultivation, whether carried out by lords, priors or peasants, was the dominant factor of social life. There was significant urban expansion too. Many new towns appeared in the twelfth and thirteenth centuries, among them ports like Newcastle, Hull, Lynn and Boston which thrived on growing foreign trade, and a number of 'planned' or 'planted' towns, of which no less than 172 have been identified. A classic example of the latter was 'new' Winchelsea in Sussex, laid out between 1281 and 1288 in thirty-nine rectangular lots: its chequer-board pattern of streets is still visible, preserved by the misfortunes in its later history. Other new towns included Stony Stratford and Devizes.

Nevertheless, country rather than town rhythms continued to dictate the pace of life during the twelfth and thirteenth centuries. Some of the most important trading activities took place at country fairs, glorified markets which involved the same medieval mix of activity and conviviality as did the guilds inside the towns. Domesday Book itself has practically nothing at all to say about fairs – only one, Aspall in Suffolk, is mentioned specifically – but by the end of the thirteenth century there were many of them, including the St Ives fair, founded by Henry I, and the great Stourbridge Fair near Cambridge, founded in the reign of John, which lasted for three weeks every September. Some fairs were, of course, held in towns, like the great Winchester St Giles Fair, with one section famous for its wines and spices, and Bartholomew Fair in London held in Smithfield. Religion directly influenced the location of fairs, the booths often being grouped around the church. It also determined their timing on days of festival.

Villages, the everyday life of which still centred on the seasons, varied like towns in site, size, appearance and fortunes – there were 13,000 of them already registered in Domesday Book – and by the end of the thirteenth century compact village settlements were to be found in most of lowland England. A few were new, like Fleet in Lincolnshire; most were old. They were often physically unattractive settlements with rough-and-ready cottage dwellings, sparsely furnished inside and filthy outside, but there were also gardens and fruit trees. The simplest dwellings would be made of mud and clay with a thatched roof, but by the thirteenth century the manor house might be built of stone, as might the barn. It was a sign of luxury when the lord of the manor installed better quality roofs, ornamental tiles and floors, strewn with rushes or straw, and cobbled yards; he would often plan expensive enclosed deer parks as well. One at Cold Overton in Leicestershire, first mentioned in 1269, covered 200 acres and had banks 30 feet in width. Inside the manor the great hall was still the centre of life for much of the year, a place for meeting and even sleeping, as well as eating and feasting. Windows were small and high, and glass was used in churches before it was used in domestic buildings. There was little furniture except wood-framed beds, benches and chests.

In some parts of the country, such as the Lake District and Cornwall, most of the population lived in scattered small hamlets rather than villages. Wherever there was a village, however, it was taken for granted that the individual's interests would in certain respects be subordinated to those of the community. The village, like the town, was not simply a collection of individuals or of families of unequal status and wealth. Community obligations, such as road and bridge maintenance, were taken for granted, while the operation of the legal system involved the participation of villagers in juries – for example, those to inquire into mysterious deaths. In the thirteenth century, under Henry III and his son Edward I, villages were required to mount watches to protect life and property, and later they were also called upon to provide one man for the army and pay his wages. Villagers might reach common decisions enshrined in their own by-laws about access to land or the use of the meadows without any pressure from above, or join together in raising funds for a new church. It has been suggested, indeed, that the dynamic element in village life in some parts of the country was more often the community than the lord.

This picture of social order in the medieval village of the thirteenth century has recently been redrawn by an English social anthropologist, Alan Macfarlane, who has argued that 'the majority of ordinary people in England from at least the thirteenth century were rampant individualists, highly mobile both geographically and socially, economically rational, market-orientated and acquisitive, ego-centred in kinship and social life'. Tied though villagers were to the land, they were not, according to Macfarlane, peasants of the kind to be found in contemporary peasant societies: custom was not all-powerful, kinship under patriarchal direction was not the main social bond. Villagers bought and sold land, there was no rigid division between villeins and non-villeins in the holding of their land, and, according to the law, women were able to carry out transactions as well as men.

Macfarlane implies, in the tradition of the great nineteenth-century historian Maitland, that many legal statements of the time corroborate aspects of his suggested sociology, economics and psychology. Thus, he argues, there was no link between family and land under common law; 'peasant land charters' reveal that there was an extensive land market in some parts of the country in the late twelfth and thirteenth centuries; and the great thirteenth-century lawyer Bracton could assert that 'a citizen could scarcely be found who would undertake a greater enterprise in his life-time, if, at his death, he was compelled against his will to leave his estate to ignorant and extravagant children and undeserving wives'.

While there is ample evidence of both social and geographical mobility, this stimulating alternative picture, relating also to later centuries and very different from that of historians like Rodney Hilton, begs many questions. If it is sensible to be sceptical about calling English villagers peasants, is it not equally sensible to be sceptical about the attribution to medieval Englishmen and Englishwomen of qualities like 'rampant individualism', 'market orientation' and 'ego-centricity', terms derived from the relatively recent language of sociology, economics and psychology? The word individual itself did not emerge in its contemporary sense until the late seventeenth century; in the thirteenth century it meant indivisible.

There were, in fact, many medieval constraints on the individual. The social nexus was tightly conceived at the time and status was carefully nuanced, so much so that two recent historians were able to list no less than twenty-one status terms within a group of Cambridgeshire villages in the year 1279. Nor was status the only constraint. The King's Courts would not afford the villein protection against eviction, nor award him damages against his lord; and he had no standing in the public courts against the lord unless the latter's actions went beyond all reason (for example, maiming and killing). Men's self-estimations were not necessarily those of either their lords or the lawyers.

Economic and social historians have argued also about the implications of change within the village and the manor between the Norman Conquest and the end of the thirteenth century, focusing more on the attitudes of the lord than his dependants. During most of the twelfth century many lords ceased to manage their land directly and rented it out. During most of the thirteenth century, by contrast, many lords managed their demesne land directly in order to secure the greatest returns from it. Such shifts of policy were influenced by demand, which was itself influenced by population, but inevitably supply factors – the quality of land and the costs of labour – came into the reckoning. So too did prices, which reflected these different forces, for there was rapid inflation between 1180 and 1220, and during the thirteenth century as a whole prices more than tripled while wages remained static. Enforced labour services had already been giving way to wage labour as villeins commuted their labour dues by paying money to the lord instead, so that by the early thirteenth century over half the adult male population was working full-time or part-time for money wages. While the pattern could change – in order to profit from increased demand lords often reverted to requiring labour services – over the period as a whole grants of freedom multiplied alongside commutation, and some of the freed were able, energetic or lucky enough to buy land and prosper as yeomen, passing on their land to their heirs.

Whatever the circumstances – and many people were living on the edge of subsistence – this was a period of substantial economic activity. Wheat was actually shipped overseas from Ipswich and wool was such an overwhelmingly important national export that when the barons were arguing with Edward I in 1297 about

taxation and government, they could claim, with some exaggeration, that half the country's wealth derived from it. Thirty
thousands sacks were shipped abroad every year, nearly all to
Flanders, where there was a highly developed cloth industry
dependent upon English wool. The trade had begun to prosper
during the previous century, and several great English estates,
like Crowland Abbey, specialized in sheep farming: the flocks
there increased from 4,000 to 7,000 between 1276 and 1313. Hull,
Lynn and Boston were the most important export centres that
grew up during this period.

The special place of wool in English history was to be recognized in many ways. The first customs duty levied on its export in
1275 became known as the *Antiqua Custuma*, and already at that
time control of wool was a political weapon. Judges and the Lord
Chancellor in the Great Council sat on a wool sack. It is not
surprising that the first chapter of the much used early twentieth-
century textbook *The Golden Fleece* was called 'The Wool Pack in
the Making of England'.

Furthermore, when wool began to be made into cloth in
England rather than exported as raw material, it stimulated the
growth of industry. England was far behind Flanders in the
production of cloth in the late thirteenth century, but there was
enough development, including the building of new fulling mills
worked by water power to shrink felt and to scour cloth, for a
distinguished scholar to suggest that there was an industrial
revolution in the thirteenth century. The industry was spread
through the countryside rather than concentrated in the towns,
and the sources for its early history are, therefore, manor rather
than borough records. One of the first mills at work, as early as
the reign of John, was at Elcot, near Marlborough; and by the end
of the thirteenth century there were significant concentrations in
West Yorkshire, the Lake District, Cornwall, Devon, Somerset,
Wiltshire and the Cotswolds.

Despite this marked surge of economic development, most
economic historians have argued forcefully that the expansion
and the population growth it supported could not last. Problems
multiplied more than opportunities. In particular, landlords'
appropriation of land on the commons (to which all villagers held

grazing rights) for arable farming raised complex questions of common rights, while the extension of cultivation carried with it economic penalties, notably exhausted land and falling yields. The first of these issues was clearly decided in favour of the lords by the Statute of Merton of 1235, which laid down that a lord was entitled to appropriate the whole of the commons provided he left sufficient grazing for any freeholders who pastured their animals there. But the second, agricultural productivity, was beyond the reach of the law, just as industrial productivity in the twentieth century has remained beyond the reach of politicians. If and when soil became exhausted (particularly on marginal lands which were by definition poor lands) and the supply of animal manure dropped because there was less land available for animal pasturing, high farming was bound to be in trouble.

The theory that soils became exhausted and agricultural yields began to decline during the last years of the thirteenth century has been seriously questioned in the light of recent detailed evidence, and a number of historians have disputed the conclusion that England (along with other European countries) was over-populated at the end of the thirteenth century in relation to its resources and technology, with the kind of consequences that Thomas Malthus was to identify in the late eighteenth century – growth checked by famine. There were densely populated parts of the country with large numbers of small-holdings where there were no signs of a Malthusian outcome (fenland communities, for example, with a population density comparable to that of the twentieth century) and which remained prosperous into the fourteenth century. Furthermore, the level of rents did not suddenly and generally begin to fall at the end of the thirteenth century. Much depended on the state of the annual harvest, but there was no general day of reckoning with nature.

There were even two new features in thirteenth-century experience which, while they did not yet contribute significantly to economic output, were later to become of vital importance in the English economy. In different ways they both suggested that nature might even be tamed. First, there was the burst of new industrial activity in the countryside, offering a supplementary or alternative livelihood to that derived from the land, which

depended on a new power-driven technology: fulling mills superseded fulling 'under the feet of men', as one contemporary
expressed it. It raised questions about the ownership of power
that were to be raised again 500 years later with the development
of steam power; the Dean in a story of Jocelin de Brakeland
argued that 'the profit which may come from the wind ought to
be denied to no man'.

Second, throughout the thirteenth century there was increasing
interest in agricultural improvement. Careful attention began to
be paid to the technology and economics of farming, partly under
the pressures of inflation and shortage of land and partly encouraged by the incentive of rising incomes. In consequence, there
were many switches from a two- to a three-field rotation system,
both to accommodate new land brought into cultivation and to
reduce the amount of land under fallow. In addition, there were
changes in cropping, including marling (fertilizing) the soil,
substituting new seed corn each year and growing more peas,
beans and vetches. 'Change your seed every year at Michaelmas,'
wrote Walter of Henley in his influential thirteenth-century
textbook on stewardship and husbandry, 'for seed grown on
other ground will bring more profit than that which is grown on
your own. Will you see to this?'

The last question was a pertinent one. Walter of Henley was
anxious not only to give advice, but also to ensure that it was
followed. Good management, including auditing, mattered as
much as new techniques. 'The hayward,' he emphasized, 'ought
to be an active and sharp man, for he must, early and late, look
after and go round and keep the woods, corn and meadows and
other things belonging to his office.' Duties were clearly set out
for every specialized office, and their number and range were
increasing in the thirteenth century. On the negative side, it was
stressed, cheating had to stop. On the positive side, production
targets could be fixed. Monasteries sometimes led the way in
good management, and it is interesting that Walter was writing
in Canterbury: Henry of Eastry, the Prior of Christ Church,
Canterbury, was one of the most astute stock-keepers and
managers of his day.

Walter was concerned with workers as well as with managers,

and his advice touched all aspects of farming at every level. 'The dairymaid,' he observed for example, 'ought to be faithful and of good repute, and keep herself clean . . . She ought not to allow any under dairymaid or another to take or carry away milk or butter or cream, by which the cheese shall be less and the dairy impoverished.' Dairying was never the only female occupation in the countryside. Women carried out other work on the farm, including hoeing. And there were women, too, who supervised landed estates, as well as household servants, with great ability. A monastic chronicler wrote of Hawisa, Countess of Aumal in her own right, who in 1180 married the Earl of Essex, that she was 'almost a man to whom nothing masculine is lacking save virility'. But at the same time the formal position of women within society, as laid down by law, had been considerably eroded since the Norman Conquest, due both to the introduction of land tenure based on a military order and to Christianity. Women in both canon and civil law were deemed to be 'under the rod' of their husbands, and canon law specifically permitted wife-beating. Adam had sinned, it was maintained, because of Eve's pressure.

Much information about thirteenth-century social life comes from many sources besides monastic chronicles. There was no single inquiry comparable to Domesday in the thirteenth century, but regular and systematic records multiply. Perhaps the best known are The Pipe Rolls, court rolls, chancery records and account books that exist for this period. The Pipe Rolls were originally long rolls of sheepskin, recording moneys received by the Treasury from the shires: they go back to 1129–30 and as a complete series to 1154. Chancery records included details of charters, wills and contracts. The Curia Regis Rolls were the records of a highly organized system of law which by Edward I's reign rested firmly on the king's authority: they covered cases in which the king was not a party. Manorial courts continued to dispense feudal justice and ecclesiastical courts universal canon law (with the power of excommunication), while borough courts had local urban jurisdiction. Yet it was the king's courts, including the high court of Parliament, which upheld the law of the land. There was also a system of judicial visitation, and Edward's reign began with an Eyre of 1274, an itinerant inquiry into royal

estates and royal rights, which has been compared with Domesday. Important statutes were enacted in his reign. Among these
were the Statutes of Westminster, which fixed three yearly
assizes, and of Winchester, which tightened the machinery of law
and order, including a jury system. There was still a basic
emphasis on old law, however, rather than new, and complaints
about the law were always conservative in nature: either that the
law was not being observed or that it had fallen into disuse.

There are four surviving originals of the most famous thirteenth-century document, Magna Carta, sealed – not signed – by
John in 1215. (Seals, like coins, provide valuable historical evidence.) Two copies are in the British Museum, but the best copy
is in Lincoln Cathedral. Its reissue in 1225, when it was cut down
in size by a third, and its confirmation by Edward I in 1297, when
it was enrolled in a new series of statute rolls, recall the frequent
struggles between king and barons during the twelfth and thirteenth centuries. Kings had patronage at their disposal, but when
they were felt to have distributed it unwisely they could be under
threat. In 1264 Henry III, unpopular because of his foreign
expeditions, was actually defeated by Simon de Montfort, Earl of
Leicester, at the Battle of Lewes, although in his turn Edward I, a
tough ruler, raised an army, defeated Simon's forces at Evesham,
killed him, and erased 'the viper's brood' of the de Montforts from
the list of great landlords.

Simon de Montfort's wife, Eleanor, sister of Henry III, who
married for the first time at the age of nine, left a fascinating
household account. It not only gives careful details of supplies and
their prices, but notes frequent changes in the personnel of the
household. It is the kind of source, therefore, which enables us to
reconstruct past ways of life. We can study the elaborate hierarchy
of household servants, who included Simon the cook, Andrew
the butler and Ralph the baker, compare the items in daily
household fare, and journey with Eleanor from one great house to
another. The fare is particularly interesting. While the poor were
living very simply, eating daily (at best) up to five pounds of
coarse (but nutritious) bread made out of wholemeal barley or
maslin (wheat and rye or beans) together with some meat, cheese,
milk and butter, vegetables and lots of weak ale, the de Montfort

household, which also consumed vast quantities of bread, was supplementing it amply with meat, fowl of all kinds, fish, and delicacies like pike and partridge. There were no forks or earthenware plates.

Rice was so special that it was kept under lock and key. Spices were expensive (the price of pepper fluctuated from 10d. to 2s. 4d. a pound and that of ginger from 10d. to 1s. 6d.) but were considered necessary. (The Crusades had added to their range and to the range of fruits.) Sugar could fluctuate in price from month to month, and the weight of sugar consumed in a year was only just larger than the weight of pepper. Many of the dishes on the table at this time were not only highly flavoured, with vinegar as well as spices as an active ingredient, but also highly coloured, either by bright yellow saffron or, perhaps less attractive, crimson blood. Pastry was predominant. Gascon wine, which was imported in very large quantities from England's empire in France, was a major drink, and the household brewed its own ale, though hops were not used in ale-making as early as the thirteenth century. Fruit and vegetables from the orchard and garden were not itemized in the accounts: they were taken for granted. It is interesting to note that while the price of luxuries varied so much, the prices of bread and ale, the two staple commodities for both rich and poor, were controlled (with reference to grain prices), as were standard weights and measures. After the Crusades they were calculated in Arabic numerals.

Monastic records, including account rolls, are packed with information of every kind and cover far more topics than the monastic chroniclers selected. At their best, they reveal much about the use of time, about rents and yields of crops, labour services and wages, and about their variations from season to season and from place to place. At Canterbury, for example, Archbishop Peckham's archives might suggest that he was as interested in the rent rolls as in the spiritual welfare of priests, and by the thirteenth century there were less well-known abbots who were efficient managers of estates. Yet it was always stressed that the monastery existed for the 'government of souls', not for good management, and that the abbot would be called to account, both for his own teaching and for 'the obedience of his disciples', for prayer as well as for work. When the mendicant friars came to England they stressed the need for poverty and simplicity, and the Franciscans, in particular, were pledged not to 'make anything their own, neither house nor place, nor any other thing'. They were expected to 'beg alms, like pilgrims and strangers in this world, serving our Lord in piety and humility'. It was a sign of the times that when they first arrived, they were not always welcomed; at Dover, for example, they were locked up as 'vagabonds' and 'idiots', familiar 'marginal groups' in twelfth- and thirteenth-century England, and at Oxford they were mistaken for mummers, another familiar group along with jugglers and tinkers, and were driven away. It was a sign of the times too that they found it difficult to avoid having houses thrust upon them, by Henry III at Reading, for example, and by the burgesses at Southampton. By the middle of Edward I's reign there were one hundred houses in the hands of friars, always in towns where they had a special message to preach.

The earliest municipal records date back to the end of the twelfth century, with nearly fifty charters going back to the reign of Henry II. They were no more standard in form than towns were standard in size, but they usually involved the privilege of appointing municipal officials and organizing markets. Freedom from tolls was a major privilege. However, it was through their own organization, different from the countryside though dependent upon it, that the towns reinforced their authority. In 1200, for instance, the congregation of citizens of Ipswich elected two bailiffs, four coroners and 'twelve chief portmen' to manage the town's affairs. The bailiffs were to be replaced later by a single magistrate called a mayor. Unlike bailiffs and reeves, mayors had responsibilities to no one but the citizens of their own community.

London, never in its history a paradigm of English urban development, was by far the biggest and wealthiest town, both at the time Domesday Book was drawn up and in 1300. There were already complaints in the late thirteenth century that its buildings were so close together in many places that there was 'no vacant land' and that some occupied 'a neighbour's walls where they have no right at all'. The first mention we have of a Mayor of

London is an accusation in the last decade of the twelfth century that one of its citizens claimed, 'Come what may, London will never have any king but the Mayor of London'; and the city's liberties, though confirmed in Magna Carta, were still under threat in the thirteenth century.

The biggest towns could be turbulent as well as busy places. In 1202 there were around 430 report cases of crime in Lincoln, including 114 cases of homicide and forty-five of rape. A little earlier, the Jew in Richard of Devizes's *Chronicle* (1193–8) had advised a Christian French boy that 'if you should come to London, you will quickly pass through it': it was full of 'stage-players, buffoons . . . musical girls, druggists, lustful persons, fortune-tellers, extortionists, nightly strollers, magicians, mimics, common beggars, tatterdemalions'. They were particularly prominent on holy days. May Day was one. At Candlemas there might be a week's holiday and at Christmas twelve days. Richard of Devizes's account was one-sided, of course, omitted both the clergy, who held substantial estates in London, and the two key groups in the towns – merchants and craftsmen. Dress, including head dress, identified roles.

There were foreign communities also with privileges of their own in the larger towns; Henry II, for example, allowed the merchants of Cologne to have a guildhall in London as early as 1157, and in 1283 the Statute of Markets gave further encouragement to foreigners to settle and set up in business. There were many signs, however, of anti-foreign and, in particular, anti-semitic feeling. The first Jewish communities, as dependent on the king for security as he was on them for capital (at high rates of interest), were established in the reign of William I, and by 1200 there were probably a total of 2,500 Jews. In the twelfth century they were to suffer appallingly from the anti-semitic pogroms that followed accusations of ritual murder at Lincoln, York and Stamford; and in 1290 they were expelled.

The guild merchant was a characteristic medieval institution, at once a group protecting the economic interests of the merchants in a particular town and a fraternity offering all the pleasures of conviviality. It inspected markets and measures, judged the quality of merchandise and laid down rules both of business and manners, while always protecting and, in so doing, restricting, local trade. It also often maintained a school, sometimes to become a grammar school in later centuries. One of the first recorded guild merchants set up by charter was in the now small and beautiful Oxfordshire town of Burford, whose lord granted the charter along the same lines as 'the burgesses of Oxford have in the guild merchant'. But the guild was not identical with the borough authority: there could be burgesses who were not members of the guild, as at Ipswich, and guildsmen who were not burgesses. And it did not exist everywhere; there was no guild merchant in London or Norwich, for example. The trade controlled by a guild might be very small or great, and where it was great the restrictions would be very precise. Thus, at Southampton, it was laid down that 'no one shall bring into the town of Southampton to sell again in the same town unless he be of the guild merchant or of the franchise', while at Shrewsbury no one was allowed to erect booths or to adopt other devices whereby 'to have better sale than any of the other combrethren'.

The idea of fair or just prices for traded products, reasonable alike to buyer and seller, was fundamental to medieval thought, although there was, as always, a gap between theory and practice. The frequency with which middlemen were attacked for forestalling (intercepting goods before they reached the open market), engrossing (cornering by buying up large quantities) and regrating (buying wholesale to sell retail) shows how wide the gap could be. Indeed, it was difficult to draw the line between legitimate and unreasonable business activities. Nor was it always easy to deal with the differences between crafts, which were concentrated in particular streets and in some towns had separate guilds of their own; London led the way as early as the 1260s. Craft guilds were to regulate not only standards and prices but apprentices and wages as well; in most crafts a seven-year period of apprenticeship was deemed to be essential for the 'mystery' of a craft to be acquired.

The language of apprentices' oaths could be French or English, for the third and fourth generations of Normans were bilingual. Richard Fitzneale, writing in the twelfth century, claimed that 'with the English and Normans dwelling together and marrying, the races have become so fused that it can scarcely be discerned at the present day – I speak of freemen alone – who is English and who is Norman by race'. Nevertheless, Norman French and Latin were, at the end of the thirteenth century, still the languages of the law, of the court and of education, and a proclamation on the Provisions of Oxford of Henry III, circulated in English in 1258, was picked out by a Victorian account of the Middle Ages as 'our one native oasis in a howling wilderness of French and Latin'. English dialects continued to thrive, however, and began to work their way back up the social scale; but it was not until the middle of the fifteenth century that East Midlands dialect was accepted as a written standard by writers of official documents. The future was not clear. *A Song of Lewes* in support of Simon de Montfort and claiming that 'England breathes again, hoping for liberty', might be written in Latin, but Englishmen were already singing, in English, 'Sumer is icumen in'.

4

ORDER AND CONFLICT

It was a marvellous and terrifying thing to hear the thundering of horses' hooves, the cries of the wounded, the sound of the trumpets and clarions and the shouting of the war cries.

> Sir John Chandos, on the Battle of Poitiers, 1356

O just God, mighty judge, the game was not fairly divided between them and us. Their surfeit was our famine: their jousts and tournaments were our torments . . . their feasts . . . our fasting.

> John de Bromyarde, Dominican friar, *c.* 1420

> I was so high upon my whele,
> Myne owne estate I cowd not know,
> Therfor the gospelle seyth fulle welle
> Who wille be high, he shall be low
> The whele of fortune, who may it trow,
> All is but veyn and vanitye.

> *Lament of the Duchess of Gloucester*, 1441

WILLIAM MORRIS looked back longingly to the fourteenth century when he conceived of his late Victorian utopia in *News from Nowhere*, and good words were written about the fifteenth century by his contemporary, the economic historian Thorold Rogers. Yet in recent years historians (with notable exceptions) have laid their emphasis on the tearing apart of the social tissue in a calamitous fourteenth century when, as William Langland's poem *The Vision of Piers the Plowman* implied, the world was coming to an end, and a bizarre fifteenth century, which has been said to bear 'the mixed smell of blood and roses'. 'Wherever we look,' one historian, Barbara Tuchman, has recently written, we see 'panic, brutality, violence in the streets. This was an upside-down world, a troubled, feverish world.' 'Right wild' was how one fifteenth-century gentleman put it.

Any account of the 'waning of the Middle Ages' usually starts with the Great Plague of 1348 and 1349, carried by black rats from continental Europe, which was followed by further pestilences in 1361, 1368–9 and 1375. Its most important effects were on population; within the space of a single generation probably between a third and a half of the population was wiped out. And there is evidence from this time and later too that young people were particularly vulnerable to the plague: indeed, the second pestilence of 1361 was known as the 'pestilence of the children'. (They figure little in the writing of the period except in this context.) The total population of England, which may have reached 4·75 million before the Great Plague, may have fallen to around two million by the end of the century.

It was an episode of exceptional catastrophe. Yet some of the consequences attributed to it were apparent before it took place. Population, for example, may have ceased to grow earlier in the fourteenth century; moreover, the resistance to epidemic disease, including the plague, may have been lowered by chronic under-nourishment. There was a marked fall in temperatures at the beginning of the century, which produced what has been called 'a little ice age', and between 1315 and 1317 there were great floods, compared by contemporaries with the Biblical Flood. Harvests failed, and there were also sheep and cattle plagues, the former beginning in 1313, the latter in 1319, when it is said that in some places horses, which were immune to the plague, had to be substituted for oxen to draw the ploughs. Together these disasters caused what some historians have considered to be the worst agrarian crisis since the Norman Conquest. Scarcity affected the towns as well as the country. The chronicler of the *Annals of Bermondsey* told how the poor ate dogs, cats, the dung of doves and their own children. And matters were made worse by the fact that alms were reduced. The supply of charity dried up.

The movement from arable cultivation to pasture and the retreat from marginal lands that characterized the post-plague years were apparent in various places before 1348, in counties as far apart as Shropshire and Sussex, although, as always, the pattern varied from one part of the country to another. A deserted windmill at the village of Ibstone on the Chiltern hills was a symbol of the times: the Fellows of Merton College, Oxford, had invested in it during the 1290s, but thirty years later it was derelict. Deserted villages were not a new phenomenon in the fourteenth and fifteenth centuries, but there were far more of them. The processes of desertion can also be traced back to pre-plague years: in 1334 the tax assessments (which reflect the size of population) in four Norfolk villages were less than one-fifth of those paid by their neighbours, and when the church in one of these villages, Pudding Norton, fell into disuse in 1401, 'the fewness and the poverty of the parishioners' was blamed on the soil. Villages were safe only if they had quality corn land, or if their economy depended on other products besides corn.

Even the very first decade of the fourteenth century had revealed difficult economic problems, although their extent has been debated as vigorously as the effects of the agrarian crisis of 1315–17. The main initial problem was inflation, for in some places both grain and livestock prices almost doubled between 1305 and 1310. It is only with the invaluable help of a price index computed in the twentieth century that we can estimate its impact, since contemporary memories of the earlier period of inflation between 1180 and 1220, described by William Beveridge as the most alarming inflation of the Middle Ages, had gone. Prices (with 1415 as a base line of 100), which stood at 83 in 1264 and 105 in 1310, reached peaks of 216 and 215 in 1316 and 1317 respectively. These were higher than the post-plague figures.

Whatever its causes (one of them was said to be an influx of foreign silver), inflation added to the burdens of the poor, who were already suffering from increased tax demands generated by unsuccessful war in Scotland. Prices remained high until 1338, then dropped and stayed low for twenty years, during which lords of the manor were to complain just as bitterly of deflation as the poor had complained earlier of inflation: goods, though abundant, could not then be sold. Prices rose for another twenty years in the third quarter of the century, following the Great Plague. Within these broad movements, however, there was an extraordinarily wide range of fluctuations, determined largely by the state of the harvest, which remained the main fact of life. Wheat prices, which had peaked at 15s. 5d. a quarter (the main unit of measurement) in the famine year of 1316, were as low as 2s. 10d. in 1357, a year of an exceptionally good harvest: only if we take five-yearly averages do the fluctuations begin to sort themselves out.

The biggest landlords were, of course, in a far more powerful position to complain than the poor, and so too were the knights. For this reason, politics were as confused as economics during the unhappy reign of Edward II (1284–1327). Indeed, Edward's reign, which ended in his deposition, the first since 1066, and his murder three years later, was a period of civil strife as 'vicious and violent' as the reign of Stephen in the twelfth century or as the barons' wars of the mid-thirteenth century, with the difference that feudal ties were snapping: feudal military service was no longer as important as it had been. There was urban discontent as well, with townsmen's risings in 1327 in Bury St Edmunds and in other monastic towns where there was a long history of conflict between Church and citizens. 'Alas, poor England,' wrote a contemporary chronicler. 'You, who helped other lands from your abundance, now poor and needy, are forced to beg.' The first three years of the long reign of Edward III (1327–77), then a minor, were equally violent. Indeed, after Edward had laid claim to the French throne in 1337, challenging 'Philip of Valois who calls himself King of France', what came to be known in the nineteenth century as the Hundred Years War began. It was, in fact, a series of wars, beginning with victories but ending with a series of 'various adversities . . . long undergone'. The cost of the Hundred Years War provoked *The Song against the King's Taxes* with its bitter message 'people are reduced to such ill plight they can give no more. I fear if they had a leader they would rebel.'

Nonetheless, war could appeal to landlords and knights as an escape from the bewildering economic and social circumstances at home and as a possible, even likely, means of personal profit through plunder. It was attractive for other reasons too. Successes – and there were many of those before 1360 – stimulated national feeling, and in the field warfare appealed through the codes of chivalry to loyalty, honour and valour. Edward made every effort to conciliate as well as to impress the great magnates on whom he depended, creating six new earls when he invaded France, 'each one content with his rank under the king' according to one contemporary. In the very year of the Black Death, Edward decided to create a new order of chivalry, the Knights of the Garter, of whom he was one. The first meeting of the twenty-six knights, including the king, was held on St George's Day in a newly-built 'noble hall' at Windsor, where it was claimed that Arthur, whom Edward greatly admired, had founded his great castle with its Round Table. Like the king and knights of lesser status, almost all the magnates were caught up in pride of precedence and in the heraldic arms and codes of chivalry that went with it. Society was becoming more hierarchical, more fascinated by 'descent'.

In August 1346, on the eve of the Black Death, which challenged all hierarchies, one of the greatest victories the English ever achieved in France was won at Crécy in Picardy, where the full array of French chivalry was destroyed by Edward's archers. It was a triumph of infantry over cavalry, a victory of the long bow against the newly introduced gun, which had also been used by the French during their sack of Southampton in 1338. In 1347 the town of Calais, which had been besieged for a year, fell to the English too. And in 1356 the French king was brought back as a prisoner to London after the victory of Edward III's formidable son, 'the stern and gloomy Black Prince', at the battle of Poitiers. Jean Froissart, the great chronicler of chivalry, believed Poitiers to be an even greater victory than Crécy because there were greater feats of arms, 'with the result that fewer great men were killed'. Certainly at Crécy, where many men were 'slaughtered regardless of their rank . . . the number of dead lords was very great'.

To his contemporaries the Black Prince, who was only sixteen years old when he fought at Crécy, was 'fell and cruel' and 'the flower of earthly chivalry'. 'To serve him as a knight,' wrote one chronicler, 'was to be a lord.' Another outstanding warrior magnate was Henry of Grosmont, Duke of Lancaster, a founder Knight of the Garter, who had joined crusades which took him to Lithuania as well as to Spain and the Near East. Posterity remembers him less for his 'war-like deeds and great exertions', highly estimated by his contemporaries, than for his remarkable book of meditations and confessions, describing vividly the tensions and delights of a life which combined warfare and faith. He was also the main founder of Corpus Christi College, Cambridge.

The Black Death proved more 'fell and cruel' than any prince. It was known at the time not as 'the Pestilence' but as 'the Great Mortality', and as it made its way inland from Southampton and Bristol, it killed nine out of ten of its victims. Wherever it moved, it was a 'wretched, fierce, violent' pestilence. In the vivid and revealing words of an inscription in Ashwell Church, only the 'dregs of . . . a people survive to witness'.

People with power and influence suffered as much as the rest. The newly appointed Archbishop of Canterbury, a distinguished scholar, died within six days of his consecration (one of three archbishops to die within a year) and two out of five beneficed clergymen in the huge diocese of Lincoln were stricken down. Monks and priests suffered in other ways too, since the plague was also thought of as a scourge of God:

> God is deaf now-a-days and deigneth not to hear us,
> And prayers have no power the Plague to stay.

A thanksgiving service for the end of the plague at Yeovil was interrupted by restless 'sons of perdition', who kept the Bishop of Bath and Wells besieged in church. England's chivalry and the leaders of the mercantile community were also among the victims: all six Wardens of the Hatters and all four Wardens of the Goldsmiths died before the midsummer of 1350. The biggest direct impact of the plague, however, was on people without power. At Cuxham, a much studied manor in Oxfordshire, all twelve of the lord's villeins died within one year, and at Tusmore in the same county, the lord of the manor was granted permission to turn his fields into a park since every villein was dead.

Inevitably, therefore, there was a shortage of labour; and although surviving lords of the manor might try to overcome the problem by seeking to reinstate labour services, they could not do so. Release from labour dues became as regular and frequent as in the twelfth century. Nor could manorial lords or smaller land-owners keep down by law the wages for farm workers whose labour services had been commuted: a royal ordinance of 1349, followed by a Statute of Labourers in 1351, which tried to prohibit wages in excess of those paid before the Black Death and to lay down that alms should not be given to able-bodied beggars, were largely inoperative. Clauses like 'no-one is to be paid at haymaking more than a penny a day . . . and reapers of corn in the first week of August 2d. and the second 3d.' were impossible to enforce. (As a point of comparison, a trained war-horse, fit for a knight, at that time cost almost £100, the equivalent of a lifetime's earnings for a labourer.) The statute was as unsuccessful as twentieth-century wages and income policies. Energetic attempts to hold back commutation and wages on the spot inevitably failed, too. Competition between employers for labour was one cause, and effective protest was another: villeins destroyed mano-rial records which carefully listed laws and obligations. And so, while villeinage was shorn of many of its most cramping features and the relative economic position of the labourer improved, the revenues accruing to many lords of the manor, lay and ecclesiasti-cal, fell. The monks of Battle Abbey, for instance, lost 20 per cent of their revenues between 1347 and 1351, and another 7 per cent in the 1380s.

In such circumstances some small men prospered by buying and selling land, often in small parcels, from the lord of the manor or from fellow villagers. There was considerable variation there-fore in the wealth of smallholders: at Frisby in Lincolnshire, for example, where there were sixteen tenant families in 1381, the richest were reckoned to be two or three times wealthier than the poorest. There is also evidence that the average smallholding became larger and better. But this did not impede a wave of unrest for, as William Langland noted, the way of a poor man was hard, particularly if he held no land of his own and was 'charged with a crew of children and a landlord's rent'.

Society as well as the economy was deeply disturbed in the fourteenth century, not only by obvious inequalities but by changes in the facts of inequality. Proportionately at first, the biggest increases in wages often went to the humblest. Thus, a thatcher and his helper, who earned a penny a day before the Black Death, received two-and-a-half times that modest sum later. And although the price of horses, and the oats on which they were fed, remained stationary, payments to the threshers increased sharply. Market forces were at work, and it is not surprising, given the framework of society, that the Black Death was followed by a great deal of moralizing and a preoccupation with social status. Indeed, this, rather than economic analysis, coloured political speeches and acts of parliament. Above all, the poor were expected to keep their place. It was doubtless to try, through improved communication, to maintain law and order (a coupling of words which still survives) that in 1362 Parliament ordered all pleas to be conducted in English.

The voice of tradition had strong social and cultural supports. *The Mirror for Magistrates* stated orthodox opinion clearly:

> No subject ought for any kind of course
> To force the lord, but yield him to the laws.

Worried 'poor tenants' were supposed instead to appeal in their petitions to 'their very dear, honourable and rightful lord'.

Evidence of increasing concern for status among all groups, including the upper ranks of society, where the range of hereditary titles was extended, is apparent in the sumptuary legislation of 1363, which prescribed the clothing to be worn by different social ranks. Dress was more ostentatious and more influenced by fashion, and who wore what was deemed significant in an age when different ranks were more sharply graded than before and more conscious, within each rank, of their common identity. Earls and barons were clearly distinguished from knights, and knights from 'gentlemen', 'yeomen' and 'husbandmen'. Significant shifts in legal terminology continued through the fifteenth and sixteenth centuries also as copyholders, who held customary tenancies from their lords on a lifelong or continuing basis on terms set out in copies of entries in the old manorial rolls, became identified as another legal group with distinct interests of their own.

The more talk there was of subordination in the late fourteenth century, the more conflict was generated, however (and vice versa); and there was a violent, though short-lived riotous protest, the so-called Peasants' Revolt of 1381, which began in the remote countryside but went on to threaten the Court. It was not given this name at the time, and it was precipitated not by general discontent but, very specifically, by Parliament's attempt to levy a poll tax (a tax per head of population) that fell on all sections of the community. This was the third such tax that had been levied between 1377 and 1381, and the fact that in 1381 it tripled in size and was not graded by rank, as the 1379 tax had been, was bound to generate protest. Significantly, the Parliament that levied it met not in London but in Northampton, because officials feared popular reactions in the capital.

There were other discontents in the background. The war with France was renewed after the brief and unpopular peace of 1360. It was expensive and no longer a war of victories: much of the richest land in Gascony was lost and only Calais in the north of France remained an English possession. For these reasons the long reign of Edward III, who was by now senile, closed as turbulently, as it had begun. In 1376 two of his 'evil councillors' were impeached by the House of Commons, and the death of the Black Prince in the same year added to the gloom. The throne would now pass to the Black Prince's son, Richard, born in Bordeaux, a boy not yet eleven years old. It was more in melancholy than in anger that on Edward's death in 1377 an unnamed poet compared England to a once noble ship – with the Commons as the mast – which was now drifting, and asked rhetorically,

> Ah, dear God, what may this be
> That all things wears and wastes away.

In the same year there were French raids on the south coast, and in 1380, on the eve of the Peasants' Revolt, there was fear of a large-scale invasion.

Alarm about the possibility and likely effect of social unrest was well expressed by John Gower, one of the finest poets of his age, a conservative in temperament and outlook who almost forecast the revolt when he wrote:

It seems to me that lethargy has put the lords to sleep so they do not guard against the folly of the common people, but they allow that nettle to grow which is too violent in its nature.

'If God does not provide His help,' Gower concluded, 'this impotent nettle will very suddenly sting us.'

It was young Richard II (1377–99), only fifteen years old at the time, who ultimately had to deal with the Peasants' Revolt, which started with risings against the third poll tax in Essex, Kent, Norfolk, Suffolk and Hertfordshire. Three marshland villages near Brentwood in Essex led the way, with other villages soon following. The revolt quickly collected long-standing complaints and stimulated sweeping radical invective. It was from Kent that the revolt found its leader Wat Tyler, in the eyes of authority 'a king of the ruffians and idol of the rustics'. 'We are men formed in Christ's likeness,' he exclaimed, 'and we are kept like beasts.' The rebels marched on London and the revolt reached its climax in three stormy days, the first of them on Corpus Christi Day, 13 June. The Kent contingent had travelled to the capital through Canterbury and Rochester and camped at Blackheath; the Essex contingent was lodged north of the river. Boy king and rebels eventually met near the Tower at Smithfield, now London's meat-market.

Many essential features of the three days are lost. It is not clear, for example, though rumours abounded, how much support the rebels actually secured from the faction-torn citizens of London. There is enough recorded incident, however, to permit reconstruction of the events and even to catch glimpses of individual personalities. The one specific and consistent demand was that the legal bond of villeinage should be broken. One rebel clergyman, John Ball, also demanded that the country should be rid not only of lords but of archbishops, bishops, abbots and priors. Both the Archbishop of Canterbury (who was also Chancellor) and the Treasurer of England were murdered. Richard proved himself brave and confident when he met the rebels face to face, and Wat Tyler was killed by the sword of the Lord Mayor of London.

The surviving rebels were punished severely, but villeinage, if not abolished, was soon to lose most of its backing and the poll tax was dropped. Thereafter the Commons came to argue even more strongly than before that 'the king should live of his own', by which they meant – and the emphasis, if not the phrase, was new – that he should live on the known revenues of his hereditary rights and properties, supplemented only in exceptional circumstances, and if Parliament approved, by customs duties, subsidies and levies. The political necessity of keeping within this framework was to impose long-term difficulties on royal government and was to be an important contributory factor to the late-sixteenth- and seventeenth-century conflicts which culminated not in another Peasants' Revolt but in civil war.

There are several vivid accounts of the 1381 revolt, each with its own gloss on the events. 'The rebels, who had formerly belonged to the most lowly condition of serfs,' wrote Thomas of Walsingham, 'went in and out like lords; and swineherds set themselves above soldiers, although not knights but rustics.' There is mixed evidence, however, on such matters. While there were demands that 'no lord should have lordship, but that it should be divided among all men, except for the king's own lordship', in many places the rebels tried to secure the support of the gentry. The gentleman, as such, was never the prime target of peasant hostility in 1381. Froissart, the chronicler of chivalry, surveying events at a distance, was interested more in the vicissitudes of personal fortune epitomized by the revolt: 'how wonderful and strange are the fortunes of this world.'

It is impossible to understand the social tensions of the four-teenth century without bringing in the Church at every point, for while there were priests such as John Ball who were capable of rebellion, and poets like William Langland who kept their bright vision of salvation, at the very centre of power there were often clerical ministers governing the kingdom. The Church itself was a hierarchy composed of its own great lords, some of them combining spiritual authority with administrative, political and economic power; below them came lesser lords, who were influential in their own areas, with large numbers of liveried attendants; and then the clergy, the underprivileged priesthood and the mendicant orders, who still favoured, in theory at least, a return to the simple poverty of the Apostles.

There was always scope not only for anti-papal but for anti-clerical feeling, not least in Parliament, where in 1371, ten years before the Peasants' Revolt, there was a sharp conflict about taxation of the clergy following the dismissal from the Chancellorship of the powerful prelate, William of Wykeham, and there were even suggestions of the confiscation of Church lands. There was to be a further scandal in 1378 when the Church divided, leaving two Popes, one in Rome and one in Avignon in enemy France, and in 1393 the statute of Praemunire insisted that the Crown had 'no earthly master'. There was radical anti-clericalism too: thus, in the *The Complaint of the Ploughman*, a poem shot through with social criticism, the anonymous poet criticized 'Peter's successors', 'high on horse', for changing their clothes every day and for punishing the poor:

> Of holy church make they an hore
> And filleth her wombe with wine and ale.

There were many different strands in Lollardy, the most organized fourteenth-century religious protest. The first Lollard, John Wycliffe, had in 1372 taken a Doctorate of Divinity at Oxford, where he had learned much from critical scholars, but he did not begin preaching what were considered heretical ideas until 1378. Going far beyond chauvinistic anti-clericalism, he focused on the Bible as the one sure foundation of belief, urging that it should be placed, in English, in the hands of everyone, clerk or layman. Other points followed from this: he questioned the doctrines of the Mass (the central service of the Church), he demanded a dissolution of its corporate wealth, he condemned monasticism, and he advocated the marriage of the clergy. He stopped short of a broader critique of contemporary society and government, however, first because it was pressing spiritual matters that most concerned him, second, because he believed, that 'all things not to the will of the Lord must end miserably' (a good motto for his age), and, third, because he placed great trust in 'the Prince'. In his translation of the Book of Genesis, where the seventeenth-century Authorized Version of the Bible was to read 'chief captain of his host', Wycliffe had 'prince of all his chyvalrye'.

It was inevitable that Wycliffe's ideas should be condemned, and by 1411 academic heresy was stamped out in Oxford where it had originated. The Archbishop of Canterbury warned that if Lollardy was not eradicated there would be further social disturbance, but, in fact, while the Lollards wanted to see far-reaching changes in ways of thinking and behaving, like Wycliffe few of them were identified with social revolt. The rebels of 1381 did not share many of Wycliffe's religious views; his ideas had more support in the Parliament that had provoked the Peasants' Revolt.

It was in the fifteenth century, not the fourteenth, that Wycliffe's ideas took root among small radical minorities, attracting disciples not just in anti-clerical London but in country areas like the Chilterns in Buckinghamshire and the villages around Tenterden in Kent. In Berkshire too there was 'a glorious and secret society of faithful followers'. The demand for an open Bible, in English, was at the heart of what became a Lollard heritage, and, despite all efforts to suppress Wycliffe's Bible, the first complete Bible in English, over a hundred copies survived. Although Lollardy had not achieved any of its immediate aims, it prepared the way for – even anticipated – the popular dissent that was to figure in the background of the sixteenth-century Reformation.

The fifteenth-century suppression of Lollardy left behind it heroes. One of them was the warrior knight Sir John Oldcastle, a friend of Henry V (1413–22) before he came to the throne. Oldcastle was an intrepid character, and when the Archbishop of Canterbury tried in 1413 to serve him with a final summons to trial as 'the principal harbourer, promoter, protector and defender of heretics', Oldcastle shut the gates of his castle. Tried and convicted, he escaped, unsuccessfully attempted rebellion with the help of craftsmen and ploughmen, went underground, was captured late in 1417 and after appearing before Parliament was hanged and burnt at the Tower of London. There are elements in the story of Oldcastle which throw light on the medieval 'underground'. Becoming an outlaw, whatever the cause, was a popular theme in the late fourteenth and early fifteenth centuries. These were the years when Robin Hood and other similar legends circulated widely; as early as 1377, the poem *The Vision of Piers the*

Plowman refers to 'rymes of Robin Hood'. Several of them hold him up as the upholder of justice who is seeking not to destroy society but to redress its manifest wrongs; but there have been suggestions that he was the hero of the gentry rather than the poor and that his 'merry men' were poaching, not for food but for sport. Yet his advice was plain enough. 'Do no husbande harm, that tilleth with his ploughe.'

Most outlaws were clearly not of this kind; the reality of their existence was as far removed from romance as the facts of war in France were at odds with the language of chivalry. The preamble to a 1378 statute described how armed bands were taking possession of houses and manors, 'having no consideration of God, nor to the laws of the Holy Church, nor of the land, nor to right, nor justice'. And the lord of the manor himself might, in the right circumstances, employ the same methods as the outlaw. Not very far from Nottingham, for example, Eustace Folville, one of seven sons of the lord of the manor of Ashby Folville, in Leicestershire, had been involved in crimes that included robbery, kidnapping, rape and murder, the success of most of which depended not only on team effort, but on support in higher places. Folville was, in fact, pardoned three times because he had fought against the king's enemies (for which he was knighted) and on more than one occasion he was hired by local people with power, including the Canons of Sempringham.

As the Hundred Years' War continued, straddling the four-teenth and fifteenth centuries, it was seen as perpetuating a sense of disorder at home rather than diverting violence to France. Other factors were at work also, for there were dramatic domestic events between 1381 and 1413. Even in 1381 feuding between great magnates loomed larger than peasant protests, and there were two great shifts of power later in the reign of Richard II, in 1388 and 1397 (the latter involving the redistribution of estates by the crown on a huge scale) before the king was deposed and replaced by the Lancastrian Henry IV (1399–1413). The manner of Richard's deposition suggested injustice, however, and Henry IV's reign was an uneasy one. The chronicler Adam of Usk's claim that the sacred chrism used at Henry's coronation produced in the king's hair a crop of tenacious lice and his interpretation of this as an evil omen throw an interesting sidelight on the insecurities and fears of the age.

Under Henry V the English won great victories in France, one of them in 1415 at Agincourt, where English bowmen triumphed against overwhelming odds; and in the years that followed lands in France were distributed among great English magnates in a kind of Norman Conquest in reverse. Henry's two-year-old son Henry VI (1422–61) was nominally king of both England and France after victory at the Battle of Vermeil in 1424, as a result of which Sir John Fastolf was said to have won 20,000 marks by 'the fortune of war'. But this was the last significant English victory in the Hundred Years War. The subsequent story is that of Joan of Arc, the rehabilitation of the French monarchy, the growing strength of French cannon and gunpowder, the French recovery of Normandy, severe financial strain in England and the loss of the whole of France by the English (except for Calais) by 1453, the year of the fall of Constantinople to the Turks.

The story in England itself was also a sad one from the English point of view. In 1450 there was another rural revolt, this time in Kent, led by Jack Cade, who claimed to be a cousin of the Duke of York. For its leadership it drew on esquires and gentlemen rather than peasants, but Cade's demands included the abolition of the Statute of Labourers and the resumption into the king's own hands of royal lands which had been granted away. The rebels entered London and executed the Lord Treasurer before being dispersed, and Cade was killed. Twenty-one years later, sporadic dynastic wars, which had their distant origin in the succession of Henry IV, split the aristocracy between support for the Houses of Lancaster and York and weakened the monarchy. There was more talk, indeed, while they lasted, of 'false authority', as a contemporary poem, *On the Corruption of the Times*, put it, than of order. The Yorkist Edward IV (1461–83) won the throne through rebellion, and the first of his parliaments passed acts of attainder for treason against no fewer than 113 people, including thirteen peers.

During the Wars of the Roses, great men attached lesser men to their service by life indentures; the Duke of Lancaster had pointed the way in the late fourteenth century when he indentured large numbers of knights and esquires, most of them retained for life in his service and in war and peace. Such 'bastard feudalism', as this has been called, was quite different from feudalism. The retainer was not a vassal who received land from his lord, owed loyalty to him and was linked to him through ties of mutual obligation. He rather looked to his lord as his patron. He was his lord's follower, wearing his livery and being maintained by him in return for a contract to serve for life or for a fixed period under stipulated conditions. Payment for service in instalments was the quintessence of the system, although it could not have worked had there not been men, often veterans of the Hundred Years War, who preferred service under a lord of their own choosing, sometimes a soldier of fortune but more often a great lord of their own locality. Once the maintained men put on their lord's livery, they demonstrated his power, and one lord could vie with another in the numbers of his retainers and display. 'Worship' was as important as display and carried very different connotations: it was reciprocal, and loss of it on the part of the lord meant shame for both sides.

There was an unavoidable element of instability – or fluidity – in the system, since retainers could change from a losing lord to a winning one and a strong king could control through balancing one side against another. This was a worldly and restless society which, for all its attachment to heraldry, favoured ambitious men – those who, in the words of a contemporary, were able to seize their opportunities, 'some by their prudence, some by their energy, some by their valour and some by other virtues which . . . enoble men'. The Paston letters, much quoted by historians, describe three occasions on which members of the Paston family, who lived in East Anglia, were besieged in their own homes by armed bands despatched by members of the peerage.

Nonetheless, the extent of both unrest and revolt in the fifteenth century can be greatly exaggerated. The Pastons were not a typical family, even if their preoccupation with property was generally shared. Nor was everyone driven by ruthless ambition. Many of the key events in the fifteenth century are surrounded by myths that originated under the Tudors after Henry VII (1485–1509) came to the throne, and the conditions of life then can be seriously misrepresented. There was less blood-shed in the late fifteenth than in the mid thirteenth century or, earlier still, in the reign of Stephen; and the Wars of the Roses did not directly affect large sections of the population. Towns were not sacked, nor were churches desecrated. The appeal of Lancastrian and Yorkist claims in different places and at different times can be understood only in terms of local family feuds which drew in dependants as well as relatives in what was called at the time 'vicious fellowship'. Moreover, the numbers involved in the battles were small. At St Albans in 1455, for instance, when the Duke of York defeated the forces of Henry VI under the command of the Duke of Somerset, York had only 3,000 men under his command and Somerset, who was killed, about 2,000. The best description of the battle is brief: 'a short scuffle in a street'. Only at the Battle of Towton in 1461 were there clearly defined ranks.

There were many people who were both comfortably off and able to stay out of the turmoil and the feuding, and for them life could be agreeable. In one of the few friendly accounts of the fifteenth century written in the 1920s, C. L. Kingsford described Sir William Stonor's life as a country gentleman busy with the management of his estates, taking his share in the work of local administration, living in friendly intercourse with neighbours in like circumstances to himself, growing rich with his profits as a sheep grazier, and spending money on the rebuilding of his house and the laying out of his garden.

Another section of the community, the monks and the clergy, were less harassed in the fifteenth century than they had been in the fourteenth. Moreover, though Rome demanded a subsidy from the English clergy on twelve occasions between 1450 and 1530, they responded only twice through their assembly, Con-vocation. While the number of monks fell, their standard of living often rose: early in the sixteenth century the Cistercians at Whalley Abbey in Lancashire were spending two-thirds of their income on food and drink. At St Albans, lying on the main road to the north, there was lavish hospitality. Two Dukes were entertained there, each with 300 attendants, in 1423–4 and in 1436, and in the last of these years nine Bishops and the whole of

Convocation. The young Henry VI stayed there for nine days with his mother in 1427–8.

Wage labourers, many of them employed by abbeys, were a third section of the population who were certainly better-off than at any other time during the Middle Ages. Since population did not recover in the fifteenth century, the wages of both farm workers and urban craftsmen rose faster than the prices of the goods they demanded. Indeed, real wages in the building industry doubled between the Black Death and Agincourt and remained high throughout the fifteenth century. There was no inflation. Meat was in plentiful supply, as was poultry. Cereal prices were low and steady until a series of bad harvests in the 1480s broke the pattern, as a result of which the price of wheat leapt 74·7 per cent in 1482. In the 1470s the lawyer and writer Sir John Fortescue described the Commons in England as 'the best fed and the best clad' of 'any Natyon crystyn or hethen', and they were able to buy new things besides food and clothes: brass pots and pewter candlesticks were in greater demand. In other words, there was a real though limited improvement in the material standard of life. If fifteenth-century Parliaments resisted taxation or granted particular towns exemption from it, this reflected Englishmen's desire to keep their money in their pockets rather than their inability to pay. Fortescue went on to compare the English favourably with the French: in France the king could levy taxes as he pleased, nobles and clergy were not taxed and the necessities – food – were. In England prosperity, even if relative in European terms, had been made possible.

Nor had the prosperity been bought entirely at the expense of the landlords, who were sometimes critical of it. Landlords' fortunes were in fact mixed, even in the same county. Some faced difficulties; others prospered. The most able of them watched their estates extremely carefully, although the biggest estates were now mainly leased out to others. Other landlords lost income, however, at least until the last decades of the century, particularly in the grain-growing districts of the Midlands, and more villages were deserted.

There was one important incentive for farmers of ability and drive: the profitability of sheep farming, which required less labour than wheat and in which transport costs were lower too. Seven years after the Black Death 40,000 sacks of wool were exported annually, and a century later there were sheep farms with 8,000 or 9,000 sheep. Exports of raw wool fell during the fifteenth century, but exports of cloth rose fourfold. Indeed, by 1450 cloth not wool was England's greatest export. Exporting a finished product brought with it more profit – and employment – than exporting a raw material.

Complaints of sheep 'devouring' men as arable land was replaced by pasture were to be more vociferous and numerous in the sixteenth than the fifteenth century. This may have been because the process was further advanced. It may, however, have had more to do with the influence of the printing press, introduced into England by William Caxton in 1476. Certainly, the complaints had been heard in the fifteenth century before the printing press diffused them. 'What shall be said of the modern destruction of villages?' a well-known Warwickshire antiquary asked, and he could answer himself with confidence. 'The root of this evil is greed. The plague of avarice infects these times and it blinds men.' It was a charge that was often to be made throughout the long history of the fencing-in of land to consolidate and control its use, a process known later as enclosure.

Obvious conflicts of interest in the sheep fields were reflected in poetry and prose. A contented clothier could declare,

> I thank God and ever shall
> It was the sheep that payed for all.

But neither shepherds nor clothworkers were necessarily quite so contented. In an early fifteenth-century nativity play the shepherd complains,

> But we silly husbands that walk on the moor,
> In faith, we are nearhands out of the door;
> No wonder, as it stands, if we be poor,
> For the tilth of our lands lies fallow as the floor
> We are so hammed
> For taxed and rammed
> We are made hand-tamed
> With these gentlery-men.

The way of life of the shepherd, and of the ploughman, did not change much in the fifteenth century, but that of the clothworker did. There could be as big an economic gulf between the great clothier and the journeyman as there was between the lord and the farm labourer. There was also an argument about the number of apprentices a master might employ and about access to the trade. An act of 1388 had laid down that all who served in husbandry until the age of twelve should not be permitted entry to a 'mystery', while an act of 1406 laid down that no one might send his son to be apprenticed 'except he have land or rent to the value of twenty shillings a year at the least'. Once in the trade an apprentice could look forward to becoming a journeyman, and a journeyman to becoming a master (or at least this was the approved pattern), yet there were also permanent groups of wage earners who had 'sufficient cunning and understanding in the occupation and exercise of their craft' but who lacked the financial means to progress in the trade.

Many of the towns that rose in importance during the fifteenth century were cloth towns such as Southampton, which had a long history as a chartered borough, although other old cloth towns like Lincoln, Beverley and Winchester decayed. Historians have talked, indeed, of an 'urban crisis' affecting old cities like York, Canterbury and Coventry, noting that the urban centres of the wool trade which prospered most did not have a municipal constitution. Among them was Lavenham in Suffolk, shortly before this time an insignificant village, then suddenly one of the fifteen richest places in the country, but constitutionally still a village governed through a manorial court. Early in the following century Thomas Spring, a Lavenham clothier, was the richest man in Suffolk after the Duke of Norfolk. And not far away from Lavenham, which was virtually rebuilt in a single architectural style, were other great cloth centres such as Long Melford, also dominated by its wonderful parish church. There were great churches also in the Cotswolds, another important wool area, which from 1399 was linked with Calais, the great wool-staple town (the authorized entrepôt for all wool passing to the continent) by a route that followed the ancient Ridgeway to Sandwich. There were links also with Southampton, where there was a great

Wool House which was to survive the bombing of the city in the Second World War.

Non-ecclesiastical architecture flourished in all these areas. Thus, William Grevel, 'the flower of the wool merchants of all England', who contributed generously to his parish church, built an imposing house for himself at Chipping Campden and William Browne of Stamford, 'a merchant of very wonderful richness', built a 'hospital' for the poor brethren. They each have their brasses in their local churches. It was the new churches, designed as they often were in an English style, Perpendicular, that could produce the most magnificent effects. Indeed, in a century when there was persistent preoccupation with death (plagues continued to rack town and country alike, and chantries involving Masses for the dead were the favourite religious endowment), Perpendicular architecture let in grace as well as light. St Mary Redcliffe, Bristol, vaulted throughout, has been described as 'the most splendid of all parish churches' and the chapel of King's College, Cambridge (Henry VI was the king), carried what has been described as an architectural revolution, begun by monks at Gloucester, to its logical end. There was light too in Nottingham's carved alabasters, which were bought as eagerly abroad as at home, although alabaster was used extensively to produce monuments of the dead.

Meanwhile, castles, of which the last examples were concerned with prestige, not with defence, were giving way to country houses everywhere at the end of the fifteenth century, and greatly improved farmhouses were dotting many rural landscapes. In the port towns there were new wharves, and at Southampton a new guildhall; in some favoured older towns there were whole new groups of houses, as at Norwich. In London there was the magnificent Guildhall, parts of which were to survive the great seventeenth-century fire and to be embellished in medieval fashion in the nineteenth century.

As in the twelfth and thirteenth centuries, only one in ten of the population lived in towns. They were expensive places to govern (which made some businesses move out of them) since they had to maintain lavish traditions of ceremony and hospitality – this was particularly true in the case of London, which remained far bigger and richer than any other town – and they were characterized by increasingly complex patterns of urban control. Even in small towns like Beverley, there were street and traffic laws to protect the streets, laying down, for instance, that 'no cart shod with iron be driven or enter the town by any burgess', while in London it was ordered that 'no carter within the liberties shall drive his cart more quickly when it is unloaded than when it is loaded'. At Scarborough there were complaints that a private solar overhung the road 'so low that it is an obstruction', while a later rule of 1467 at Beverley anticipated nineteenth- and twentieth-century by-laws and legislation to deal with air pollution. It laid down that 'no one henceforth here to build any kiln for burning brick . . . under penalty of 100s.' because of the danger of attendant fumes. The injunction spoke frankly of 'the stink and badness of the air to the destruction of fruit trees'.

The recognition of such problems and pressure for controls often came from residents. Thus, in London, where there were still fields between the city and Westminster, with its great abbey building, a citizens' petition of 1444 complained of 'swannes, gees, herons, and ewes and other pultrie whereof the ordure and standing of them is of grate stenche and so evel savour that it causeth grete and parlous inffecting of the people and long hath done'. The petition may be compared with a writ of 1372 sent by Edward III to the Mayor and Sheriffs, ordering them to keep Tower Hill free from dung and filth and noting that he had been told it was in such a state as 'to fill those dwelling about with disgust and loathing'.

Towns were often thought of as places of greater social division rather than of tighter social control. Craft guilds, which became increasingly important during the fifteenth century, did not necessarily share the same interest as merchant guilds. Thus, there were open conflicts during the 1440s between merchant drapers and artisan tailors, in London, Coventry and Norwich, for example. There were other divisions also. As livery companies developed in towns as well as in the country, distinctions began to be drawn between those who were allowed to wear the livery and those whose lack of means excluded them. Journeymen often began to organize themselves separately. At Coventry a brotherhood of St Anne formed by journeymen was repressed, but revived again under a different name, and even earlier in the late fourteenth century a journeyman cordwainer who refused to join a journeymen's guild was so violently assaulted that he barely escaped with his life.

The final source of division was conflict between organized economic interests and the county and civic authorities. Economic ordinances could be highly restrictive, as in the past, like the rule of the cordwainers and cobblers that no person who 'meddled with old shoes' should sell new ones. Legislation was passed in 1437, ordering 'the masters, warden and people of the guilds' to submit their ordinances to the justices of the peace in the counties or to the 'chief governors of cities and towns', and a further act of 1504 was to refer backwards to the many times in the past when guilds had 'made themselves many unlawful and unreasonable ordinances as well in prices of wares as other things, for their own singular profit and to the common hurt and damage of the people'.

Guild life in the fifteenth century expressed itself culturally, and alarm was sometimes expressed at the expense of the often elaborate plays and pageants, which were held on special feast days, particularly at the great midsummer festival of Corpus Christi, first established as a feast in 1311. Arrangements for 'mystery' plays, which at Chester and Coventry went back to the 1370s, had by the mid fifteenth century often passed from the clergy to the laity, and they were great urban occasions. They were performed in different parts of the cities with musicians also taking part. Organization was complex, but the aim was simple enough – to present a moving Christian vision of the fall and redemption of man. At York, for instance, where there was a cycle of plays, as at Chester and Coventry, the 'Shipwrights' presented the building of Noah's Ark and the 'Fishery and Mariners' the Flood. The Shepherds' plays, in particular, passed from the simplicities of existence – 'Lord, what these weathers are cold' – to the raptures of assured faith: 'Hail, sovereign Saviour, for thou has us sought!'

Other medieval drama included miracle plays dealing with the lives of saints and, in the late fifteenth century, morality plays, of which the most famous was *Everyman*, the great allegory which was first to be printed early in the following century. Everyman is stripped of all his Good Deeds in order to be saved at the reckoning:

> And he that hath his account whole and sound,
> High in Heaven shall he be crowned.

We now classify *Everyman*, along with *The Vision of Piers the Ploughman* (with its dream of 'a fair field full of folk'), as 'literature'. In the fourteenth century, however, when the term was first used, it had the sense of learning from reading and was close in meaning to the twentieth-century word literacy. ('He has not sufficient literature to understand the scripture', we read as late as 1581.) *Everyman* was for every man, and it was spoken in an English that could be generally understood, grammatically far simpler than that of earlier generations but at the same time far richer in its vocabulary.

The memorable Paston letters, a collection of over 1,000 letters that illuminate the lives of the Norfolk Paston family between 1420 and 1503, were also written in English. The remarkable level of linguistic competence they display seems to have been shared by the members of the family who had been to university or an Inn of Court and those, including Margaret Paston, who had not. 'Right reverand and worshipful husband', she would begin her letters, but her writing and that of her relatives and agents was often close to direct speech. 'I may more leisure have to do writen half a quarter so much as I should sayn to you if I might speak with you.' 'I suppose the writing was more ease to you,' she adds generously. We can almost hear the Pastons talking in their letters, just as we can hear the talk of the Celys, wool-staplers who lived in Essex and ran their business in Mark Lane, London, through their correspondence.

It is Geoffrey Chaucer's poems, however, which introduce English literature as most people know it – fresh, bright, pictorial, packed with memorable characters, bristling with humour. If we were to rely on documentary evidence other than the poems, we would have little reason to believe that Chaucer had written them. He was born around 1343 in London's Vintry, the quarter of the wine dealers, when French was still the language into which Latin had to be construed in schools, and his father had been in attendance on Edward III. His own fortunes, as a page who became a civil servant, followed the political fortunes of those on whom he depended:

> This wretched worlde's transmutacioun,
> As wele or wo, now povre and now honour,
> Withouten ordre or wyse discrecioun
> Governed is by Fortunes errour.

Although he was deeply read in Latin, French (both of France and of Stratford-atte-Bowe) and Italian, it is through his mastery of English – and he knew many of its regional variants – that Chaucer can still draw us back to his own century.

He has left us not only with *The Canterbury Tales*, a collection of pilgrims' tales, but with a gallery of unforgettable profiles. The tales take us back to the pilgrimages of that time, some of them linked to holy days, all of them to sacred sites. 'Then longen folk to goon on pilgrimages', Chaucer noted, to Canterbury, and further afield to Santiago de Compostela and Jerusalem. It is often forgotten how frequently, and how far, medieval Englishmen travelled on pilgrimages. 'Right heartily beloved wife,' one real pilgrim wrote in 1456. 'I greet you with a thousand times, letting you wish that at the making of this letter I was in good health, blessed by God, and that is great wonder, for there was never men that had so perilous a way as we had.' The perils of pilgrimages were real enough. The keynote of *The Canterbury Tales*, however, is jollity. Chaucer's pilgrims could forget any hazards there might have been as they listened to the Prioress or the Wife of Bath, the Franklin or the Pardoner:

> This pardoner had hair as yellow as wax,
> But smooth it hung, as doth a strike of flax . . .
> And in a glass he had pigs' bones,
> But with these relics, when that he found
> A poor person dwelling up on land
> Upon a day he got more money
> Than that the parson got in two months . . .
> He made the person and the people his apes . . .

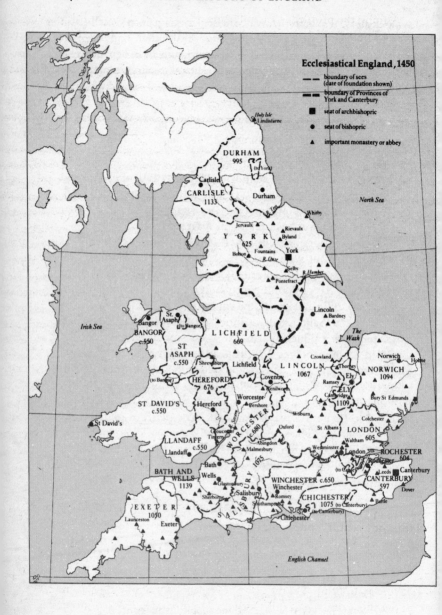

Ecclesiastical England, 1450

- – – boundary of sees (date of foundation shown)
- – – boundary of Provinces of York and Canterbury
- ■ seat of archbishopric
- ● seat of bishopric
- ▲ important monastery or abbey

DURHAM 995 (to York)

Holy Isle Lindisfarne

Carlisle

CARLISLE 1133

Durham

North Sea

Jervaulx

Whitby

Rievaulx

Byland

YORK 625

Fountains

Bolton

York

R. Ure

Selby

R. Humber

Pontefract

Lincoln

Bardney

BANGOR 550

Bangor (to Bangor)

St. Asaph

ST ASAPH c.550

Shrewsbury

LICHFIELD 669

The Wash

Lichfield

LINCOLN 1067

Crowland

Norwich

Hulne

NORWICH 1094

(to Bangor)

HEREFORD 676

Coventry

Kenilworth

Thorney

Ely

ELY 1109

Ramsey

Cambridge

Bury St Edmunds

ST DAVID'S c.550

Worcester

Pershore

Woburn

St Albans

Colchester

Hereford

Oxford

LONDON

St David's

WORCESTER c.680

Gloucester

Tintern

Abingdon

Malmesbury

Westminster

Waltham 605

London

ROCHESTER 604

LLANDAFF c.550

Llandaff

Bath

Rochester

Leeds

Canterbury

BATH AND WELLS 1139

Wells

SALISBURY 1075

WINCHESTER c.650

CANTERBURY 597

Glastonbury

Winchester

Romsey

Dover

Salisbury

CHICHESTER 1075 (to Canterbury)

Battle

Sherborne

Southampton

(to Canterbury)

EXETER 1050

Chichester

Launceston

Exeter

Irish Sea

English Channel

Among the profiles of the pilgrims, the medieval knight lives today more in Chaucer's words than through any real knight's chivalrous deeds:

> A knight there was, and that a worthy man
> That from the time that he first began
> To ride abroad, he loved chivalry
> Truth and honour, freedom and courtesy.

For other pictures of knights we can turn to the springy, alliterative metres of *Gawain and the Green Knight*, which was written by an anonymous author in the dialect of the North West Midlands area, and to the direct and simple prose of Malory, whose *Morte d'Arthur*, written in 1469, was printed by William Caxton in 1485.

'I, William Caxton, simple parson, present this book following which I have emprised t'imprint', Caxton wrote in the preface. He had started his career as a merchant in Bruges; the first book that he printed, in Cologne, was a *Histories of Troy*, but already by 1478 he preferred to print *The Canterbury Tales* rather than a new edition of Ovid or Virgil. Caxton's self-styled 'simplicity' is suspect, and as a translator and critic he could get things wrong (he praised Chaucer, for example, for his 'ornate' eloquence), but the books he printed in whatever language (and many were translations from Norman-French) reveal as much about the age as about printing.

Like all major inventions, printing was controversial and its effects are as difficult to disentangle as those of television in the twentieth century. 'The art of Printing will so spread knowledge,' it was to be argued later (in 1642), 'that the common people, knowing their own rights and liberties, will not be governed by way of oppression.' That comment, however, was made in a century not of limited social conflict but of civil war. In the fifteenth century preservation may have been the single most important immediate effect of printing: a press was more effective than a *scriptorium*, where texts were laboriously, but often lovingly, copied by hand. More information was stored as script gave way to print. Yet diffusion was of greater importance even in the short run. Old books as well as new books reached more readers. Most other generalizations about printing are suspect: the image, for instance, was not immediately overcome by the word, nor the pulpit by the press. Moreover, during the first years of printing it had as strong an influence on 'the home', a developing concept, as on public events. The family, if it could afford books, was now open to books on manners and morals (Caxton translated a French text on the first of these in 1487), on health (his *Journals of Health* appeared four years later) and, above all, on religion. Priests and members of universities might lose ancient privileges of access to knowledge although universities as institutions were to be given new rights as printers and publishers. The social perceptions of those who could read were bound to diverge from those who could not; in other words, a new inequality was added to all the existing inequalities of lay society.

One of Caxton's books, *A Description of Britain*, was extracted from John Trevisa's translation of Ralph Higden's *Polychronic*, and he rearranged Trevisa's order of the British realms in it so that England, rather than Ireland, came first. It not only included complaints that 'a yeoman arrays himself as a squire, a squire as a knight, a knight as a duke and a duke as a king,' but went on to argue that the unity of the English people still seemed incomplete. 'Men of the South beeth esier and more mylde; and men of the North be more unstable, more cruel and more uneasy; the myddel men beeth some dele partners with bothe.' Yet this picture of the Kingdom of England was to change radically during the next century. By 1559, John Aylmer, later Bishop of London, could write from exile with a firm sense of national identity.

> Oh, if thou knewst thou Englishmen in what wealth thou livest, and in how plentiful a country: Thou wouldest VII times a day fall flat on thy face before God and give him thanks that thou were born an Englishman, and not a French peasant, nor an Italian, nor German.

5

PROBLEMS, OPPORTUNITIES AND ACHIEVEMENTS

We Englishmen beholde
Our auncient customs bolde,
More preciouser than golde
Be clene cast away
And other now be fownd
The which (ye may understand)
That causeth all your land
So greatly to decay . . .

From *Now A Dayes*, a ballad of 1520

Elizabethan Englishmen were conspicuous for some of the qualities that we nowadays associate with the Japanese.

C. M. Cipolla, *Clocks and Culture*, 1965

We were just in a financial position to afford Shakespeare at the moment when he presented himself.

J. M. Keynes, *A Treatise on Money*, Vol. II, 1930

IT WAS in 1587, a year of strange 'preordained' eclipses and conjunctions of the planets, on the eve of the Spanish Armada, that an Elizabethan prayer referred proudly to 'the Commonwealth of England, a corner of the world, O Lord, which thou hast singled out for the magnifying of thy majesty'. The prayer and the sentiments it expressed were very similar to the one which was to be offered up at the opening of the Crystal Palace in 1851 in the reign of Queen Victoria. Both monarchs drew deeply on the loyalty of self-confident and divinely blessed Englishmen.

But the differences between the two queens were as great as those between the two centuries. Victoria was the mother of a large family; Elizabeth was hailed as Gloriana, the imperial virgin of classical myth, 'the phoenix of the world'. In 1851, England was the workshop of the world; in 1603 the Dutch were far ahead in economic strength. In the nineteenth century there was a *pax Britannica*; in the sixteenth century there were expensive wars against France and Spain and the internal struggle for power – religious and economic – of the Reformation. Tudor England did not, like Victorian England, profit from strength through peace. Yet there were echoes across the centuries: Victoria lived in an age of increasing democracy, while the Tudor monarchs, in particular Elizabeth I (1558–1603), were increasingly forced to recognize that they must rule with the assent of Parliament. Both centuries witnessed extraordinary population growth and, most important of all, Tudor and Victorian Englishmen shared a heightened role of national identity.

Tudor sovereigns, from Henry VII to Elizabeth I, with the experience of the fifteenth century behind them, hoped for consent but expected obedience. They regarded rebellion as the greatest danger to society as well as to their dynasty, whether it was provoked by 'over mighty subjects', as Sir John Fortescue called them in the 1470s, or fermented by discontented rural labourers. Order was considered essential to the stability and security of the state. The belief that the law of nature itself lay behind the one law of the realm lent sanctity to the whole system. Richard Hooker's *Laws of Ecclesiastical Polity* (1593), the great Elizabethan work on Church and State, summed up in magisterial style philosophies that had emerged intact from the hot crucible of sixteenth-century experience. Hooker was in no doubt, first, that 'obedience of creatures to law of nature' was 'the stay of the whole world' and, second, that 'all things do work after a sort according to law'. The laws of society, therefore, required that 'every part do obey one head or governor' and that 'order, moderation and reason' should 'bridle the affections'.

They were reinforced by paternal authority within the family and the preaching of the Church. Each household, like society as a whole, had its 'head', who, in theory at least, expected obedience in his small realm. Wives, by law as well as by custom, were held to be subordinate to their husbands. So, also, were children to parents. Indeed, according to William Perkins, the great Puritan divine, who wrote a 'domestic conduct' book on the subject in 1590, the definition of a husband was 'he that hath authority over the wife' and of parents 'they which hath power and authority over children'. The Bible, which was held to justify this natural 'order', was preached every Sunday from the pulpit: Perkins was one of the greatest preachers.

Order, therefore, lay at the centre of all things. This orthodox hierarchical view of society, not new, was more tenaciously held, more firmly articulated and, because of inflation, improved communication and religious reformation, more widely diffused than ever before. 'Take away order from things,' said Sir Thomas Elyot in his *Boke Named the Governour*, which went through ten editions between 1531 and 1600, 'what then should remain?' Many of Shakespeare's most rousing passages deal with dynastic, social and natural order, like the often quoted lines in *Troilus and Cressida*:

> The heavens themselves, the planets, and this centre
> Observe degree, priority and place . . .
> But when the planets
> In evil mixture to disorder wander,
> What plagues and what portents! what mutiny!
> What raging of the sea! shaking of the earth! . . .
> Take but degree away, untune that string
> And hark, what discord follows! Each thing melts
> In mere oppugnancy.

When Elizabethans wrote like this, directly linking the order of nature – God's dispensation – with the order of men, they were not merely expressing an ideal. They also had in mind the experience of their immediate ancestors and remote forebears (real or legendary), in whom they were increasingly interested. 'During the last twenty years,' wrote a Venetian observer of early Tudor England, 'three Princes of the blood, four Dukes, forty Earls, and more than three hundred other persons have died by violent death.' Statecraft demanded greater discrimination.

Henry VII married Elizabeth of York and in 1499 disposed of the last Yorkist with a title to the throne that was better than his own; Henry VIII (1509–47), whose momentous divorce from Katharine of Aragon and marriage to Anne Boleyn, contrary to current popular myth, reflected anxiety to secure a male heir as much as infatuation, eliminating many other people with royal ancestry; and Elizabeth was in 1587 reluctantly forced to sign the warrant for the execution of her cousin, Mary Queen of Scots, after her involvement in a Catholic conspiracy against the throne. In fact, Henry VIII's three children, Edward, Mary and Elizabeth, were to follow him in natural succession.

Yet violence was never exorcised in the sixteenth century at any level. It was part of the texture of everyday life. Private armouries and armed gangs were taken for granted. Non-political brutal crime and equally brutal punishment were commonplace; homicide rates were high and in the prisons people were kept 'lying in filthy straw, worse than any dog'. There were frequent local riots and disturbances, both in the countryside and in the towns, and intermittent large-scale rebellions. In 1536–7, beginning with a revolt in Lincolnshire, the Pilgrimage of Grace associated in instantaneous but uneasy alliance peers, gentry, yeomen, peasants and clothiers in the North of England, with Yorkshire soon in the forefront; and in 1549 two separate rebel armies were in the field, one in the west, following an uprising in Devon and Cornwall, the other Robert Ket's in East Anglia, urging relief for 'your poor Commons'. There was a further Northern rebellion in 1569 followed by 400 executions. Five years later, Sir Thomas Wyatt led rebels from Kent across the river at Kingston and reached Charing Cross. Oxfordshire villagers rioted against enclosure in 1596 at the same time as London apprentices were rioting against the City government. Nonetheless, the 1570s and 1580s were relatively orderly, despite the Spanish Armada scare of 1588, and there were fewer disorders than might have been anticipated during the crisis years of the 1590s. In 1601 the rebellion of the Earl of Essex, who 'concentrated the pride, the quarrels, and the popularity of the age', had no aftermath of violence. After his peers condemned him to death it was left to the ballad writers to lament his loss.

The loss of direct control over arms and men by the nobility was one of the reasons why chain reactions became more difficult. As Sir Walter Ralegh, himself tried and found guilty of treason in 1603, put it,

> the lords in former times were far stronger, more warlike . . . than they are now. There were many Earls who could bring into the field a thousand barbed horses; whereas now very few of them can furnish twenty to service the king.

The fourteenth- and fifteenth-century retaining system had survived the reign of Henry VII only as a 'feeble shadow of its former self', following a series of measures designed to emasculate the military power of the nobility. A Statute of Liveries of 1504 directed that persons practising livery and maintenance should be summoned before the Council in Star Chamber: defendants might be found guilty of 'confession, examination, proofs, or otherwise'. The Act lapsed in 1509, but by then it and a series of other measures had achieved their object – that of drastically reducing the number of the crown's subjects answerable to lords other than the monarch. Inflation assisted the process.

The Tudor sovereigns' overriding concern with public order was testified as much by their deeds as by their proclamations and homilies. Henry VIII went on to appoint Lord-Lieutenants to supervise the military organization of the realm, and their powers were continued by statute under Edward VI (1547–53), Mary (1553–8) and Elizabeth. Below the Lord-Lieutenants were the justices of the peace, who had their origins in the fourteenth century: they exercised both administrative and judicial functions. The Tudors' increasing use of the gentry as justices should be seen not as a concession to a new social group, increasing in size and importance, but as an attempt to maintain order effectively and cheaply; they were used to keep an eye on 'disorderly alehouses' and 'unlawful games' as much as to watch for signs of social and political protest. Meanwhile, the Tudors set out to employ men of talent at the centre of government, irrespective of their social origins. Thomas Wolsey, Thomas Cromwell and William Cecil all came from the middle ranks of society. Yet such men were wielders of royal power, not representatives of their 'order'; indeed, Cecil would have reserved public office for the aristocracy and barred people of his own humbler background from the kind of education that would fit them to enter public service.

Whoever the agents of government were (and the number of permanent salaried officials of the crown remained small), the law and the lawyers were always in the background. Admission figures to the Inns of Court multiplied by five in the sixteenth century to reach a figure of 200. The law itself was venerated (and much resented too by individuals) even if it was not always observed or enforced; and if it sometimes lagged behind social facts, its strength was its uniformity, whether it was dispensed by the local justices of the peace or by the judges in the higher courts of the realm. There were still manorial courts (although their jurisdiction was limited) and ecclesiastical courts, which dealt *inter alia* with sex offences even after the break with Rome, but the only real challenge to the common law came from new prerogative bodies. These included the Council in Star Chamber, which dealt, often very summarily, with the disorderly, the Court of Requests, deputed to deal speedily with cases affecting poor men, the Court of Wards, which extorted large sums of money from reluctant landowners, and the regional Councils of the North and of Wales. All these bodies were, in time, to be attacked bitterly by defenders of the one overriding common law, but that challenge was to come later. The efficiency of their procedures was an early recommendation.

The laws of nature and society also required respect for social 'degree, priority or place', although the relationship between systems of ranking and the ways to social mobility for individuals within the systems is difficult to establish. In the middle of the fifteenth century there had probably been around 5,000 knights, members of the gentry; by the early nineteenth century there were more than twice as many. Yet there were considerable variations from place to place, even within the same county. In parts of Kent near the metropolis only one-third of the late-seventeenth-century gentry were indigenous, but in East Kent only 3 per cent were not of native stock. In Leicestershire the leading families of the gentry were well established, but in neighbouring North-amptonshire, which, according to William Camden, the greatest scholar of his age, was 'everywhere adorned with noblemen's and gentlemen's houses', 'only the slenderest thread of blue blood flowed through county society from its medieval sources'. Half the county had formerly been royal forest, and many of the new estates with their great new houses were in or near the old forest areas.

At the lower levels of society there was enough social mobility in some parts of the country, particularly in and around the metropolis, for hierarchy itself to be difficult to buttress. Of 881 persons admitted as freemen of London in the years 1551 and 1553, forty-six were the sons of gentlemen, 136 the sons of yeomen and 289 the sons of husbandmen. Some people, as always, were coming down, others were going up. Both processes require more complex imagery than that of the social ladder. A younger son apparently coming down might often become his elder brother's master, or at least his better in wealth if not in honour and reputation; those who were successfully going up might move from commerce to landowning or seek to ensure that their children did so once they had accumulated sufficient wealth. There was relatively flexible entry into the ranks of the gentry, if not to the higher aristocracy, and many of the distinctive features of English society, when viewed comparatively, were and have been related to this characteristic.

Since the ownership of land continued to confer the greatest social status, the effects of social mobility on the hierarchical system of society were obviously just as apparent in the countryside as in the towns. The dissolution of the monasteries (1536–40) widened the land market in many parts of the country to the benefit of the gentry, and the market undoubtedly boomed again from the 1580s onwards. Of course, there were obvious manifestations of degree other than ownership of land. To whom did you raise your hat? Where did you sit in church? What clothes did you wear? It was always difficult in Tudor times to enforce sumptuary laws, which prescribed what different groups could or could not wear, like the act of 1463 which had restricted velvet and satin to men above the rank of knight and their wives, even though heavy penalties were attached to them. (The last such act was passed in 1597). When one *arriviste*, Thomas Dolman, chose to display classical mottoes over the entrance of his new mansion, he selected a revealing self-confident text, 'the toothless envies the eater's teeth'.

Given the welter of examples of individual *arrivisme*, there was ample scope for contemporaries to generalize about upward mobility. Thus, Sir Thomas Smith, lawyer and government official, stated tersely in 1560 that 'gentlemen be made good cheap in England' – 'whosoever . . . can live idly and without manual labour, and will bear the port, charge and countenance of a gentleman, he shall be called master.' For Smith and many others what was happening was not amiss. But the process had its critics. Edward VI, for example, referred to 'merchants become landed men' who called themselves 'gentlemen though they be churles'.

One of the best-known expositions of the framework of social hierarchy was that of the country parson William Harrison, who later became Canon of Windsor. 'We divide our people commonly into four sorts,' he wrote in 1577. The first sort were gentlemen, with 'the prince at the head . . . the nobility next . . . and next to them knights, esquires and simple gentlemen'. Second came 'citizens and burgesses . . . of some substance to bear office' and third 'yeomen' of the countryside. At the base were members of the fourth group, people 'to be ruled and not to rule others' – 'day labourers, poor husbandmen, and all artificers, as tailors, shoemakers, carpenters'. 'These,' Harrison went on, 'have no voice or authority in our commonwealth.'

Harrison, who allowed for wealth as well as birth in the determination of his hierarchy, left out professional people and the clergy, and he was less interested in what was happening at the lower end of the social scale than what was happening at the top. Here he recognized that there was homogeneity: peers were gentlemen, if gentlemen were not peers, and they had legal identity since they received individual writs of summons to Parliament. They had no special judicial or territorial powers, however, and their fortunes varied. The numbers of the high aristocracy – dukes, marquesses, earls, viscounts and barons – remained constant during the sixteenth century. (There were fifty-five peers in 1485 and the same number, though with many new names, in 1597.)

'Gentlemen' accounted for around only 2 per cent of the population of two counties as widely separated as Kent and Lancashire in the early seventeenth century, although their numbers there too were increasing. They were not a legally defined group, yet the distinction between 'gentlemen' and the rest was for Harrison the crucial one. Their strength lay in their ownership of land and the social and economic influence that went with it. But they also did not all share the same fortunes or outlook: it is not possible to generalize about the 6,000 men to whom the College of Heralds, the guardian of titled status, granted arms between 1560 and 1640. Some of the gentry, old or new, stayed at home; others were drawn into the life of London and the Court, whose values were set against the values of 'simple life' in the countryside. After 1611 some of them were to become baronets, hereditary knights granted a new title. And while some of the gentry felt special concern for the 'meaner sorte', others lacked a sense of obligation.

The yeoman, who ranked next to the gentleman, like him did not have a legally defined rank and, unlike him, did not bear a coat of arms, but he could be wealthier, and he too could be called to public service as constable, churchwarden or juror. Below the yeoman were working husbandmen, with land of their own, descendants, romantic legend was to have it, of the archers of Crécy and Poitiers, though their numbers were decreasing. And alongside and below the working husbandmen there were many varieties of powerless poor men, dependent at best on wage labouring. The worst off were survivors from older systems. Thus, three bondsmen or villeins on one Norfolk manor provided feudal services until 1575, and the last case concerning villeinage was handled in the royal courts as late as 1618. Harrison had nothing to say about other distinctions within the fourth of his social groups, although it clearly had its own hierarchies. It seemed enough to comment simply that these people were left out of government. 'The meaner sorte' were clearly a huge majority of the population, but they were at best a chorus, with individuals rising occasionally to sing unrehearsed parts of their own.

Their economic powerlessness was certainly as striking at all times as their political powerlessness:

> From pillar to post
> The poor man he was tossed:
> I mean the labouring man,
> I mean the ploughman,
> I mean the handycraft man,
> I mean the victualling man
> And also the good yeoman.

The lament for the plight of the poor, missing for much of the fifteenth century, was a recurring theme in the sixteenth century. So too was vagrancy, which was a perpetual concern of the justices of the peace. Hitherto, the Church in particular, through the monasteries and through urban charity, had concerned itself directly, if not systematically, with provisions for the poor. So too had the guilds, and while charitable giving may have declined in real terms after the Reformation, relief provided by public authority at a local level increased. It was often initiated by local justices of the peace and town councils before Parliament itself introduced major legislation in 1572 imposing compulsory poor rates. York, for example, levied a compulsory rate as early as 1561. Between 1546 and 1557 London, which had taken the lead with a poor relief scheme of 1552, also reorganized its hospitals: St Bartholomew's was for the 'impotent poor' and St Thomas's and Bethlehem (Bedlam) were for the insane.

National legislation on the subject became increasingly sophisticated. Thus, a statute of 1531 distinguished between vagrants and the sick and unemployed poor, only the latter being allowed to beg in their own parishes, while a statute of 1552 ordered parishes to register their poor and to meet their responsibilities in relation to the local resources available. Evolving policies culminated in important acts in 1597 and 1601 recognizing that the poor did not all belong to one category, confirming the parish as the unit of poor law administration, and empowering justices of the peace to levy poor rates and to pay for work provided for the able-bodied poor. This Elizabethan legislation became known as 'the old poor law', and it remained in force with changes (some of them substantial) until 1834. Overseers of the Poor were now appointed annually by the local justices, under penalty of fine, and took their place alongside churchwardens as busy, unpaid and necessary local officials.

In some earlier Tudor poor law legislation there had been a harshness of tone which reflected both the fear that the numbers of the poor were increasing in town and countryside and the belief that they were a threat to public order because they included 'rogues and vagabonds' as well as 'impotent poor' (the contemporary term for people of good character and goodwill who were sick or could not find employment). It also reflected in part, however, the sense that there were limits to what government could do to alleviate the problem of poverty. It is to this period that we can trace back a clear awareness that economic and social policy might not always move in the same direction.

Ideal and practice could clash in other issues. In theory, according to the laws of natural and mutual obligation, the community, local or national, was one. 'Note,' the preacher Hugh Latimer told his hearers, 'that our Saviour biddeth us to say "us".' The use of the word 'Commonwealth' was as common as the use of the word 'Empire', and Elizabeth herself stressed that 'it was the duty of a prince to hold an equal hand over the highest and the lowest.' Shakespeare was not alone in pointing out that in death all trappings and ceremony disappeared and all people were in the same condition. 'Lordes, ladies and gentlemen, learned or unlearned of what estate or degree so ever you be of,' Andrew Boord told his readers in his *Breviary of Health* (1547), 'think not that no man can be holpen by no manner of medicines, if so be God do send the sickness, for he hath put a time to every man.'

Boord was aware, however, as Latimer was, that as long as people lived, some could get all manner of medicines and others could not: 'at our tyme physic is a remedy only for rich folks.' Theories of obligation did not necessarily work easily in practice, for, in fact, inequality expressed itself in contrasts that started with chances of life and death and extended through sex, work, diet, clothes and shelter to education and taste. Natural order could be used also as an argument against government intervention. As one sceptic argued in 1550, when an attempt was made to regulate prices of cheese and butter by proclamation, 'Nature will bear her course . . . and never shall you drive her to consent that a *penny-worth* of new shall be sold for a farthing.' Thomas Nashe, poet, pamphleteer and dramatist, expressed similar scepticism about the way theories of natural obligations worked in practice.

> In London the rich disdain the poor. The courtier the citizen. The citizen the countryman. One occupation disdaineth another. The merchant the retailer. The retailer the craftsman. The better sort of craftsman the baser. The shoemaker the cobbler.

Social contrasts were obvious enough, even on the surface. One of the most obvious was pointed out by Harrison. The 'gentilitie' ate wheaten bread; 'their household and poor neighbours rye or barley bread, and in time of dearth bread made . . . of beans, peas or oats'. Moreover, as the sixteenth century went by, this particular contrast was sharpened. Only a small section of the population could contrive to wear (let alone pay for) starched ruffs, padded doublets and farthingales (framed hoops worn under the skirt). There were best wool, fine linen and silk at one end of the scale, and leather and rags at the other – and this in an age when bright clothes were particularly prized. Houses contrasted equally sharply. The differences were there too in hours of eating. The nobility and gentry, according to Harrison, dined and supped earlier than the merchants, and the husbandmen dined 'at high noon as they call it' and 'supped at seven or eight . . . As for the poorest sort,' he concluded, 'they generally dine and sup when they may, so that to talk of their order to repast, it was but a needless matter.'

One of the courtiers of Philip of Spain (Mary's husband) was struck by the contrast between English labourers' 'large diet' and their houses 'made of sticks and durte', while at the other end of the scale, for Harrison, 'every man almost' was 'a builder' and 'the basest house of a baron dooth often match in our daies with some honours of princes in old time'. Indeed, it is to the builders of this period that we owe some of our most characteristic English domestic buildings. There was a competitive spirit behind much of the building, and it is significant that in four widely separated counties – Derbyshire, Essex, Somerset and Shropshire – more new country houses were built between 1570 and 1620 than in any other half-century. The size and management of large house-holds changed less than might have been expected, but there were physical changes, like the introduction of galleries and lodges. There were also signs of an increasing desire for privacy, impossible for the poor.

Education, like diet, costume and shelter, was socially and culturally stratified, and the proliferation after the Reformation of a wide range of educational institutions, from small private establishments, often kept by a single master, to well-endowed grammar schools – over 300 new schools were founded between 1500 and 1620 – on the whole exaggerated rather than reduced inequalities. Literacy, however, increased during the 1560s and 1570s, and although the rate of growth may have slackened off between then and the end of the century, there is evidence that 47 per cent of at least one major social group, the criminal class of London, could read soon after the beginning of the next. The book trade expanded – 259 books were published in the year 1600 alone – as did the business of printing broadsheets. Yet there was a substratum of illiteracy. It is interesting to note, for example, that Shakespeare's father always marked rather than signed documents.

There was also a distinct increase – with a setback in the last decade of the sixteenth century – of the total number of under-graduates receiving university education. Yet access was not easy, for the education offered was costly. As Harrison put it in 1577, 'it is in my time an hard matter for a poore man's child to come by a fellowship (though he be never so good a scholer)'. The Inns of Court were even more exclusive, since they offered no scholarships, and in the early seventeenth century nine out of ten of the students there came from the aristocracy and the gentry.

Shared education, if only for the exclusive few, brought with it both increased cultural cohesion and a widening of interests among the gentry and the aristocracy; and although there were local variations in culture and style, there were now country gentlemen who through their literary and artistic interests could form something of a 'dispersed university'. Non-verbal culture was not despised: the complete 'Renaissance man', epitomized by

Sir Philip Sidney, was expected to combine bodily and verbal skills – to dance as well as to read, to use the bow as well as the pen.

There were already 'high' and 'low' elements in the national culture. Musicians, writers and painters looked for patronage to courtiers and gentlemen, either in London or in the great new country houses. Neither music nor painting were thought of as arts in the modern sense, but, as they began to secure new influence outside the Church or the City, they were now fitted into a privileged social context. The fashionable Elizabethan lute was an expensive instrument; so too were the virginals. Painting from Holbein onwards was for kings, courtiers and gentlemen, and Nicholas Hilliard, official miniaturist to Elizabeth (himself the son of a sheriff of Exeter), expressed the wish that 'none should meddle' with limning (miniature painting) but 'gentlemen alone'. Within this increasingly distinct 'high culture' there was always a dividing line between the artist as gentleman, including the gentleman–author, and the artist as craftsman, whatever the art, or as performer. Thus Queen Elizabeth would admire the dancing of a courtier but not of a professional dancing master. 'I will not see your man,' she once told Leicester, who invited her to watch his dancing master dance. 'It is his trade.'

Literature, architecture and gardening as well as music and painting explored the language of allegory. The poet Edmund Spenser introduced many allegorical devices into his ingenious *Epithalamion*, describing in twenty-four stanzas the twenty-four hours of his wedding day, and the recusant Sir Thomas Tresham (who had the number *tres*, representing the Trinity, concealed in his name) built a three-storey triangular lodge at Rushton in Northamptonshire, each side of which measured thirty-three feet, had nine windows (three on each storey) and bore an inscription of thirty-three letters.

Local culture in small towns and villages still had its roots in tradition. Once Latimer could not preach in a village because the parishioners were celebrating 'Robin Hoode's day', while the Elizabethan Puritan Phillip Stubbes always watched with horror parishioners gathering round 'their Maie pole, which they bring home with great veneration'. Popular culture in the towns suffered as a result of the Reformation, but there were new leisure pursuits. Organized horse racing, for example, began at York in 1530, and bowls was becoming more common by the end of the century. Stubbes thought that football was more 'a freendly kynde of fight' than a recreation, but he was biased. Alehouses multiplied, and hops, dismissed earlier as a 'wicked and pernicious weed', became a staple ingredient of beer, criticized by conservatives:

> Hops, Reformation, Beys and Beer
> Came to England in one bad year.

The Reformation was the biggest of these three major agencies of change, and change acquired a new significance in the sixteenth century, whether or not it was consciously planned. Religious change was certainly fully understood by contemporaries, one Venetian observer describing it as 'the greatest alteration that could possibly arise in the nation because a revolution in customs, laws, obedience and, lastly, in the very nature of the state itself, necessarily follows'. Population growth, also clearly visible at the time, was the second agent of major change, although it was difficult to explain. The third, which puzzled and baffled the century, was inflation.

Henry VIII's break with Rome, the prelude to the Reformation, was essentially political rather than doctrinal – the crucial issue was the dynastic succession – and doctrinal change followed only later and hesitantly: few people wanted it. The first of the great changes was in fact, political, in the 'very state itself', for the king now became Supreme Head of the Church of England, which was deemed sufficient of itself 'without the intermeddling of any exterior person'. Church property too was transferred to the State, although much of it soon made its way from the Crown into the hands of the laity.

Yet even during this first phase, when sweeping changes in the power and position of the Church, masterminded by Thomas Cromwell, merchant and soldier before he became an administrator, were effected through the agency of one long Parliament sitting at intervals for seven years, the Reformation had other dimensions. The changes were carried through on a ground-swell of anti-clericalism, and there were imported influences too, for

Calvinism and Lutheranism, which Henry VIII had opposed, already had their adherents in England. While most, but not all, of the clergy were prepared to accept the change, the views of the laity were inevitably divided and the Church of England was not to become firmly established for another thirty years. Cromwell himself was to lose his head in 1540, and there were further religious struggles during the reigns of Henry's Protestant son, Edward, and his Roman Catholic daughter, Mary. The Mass became the Holy Communion in Edward's reign, when Archbishop Thomas Cranmer's new Prayer Book was intro- duced with its beautiful haunting English, threatened only in our own century, but there were many people who opposed the change, like the disgruntled Cornishman who complained to Cranmer that the new service was 'but a Christmas game'. Mary's attempts to restore the Catholic faith failed, however, and in retrospect at least seem doomed to have done so.

It was only with the Elizabethan Church settlement of 1558, initially a compromise between contending forces, that the Church of England found the basis on which it could acquire enduring support, but even then there were always parties within it. Religion in England could never be completely controlled from above, and the desire for religious change continued to serve as a driving force, both in the attempt to restore an older Roman Catholic order and in the struggle by Puritans – the word was current in England from the 1560s – to push the Church further in a reformed direction with the open Bible in the home as well as in the parish church.

The biggest economic change resulting from the Reformation, directly affecting not only the state but the balance of social forces inside it, was the dissolution of the monasteries, a two-stage operation beginning with 374 lesser houses, with an annual income of less than £200,000, in 1536 and continuing in 1538–40 with the 186 'great and solemn monasteries'. The last to go was Waltham. The object of this Cromwellian exercise was not to reform the Church but to enrich the crown. The monastic houses, which collected about half the total income of the Church, were an obvious target, even though there were striking variations between rich and poor monasteries just as there were between rich and poor dioceses. The first effect of the dissolution was to augment substantially royal annual income from monastic lands; and it needed a new agency, the Court of Augmentations, to deal with it. The assets could have provided a long-term relief to royal revenues, although the social consequences would have been uncertain.

But the crown did not keep what it had acquired: a small part of the land was given away subject to feudal knight service, more was exchanged, and a large part was leased or sold at market prices, fixed at a minimum of twenty times the annual rent. Two out of every three peers were either granted or purchased monastic estates, and by the end of Henry VIII's reign two-thirds of the new wealth had been alienated in land market operations of unprecedented scale and speed. The freed lands passed for the most part not into the hands or pockets of 'new men' and speculators but into the hands of existing local landowners, the peerage and gentry. In Yorkshire, where there were marked local variations between one part of the county and another, over a quarter of the gentry families of 1642 owned property which before 1540 had been held by the monasteries.

Once seized, there was no chance that the property would revert to the monasteries again; old believers were just as unwilling to part with their acquisitions as Protestants. Naves speedily became farmhouses, chantries became parlours and towers became kitchens. A Gloucester clothier, Thomas Bell, turned a Dominican priory into a factory; a furnace and forge were set up on the site of a Sussex monastery at Robertsbridge; and the end of the Black Friars' franchise in London released properties for use as theatres. Where monastic land continued to be leased under lay hands, shortened leases, racked rents and evicted tenants were common. Thus, the properties of St Albans Abbey were a century later worth eighty times their value at the time of dissolution.

A further dissolution of chantries, free chapels, colleges, hospitals, fraternities and guilds in the reign of Edward VI completed the process of property transfer, although some of these institutions suffered more than others. Chantries, a favourite form of late medieval endowment, suffered more than guilds. Some of the income from this second dissolution was used to found grammar schools, hospitals and almshouses. Yet much land passed on to the market, and private individuals benefited directly as they had done during the 1530s.

Inevitably, the dissolution of the monasteries led also to social unrest, since the monasteries had been important employers and exercised many charitable functions, particularly in rural areas. The Pilgrimage of Grace had its origins, in part at least, in the closure of the great monasteries in the North of England. And if economic change brought with it social discontent, doctrinal change brought with it social division. The Reformation had both Catholic and Protestant martyrs: on the one side Sir Thomas More and Cardinal Fisher, who were executed in the reign of Henry VIII and, on the other, Latimer, Ridley and Cranmer, burnt at the stake during Mary's reign and commemorated in John Foxe's *Book of Martyrs*. Less well remembered but just as significant, shires, villages and families were divided. In the reign of Mary, who was advised by the Holy Roman Emperor to be '*une bonne anglaise*', many Protestants of all ranks moved into exile: of 472 people known to have fled, 166 were gentry, sixty-seven clergy, forty merchants, 119 students, thirty-two artisans and thirteen servants. Some of them were zealously determined that 'the walls of Jerusalem should be built again in England'.

In earlier and in later years idolatrous church images were destroyed, religious texts replaced medieval paintings on church walls, church plate was sold, altars gave way to communion tables, marriage was legalized for priests (in 1547 and again in 1559) and the Mass was no longer said in Latin. Yet, however great the zeal of reformers, much was carried over from the past, especially in the 'dark corners of the land', as the Puritans called them, counties like Lancashire and Shropshire. Elizabeth herself kept candles and a crucifix in her private chapel. The hierarchy of the Church, from bishops to parish priests, survived everywhere and retained much of its influence: five new dioceses – for a time six – were created following the dissolution of the monasteries. The ecclesiastical courts and Convocation kept their influence too. The clergy never became a salaried body as they did in many other European Protestant countries, and they continued to be supported by tithes, endowments and income from their glebe lands.

Some lay patrons chose clergy for the colour of their church-manship – and many of them were far better educated in Queen Elizabeth's reign than they had been in her father's – but in much of the countryside old religious beliefs and customs prevailed. There were still services in the fields, for example, at Rogation Tide, and the parish boundaries were still perambulated. Screens which separated ministers and the people might be destroyed in Edward VI's reign, but in the reign of Elizabeth some of them returned despite Protestant objections. A 'witchcraze' in England began while the Reformation was still in progress – around 1550 – and continued for a century. Between 1563 and Elizabeth's death in 1603, in the county of Essex alone, 174 persons were indicted for black witchcraft, which was a capital offence, although only half that number were executed. White witchcraft was generally acceptable as were the 'cunning' men and women who practised it. Awe and superstition did not disappear either from the society or the culture.

During the first phase of the Henrician Reformation, Thomas Cromwell ordered parish priests to keep registers of marriages, baptisms and deaths, a measure that was resented by many of the gentry as an infringement of individual liberties. Through sys-tematic analysis of these registers, dating from 1538, historical demographers have been able to determine more accurately than for any previous period population trends and patterns during this period. It is clear even without them, however, that the sixteenth century saw a dramatic growth in population which was to have far-reaching effects. By the 1470s population had started rising for the first time since the Black Death. Growth continued through-out the sixteenth and early seventeenth centuries, although there was a sharp setback from 1557–9, years of epidemic disease in which burials were more than double the annual average, and there was also some slackening off of growth during the 1590s. By 1603 the population of England had probably passed the four million mark and was still growing. Rates of growth were not equal, of course, throughout the country, but to take one main farming county, Leicestershire, as an example of a not uncharacteristic scale of growth, population increased by 58 per cent between 1563 and 1603.

In the early sixteenth century there had been talk of depopulation; now there was talk of over-population. For the geographer and historian Richard Hakluyt, writing in 1584, 'wee are growen more populous than ever heretofore'. For Sir Humphrey Gilbert, who wanted people to emigrate, England was 'pestered with people'. Local migration, particularly to places where there seemed to be available common land – and there was much of this – could lead to bitter litigation as well as sad complaint. Yet there was no serious Malthusian problem of mass starvation and unemployment, since the Tudor economy successfully absorbed a rise in population which was markedly less than that in twentieth-century under-developed countries. As the number of people increased – and with them the numbers of cattle, sheep, horses and pigs – there was less vulnerability to famine than there had been earlier. Mortality was higher in the terrible crisis years of the middle of the century, 1557–9, than it was in 1596–8, when the national population was greater.

Fluctuations in rates of population growth can be traced back to bad harvests and to epidemics, and the two were still closely related to one another: 'first dearth and then plague'. If dearth was diminishing, so too was the incidence and intensity of the plague. There seems to have been relatively little change in the underlying structural patterns of demography at this time, although the expectation of life may have risen and the age of marriage was one or two years lower than it was a century later.

Analysis of the parish registers has also given us a unique insight into the structure of the population and family patterns. Families were not large, and they were nuclear (consisting of parents and children) rather than extended (hosts of relatives living together). Infant and child mortality rates were high, although there were marked differences between parishes. Over half the population was under the age of twenty-five while only 8–10 per cent were over sixty. Very young children from poorer families were expected to work from the age of six or seven.

Marriages in families of status and wealth, often involving

property deals, were usually arranged, but there were arranged marriages at other levels of society as well. The ceremony itself was a festive and public occasion. Marriage practices were local-ized and, while there were contemporary complaints of early and hasty marriages, most people, either ordinary or privileged, did not marry much younger than we marry now; they were, indeed, very much older in relation to their expectation of life. At the same time, illegitimacy rates were low until the last years of the sixteenth century, when limited evidence suggests a sharp rise continuing into the seventeenth century. There was a large minority of unmarried people and of children with only one parent alive.

The family was the basic unit of production, although viewed within the context of other Western European countries there was a relatively high number of family groups which were not production units. Within each household there were non-members of the family, servants and dependants, the number varying with wealth and status so that the poorest households tended to be the smallest. The more children, the greater the strain. Not surprisingly, there was considerable migration of the landless poor. The areas to which they migrated were more 'open' in social atmosphere than the old 'fielden' areas of the Midlands. Trade was a magnet.

It is far more difficult to generalize about actual behaviour within families, particularly among poor families, than it is to identify demographic trends. The marriage system allowed for considerable play of personalities, although always within the context of the authority of the head of the household. There is ample evidence from Shakespeare's plays of individual women who ruled their husbands, and servants might rule men too. Likewise, while girls were in general not as well educated as boys, there were significant exceptions, including Anne Boleyn and the learned daughters of Sir Anthony Cooke, one of whom married William Cecil, later Lord Burleigh. The beating of children by their parents could be recommended or frowned upon even in books of guidance, and there were many examples in practice of parents actually demonstrating signs of love for their children. There were also examples both of generational conflict, not surprisingly in an age which flaunted youth and venerated age, and of cross-generational sympathy. Apprentices were one of the most interesting groups in society. 'If there were any good to be done in these days,' wrote an Elizabethan minister, 'it is the young men that must do it, for the old men are out of date.'

Contemporary generalizations about the balance of the population were often linked to lively and concerned comment about the price rise, the third major agent of change in this period. This was particularly true during the decades in which prices rose most rapidly: the 1540s, 1550s and 1590s. Following a period of stability in the fifteenth century, when the total population was relatively low, prices began to rise throughout Western Europe, starting with Spain. Taking the selective Phelps Brown/Hopkins price index for England, with 1451–75 prices as the base line of 100, the index had risen to over 160 by 1520 and to 170 by 1555. And there were two extraordinary years in the middle of the century: in 1556 the index reached 370 and in 1557 a peak of 409. The index had dropped back to 281 by 1594, but rose to 505 two years later and 685 in 1597. These, of course, were fluctuations related to those in population rates. The trough never fell below 400 again and was to reach a mid seventeenth century peak of 839 in 1650.

When compared with late-twentieth-century inflation this upward movement may seem mild rather than revolutionary, but it has been identified, nonetheless, as the highest betweeen 1250 and 1900, and it significantly disrupted social relationships. Economic historians have argued as much about the causes of the inflation as social historians about its consequences, but there is now common recognition, first, that the economy still included a large subsistence sector affected by the change only to a limited extent; second, that there were marked geographical differences; third, that the prices of different commodities did not move uniformly; and, fourth, that movements of wages and rents, as well as movements of prices, have got to be taken into the reckoning at every stage.

No simple explanation seems adequate. Contemporaries attached special significance to the import of large quantities of Spanish treasure from across the Atlantic and to the debasement of the coinage. Recently, however, emphasis has shifted to the effects of the growth of population on increased demand, but the fact that the far more spectacular population growth two centuries later did not produce a comparable rate of increase in prices over a long period suggests that this alone cannot have been responsible. And if debasement was more a symptom of trouble than a cause, it is nonetheless true that the velocity of circulation of money was speeded up by Henry VIII's debasements of 1526 and 1544–6 which broke a long tradition of standard metal coins and reduced the fineness of silver first by a half and next by two-thirds. Later debasements by Protector Somerset reduced the proportion of silver to a quarter. Clearly, it is the relationship between population, resources and fiscal policies of the crown that is important. Tudor governments spent large sums of money: Henry VIII's army in France in 1544 was bigger than any earlier English army that had set foot on the Continent and there was no plunder to collect. Moreover, the demand for monastic lands after the dissolution of the monasteries certainly pushed up land prices and rents: meadow land in Derbyshire fetched a rent in 1584 four times that of 1543, while rents in parts of Kent near to the metropolis rose sharply enough for William Lambarde to anticipate later theories of rent as an unearned surplus. It was not 'the quantity of their possessions or the fertility of their soil' which enriched the gentry there, he suggested, but 'the benefit of the situation of the country itself'.

There has been protracted debate about the effects of price and rent rises on the different orders of society. The fortunes of the landowners, including the high aristocracy, varied and so did their expenditures. Some peers spent ostentatiously on building, clothes, food or drink and got into aristocratic debt, although this was not always a sign of poverty. A few peers of ancient lineage, like the Berkeleys, found themselves in serious difficulties, selling manors and dismissing servants; their plight was explained by their inefficiency as much as their extravagance. Others, like the Spencers of Althorp and the Russells of Woburn, built up their estates and their wealth with them. Older landlords with scattered estates were often able to balance profits from some against losses from others.

These were times when the industrious, the enterprising and the lucky – and perhaps, above all, the lawyers – could exploit the situation, justifying John Stow's generalization that 'there was no want of anything to him that wanted not money.' The unlucky victims however, were not necessarily unindustrious or unenterprising; they included people with fixed incomes, or income from tithes expressed in kind, and people with insecure land tenures. Cottagers and wage workers, both in the countryside and in the towns, suffered seriously since wages lagged behind prices and they had no other ways of supplementing their meagre incomes. Furthermore, with the rise in population, labour lost the bargaining advantage it had enjoyed during the late fourteenth and fifteenth centuries: the Phelps Brown/Hopkins real wages index reached its lowest point in seven centuries in 1597, the year of Shakespeare's *A Midsummer Night's Dream*.

For the crown, there were major financial problems. As in the thirteenth and fourteenth centuries, monarchs found it difficult to live on their own. Henry VIII was forced to raise a 'subsidy' in 1512, a Parliamentary tax based on an assessment of individual wealth; Wolsey extorted an 'amicable grant' in 1525; and the King spent twice as much on futile war during the last eight years of his reign as the total yield of taxes and loans. Although Elizabeth's reign began peacefully – and the costs of government fell – she too had to turn to Parliament for financial support increasingly as her reign went by. In 1576, the Speaker of the Commons congratulated her on having 'most carefully and providentially delivered this kingdom from a great and weighty debt . . . a cancer able to eat up not only private men and their patrimonies . . . but also princes and their estates', but this was before the years of war against the Spanish, and when Elizabeth died the country was left with a debt equivalent to more than one year's income.

The quest of the Crown for new sources of income was bound to provoke argument with Parliament, and, as in earlier centuries, it raised constitutional issues both of political representation and of individual rights. The House of Commons was always suspicious of extended feudal dues and it did not easily yield to demands for extraordinary purposes through subsidies; at no time did it offer financial support for a standing army in peace-time. It was also suspicious of any new forms of taxation. The most important of these were monopolies, which were conferred by the Crown in return for cash, a device originally introduced by Henry VIII to protect skill and to encourage innovation. Ship money, an extension to the whole country of a fourteenth-century impost to outfit ships for the protection of the coasts, originally only levied on port towns, was revived by Elizabeth, and also became a bone of contention in the next century. It was in Elizabeth's reign that the attack on monopolies began; and she faced difficult parliaments in 1593, 1597 and 1601 when she tried to get increased support from them. In 1601, for example, when Members of Parliament were told that the Crown had granted monopoly patents for a long list of items ranging from currants to playing cards (the latter a monopoly enjoyed by Sir Walter Ralegh), one Member provoked a memorable exchange when he called out, 'Is not bread there?' 'Bread?' asked other Members. 'No,' replied the first, 'but if order be not taken for these, bread will be there, before the next Parliament.'

The relationship between the income of the Crown and the income of its subjects was bound to change in a period of economic and social change, and in Tudor times the changes began not with playing cards or with currants – or for that matter with bread – but with wool. 'The web of our life,' wrote Shakespeare, 'is a mingled yarn, good and ill together,' and in sheep farming there was ample evidence of both.

It was a rise in the price of wool that encouraged the first sixteenth-century expansion in flocks and pasturage between 1510 and 1520, and after a contraction there was a further burst which lasted until 1551: 'of all stock the rearing of sheep is most profitable,' wrote Fitzherbert in his *Book of Husbandry* in 1579. (By then the Spencers had 13,000 sheep.) Yet there was a serious enough contraction of demand for wool after 1551 to lead to considerable unemployment in the clothing industry, a fall in the sheep population and a shift among sheep farmers to meat and cheese production. Grain prices too rose faster than wool prices between 1548 and 1600.

The protracted argument about enclosures revealed the same sharp differences of values as in the fifteenth century, particularly in the Midland counties in the heart of 'open-field' England. A statute of 1489, often echoed in later statutes, had forbidden all depopulation and conversion of arable to pasture, but it could not be enforced, and Leicestershire, where some 140 villages or hamlets out of a total of 270 were partially or completely enclosed between 1485 and 1607, was one of the main storm centres.

Already in 1520 a ballad described how:

> Gret men makyth now a dayes
> A shepecott in the churche.

And a generation later complaints could be heard that there were men 'that live as though there were no God at all'. 'They take our houses over our heads, they buy our grounds out of our hands, they raise our rents, they levy great (yea unreasonable) fines, they enclose our commons. No custom, no law or statute can keep them from oppressing us.'

Thoughtful contemporaries were at pains to distinguish between a farmer's enclosure of his land for 'improvement' and rich men's enclosure of 'other men's commons'; they also drew distinctions between enclosure by force and enclosure by consent. But as common rights were lost 'greed' often seemed more in evidence than the desire to improve the land evident in books like Thomas Tusser's *A Hundred Good Points of Husbandry* (later expanded to 500 points, few of which were original), which first appeared in 1557. Not surprisingly, there were serious anti-enclosure riots, for example in 1548–9.

The increasing prevalence of usury (lending, usually at high rates of interest) seemed to be a related problem, and after Parliament had legalized it in 1571, reviving an act of Henry VII repealed in 1552, Harrison could observe that 'usury, a trade brought in by the Jews, was now perfectly practised almost by every Christian and so commonly, that he is accounted for a fool that doth lend his money for nothing'. There were forces restraining as well as sharpening economic appetites: thus, Sir John Gostwick, a Bedfordshire squire, who benefited from monastic spoils in Henry VIII's reign, could advise his heirs 'to heighten no rent unless your farmers have heightened theirs to sub-tenants'. Yet by the end of the century there was increasing resistance to interference from government in matters like enclosure and usury, although dislike of 'middle men' was as strong as ever. Sir Walter Ralegh was not alone in urging that every man should be left free, 'which is the desire of a true Englishman'.

This cry was to be raised in the future mainly in relation to industry, a term not yet used in the sixteenth century, when most 'industries' were still linked with agriculture, operated on a small scale and were at a craft stage.

Textiles were still the biggest of them. Camden called their manufacture 'one of the pillars of commonwealth', and they were the main source of livelihood, not so much now in the most important wool growing areas as in parts of Western England and the North, where there was a reserve of labour and cloth could be made more cheaply. The expansion of the market led not to the concentration of production in factories but to work being 'put out': clothiers with sufficient capital collected orders, hired out looms and depended on the manufacture of others for their sales. English cloth remained the country's most valuable export, with a steady overseas level of demand from 1559 to 1603, followed in the early sixteenth century by a further boom that generated rapid economic growth. This was the period when immigrant craftsmen, a source of strength to the economy in this as in other industries, introduced the so-called 'new draperies' with names like 'beys', 'perpetuonos' and 'shaloons', fabrics which were cheaper, lighter, and less durable, and highly amenable, therefore, to changes of fashion. Fashion might be dismissed by Harrison as 'a fantastical folly', but its exploitation could be highly profitable and the new draperies were there to stay. So also were the immigrants who first made that manufacture possible. 'What country in the world is there,' a Member of Parliament asked in 1596, 'that nourisheth so many aliens from all parts of the world as England doth?'

In one flourishing branch of the textile industry, hosiery, there was one indigenous invention that was a portent of things to come. A clergyman, William Lee, 'the first English mechanician of his own or any preceding age', invented a knitting frame in the late sixteenth century, and it was quickly adopted in the flourishing hosiery industry in the East Midlands. There are many myths about Lee's invention and the motives which inspired it: one was that he was distressed to see his wife endlessly knitting stockings by hand to supplement his meagre income. There was no myth, however, in the misfortunes of his later career, which anticipated those of later inventors. He died in poverty in France in 1610.

Other genuine 'new industries' were assisted by foreign immigrants: they included paper making, printing, gun founding and the manufacture of gunpowder. (Francis Bacon was to describe gunpowder and printing as two of the three great inventions of his age, the mariner's compass being the third.) Development in these industries was overshadowed, however, by the substantial growth of the lead, copper and iron industries. There was a growing demand for products made out of all these metals from cast-iron cannons to pots and pans. One of the most important suppliers was not a new man but the sixth Earl of Shrewsbury, who also opened glass works and coal mines.

The introduction of the blast furnace at the very end of the fifteenth century had been a significant new technical development in the iron industry, and a century later there were more than sixty furnaces in operation, most of them alongside finery forges in the forest of the Weald in Kent and Sussex. It was in that area too, where iron had been produced for centuries, that steel was first produced (with the help of German craftsmen) in 1565, and a slitting mill opened in 1588. Whether or not iron production was already beginning to be held back by lack of the timber necessary for the charcoal used in the bloomeries and blast furnaces has been much disputed. It has been persuasively argued that the extent of woodland did not, in fact, diminish as the result of the ironmasters' operations; timber prices actually rose more slowly than those of any other agricultural product.

Harrison wondered why the Weald did not use coal, the product of the biggest and most concentrated of the mining industries. The increase in coal output, with Durham and Northumberland in the lead in distribution, was big enough for some historians to have written of an industrial revolution; and while coal was not yet directly associated with the iron industry, as it was to be in the eighteenth and nineteenth centuries, its domestic use was already darkening the skies of London. In 1563–4, 33,000 tons were shipped to London from Newcastle and in 1597–8 163,000 tons. In the absence of the steam engine, which both depended on coal for fuel and enabled deeper coal mines to be pumped and brought into use, there were, however, inevitable limits to growth.

The working lives of miners and their feelings as communities reveal continuities both before and after the advent of the steam engine, particularly in the North-East. They were already a tightly knit group in Tudor times, as conscious of their bargaining power as they were of the risks of their occupation. Coal was their life.

Yet coal mining was not the only industry to flourish outside the towns. The woollen industry too was not as closely associated with towns as it had been in the Middle Ages and was to be again in later centuries: Worcester was quite exceptional in having almost half its identified craftsmen working the textile industry in the second half of the sixteenth century. Some old corporate towns, like Coventry, were shrinking in size and losing in economic importance, therefore, in relation to the countryside or to smaller unincorporated towns like Birmingham; and there were public complaints in York that weavers were moving across the moors to Halifax, where there was abundant water power. Sir John Clapham has suggested that water power was 'a solvent of guild power from the days of the first fulling mill', although there is little evidence that the craft guilds of York or those of Norwich, England's second city in population, were a brake on progress during the sixteenth century. Norwich, however, had an immigrant population of about one-third as early as the 1570s.

Some historians, seizing on observers' comments or complaints from the towns themselves and on expressions of concern on the part of central government, have discerned 'an acute urban crisis' during the period from 1520 to 1570 or even later. Others have spotlighted the oligarchic character of urban government which excluded the many and carried with it costly obligations for the few. Once again, however, they confront a complex and variegated pattern of problem and opportunity.

The decline of Winchester and Lincoln which had started in

earlier centuries was associated in part, at least, with the Reformation. Yet cities like York and Norwich, where there were the same sharp breaks, soon took on new functions and acquired new activities. York was the headquarters of the Council of the North, Norwich a centre of the new draperies. Each of them began to exert an increasingly strong pull on the local gentry and the aristocracy through the provision of leisure facilities, shops and even of town houses. And while Southampton was declining in size, Newcastle was emerging as a thriving port linked to the coal trade. Manchester was already described by John Leland, eager explorer of his own country, as 'the fairest best builded, quickest and most populous town of all Lancashire'. It remained under the control of a manor court, however, while smaller and far less commercially important places, like Grampound in Cornwall, became new parliamentary boroughs.

There was much new urban building, along with other improvements like paving, lighting and 'scavenging', in smaller towns as well as in regional capitals and county towns. Leland used the term 'suburbs' when he was describing urban expansion, and for one writer in 1579 these were no longer simply places for the poor 'outside the walls' but were for the rich who wanted fresh air and less noise. The centres of towns were still crowded places where different social groups lived in close proximity and where different social activities were carried out in juxtaposition, in churches and markets, houses and warehouses, shops and brothels. But there was a rural flavour too. Gardens were commonplace and pigs could still wander through the streets. The framework of control was, of course, being further extended – with a multiplicity of provisions. Thus, as a fire precaution, the use of thatch was banned in Norwich in 1509 and in Bristol in 1574, and in Leicester it was enacted that no person of whatever degree, except officers and the watch, should be abroad in the streets after nine o'clock at night.

One city in England was still growing and increasingly dwarfed all others. London, five times as populous as Norwich in Henry VIII's reign, was twelve to fourteen times as large by 1600. In the early 1520s its population was probably about 70,000, but by 1600 it had probably passed 200,000. The first panoramic view of it was drawn in 1588, and forty years later John Stow's magnificent *Survey* of the city penetrated behind the panorama to the people and forces responsible for its change. Stow himself was seventy years old when he wrote it, so he could remember how things had changed. Not surprisingly, London inspired and provoked contradictory reactions. Edmund Spenser penned the immortal line 'Sweet Thames! run softly till I end my song,' but his view contrasted sharply with a foreign ambassador's judgement that the city stank and was 'the filthiest in the world'.

The main complaint about London was that it was 'swallowing up all the other towns and cities', particularly the other ports. 'Soon,' James I was to remark, 'London will be all England.' The complaint was exaggerated, but the fear that the city would serve as a centre of crime, disorder and disease, all of which would spread, was real enough. At least one-third of London's immigrants were scraping a bare subsistence there. Yet proclamations of 1580 and 1602 banning further building within three miles of the gates of the City of London, prohibiting multiple occupation of existing properties and ordering lodgers who had arrived during the previous seven years to leave, could not hold in check the human flow.

Towards the end of the Tudor period there were signs of increasing, though still incomplete, national integration. Local economies were becoming more specialized and more complementary, although in general the richer South and East were drawn into the emerging unified pattern more than the poorer North and West. Increasingly, different parts of the island were being linked by the expanding coastal trade, although parts of the Midlands far from the sea, including, for example, Wigston Magna, were still tied essentially to subsistence rather than to exchange, and in the most flourishing section of the coastal trade, the coal trade between London and Newcastle, different measures were used at each end.

The surge of exploration and discovery, heralded by Henry VIII's development of the navy, which led Elizabethans like Frobisher, Drake and Davis to cross the oceans, began in England itself as a growing interest in its geography and history. This interest in the kingdom as a whole is apparent in every page of John Leland's *Itinerary*. 'I was totally inflamed,' Leland had told Henry VIII, 'with a love to see thoroughly all those parts of your opulent and ample realm that I had read of . . .' Half a century later, Christopher Saxton produced his first county maps and historians began to produce county histories.

Under Elizabeth, the Church once more became an agent of national integration: it was 'by law established', that is by the Second Act of Supremacy in 1559, that the unity of the Church and of the realm were deemed to be not complementary but identical. Elizabeth's birthday became a holy day of the Church in 1568, and the royal arms were displayed in every church. At Tivetshall in Norfolk, where they still survive, they were painted perhaps significantly on the reverse side of a medieval Doom picture. After 1559 attendance at church was compulsory by statute and non-attendance punishable by fine and imprisonment; outward conformity rather than opinion was the crucial factor. As Camden put it, 'there can be no separation between religion and the commonwealth,' and after a few years there were very few recusants or would-be separatists.

Language was also becoming more standardized, partly as a result of the development of poetry, though Cornish continued to be spoken and different words continued to be used in different parts of the country (sometimes even in the same county) for cattle, clothes and domestic objects. The power of language in Elizabethan prose owed much to its closeness to folk speech, 'to the English of ploughing, carting, selling and small town gossip', as one historian has put it. But that was only one of its debts. The boy who drove the plough might well have turned for his imagery to the Great Bible of 1539 or the Book of Common Prayer, and the merchant might have picked up words like chocolate, tobacco and potato from across the Atlantic. Shakespeare himself, who could coin unforgettable phrases, each of which was to have its own later history (like 'we have seen better days' or 'brave new world'), turned often to the law. Scholars were among the enthusiasts for the language: 'Why not all in English?' asked Richard Mulcaster, who became High Master of St Paul's. The English tongue was 'no whit behind either the subtle Greek for couching close or the stately Latin for spreading fair'.

Social integration was expressed in the new art of the theatre, which brought together different sections of the population. There were links between Elizabethan drama and medieval miracle and morality plays, but there was one great difference: Tudor drama was essentially secular. In 1545 the Master of the Revels became responsible for overseeing players and playhouses and soon found himself responsible – under the Lord Chamberlain – for the censorship of plays. In this way a lay officer took over a function hitherto exercised by the Church. By the end of the century, the most famous actors were being condemned by both their religious and their lay critics for dealing in 'profane fables'. It was in London in particular that a new theatre-going public emerged. In 1576 James Burbage built 'The Theater' in Finsbury Fields, and other theatres like the Swan and the Globe, most famous of all playhouses in Southwark, followed in its wake. Actors were acquiring social status and, in a few cases, fortune. Richard Burbage left a large sum at his death; Edward Alleyn, who retired before he was forty, bought a manor and founded a college at Dulwich.

The Elizabethan world often seemed to contemporaries less like a 'world picture', as scholars have seen it subsequently, and more like a performance on a stage. Most famous of all such images are Shakespeare's lines from *As You Like It*:

> This wide and universal theatre
> Presents more woeful pageants than the scene
> Wherein we play in.

But it was the poet Sir Walter Ralegh, explorer, historian and courtier, who carried it furthest:

> What is our life? A play of passion:
> Our mirth? the music of division.
> Our mothers' wombs the tiring-houses be
> Where we are dressed for life's short comedy.
> Heaven the judicious sharp spectator is,
> That sits and marks still who doth act amiss:
> Our graves that hide us from the searching sun
> Are like drawn curtains when the play is done.

While it is important for the social historian to recognize the value of a poet's reactions to his society as historical evidence, they need especially close critical scrutiny. They may encompass uncommon views of common experience and common views uncommonly, even dazzlingly, expressed. It is a mistake, therefore, to use labels like 'the age of Shakespeare'. Shakespeare belonged to more than one world. He was a man of his time, but he was not limited by it, and his plays, which draw deeply from a quarry of historical as well as of current material, have meant new things for new generations.

In his own generation, however, he could appeal to the same English pride that Elizabeth stirred. No other sovereign since 1066 had so little foreign blood, and she was so much at the centre of the stage, claiming her subjects' love as well as their obedience, that if any label is to be attached to the age it must be that of 'the age of Elizabeth'. She left no heir. When Henry VII, her grandfather, had crossed into England from Wales with a small army, carrying Cadwaladr's red dragon on his banner to defeat Richard III and to found the Tudor dynasty, he had come as an illegal claimant, but when James VI of Scotland marched south from Scotland, it was at the invitation of the English Parliament. Ironically, however, the Stuart kings were never to achieve the popularity of their Tudor predecessors.

6

REVOLUTION,
RESTORATION AND SETTLEMENT

———————

We found that we that till that hour lived in great plenty and great
order found ourselves alike fishes out of the water, and the same so
changed, that we knew not at all how to act any part but obedience.

Anne, Lady Fanshawe, *Memoirs*, 1600–1672

What will not all oppressed, rich and religious people do to be
delivered from all kinds of oppression, both spiritual and temporal, and to be restored to purity and freedom in religion, and to the
just liberty of their persons and estates?

Richard Overton, *A Remonstrance of Many Thousand Citizens*, 1646

I cannot forbear carrying my watch in my hand in the coach this
afternoon, and seeing what o'clock it is one hundred times and am
apt to think with myself, how could I be so long without one.

Samuel Pepys, *Diary*, 13 May 1665

'I think it fit to begin with the poorer sort from whom all other
sorts estates do take their beginning, wrote Robert Reyce in
an account of Suffolk in 1618. 'As well the poor as the rich
proceed from the Lord . . . The rich cannot stand without the
poor . . . and the humblest thoughts which smoke from a poor
man's cottage are as sweet a sacrifice unto the Lord as the costly
perfumes of the prince's palace.'

Both his content and language belong unmistakably to the
seventeenth century. The poor were often to be heard, asserting
claims of their own, not always humble in tone, during the late

1640s and 1650s, and religion, usually more militant than con-
soling, was to colour most of the social comment and almost all
of the social protest then and earlier. The magnificent Authorized
Version of the English Bible of 1611 preceded by thirty years the
most unauthorized uses made of it, and it was to survive them all.
Yet the century was not all of one piece. Long before it ended, the
demands of the poor were not heard so loudly. Indeed, they were
often not heard at all. Nor was radical religion any longer a major
driving force 'turning the world upside down'. Taking the seventeenth century as a whole, economic progress rather than the
force of religion was the major determinant of social change. A
modern historian has concluded that 'for all save the "Poor" – and
their numbers remained very large – life was a little more varied, a
little less primitive' in 1700 than in 1600. The generalization was
true; the qualification was necessary. The cottage was still the
great exception.

It would be misleading, however, to try to write the social
history of the seventeenth century entirely in terms of social
structures and social processes, for, above all else, this was a
century of dramatic and unprecedented events: a civil war which
drew in broad sections of the population; the execution of Charles
I (1625–49) and the rule of and offer of the kingship to Oliver
Cromwell, born a farmer; the return of Charles I's heir from
foreign exile in 1660. Even then there were still unprecedented
events in the offing. Edward Hyde, first Earl of Clarendon, told a
new Parliament at the beginning of Charles II's reign (1660–85)
that he hoped it would join in restoring 'the whole nation to its
primitive temper and integrity, to its good old manners, its good
old humour and its good old nature', but twenty-eight years later
there was a second revolution. After Charles II's brother James II
(1685–8) had tried to rule the country not through Anglican
squires and parsons but through Roman Catholics and dissenters,
a new king, William III (1688–1702), was brought in from
Holland, a Protestant country against which England had fought
three wars earlier in the century.

For contemporaries this 'Glorious Revolution' did not require
the kind of explanation Clarendon had offered for the Civil War –
that it was influenced by so many 'miraculous circumstances' that

'men might well think that heaven and earth and the stars designed it'. To most men in the know, and to many who were not, the revolution of 1688 was a victory of pragmatism and human reason responding to a clearly perceived threat to 'the Protestant religion and the laws and liberties of this kingdom', and its effect was to settle issues of contention that had profoundly disturbed earlier generations. A 'balance' was established which was to be maintained for years to come. During the nineteenth century, the historian Macaulay, presenting a Whig interpretation of history, was to speak of it as making Englishmen 'different from others': 'because we had a preserving revolution in the seventeenth century . . . we have not had a destroying revolution in the nineteenth.' For some twentieth-century historians of the seventeenth century, however, it marked the end of 'the heroic age' of English politics.

Not surprisingly, the events of the seventeenth century, more dramatic than anything on the Tudor stage, left vivid memories. They could also leave people breathless, even exhausted. Thus, Sir John Reresby, member of the established landed gentry, could write in the 1690s that he had seen so many changes 'and so many great and little men removed in my time, that I confess it began to cool my ambition, and I began to think there was a time when every thinking man would choose to retire and to be content with his own rather than venture that and his conscience for the getting of more'. He concluded with the conviction 'that safety was better [than] greatness'.

All the great events had provoked argument, sometimes fundamental argument; or rather, perhaps, the events themselves were the outcomes of argument, not all of it resolved or even exhausted, much of it conducted from the pulpit or through the medium of the printed word. This was a reflection of the greatly increased literacy of the period. 'When there is much desire to learn,' wrote John Milton, the great Puritan poet, a pioneer of free speech, 'there will of necessity be much arguing, much writing, many opinions; for opinion in good men is but knowledge in the making.' There was vigorous censorship of the printed word during the 1630s, but it could never control completely either pulpit or tavern, and when censorship came to an end in 1641 the great age of the pamphlet followed. Twenty-two pamphlets were published in 1640, 1,996 in 1642. This application of the printing press to the requirements of social and political struggle enlivened both religion and politics. It also provided massive material for historians.

The argument ranged widely over taxation, the law and the liberties of the subject, religion, land and trade, authority and property. Many of the economic arguments early in the century originated in the financial difficulties of the Crown, which was placed in an increasingly awkward position by the rising costs of government. Nor were matters made any easier by the fact that the price rise of the sixteenth century was slow to come to an end. Indeed, when prices flattened out in the 1620s, this was a sign not of stability or of improvement but of economic strain. The highest recorded exports of cloth were in 1614, but eight years later the figure had been cut to a half. These were years of an adverse balance of trade, frequent bad harvests, and distress, particularly in the woollen industry. Jacobean houses and furniture might impress their own and future generations by their weight and permanence, but the economy was volatile even when it was not under pressure. There were 'seven fat years' from 1629–35, but many hard times thereafter. The years 1642, when the Civil War began, and 1649, when the king was executed, were particularly bad years, for example, as was 1659, the year before Charles II returned to the throne.

Economic historians have noted 'a real and prolonged crisis arising from a radical readjustment of England's foreign trade,' but contemporaries blamed the plague and the bad harvests, which for obvious economic reasons reduced home demand and led to a withdrawal of gold specie to pay for grain imports. 'Scarcity of money' was another regular complaint. There were personal villains too, perhaps most notably Alderman William Cockayne and his partners, who, having promised much in an attempt to win over the cloth finishing trade from the Dutch, failed disastrously. The land of Cockayne, which had long meant a land of make-believe, acquired a new contemporary relevance.

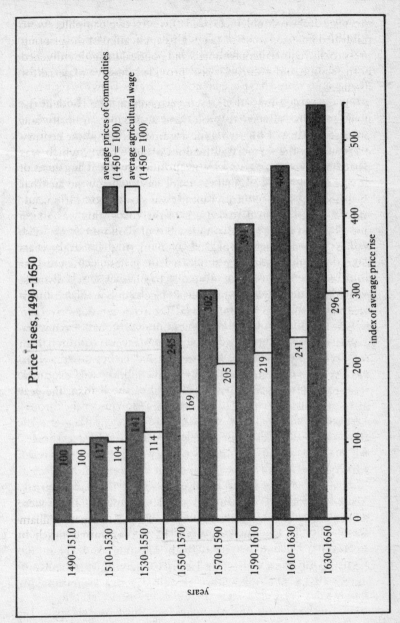

Price rises, 1490-1650

average prices of commodities (1450 = 100)

average agricultural wage (1450 = 100)

years	
1490-1510	100 / 100
1510-1530	117 / 104
1530-1550	141 / 114
1550-1570	245 / 169
1570-1590	302 / 205
1590-1610	391 / 219
1610-1630	404 / 241
1630-1650	/ 296

index of average price rise

James I was aware from the time of his succession to the English throne of what he called 'the canker of want'. Yet in 1610, when the debt which he inherited from Elizabeth had increased threefold, he could not secure a 'Great Contract' by which feudal dues would have been renounced by the crown in return for proper fiscal compensation on a regular annual basis. Both he and Charles I thereafter attempted to raise revenue by 'shifts and devices' such as ship money, which were bound to provoke opposition, and by delegating the raising of revenue to tax-farmers, who appropriated a large proportion of it. The other side of the picture was, of course, that Parliament refused to think realistically in accounting terms. Fiscal issues were turned into constitutional issues, therefore, very early in the story. 'All our liberties were now at one dash utterly ruined,' wrote Sir Simonds D'Ewes in his *Autobiography*, 'if the King might at his pleasure lay what unlimited taxes he pleased on his subjects, and then imprison them when they refused to pay. What should freemen differ from the ancient bondsmen and villeins of England if their estates be subject of arbitrary taxes?'

Much, although not all, of the argument between King and Commons was conducted in the language of common law, especially since matters of precedent and rights raised in that argument were referred to the law courts. Sir Edward Coke, who had been appointed Lord Chief Justice of the King's Bench in 1613, obstinately refused to behave like a 'lion under the throne'. Concerned above all else with the due process of law and the liberties of the Commons, he looked back for inspiration to Magna Carta. In 1616, at the age of sixty-four, he was dismissed. Five years later he became a Member of Parliament.

The accession of James I had been seen by both Puritan and Catholic dissidents as an opportunity to try and win the concessions they had long wanted under Elizabeth, and the outlines and language of the religious argument that was to persist throughout the century began to emerge in the first decade. At the Hampton Court Conference of January 1604, King and Puritans failed to agree, after wrangling with each other, and a year later Guy Fawkes was executed after the discovery of a Catholic plot to blow up the Houses of Parliament. The Puritans, who were the bigger and more dangerous group, well represented in Parliament itself, demanded that 'God, that choose this corner of the earth to plant his truth in' be besought to preserve it. As the century went by, the variety of extant Protestant versions of the truth, most of them claiming the authority of the Bible and the number of Protestant sects, not all of them with a long-term future, increased sensationally. They included Independents, Presbyterians, Baptists and Quakers and radical Millenarians and other groups with still more exotic names, like Ranters, Seekers and Muggletonians, who have long since passed into oblivion. The 'womb of teeming birth', as the poet John Milton called it, could not be sealed. The sense of truth versus error remained dominant on both sides. For Milton, as for many of those participating in the Civil War on the Parliamentary side, this was essentially a war of good against evil, not of one set of interests or even of opinions against another. 'God may leave a nation that is but in outward covenant with him, and why not England?' the preacher Thomas Hooker had warned his congregation in a farewell sermon of 1641. 'The Word and the Sword must be joined,' a Puritan preacher thundered in 1645. There were equally strong views on the other side, too. Charles I could be treated as a saint.

Historians have at different periods concentrated on the constitutional debates in Parliament and on the religious ferment in the country in their attempts to analyse the causes of the Civil War, but they have also raised questions of social and economic interest and traced continuities before and after 1660. It was members of the nobility and gentry who drew England into the Civil War and while many would have preferred to stay out of it, it was they who profited from it. Indeed, Parliament's confirmation after the Civil War of the abolition of institutions like the Court of Wards, 'that great bridle of feudality' which had been abolished by the Long Parliament before the Civil War, has been described as 'probably the most important single event in the history of English landowning'. Landowners were now free not only from the burdens of feudal service but from monetary substitutes for it; and by the end of the century, when all barriers to hereditary title had disappeared, the claims of private property, and of large estates in particular, were more firmly established than they had been at the beginning of it. By then, there were also new theories to justify the claims of property and new legal defences to protect them. In fact, they needed no protection. As Bernard Mandeville put it succinctly in the early eighteenth century, 'Dominion follows property.'

The earliest explanation of the eventual line-up in the Civil War as a conflict of social and economic interests was that of a contemporary, James Harrington, in his book *Oceana* (1656), which claimed that war had broken out because of shifts in the ownership of land from the Crown and Lords to the Commons, resulting in a transfer of power. In the nineteenth century he was followed by Karl Marx. Under the Tudors, in Harrington's words, 'the nobility being abated, the balance fell into the power of the people'; according to Marx, the English struggle was that of bourgeois against feudal England. 'Power follows property.'

Harrington included the gentry in his 'nobility', but historians of the 1940s and 1950s often sharply distinguished between the two, referring to 'the crisis of the aristocracy' and 'the rise of the gentry'. They examined closely and compared in detail the fortunes and attitudes of both 'nobility' and 'gentry' between the death of Queen Elizabeth and the outbreak of the Civil War. After fierce historical debate (as fierce at times as the seventeenth-century debates in Parliament) it is plain that there were no significant economic differences between landowners who initiated the Civil War and that some of the issues, at least, in the historical debate seem to have been ill-chosen. In particular, neither the view that the Civil War was caused by the rise of the gentry nor the diametrically opposed view that it was caused by the economic decline of a part of the gentry, now seems tenable. It is difficult to classify Roundheads and Cavaliers in terms of rising or declining gentry or of 'feudal' and 'bourgeois' landholders. In each case the methodology employed to advance the case, particularly the counting of manors, has been criticized as much as the conclusions.

Argument still continues, however, about Marx's concept of a 'bourgeois revolution' led by 'progressive' elements in society, and, in particular, about the extent to which merchant interests supported Parliament against the King. There were certainly links through London and the ports, and through the printing press, with the politically conscious bourgeoisie of Geneva, Strasbourg and Amsterdam, but English merchants do not seem to have had the same group political awareness and there were always divisions within their ranks. Furthermore, those who did have a voice in Parliament were a minority there, sitting alongside the gentry from the shires. The merchant classes may have been particularly inclined towards the adoption of Puritan values, to 'inveighing against idleness', for instance, and to believing in their occupations as a divine 'calling', and some, at least, of them had long shown that they had little patience with hierarchy in Church or in State. But there were divisions within the mercantile community which persisted after the Civil War broke out. While it is true that the economically 'advanced' South and East of the country supported Parliament more firmly than the economically 'backward' North and West, within each of these regions there were forces on the other side. Thus, there were Roundhead enclaves in the royalist textiles district of West Yorkshire and there was a Cavalier uprising in King's Lynn, Norfolk, in Parliamentary territory.

It was unquestionably of crucial importance to the success of the Parliamentary cause, however, that rich London was behind it from the start and remained so. Some London merchants had earlier had strong links with the Crown, but if we leave on one side the twelve 'monopolist' Members of Parliament who were expelled in 1641, eighteen of the nineteen remaining London MPs supported Parliament in 1642.

Other historians have taken a different angle of approach, recognizing that while social and economic groups defend their interests, a greater emphasis must be placed on cultural identity and the desire for political influence. They have seen tension between Court and Country as a widening and eventually unbridgeable divide that eventually led to civil war. That tension had certainly existed from the beginning of the reign of James I. The Puritan Lucy Hutchinson described James's court as 'a nursery of lust and intemperance' and Sir Walter Ralegh, who was in a position to know, condemned it just as strongly.

> Say to the Court it glows
> And shines like rotten wood

'Alien' influences there were attacked too; and there were certainly stronger continental links in politics and in style in James I's and Charles I's courts than in that of Elizabeth. The great Whitehall Banqueting House and the Queen's House at Greenwich, the work of Inigo Jones, were directly inspired by the classicism of Palladio. So too was Covent Garden, London's first square.

The Court then and later was sustained by an intricate network of courtiers, ministers and officials – with no distinction between civil servants and politicians – and although for financial reasons it should have saved money, as Elizabeth had tried to do, it often spent it conspicuously, both at home and abroad. James I's favourite, the Duke of Buckingham, was a collector as well as a key figure in foreign policy, and Charles himself was a great patron of foreign art. The Country too had its own tangle of families and connections at the county level and its own chains of influence and dependence – and some members of the aristocracy and gentry were themselves influenced by foreign styles – but it did not usually have the same messy entanglements with finance and business. Lionel Cranfield, for example, one of James's most able ministers, who struggled hard to curtail waste, had accumulated a private fortune as a trader and speculator before becoming a state servant and continued his business activities throughout his career until it ended in impeachment, imprisonment, release and retirement.

The Court offered all the opportunities of Place, the Country all the satisfaction of Independence. Not all Place was highly lucrative, but all Place carried with it status, much of which was secured, in Francis Bacon's telling phrase – and he knew from experience – by 'a winding stair'. Not all Independence was shabby, for there was a rise in landed income both from direct farming and from rents in the early seventeenth century. Most country gentlemen fared well, but they did not have to be in straitened circumstances to dislike bitterly the way in which property could follow Place.

During Charles I's reign there were increasing signs of the cultural gap between Court and Country. The arts of the Court were for the few – and all were expensive. Science, a subject of practical as well as of speculative interest among the gentry and in the towns, was kept out. Satire was too, in preference for the formal masque, with all its 'ingenious speeches', 'melodious music' and 'delicate devices', much to Ben Jonson's distaste (though he wrote masques himself, designed by Inigo Jones).

> Painting and carpentry are the soul of masque!
> Pack with your piddling poetry to the stage!
> This is the money-get mechanic age!

It is difficult to claim, nonetheless, that the civil conflict which eventually took place can be explained simply in terms of Court versus Country, 'ins' versus 'outs'. Motives were complex and they were certainly not always dominated by a sense of envy or distaste, or a feeling of exclusion. There were shifts of opinion too, so that political forces were aligned in different ways in the years 1625 and 1640 and in the years 1640 and 1642. What happened between mattered crucially.

Historical interpretations that concentrate exclusively on the great debates and on the economic and social divisions of the early seventeenth century tend to take the inevitability of war for granted. In fact, a step-by-step analysis of what happened is just as necessary for the social historian elucidating shifts in social relationships as it is for the political historian tracing sequences of events. It is crucial to identify and distinguish between the various stages in the sequence of developments before the Civil War, recognizing that in each of them the participants were concerned with quite different immediate issues.

One stage was of crucial importance in relation both to social alignments and the unfolding of events. Following the framing by the Commons of a Petition of Right in 1628, cataloguing grievances and demanding an end to unparliamentary taxation, martial law and unregulated powers of imprisonment, which Charles was forced to accept because of financial difficulties, he insisted in 1629 that he would grant no new liberties but only confirm ancient ones. The House of Commons went on forcibly to assert its claims by pinning the Speaker to his chair when he refused to adjourn. 'So,' the historian Keith Feiling has written, 'broke down the medieval constitution.' As a result, between 1629 and 1640 Charles I ruled for eleven years without Parliament. His two chief agents were Archbishop Laud, born in 1573 and promoted to the see of Canterbury in 1633, and Thomas Wentworth, whom he created Earl of Strafford in 1640. Laud's coherent views both on Church doctrine and Church (and university) order were diametrically opposed to those of the Puritans long before he was appointed, but Wentworth, who had sat in every parliament since 1621, had hitherto been a critic of the king acting without Parliament's assent.

Now the two men had to fall back on the king's authority, enforcing policies which were often unpopular by methods which were often arbitrary. Laud's call to establish Church discipline in the name of 'the beauty of holiness' provoked a display of revenge on the part of Puritans, who objected to railing off a communion table to make an altar and to bowing to it, while his and Wentworth's paternalistic economic and social policies alienated both men of enterprise in the City of London and country gentlemen and yeomen who objected to paying more tithes. Above all, tough censorship and the muzzling of critics repressed opposition without suppressing it. The lawyer and pamphleteer William Prynne, a critic both of bishops and of stage plays, lost his ears in 1634 and was put in the pillory for his book on stage plays, seen by Laud to reflect badly on the Queen; John Hampden, a wealthy gentleman, became a national hero through his opposition to paying ship money in 1636. And since the king lacked the apparatus of bureaucratic support which the kings of France and Spain had at their disposal, he was forced to find his civil servants among the bishops, disparagingly satirized by their contemporaries as 'stall-fed doctors' and 'crown'd divines'. In consequence, they became even more unpopular than they had been in James I's reign. It was at this stage that the regime became offensive to many persons of 'honour and quality', as Clarendon was to describe them.

There was a consequent loss of moral authority at a time when there were many other signs, local as well as national, of cultural fragmentation and of the erosion of middle ground that men of moderation and goodwill had once occupied, as one historian has put it. Because there were determined people at each extreme who were wary of compromises the two cultures eventually became two warring camps. Strafford could speak contemptuously of 'your Prynnes, Pyms and Bens [sic] with the rest of that generation of odd names and natures', while Lucy Hutchinson on the opposite side could refer to 'needy courtiers', 'proud encroaching priests', 'thieving projectors' and 'lewd nobility'.

Even by 1640 the die was not cast. In that year Charles sacrificed Laud and Strafford after being forced to summon the so-called Short Parliament, which lasted for three weeks before being controversially dissolved, and a second Parliament, subsequently to be known as the Long Parliament, which was called on the advice of a Council of Peers and which was not to disappear formally until 1660. But the effect of the execution of Strafford in 1641 and of the impeachment of Laud (who was himself to be executed five years later) was the opposite of that intended, as Cardinal Mazarin noted across the Channel. Parliament went on to take control of taxation and to abolish the prerogative courts. Although some of Strafford's sharpest critics dissociated themselves from a now divided Parliament, it went on to pass a Root and Branch Bill to abolish the episcopacy and to publish and distribute a Grand Remonstrance late in 1641. The Remonstrance was passed by only eleven votes, and one of those who opposed it exclaimed:

> When I first heard of a Remonstrance, I thought to represent unto the King the wicked counsels of pernicious Councillors, the treachery of false judges. I did not dream that we should remonstrate downwards, tell stories to the people and talk of the King as a third person, I neither look for the cure of our complaints from the common people nor desire to be eased by them.

It did not need 'remonstration downward' to mobilize the discontented forces in the country. When, following the Grand Remonstrance, the King failed in his attempt to arrest five Members of Parliament (among them Hampden and Pym) and moved out of London, there were many people psychologically and morally prepared for the fray, if still reluctant to start it. And there were enough divisions, not only between different parts of the country but even within families in the same areas, to ensure that if and when war came it would not be won easily.

The battles of the Civil War, fought as three military campaigns, took place not in London but in the counties. The King's standard was first raised at Nottingham in 1642 and, when he could not get to London, Oxford became his temporary capital, with seventy peers and 170 Members of Parliament close at hand. Oxford fell in 1646, by which time Charles had already surrendered and had passed into the hands of the victorious New Model Army, 22,000 strong after 1645, which went on to take possession of London and install its commander Sir Thomas Fairfax as Governor of the Tower. His second-in-command was Oliver Cromwell, the great military leader who was to become Lord Protector after the execution of Charles in 1649. England became a republic, the House of Lords was abolished and religious toleration proclaimed.

All in all, in four years of struggle around 100,000 Englishmen had been killed. Their ghosts have continued to haunt even the twentieth century: T. S. Eliot, for example, turned back to them when he pondered on the meaning of time and history.

> If I think of a king at nightfall,
> Of three men, and more, on the scaffold . . .
> And of one who died blind and quiet,
> Why should we celebrate
> These dead men more than the dying?

Yet most Englishmen had not taken part in the military campaigns and, as they continued, there had been signs of war weariness. There were many signs of ignorance too. At Marston Moor, where parliamentary forces won an important victory in July 1644, it is said that a husbandman, warned off the field because battle was about to begin, asked, 'What! Has them two fallen out then?'

Nevertheless, feelings ran high, and extraordinarily radical and violent opinions were expressed both during and after the Civil War. 'I hope,' said one Northamptonshire rebel, for example, 'within this year to see never a gentleman in England.' But the true colour of the <u>unique political and religious radicalism</u> of the <u>1640s</u> is best revealed by the series of debates at Putney in 1647, at which a congregation of soldiers from the New Model Army, fresh from the experience of civil war and free from local attachments and social restraints, hammered out sharply contrasting propositions about religion, government and property. 'God hath appeared with us and led us and taken delight in the work by us,' the soldiers believed, but that did not stop them from differing radically with each other not only about the social significance of the war which they had just fought but even about the social and political significance of the Norman Conquest.

Some of the views expressed came from the lips of men without social and political power. 'It seems now,' one speaker complained, for example, that, 'except a man hath a fixed estate in this kingdom he hath no right in this kingdom. I wonder we were so much deceived. If we had not a right in this kingdom we were mere mercenary soldiers.' A second speaker, Henry Ireton (Cromwell's son-in-law), replied to him equally frankly, putting forward a different point of view. 'No person has a right to an interest or share in determining or choosing those that shall determine what laws we shall be ruled by here . . . that hath not a permanent fixed interest in the kingdom.'

The more extreme republicans in the New Model Army, the 'Levellers' as they were called, were in agreement with the first speaker. They had their manifesto, the Agreement of the People, and they rallied together to defend the rights of 'hobnails, clouted shoes and woollen aprons', to press for manhood suffrage, which might have made Parliament a very different (possibly at that time a more conservative) place, and to demand the abolition of tithes, which would have broken the power of any established Church. 'If we take not advantage of this time,' they urged, 'we shall never have the opportunity again.'

The Diggers, a far smaller and still more radical group, opposed the private ownership of property altogether and struggled to 'set the land free'. And they did not stop at words. They squatted on manorial common lands and felled feudal trees. Charles I, they maintained, had been the legatee of William the

The Civil War, 1643-5

Conqueror. 'If the common people have no more freedom in England but to live among their elder brothers and work for hire,' asked Gerrard Winstanley, one of their chief spokesmen, 'what freedom can they have in England more than they can have in Turkey or France?' 'The poorest man,' the Diggers insisted, 'hath as true a title and just right to the land as the richest man.'

The language of radicalism which burst out between 1640 and 1645 alarmed conservatives of all kinds. Decades before the Civil War, fear had been expressed by influential, if not 'average', men that 'the loose and needy multitude' might all too easily be transformed into a 'senseless and furious beast . . . with many heads'; and at least one critic of the king changed sides before the Civil War because he believed that 'the necessitous people of the whole kingdom' would 'presently rise in mighty numbers' and 'within a while' would 'set up for themselves to the ruin of all the Nobility and Gentry in the Kingdom'. Indeed, the radicalism tapped veins of conservatism in people who were not conservative by the standards of the early century and who often held radical religious convictions. 'If the unruly rout have once cast the rider,' it was claimed, 'it will run like wildfire through all the counties of England.' Oliver Cromwell himself, a 'Root and Branch man' in religion, was a reluctant republican, anxious to preserve 'the ranks and orders of men whereby England hath been known for hundreds of years: a nobleman, a gentleman, a yeoman'. And in this, as in so many things, he may simply have been showing his 'resemblance to the average man'. S. R. Gardiner called him the most typical Englishman of all time.

However, it was not 'the beast with many heads' but the 'Nobility and Gentry' who eventually profited from the Civil War and the Interregnum between 1649 and 1660. The Diggers failed in all their ventures and the Levellers were suppressed in 1649 after they rebelled against Cromwell and the other army leaders. Nor did radical religious groups like the Ranters create a new Sion. There were some notable innovations: religious toleration was extended to a large number of the less radical Puritan sects, enormous areas of confiscated ecclesiastical and royalist lands changed hands, Cromwell welcomed Jews back into the country (although they did not receive citizens' rights), and there were legal reforms. But Cromwell, who remained in power as 'the father in this family', 'the constable in this parish', until his death in 1658, was essentially conservative and Parliament continued to have a chequered history, purged, nominated, dissolved, reformed. And there was certainly no appreciable change in the condition of the have-nots.

From 1655, England was divided not only into its traditional parishes, but into districts, each with a soldier Major-General exercising authority in the name of 'godliness and virtue'. In the country and the town alike, successive regimes enforced the Sabbath Day protection and anti-gambling rules (introduced under the Tudors), closed alehouses and, for several years, theatres, banned race-meetings as well as cock fights and duels, exercised censorship, severely punished those people found guilty of immorality (or swearing), and suppressed 'rowdy' or 'superstitious' practices like dancing round the Maypole or celebrating Christmas. 'Who would have thought to have seen in England the churches shut and the shops open on Christmas Day?' we read in a letter of 1646. But the Puritan excesses of the Major-Generals and their unpopularity can be exaggerated: they certainly were at the time of the Restoration. Cromwell himself, who was born at Huntingdon not far from the Fens, loved horses and hawking, and although he served 'plain fare' at his table, he and his household consumed substantial quantities of wine – and listened to music (except in church).

It proved difficult to suppress custom and to turn England into 'a land of saints and a pattern of holiness to the world', as the Puritan Richard Baxter had hoped. Alehouses might be described, not for the first time, as 'nests of Satan', but in the attempt to suppress them the gap between 'local notables' and 'common people' widened, as it often did when the same notables tried to get the 'common people' into church to listen to sermons which they might not understand. 'Not one in twenty . . . go to any place of worship on the Lord's Day, but sit in their own houses,' complained one minister to his Major-General. In some places, indeed, the attempt was abandoned, and the services, which followed no uniform pattern, became exclusive to small groups of believers.

Many of the changes of the Interregnum were short-lived. The ecclesiastical and royalist lands confiscated by Parliament during and after the Civil War were for the most part regained by their owners – some before, but most after the Restoration. There were, therefore, no profound long-term shifts in the pattern of land ownership as there had been and were to be in other revolutions. By the end of the century, however, the great estates were getting bigger and systematic attempts were being made to exploit them through their tenants. According to the pioneer statistician, Gregory King, landlords' rents and farmers' profits then accounted for about half the country's income, a figure close to recent twentieth-century estimates of 43 per cent. He estimated the cultivated land, including woods, orchards and gardens, at twenty-five millions acres, which, he calculated, maintained twelve million sheep, 4·5 million cattle and two million pigs, worth together about £15,000,000, and base crops worth about £9,000,000. Interest in agricultural improvement, with some of the methods taken from Holland, was expressed in a wide range of books on profitable husbandry. The game could not be counted, but shooting meant that more of them could be quickly destroyed. The 'landed interest' was secure and well-established, though gentry and owner occupiers suffered from generally low levels of prices.

At the peak of the social pyramid were 160 peers. Their numbers had been increased by James I in inflationary fashion from fifty-five to 126, and were now not to increase for a century. Below them there were another eighty to a hundred non-noble families owning 10,000 acres or more. The greatest landed families could benefit directly from marriages outside their privileged rural circle. Thus, in 1695 the fortunes of the Russells, Dukes of Bedford, were powerfully reinforced when the young Marquis of Tavistock married Elizabeth Howland, the daughter of a wealthy London merchant.

The gentry were now beginning to be thought of as a 'squire-archy'. They owned about half the land in the country, and when they served as justices of the peace they exercised an even greater degree of local power between 1660 and 1685 than they had done before 1640. The justices were also in charge of the local militia, the only substantial armed force in the country.

Gregory King demonstrated also that in 1688, while the power of property was being consolidated after the Revolution, about half the families in England were not earning 'a subsistence'. And long before then, the poor law and the poor rate had become accepted facts of life at all times, not just in emergencies. An Act of Settlement, passed in 1662, empowered any justices of the peace, upon complaint to the Overseers of the Poor, to eject any newcomer to a parish who had no means of his own to return to the parish where he was last settled, a measure intended to deal with the whole population of the poor as only rogues and vagrants had been dealt with previously.

That old contrasts of circumstance were not weakening is revealed by the fact that the poor, who had suffered appallingly in the dearth of 1659, suffered even more during the last years of the century when bread prices doubled between 1693 and 1699. (Thomas Muffett had written in 1655 that 'Bread and Cheese be the two targets against Death.') These were exceptional years in a period of agricultural improvement when corn yields were increasing and marginal lands brought into cultivation. In general, there had been a downward trend in grain prices, and export subsidies were introduced by the government in 1673 and renewed in 1689 after a lapse. Yet while the fall in prices had helped the poor, both they and some of the people who were not so poor suffered as a result of the tightening up of the game laws; the so-called Cavalier Parliament of 1671 prevented all freeholders of less than £100 income a year (the great majority of them) from killing game even on their own property. The use of the shotgun, which was to supersede hawking, was to be restricted to their 'betters'. It was only a limited consolation to be told that lack of food might be compensated for by a 'variety of divertissements, sports and recreation' as Edward Chamberlayne wrote in 1687.

Those 'divertissements' which were encouraged had another purpose. A series of notes prepared by the Duke of Newcastle, a survivor from the reign of Charles I, suggested that the revival of 'May games, Morris dances, the Lord of the May and the Lady of the May, the fool and the Hoby Horse, Whitsun Lord and Lady, threshing . . . at Shrove Tide, carols and wassails at Christmas, with good plum porridge and pies', which had been 'forbidden as profane' would 'amuse the people's thoughts and keep them in harmless actions which will free your Majesty from faction and rebellion'. It was welcome advice. A recent historian of the period between the 1660s and 1685 has noted that the politicians of the period, like revellers in a carnival, were assumed to be wearing masks to conceal their features: 'sham' was a favourite new word of the period, another was 'plot'. It was applied in 1678, for example, to the Popish Plot, when Titus Oates alleged that Jesuits were planning to murder Charles II and install his brother James, and in 1683 to the Rye House Plot, another alleged conspiracy to assassinate the king. The word 'cabal' also originated in this period; it was an acronym for the group of ministers in power from 1667–73, derived from the initial letters of their five surnames.

Given that one of the main fears throughout the period was Popery (it roused even Milton from his retirement), there was an element of sham at the very centre of society since we now know that Charles II, the Defender of the Faith, was a secret Roman Catholic. His brother James II was an open Roman Catholic, who, after getting into difficulty with his first Parliament, did not summon a second; and looking for effective political alliances, he replaced nearly half the justices of the peace by his own nominees, a more drastic change of office holders than any attempted earlier in the century. If he had succeeded in establishing royal absolutism, supported by a strong army – while relying in the process on people outside the Church of England, Puritans as well as Roman Catholics – then independent country gentlemen would have been at the mercy of salaried officials and England would have become more like some other European monarchies. But there was no chance of this: the Anglican gentry was too strong. They went on to forge an alliance with the landed aristocracy and reject James. The Church of England itself was also too strong; it had lost the power of its ecclesiastical courts, but it had the substantial backing of property. It was to survive both fundamental social changes and the erosion of the view that Protestantism was an essential part of the constitution and that Church and State were one.

The fact that it proved impossible for the post-Restoration Church of England to retain within it the comprehensiveness of religious outlook that it had maintained with difficulty until the Civil War implied that thereafter in English social history there would be a divide – and a contrast – between Anglicans and dissenters, or Nonconformists, the latter made up of the various Protestant sects, a divide which was to seem as important at times as that between rich and poor. The third Act of Uniformity of 1662, which laid down that all priests who did not conform to the Prayer Book liturgy by St Bartholomew's Day would be deprived of their livings, ensured the secession of nearly 1,000 'Bartholomewmen', but the dissenters were strong enough to withstand persecution and other measures, like the suppression of unauthorized religious meetings in conventicles and restrictions on their freedom to operate in incorporated towns.

Nonetheless, 'fanatical opinions' were out of fashion after 1660. The new dissenters, who, like Catholics, were excluded from public office in 1673, turned increasingly to trade and industry. Dissenters were not 'excluded from the nobility', wrote John Corbett in 1667 and 'among the gentry they are not a few. But none are of more importance than they in the trading post of the people, and those that live by industry, upon whose hands the business of the nation lies much.' They were 'patient men', wrote Sir William Petty, 'and such as believe that labour and industry is their duty to God'.

The most democratic dissenters were the Quakers, who addressed people, whatever their rank, as 'thou' and refused to doff their hats. They were to create a small but effective national network of organization; they were also to repudiate violence and, in time, to become renowned for their philanthropy. The Independents, to whom Cromwell had belonged, were locally based, with each congregation choosing its minister; they were to become Congregationalists. The Baptists were to split into 'closed' and 'open' congregations. The Presbyterians, who were strongly represented in the Long Parliament and had their own Calvinistic system of church order, were never to have the influence they exercised in Scotland, although they continued to dream of a comprehensive Church of England until 1689. Some of them were to reject the doctrine of the Trinity and to become Unitarians, thereby gaining influence of a different, predominantly secular, kind in the eighteenth century, largely in urban society.

The Toleration Act of 1689 was to allow all Nonconformists except Unitarians freedom of worship; and although they were not to secure their full religious and civil freedom until the nineteenth century (they were still to be excluded from public life unless they were prepared to communicate once a year in their parish church), in most places they avoided the play of increasingly strong prejudices and the penal laws which continued to handicap Roman Catholics. The dissenters became one among a broad spectrum of interests in society, albeit a divided interest with Quakers at one end of the spectrum and Presbyterians at the other.

There was a place in that spectrum – before and after 1689 – for the sciences and the arts. Indeed, before 1660 it could be claimed that the sciences, in particular, had benefited during the Interregnum both because there were Puritans who had long been drawn to science and, more generally, because men's minds had become more 'active, industrious and inquisitive'. As for the arts, the portrait painter and connoisseur Peter Lely, who had painted Charles I and was to flourish after the Restoration, was told by the Protector not to leave out the 'roughnesses, pimples, warts and everything' in the picture which he painted of him and had been able to secure many commissions during the Interregnum. Literature too had scarcely suffered. Nor did it necessarily focus on religious themes. Thus in 1653 Izaak Walton 'for whom England was brooks, not agonies', published his *The Compleat Angler*. In 1651, but abroad in Paris, Thomas Hobbes, tutor to Charles II, had published his *Leviathan*, a book shot through with fear of civil disorder and bound to provoke conflicts because of its atheistic and absolutist tendencies. It had an interesting future. In September 1668 Samuel Pepys recorded in his *Diary* that he had paid three times the publisher's price for a second-hand copy ('the bishops will not let it be printed again'), and eleven years after that copies were burned publicly in Oxford. Two of the greatest works of the seventeenth century date from immediately after the Restoration: Milton, who had used his talents for political purposes during the Interregnum and who was now blind, published his *Paradise Lost* in 1667, and in the following decades John Bunyan, who had been swept up into the Civil War, wrote his great Puritan work, *The Pilgrim's Progress*, which has often been described as England's most powerful allegory. Bunyan had spent more than twelve years in gaol for his faith, and his book gave a new dimension to the idea of pilgrimage presented centuries earlier by Langland and Chaucer.

Bunyan's Christian had to resist the snares of the city, and 'the merchandise of the fair' which included stage plays. While Restoration comedy was much appreciated by Charles II, who encouraged rhyming verse in drama (although he demanded 'clear, plain and short sermons' in church), it was particularly repugnant to Puritans. The language of the Restoration dramatists, like their themes, was polite and witty on the surface, but it was underscored by an often bawdy muse of comedy. 'Our way of living became more free,' commented the poet John Dryden, who approved of the change, 'and the fire of the English wit, which was being stifled under a constrained, melancholy way of breeding, began first to display its force, by mixing the solidity of our nation with the air and gaiety of our neighbours.' Yet there were complaints that too much attention was paid to effects or tricks – 'that which makes our Stage the better makes our Players the worse' – and in November 1661 a diarist wrote, 'I saw Hamlet, Prince of Denmark, played; but now the old plays begin to disgust this refined age.'

The personal diary was coming into its own as a literary form in the middle and late seventeenth century. Indeed, diarists have left us some of the most memorable accounts of life in England after 1660. Pepys, who was born in 1633, rose to be Secretary of the Admiralty and was elected to Parliament in 1679, but it is the directness of immediate comment in the diary, which he kept in shorthand between 1660 and 1669 and which was first transcribed in 1818, rather than his knowledge of the workings of government, which won him immortality. Another diarist, John

Evelyn, a voluminous correspondent, left to posterity a life-long calendar, describing vividly all the striking events of the day, such as the removal of the bodies of the Commonwealth leaders from their tombs to be hanged again on the gallows of Tyburn in 1661.

But Evelyn and Pepys do more than recount events. They catch the changing ways of life and thought of their country. Evelyn was a founder member of the Royal Society, and Pepys joined it in 1664. The Society, incorporated two years earlier with the king's blessing, aimed to 'promote the welfare of the arts and sciences' and to 'make faithful Records of all the Works of Nature or of Art'; and its prose, in contrast with that of Restoration comedy, was plain, direct and deliberately designed to avoid 'fulsome metaphors'. Yet one experimental 'natural philosopher' could write in the same year of 'Philosophy' coming 'in with a spring-tide' and 'all the old Rubbish' being 'thrown away'. As new 'sciences' evolved there was a strong sense of change. Newton, who was to produce a new system, worked away from the centre. Indeed, he spent his *annus mirabilis* in 1665–6 sheltering from the plague in his home in rural Lincolnshire. It was years later that Samuel Johnson was to say of him that 'he stood alone because he left the rest of mankind behind him.'

Evelyn and Pepys catch the immediate tempo of the age from London. Time was acquiring a new significance in the late *Clock* seventeenth century; it mattered as much to businessmen as to diarists and historians. Business – and much of secular life – began to follow the clock as relentlessly as the Church had followed the bell and agriculture still followed the seasons. Pepys was not alone in being proud of his watch and in treating it increasingly as a necessity. It was Bunyan who wrote in a *Book for Boys and Girls*:

> Behold this Post-boy, with what haste and speed
> He travels on the Board; and there is need
> That so he does, his Business calls for haste.

Puritans made more of the importance of 'time well spent' than any other section of the community. The clock pendulum and the balance spring, which enabled minute-hands to be added to hour-hands, both belong to the Restoration period.

All sectors of the community – at least of the urban community

– were becoming more interested in news. English newsbooks and *corantos*, imitations of earlier Dutch innovations (like so much else), had first appeared during the early 1620s, but under the tight censorship of both the Commonwealth and Restoration there had been strict licensing regulations, with the government seeking to treat news as a monopoly, against which Milton had argued in *Areopagitica*. The twice-weekly *London Gazette* was established in 1665 as an official vehicle for news, but by the end of the century, when news sheets were appearing in single-leaf layout, it was clear that the demand for unofficial news was increasing rapidly. Parliament allowed the restrictive Printing Act to lapse in 1679 and during six years of increased freedom there was a flood of unauthorized new publications. In 1695, after the 'Glorious Revolution', the whole system of licensing was abolished.

Ten years later, an article in the thrice-weekly *British Mercury*, published by the Sun Fire Insurance Company, was to claim in retrospect that urban population was growing proportionately during these years as the rate of increase in national population slackened off (with local variations) until the 1690s. By 1700, 16 per cent of the national population lived in towns of 5,000 people or more. There were then seven towns with a population of more than 10,000, and twenty-three towns with a population of more than 5,000. Some of these provincial towns greatly impressed the traveller Celia Fiennes, who visited them in the 1690s, a quarter of a century before the journalist Daniel Defoe published his *Tour through the Whole Island of Great Britain*. Nottingham was the 'neatest' town she saw, Leeds 'the wealthiest town of its bigness', Norwich 'a rich thriveing industrious place', and Liverpool, which had begun as a row of fishermen's houses, was 'very handsome', a 'London in miniature'.

Throughout the seventeenth century London was a crowded, unhealthy and dangerous place as well as a centre of wealth, with epidemics of the plague in 1603, 1625 and 1636 and a pall of smoke hanging over it like a canopy. The crowdedness was noted by the playwright Thomas Dekker, a characteristic Londoner in his ways of thinking and feeling, in his *Seven Deadly Sins of London*, as early as 1606: some of the sins were as noisy as the carts and coaches which made 'such a thundering as if the world ran on wheels'. Between 1600 and 1650 the population of London doubled at a time when the national growth of population was levelling off, reaching a total of 400,000 people, and by the end of the century one in nine in the English population lived there as against one in twenty at the beginning. It was at Whitehall in London that Charles I had been executed and it was above Westminster Hall that Cromwell's severed head was placed on a pole. For Bunyan, 'he that will go the [celestial] city and not pass through this town must needs go out of the world.'

We can turn to Evelyn, Pepys and Defoe for the accounts of the two most dramatic events in the London of the 1660s: the 'great plague' and the 'great fire', which came within a year of each other, in 1665 and 1666, when England was involved in a difficult (second) war against the Dutch. 'Everybody talking of the dead,' Pepys wrote simply of the first; it made 'a noise like the waves of the sea', the antiquary Anthony Wood wrote of the second. Plague and fire together, in Wood's words, had left the city 'much impoverished, discontented, afflicted, cast downe'. Yet, just as revolution had been followed by restoration, so fire was followed by rapid and imposing reconstruction. Old London disappeared; a new London was born. Christopher Wren, a member of the Royal Society, gave London a new look as he rebuilt, or superintended the rebuilding of, fifty-one of the eighty-six churches which had been burnt. His St Stephen's in Walbrook should be set alongside his new St Paul's, which, according to Evelyn, made Westminster Abbey Gothic look like 'crinkle-crankle'. Who, Evelyn asked, could deny the superiority of the great domed building 'which strikes the understanding as well as the eye with the more majesty and solemn greatness'? Gothic was all 'turrets and pinnacles, thickset with monkeys and chimeras'.

There were many obvious contrasts between the taste and the mood of the early years of the century and those of the 1660s. The first of these was in dress, although the main contrast here was not between the Interregnum and the Restoration, but between sober Puritan costume and lavish and flamboyant costume for the rich. 'A strange effeminate age when men strive to imitate women in their apparel,' wrote Anthony Wood in 1663, 'viz. long periwigs, patches in their faces, painting, short wide breeches like petticoats, muffs, and their clothes highly scented, bedecked with ribbons of all colours.' Two years earlier, Evelyn had watched a man strolling through Westminster Hall with 'as much Ribbon about him as would have plundered six shops and set up twenty Country Pedlers: All his Body was dres't like a Maypole or a Tom-a-Bedlam Cap.' The king himself complained to Parliament in 1662 that 'the whole nation seemed to him a little corrupted in their excess of living. All men spend much more in their clothes, in their diet, in all their expenses than they need to do.' However, it was Charles who set the fashions and they were not cheap.

Diet was certainly becoming more sophisticated – for the well-to-do. Old recipes were being collected, while new foods and drinks were being imported, including coffee, 'heretofore in use amongst the Arabians and Egyptians', and chocolate, 'lately much used in England'. Soon the coffee house, the first of which was opened in 1650 (in Oxford), was to become a new social rendezvous, not only in the capital but in provincial towns too: Bristol came second to London in numbers of them. 'You have all manner of news there,' a foreign visitor was to write. Yet the consumption of French wines declined drastically as a result of heavy taxation, while the consumption of spirits and beer increased. The scope and scale of dining at home can be best appreciated not from life in great noble households, but from Pepys's diary. At a New Year's breakfast in 1661 (still taken early in the day), he offered his guests a barrel of oysters, a dish of meat, some tongues and a plate of anchovies, and at a special dinner in 1663 he presented them with

> a fricassee of rabbit and chickens, a leg of mutton boiled, three carps in a dish, a great dish of a side of lamb, a dish of roasted pigeons, a dish of four lobsters, three tarts, a lamprey pie, a most rare pie, a dish of anchovies, good wine of several sorts, and all things mighty noble, and to my great content.

There were many great dinners in 1688 to celebrate the arrival in London of William, the staunch Dutch leader of the Protestant forces in Europe, who was to rule jointly with James's elder daughter, Mary, and the event was to be celebrated equally enthusiastically a century later. William and Mary were to be rulers not by divine right but on the invitation of Parliament and people. Indeed, they were presented with a Declaration of Rights before they accepted the crown. This was the essence of the 'Glorious Revolution' of 1688. Royal powers, now limited, were never explicitly defined, but the Bill of Rights, professing to declare ancient rights rather than create new or abstract ones, declared, *inter alia*, that extra-parliamentary taxation was illegal (Charles II had ruled without Parliament between 1682 and 1685) and required explicitly that Parliament must approve any peacetime standing army. The role of Parliament was further emphasized by the Triennial Act of 1694, which laid down that Parliament must be summoned at general elections to be held at least once every three years. Finally, the Act of Settlement of 1701, which required that the king should be an Anglican, sought to perpetuate the settlement: it was sub-titled 'an act for the further limitation of the Crown and the better preserving the liberties of the subject'.

If the bloodless revolution was to be remembered as 'glorious', the constitution was hailed as 'the most beautiful constitution that was ever framed', and it soon began to be revered as a landmark. Indeed, Macaulay's 'Whig interpretation' of English history (which stressed the rule of England's democratic institutions in a story of progress) was to centre on it. There would have been less reverence, however, had there been no earlier record of disturbance and conflict, and there would have been no 'Whig interpretation' without the struggles and revolution earlier in the century. The experience of the whole century was relevant to its outcome. In the final years of the seventeenth and early years of the eighteenth centuries a financial settlement also was directly related to the constitutional settlement, so that a later pamphleteer could claim that 'trade and commerce are nowhere to be found but in the regions of freedom, where the lives and properties of the subjects are secured by wholesome laws'.

Like the constitution, the financial settlement had emerged out of a longer experience than that of the last decade of a stormy century. During the Civil War it had been possible for Parliament to introduce in 1643 two new taxes, which the king would not have been able to secure before the war began. The first was a land tax replacing the old Parliamentary subsidy and the dues of wardship. The second was the excise, a tax on consumption introduced by Pym to pay for the Civil War; it was modelled, as was so much else in financial reform, on a Dutch tax. The wide range of articles on which it was levied was narrowed after 1660 to beer, cider and spirits (on which it is still levied in the twentieth century) and tea, coffee and chocolate, but it was widened again between 1688 and 1713 to cover malt and hops, salt, candles, soap, leather and paper. If the burdens of the land tax fell on the propertied, landed interest, many of the burdens of excise fell on the poor. At the same time, import duties multiplied by four between 1690 and 1704 in order to pay for the long European wars in which England was engaged after 1688, for the first time as a major European power. The debate on such subjects, which brought in the study of private and public wealth as well as the structure of 'interests', was free from criticism of 'feudal' undertones. The old idea that within a complex society the king might 'live on his own' had been dead already by the 1640s, when a wide range of pamphlets had been published on trade.

Even with the benefit of the new taxes, however, Cromwell had left a bigger debt than James I, and Charles II turned to his powerful and unpopular neighbour Louis XIV, King of France, for secret subsidies. More important in the long run, however, he, like Cromwell, turned also for loans to merchants and bankers, thereby strengthening the 'City interest', even though such loans involved risk and difficulties, as in 1672 when the Crown repudiated a part of its debt in the much criticized 'Stop of the Exchequer'.

The effects of these important changes were wide-reaching. As contemporaries fully appreciated, the growing variety of 'interests' made for a much more complex society. The mercantile interest, representing 'the great Sinews of Trade' and the City interest, concerned with credit in both private and public funds, met with suspicion and resentment, often crudely prejudiced, sometimes brilliantly expressed in pamphlets. Trade and Credit, it was claimed, were less solid than Land, and it was 'the Landed Gentlemen, Yeomen and Farmers, whose Substance is fixed in this particular part of the globe' who were 'the most settled inhabitants and the Bulk of the Nation'. The eighteenth-century politician Bolingbroke, who passed on to posterity a Tory version of English history in which the growth of the institutions and credit structures of the City of London had destroyed rather than strengthened the country, was to put it more memorably in 1749: 'the landed men are the true owners of our political vessel, the money'd men are no more than mere passengers in it'.

After the revolution of 1688, an intricate public borrowing system was devised to meet the demands of greatly increasing governmental expenditure. Holland, economically the most advanced country in Europe, once again provided a model, and in 1694 the Bank of England was set up by charter: it had a governor and directors, and its first subscription list was headed by the king and queen. There was opposition, centred in the House of Lords, and there were only two peers among the initial holders of stock. The founding of the Bank, was, while less acclaimed by the 'Whig' historians, just as important in the social history of England as the events of 1688: it made public borrowing possible on a secure and regular basis and gave government a new fiscal base. Over £14 million was borrowed between 1690 and 1700 to pay (along with £45 million in taxes) for the costs of European wars. Within a hundred years Lord North, Prime Minister during the American War of Independence, was to call the Bank a part of the constitution. 'It acts not only as an ordinary bank,' wrote Adam Smith – and by then there were many 'ordinary' country banks – 'but as a great engine of State.'

Yet the seventeenth century did not end quite as neatly as an emphasis on the constitutional, religious and financial settlements of the final decade might suggest. It was a sign of the restless spirit of the age that the Bank of England was founded one month after the Cabinet had passed a bill for a £1,000,000 national lottery with £10 tickets. (Dealers were soon to sell smaller shares.) The passion for gambling was at least as strong at this time as the pursuit of industry, and during the next twenty years there were to be more 'projects' – projects of every kind, some based on new inventions – than in any previous period of English history. Moreover, the constitutional settlement did not dampen political argument.

During the reign of James II's second daughter, Anne (1702–14), both political and religious argument was often strident: elections were keenly contested and sermons were as polemical as political speeches. If England was to move into an 'age of stability' in the 1730s and 1740s, it was to do it noisily, not quietly. Indeed, Daniel Defoe was to write in 1701 that 'whether we speak of differences in opinion or differences in interest, we must own we are the most divided quarrelsome nation under the sun.' Six years later, the 'perfect union' of England and Scotland, for which James I had expressed hopes when he became king in 1603, was realized through the Act of Union of 1707. There was to be one Parliament and one Union Jack. Nonetheless, there was to be open rebellion by loyal supporters of the Stuarts north of the border twice during the eighteenth century before union became peacefully established. Then, it was to come about not through political union, but through the quest for wealth, power and enlightenment which both countries shared.

7

THE QUEST FOR WEALTH, POWER AND PLEASURE

Men are gaining possession without your knowledge . . . Merchants ignore the interests of their sovereign, and are concerned only with their own commercial profit.

> Tsar of Russia, Ivan the Terrible, to Queen Elizabeth, 1571

> When Britain first at Heaven's command
> Arose from out of the azure main,
> This was the charter of the land,
> And guardian angels sang the strain:
> 'Rule Britannia, rule the waves;
> Britons never will be slaves.'
>
> James Thomson, *Rule Britannia*, 1740

Happiness is the only thing of real value in existence: neither riches, nor power, nor wisdom, nor learning, nor strength, nor beauty, nor virtue, nor religion, nor even life itself, being of any importance but as they contribute to its production.

> Soame Jenyns, 1765

THE SEVENTEENTH century had ended in war, as the eighteenth century was to do. England's entry into long wars against Louis XIV's France, which were not to end until 1713, raised public expenditure between two and three times and increased the national debt from £11,000,000 to over £40,000,000. Yet national wealth increased rapidly at the same time: in 1701 it was believed to have risen by 20 per cent since 1688. This wealth was in large part generated at home, but some derived from the quest for wealth and power abroad. There is much that is distinctive and ironical in the story of that quest, and much also that influenced the social history of other continents, among them Asia and Africa. And because the story is bound up with rivalry – sometimes war – with other European countries, the context of Europe is also relevant to an understanding of the processes of expansion. In 1700 the European market still accounted for 85 per cent of both English exports and re-exports, while two-thirds of the nation's imports (£0·67 for each man, woman and child) came from the same source. By 1722–4, 42 per cent of British exports were crossing the Atlantic.

The achievements – and the ironies, not to speak of the tragedies for the victims – began in the sixteenth century, the age of discovery. There was, above all at that time, a greatly enhanced sense of opportunity. While Richard Hakluyt canvassed a wide range of exports, including needles, soap, glue and locks, and advocated colonization in his *Discourse of Western Planting* (1584), his compatriot John Hawkins was trading in African slaves. English coal too was in genuine demand abroad, while cloth still deserved its name 'the golden fleece'. The explorers led the way further afield: Francis Drake in his *Golden Hind*, a ship weighing less than 150 tons, completed his circumnavigation of the globe in 1580 after a voyage of nearly three years, and in 1600, William Adams, a far less well-known figure in England, reached Japan and helped the Japanese to found a navy.

As horizons were widened attitudes were being transformed. It was not a sailor but the astrologer/scientist John Dee who as early as 1577 predicted the growth of an 'incomparable British Empire', and it was Francis Bacon, prophet of New Atlantis, who carried the idea of the map into learning itself, breaking with the traditions of scholasticism. Bacon, who was deeply and realistically concerned with 'the Greatness of Kingdoms and Estates', was also an advocate of emigration, although he warned that 'planting of countries is like planting of woods' and would take time to produce results. He was frank about the motives behind early discovery and colonization, and claimed that they did not centre on the 'propagation of the Christian faith', but on 'gold and silver, and temporal profit and glory'.

The cluster of new trading companies that had come into existence by the end of the century probably emerged not from an expansion of trade but from its stagnation in Europe. Even if the trading activities of 'interlopers', 'outleapers' and 'pirates' are taken into the reckoning, it has been suggested that the much-noted expansion of Elizabethan trade was largely a myth. Political barriers in Europe and limits to economic opportunity there pushed English merchants further across the seas. Thus, for example, it was after the cloth trade collapsed at the end of its greatest boom period in the middle of the sixteenth century and after Antwerp began to lose its dominance in the European trading network to Amsterdam that new English trade with Morocco was opened up. The first voyage to Guinea was made in 1553, and in the same year English voyagers reached the White Sea and travelled by land to Moscow. The Muscovy Company was set up by royal charter in 1555. Later in the same decade, England lost its last possession on the European mainland, the wool 'staple' town of Calais. Holland and Germany remained by far the biggest, if often precarious, markets for cloth, but trade with the Baltic and the Mediterranean was extended. An Eastland Company had been incorporated in 1579, followed two years later by a Turkey Company, which was to become part of a bigger Levant Company in 1592; an Africa Company had been launched in 1588, and an East India Company on the last day of 1600.

The biggest profits came not from exports but imports: wax, tallow, furs and hides from Russia; pitch and tar from the Baltic (and in one year, 1595, sizeable quantities of grain); wine from France and fruit from the Mediterranean; silks, spices and perfumes from the East; sugar, first from Morocco; tobacco, a new crop in 1585, from Virginia. While many of the individual items in this list excited Tudor consumers, its size and possible effect on the balance of trade worried some of their contemporaries. 'We brought in more foreign wares than we vended commodities,' suggested a Member of Parliament, not for the first or last time, in 1593.

Economic analysis does not do justice to the excitement of the quest for either wealth or power (they were usually the same) during the late sixteenth century, when 'all perils and misadventures' were accepted as 'tolerable' and all acts of piracy were welcomed as 'adventurous'. To catch the flavour of the times, it is necessary to turn back the pages of Hakluyt's massive *Principall Navigations, Voyages and Discoveries of the English Nation*, the first volume of which appeared in 1589 and the last in 1600, the year of the foundation of the East India Company. The English, Hakluyt proudly claimed, had 'excelled all the nations and peoples of the earth' in 'searching the most opposite corners and quarters of the world and . . . in compassing the vast globe', and a viceroy of New Spain said of Drake that he was 'one of the greatest mariners that sail the seas'. 'He drinks and sups to the music of viols,' he went on, 'and carries painters who paint for him pictures of the coast in its exact colours.' Daring in the age of discovery should not be confused with foolhardiness. Navigation rested on science and on scientific instruments: among the necessary inventions of the time were the mariner's compass and a new sea quadrant, which was invented by an Englishman, John Davis. The map pointed to the charting of what had hitherto been uncharted.

By 1640 shipping tonnage had more than doubled in sixty years and there were English footholds of empire in Asia, where Surat on the north-west coast of India became the first base of the East India Company (with access to Agra), and in the West Indies, where St Christopher was settled in 1624. The uninhabited island of Barbados was claimed three years later, Nevis in 1628 and Montserrat and Antigua in the 1630s; there was as much of a 'fashion for islands' at this time as there was for gardens. Further north, Bermuda, 'God's perfect garden', had already inspired Shakespeare (*The Tempest*) and Andrew Marvell:

> He gave us this eternal spring
> Which there enamels everything.

In reality there was little spiritual concern in the acquisition and development of the West Indian islands. Indeed, the fame of Sir Henry Morgan, the seventeenth-century buccaneer in the Caribbean, has been likened to proclaiming Al Capone the most famous American of the twentieth century. Buccaneering plunder was divided meticulously in terms of merit and rank, provision first having been made for the wounded: 'for the loss of a right arm 600 pieces of eight, or six slaves . . . for a finger of the hand the same rewards as for an eye'. There was a Saxon note in this.

The biggest and most ambitious early plantations were in Virginia, named after the Virgin Queen. They were set in countryside often resembling that of England to which the ideal of the gentleman could be exported, although increasingly it could be maintained only with the help of black slaves. 'In the beginning,' wrote William Byrd, 'all America was Virginia.' Yet the first settlers there faced hardship and danger: of 104 men and boys who travelled there in 1607, fifty-one were dead by the following spring. In 1632 the sponsors of the enterprise complained of 'the extreme beastly idleness' of their fellow countrymen because they did not back the venture strongly enough; indeed, they suggested that the English were 'wedded to their native soil like a snail to his shell'. Nonetheless, Virginia soon flourished, as did Maryland, which began to be settled in 1622. As the years went by, slaves provided the work while sugar and tobacco, both important crops, provided the wealth. The first Englishman to 'plant' Barbados took with him ten negroes and thirty-two Indians, and although few black slaves were imported, by 1660 there were as many blacks as whites – 20,000 of each – in Barbados with a population density higher than that in most parts of England. The gulf in lifestyles widened as the planters grew rich: indeed, five of them were to receive baronetcies between 1658 and 1665.

Very different colonies were created further north in the colder climes of 'New England'. There was little publicity for the voyagers on the *Mayflower*, a vessel of only 180 tons, which landed at New Plymouth in 1620 after a voyage of nearly two and a half months, although the fact that forty of them died during the first hard winter has kept the memory of the journey alive on every subsequent Thanksgiving Day. These first pilgrims were Independents, and there were to be further Puritan reinforcements for 'New England' before the Massachusetts Bay Company received its charter in 1629 and Providence Island its charter in 1630.

New England was deliberately different from old England: in the words of John Winthrop, an emigrant from Suffolk, who had one son in Barbados, it was 'a shelter and a hiding place for us and ours, aş Zoar for Lot'. Yet it was not democratic. Winthrop called democracy 'the meanest and worst of all forms of government', while Edward Winslow, one of the first pilgrims, stated tersely that America was a place where 'religion and profit jump together'. In fact, religion was the point of departure and no more; above all else, the immigrants *had* to be practical, and while there were to be many cultural and economic links with England – the first magistrates printed the main provisions of Magna Carta alongside their own 'fundamentals' – the American colonial experience was always sufficiently distinct to demand a separate, if related, social history. And there were varieties within America too. The New Englanders had different perspectives from the Virginians.

It was while the English Puritans were in command in their own country that the seventeenth-century quest for power and wealth reached its peak. Cromwell was an enthusiast for New England. He sent out convicts rather than pilgrims as colonists, introducing systematic procedures after 1655. English mercantile interests were paramount in the Navigation Act of 1651 (the work of the Long Parliament), which had been foreshadowed in earlier acts and which was perpetuated after the Restoration: it laid down that all merchandise imported into England from America, Asia and Africa should be imported in English ships and that all other merchandise should be imported either in English ships or in ships of the country of origin.

The wars of the Interregnum were primarily commercial in motive. The war against the Protestant Dutch of 1652–4, the first of three such wars in the seventeenth century, was designed to break their grip on trade in key commodities, and when it ended, the peace was unpopular with English merchants. Trade, conquest and colonization in the West Indies also figured prominently in the less successful war with Spain which began in 1656; Jamaica was captured from the Spanish in 1655 – to be completely refashioned. Across the Channel, Dunkirk was captured and across the oceans trade contacts were established with China, despite prejudices in London against the East India Company. Between the two, Admiral Blake, fighting Barbary pirates, bombarded Tangiers, attacked Tunis and released English captives in Algiers.

Just as important as these victories was a change in attitude towards the making of wealth. The rate of interest, which fell to 6 per cent in 1652, could now move as freely as the rate of profit, whatever the consequences. After 1660 moral or ethical debate on the permissibility of interest gave way to practical discussion concerning its level and whether or not there should be any legal limits to it; low interest rates in Holland were judged to be a main factor in that country's prosperity. The ways of making money, the possible realms of enterprise and the necessary kinds of mercantile skill were increasing in number all the time. Thomas Mun's *England's Treasure by Foreign Trade*, published in 1664 but written decades earlier, presented the merchant as master of the 'mysteries of trade', whose frugal lifestyle contrasted with that of his fellow countrymen who spent their days in 'Idleness and Pleasure'. Puritanism emphasized the importance of hard work.

Yet by 1691 Dudley North in his *Discourses upon Trade* could describe as the main spur to 'Industry and Ingenuity' what he called 'the exhorbitant Appetites of Man'. 'Did Men content themselves with bare necessaries,' he went on, 'we should have a poor World.' This was the Restoration view. In 1681, John Houghton argued boldly that 'our High-Living, so far from prejudicing the Nation . . . enriches it.' Although the political position of England in Europe weakened substantially after the Restoration of 1660, there was no substantial change in much of the economic policy devised under Cromwell. Indeed, some of the personalities involved were the same. So too were the theorists, like Sir William Petty, founder of 'political arithmetic'. The Navigation Code of 1660–63 completed the work begun in 1651, and from 1663 onwards colonists were bound to buy most of the European goods they needed in England. There were further expensive and unsuccessful Dutch Wars which, nonetheless, turned Englishmen's eyes further away from Dutch economic strength in Europe and the role of the French, who were Charles II's paymasters. The Dutch were able to attack Chatham in Kent in 1667 and to win a great naval battle off the Suffolk coast five years later.

Between the two dates the East India Company acquired Bombay. By 1680 the Company's annual investment in Bengal was £150,000; its agents there were behaving like English merchant clothiers and ordering silk 'taffeties' and cotton 'ginghams' for the English consumer market. 'The Artists of India out-do all the Ingenuity of Europe,' wrote a clergyman visitor to Surat. A decade later tea had become another favourite commodity, with annual exports to England rising to 100,500 lb. by the end of the century. Tea from the East needed sugar from the West, and as the West Indian islands boomed – in particular Barbados, which was described in 1681 as 'one great City adorned with gardens' – imports from the Caribbean more than doubled between 1660 and 1700. At the same time, it has been argued that trade in Newfoundland cod was the means by which England kept trade with the New World out of her rival's hands.

Bristol, which was described by Samuel Pepys in the 1660s as 'in every respect another London', was the main English port involved in triangular trade. It had been flourishing even before slaves became a precious cargo in the late seventeenth century but now it was given a new impetus. When the Royal African Company was founded in 1672 to ship slaves to the American planters, it was emphasized that 'the planters could not subsist without them', and soon English manufacturers were also profiting from the African market; between 1690 and 1701 one Birmingham manufacturer shipped over 400,000 knives and 7,000 swords, and by the last quarter of the eighteenth century Birmingham's overseas exports had quadrupled. By then too one-third of Manchester's textile exports were going there also. Raw cotton imports quadrupled, arriving in England through Liverpool, another centre of the slave trade.

It was as a result of the long Wars of the Spanish Succession, when Marlborough's armies were fighting great battles on European soil, among them Ramillies and Blenheim, that England secured the *Assiento*, or sole right to ship slaves to the Spanish American Empire, in 1713. Ten years earlier Portugal had been drawn into the system by the Methuen Treaty, which also ensured that port as a drink would become a prized ingredient in the eighteenth-century way of life (which had a special place for alcohol). Slaves were the key to the system, however, and more than two million of them were exported to the British colonies alone between 1680 and 1783. The profitability of the different ventures linked to this trade, some of them highly speculative, like the South Sea Company, which was set up in 1711 and took over the *Assiento* rights in 1713, has been the subject of extensive argument, most recently by quantitative economic historians.

The South Sea Bubble, which encouraged every other kind of speculation as well, left many people with nothing but paper when it burst ignominiously in 1720. The historian Edward Gibbon's grandfather was one of them: for him, 'the labours of thirty years were blasted in a single day', and for the politician Sir Robert Walpole, it was 'never-to-be-forgot or forgiven'. Many other forms of business enterprise were hit too, but the slave trade continued in other hands. 'All this great increase in our treasure,' Joshua Gee wrote in 1729, 'proceeds chiefly from the labour of negroes in the plantations.' Many fortunes depended upon it, as some of the richest merchants admitted. Thus, the Bristol merchant John Pinney, a great plantation owner in the West Indies, stated frankly that 'negroes are the sinews of a plantation' and that it was 'as impossible for a man to make sugar without the assistance of negroes as to make bricks without straw'. The planters themselves often returned to England like nabobs, displaying their great wealth ostentatiously, sometimes to the distaste of people of more modest temperament. Some economic historians have questioned the real value of the West Indies to England, suggesting that they generated a loss of £600,000 a year. Yet it is difficult to reconcile this picture with the existence of the powerful West India interest at Westminster, which drew its support not only from returning merchants but also from members of the English landed interest with West Indian possessions who remained absentee landlords, like the Lascelles, who were later to marry into the royal family.

Socially, the consequences of West Indian slavery were profound and cast their shadows into the distant future – in the twentieth century English-speaking descendants of the first slaves were to come to England in large numbers and influence contemporary patterns of life, particularly in the large cities – and in the eighteenth century there were black slaves in London. At that time more was made of the difference between black and white than ever before – the novelist Tobias Smollett could write in 1735 that the 'Africans' had manners 'as wide from ours as we should find in the planetary subjects above could we get there'. Not surprisingly, 'manners' were very different in the Caribbean and in Africa. There was nothing approaching family life, and the growth of a coloured population of mixed stock had its origins not in marriage but concubinage and sexual abuses of various kinds; a law was passed in Jamaica in 1748 limiting the amount of property which could be inherited by a concubine and her issue to £1,200. Yet Smollett also attacked the slave trade, as many other people, particularly Quakers, were to do as the century went by. The ratio of blacks to whites increased in the plantation countries, but slave mortality rates were exceptionally high. Between 1712 and 1768, for example, 200,000 slaves were imported into Barbados but the population increased by only 26,000.

Between 1700 and 1780 English foreign trade nearly doubled, and the merchant marine almost trebled with it. Although Europe still accounted for the biggest share of England's trade, the lure of high profits continued to draw Englishmen to all corners of the world; symbolically, a new gold coin was called the 'guinea' after the African territory. There were still many writers who suggested that one of the chief uses of colonies was to provide 'an Outlet, or Issue for the ill Humours which from time to time are engender'd in the Body Politick' or a means 'for employing our poor, and putting hands to work, either at home or in the plantations who cannot support themselves'. General James Oglethorp used the second argument when he urged the case for settlement in Georgia in 1730. Philosophers found other interests in the story. John Locke, who prepared a Fundamental Constitution for Carolina, quoted American experience to support his theory of property.

Although England kept out of war between 1713 and 1739, seen as a whole the eighteenth century was a century of war and diplomacy, and from 1745 Englishmen abroad were deeply involved in action on frontiers far from Europe. Slave colonies were as liable to change hands as European frontier towns. This was a time when open war with France and Spain was popular not only with many merchants and colonists but with the English public, who were roused by chauvinistic journalists, 'literary hacks' as their critics called them. They were now supported by large numbers of Scotsmen too, for they proved themselves particularly shrewd and energetic merchants and colonists. News of war in 1739 drew the crowds to the streets of London, Bristol and Liverpool to cheer the proclamation. Melodies could stir as much as words: Arne's setting of *Rule Britannia* was published a year later and *God Save the King* was first printed in 1744.

Four years after the victory of the Duke of Cumberland, George II's son, over the Jacobite Scots in the savage battle of Culloden near Inverness, the poet James Thomson, author of the words of *Rule Britannia*, was extolling England as an 'ever-sacred country':

> It knows no bound: it has a retrospect
> To ages past: it looks on those to come.

And a very different poet and hymn writer, Isaac Watts, produced words which appealed to 'God our help in ages past, our hope for years to come', words which were to retain similar patriotic connotations in the twentieth century.

King George II (1727–60) was more interested in Hanover, from where his father had come to London in 1714, than in the world of merchants, sailors and colonists. Indicatively, when he led his troops into battle – he was the last English king to do so – it was at Dettingen on European soil. Yet once his dynasty was secured in 1745 against the Jacobite armies who mustered in Scotland and marched south into Lancashire, his ministers were drawn increasingly into power struggles on a global scale, involving Europe, North America, the Caribbean, Africa and India.

The hope of many Englishmen in the 1740s and 1750s was William Pitt. 'When trade policy is at stake it is your last retrenchment,' he had proclaimed as a young politician in 1739. 'You must defend it or perish.' In the twentieth century, however, historians have demurred, echoing Samuel Johnson's dictum: 'Reason

frowns on war's unequal game.' 'If England had enjoyed un-
broken peace,' Professor T. S. Ashton used to argue, 'the industrial revolution might have come earlier.' Certainly, three major
wars of the eighteenth century, those of 1702–13, 1739–48 and
1775–83, led to a sharp contraction in the value of overseas trade,
even though they were followed by expansion. Terms of trade
moved against the English in wartime as well, and real incomes
were depressed.

Other historians have considered war an important spur to
technological advance. And 'going to war' had its immediate
prizes, particularly for sailors. The scale of naval wages did not
increase between 1653 and 1797, and press-ganged sailors were
often eager to desert, but everyone shared the booty. 'If these
French gentry do not escape me this time,' wrote one Admiral to
his wife in 1714, 'they will pay for the house and the furniture too,
besides something to save hereafter for all our dear children.'
There might be complaints that the foot soldier was 'commonly a
Man, who for the sake of wearing a sword, and the Honour of
being termed a Gentleman, is coaxed from a Handicraft Trade,
whereby he might live comfortably to bear Arms for his King and
Country, whereby he has hopes of nothing but to live starvingly.'
Yet for every such complaint there was ample patriotic talk. A
recruiting order of 1782 appealed to 'all handsome young Men,
whose Hearts beat at the Sound of the Drum, and are Above
Mean Employments'; and for those who enjoyed 'active service
life' the excitement compensated for the toughness of the in-
itiation and the discipline. That it was not just talk is suggested
by the enthusiasm of those like the young countryman William
Cobbett who wanted to become a sailor and actually became a
soldier. The Forces could attract.

The Navy was the senior service, and more money was spent
on it by England than was spent by the French: the seventeenth-
century fear of standing armies persisted and contemporaries
considered that the French held the military advantage. 'Though
our colonies were superior to those of the enemy in wealth and the
number of inhabitants,' Lord Waldegrave noted during the Seven
Years War, 'the French were much our superiors in military
discipline: almost every man amongst them was a soldier.' There

was no compulsory service for the Army, and no adequate peace-time training in England.

Yet it was the English who won the protracted struggle against the French fought in different continents between 1756 and 1763. Naval action was decisive in the capture of Fort St Louis in Senegal in 1758 and the taking of Goree, the other main French settlement in West Africa. James Wolfe's capture of Quebec in 1759, 'a year of victories', called by the actor and dramatist David Garrick a 'wonderful year', signalled the end of French power in Canada in 1760, although not the end there of French language, culture or political aspirations. Wolfe's army was smaller than that of the French and naval support was again decisive in the victory. The rich island of Guadeloupe in the Caribbean fell in the same year, and at the time it seemed a bigger prize. Two years later, Pondicherry, the French capital in India, fell also, completely ending French power there. Again, Robert Clive, the East India Company's ambitious commander in the field until 1760, had been given valuable additional leeway in his long campaign on land by the defeat of the French fleet in Indian waters during the earlier year of victories.

By this time national pride needed no encouragement from Pitt. In 1757 the clergyman John Brown had published his *Estimate of the Manners and Principles of the Times*, an anatomy of England which accused his fellow countrymen of effeminacy, and a year later he published his *An Explanatory Defence of the Estimate*, praising Pitt's achievements in rousing the nation. A year after that a Sussex shopkeeper, Thomas Turner, was writing proudly that 'no nation had ever greater occasion to adore the Almighty Disposer of all events than Albion, whose forces meet with success, in all quarters of the world.' Yet the cost of the victory was high. Land tax, which under Sir Robert Walpole, Prime Minister from 1721 to 1742, had once stood at a shilling in the pound – he believed in economy, but was, nonetheless, faced with a crisis when he planned a higher inland excise tax in 1733 – now stood at four shillings. Moreover, 200,000 troops were being paid for out of the budget. There were massive loans too. Of £160,000,000 spent by government between 1756 and 1763, £60,000,000 was borrowed. The national debt amounted to more

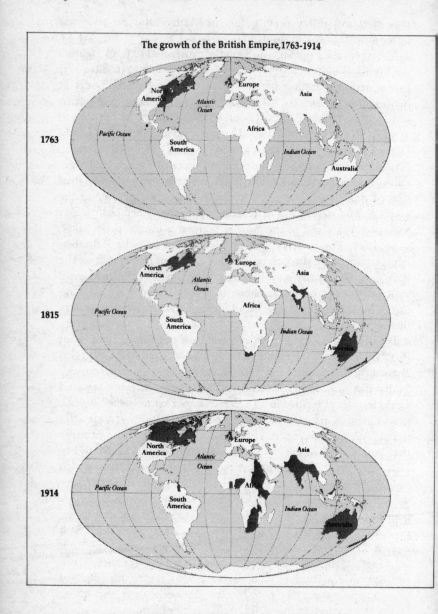

The growth of the British Empire, 1763-1914

than double that sum, though Parliament by this time had a direct interest in it, and in the annual interest repayments. So too did the scattered holders of the new 'consols', the name applied to the consolidated 3 per cent government stock of 1752. The greater part of the small individual holdings, a considerable proportion of them belonging to women, among them spinsters and widows, were held in London and the Home Counties.

Pitt fell from office in 1761, on a dispute about Newfoundland cod, and he was to complain bitterly about many of the features of the first Treaty of Paris made in 1763 at the close of the Seven Years War. Against his wishes Canada was preferred to Guadeloupe, which was restored to the French together with parts of French West Africa, and French fishing rights round Newfoundland were confirmed. Nonetheless, the British Empire reached a new peak as a result of the war. The thirteen American colonies, with far-flung lands to the north in Canada, stretched in the south to Florida and in the west towards the Mississippi. France recovered several of the Caribbean islands that had been seized during the war, but the British secured others, including Grenada, St Vincent and Tobago. Meanwhile, in the East, the riches of Bengal were being exploited as if it was a new El Dorado. Others paid the price: according to Robert Clive's many critics the increase of 'the London government's share of the spoils' had been bought at the cost of 'the late famine in Bengal and the loss of three million of inhabitants'. Clive's own advice that the 'sovereignty of India' was 'too large' for a Company did not greatly appeal to English politicians.

For all the triumphs of war and peace, the Empire as it stood in 1763 had many weaknesses. Its various parts were so different from one another that it was impossible to envisage them in terms of one single design, even a Providential one. It was an empire held together by sea power, but that alone was not enough to control it, let alone to govern it. Nor was trading supremacy guaranteed. France remained a strong rival after 1763, though some contemporaries believed that it was in the country's interest to be at continual variance with that restless neighbour, provided the contest could be limited to the operations of a sea war, in which England would be always invincible and victorious.

The North American colonies posed other problems. The population of the colonies was increasing at a dramatic rate – in 1760 it was six times larger than in 1700 – and while their inhabitants could be as patriotic as Englishmen when they talked about their shared heritage or naval and military victories, there were obvious divergences of interest. The Grenville government that took office in London in 1763 believed that for reasons of defence a permanent standing army of some 10,000 men should be kept in America and that American colonists should be taxed to help to cover the costs. It suggested too that since the Seven Years War had doubled the national debt, the increasingly prosperous colonies should not complain about making a contribution.

Modern American economic historians have challenged the view that England was seeking to place a heavy new burden on the colonies and have suggested that the real annual cost of defending the North American colonies was £400,000, five times the maximum income from them. Yet such calculations, convincing or not, were not made at the time, and the colonists, already chafing under the restrictive seventeenth-century Navigation Acts, felt increasing resentment against the tightening up of British policy after 1763: the Sugar Act of 1764 and American Stamp Act of 1765, both of which were later repealed, and the Tea Act of 1767, which was later modified, were bitterly disliked. There had been too much legislation of the kind which prompted Benjamin Franklin to remark, 'a wise and good mother will not do it'. The colonists turned with increasing fervour to seventeenth-century and even earlier English precedents for resistance; they were, they argued, 'free-born Englishmen' and should be 'co-equal in dignity and freedom'. Taxation without representation was tyranny.

The American War of Independence, which began in 1775, did not end until 1783. English failures were as important as the American victories since they undermined the English government at home; indeed, the debate in England on the war, which, according to William Pitt the Younger (the son of Pitt the Elder), had been 'conceived in injustice' and 'matured and brought forth in fury', was as bitter as the fighting on the other side of the Atlantic. When Lord Cornwallis was finally forced to surrender to George Washington at Yorktown in 1781, his troops clearly remembered the upheavals of the seventeenth century at home when they stacked down their arms to the tune of 'The World Turned Upside Down', and their feelings were echoed in a remark of 1782 that defeat had produced in England 'the strangest, though not unexpected revolution that has happened in this country for many years'. Lord North was replaced as Prime Minister first by the Marquis of Rockingham, his Whig critic, and then by Lord Shelburne, who arranged the Second Treaty of Paris. It recognized a new independent America south from the Great Lakes and west to the Mississippi. As industrial output in England soared during the 1780s, Englishmen sold more goods to independent America than they had done in colonial days under 'the old colonial system', propped up by the Navigation Act of 1660. The value of total exports amounted to £12,500,000 in 1782 and to £20,000,000 by 1790.

The Secretaryship of the Colonies was abolished in 1782, but the Empire was not abolished with it. Indeed, James Cook's discovery of Australia in 1770 added an enormous (although as yet unexplored) territory that would later become an important penal colony. In 1790 constitutional arrangements were introduced in Canada, where large numbers of 'loyalists' had settled after American independence, but their effect was to strengthen 'the principle of authority in government and of hierarchy in society'. Meantime, the Empire was still being extended in India, despite attempts by a series of governments to bring the activities of the East India Company under control. The government of Pitt the Younger, which was formed in 1784, established a Board of Control a year later to scrutinize all the Company's political operations. This was followed by the impeachment and trial of Warren Hastings, the Governor-General, 'an empire builder by design', in which the Earl of Cornwallis, who broke with the tradition of working in close association with Indians, played an unappealing part. 'Though the constitution of our Eastern possessions is arbitrary and despotic,' Pitt explained in 1795, 'still it is the duty of every administration in that country to conduct itself by the rules of justice and liberty.' A later Viceroy of India, Lord Curzon, took a different view. 'Had a Committee been assembled from the padded chambers of Bedlam,' he wrote, 'they could hardly have devised anything more extravagant in its madness or more mischievous in its operation'.

Throughout the eighteenth century it had been possible to pursue the quest for wealth as vigorously and profitably inside hierarchical England as outside it. Land remained the major source of wealth and power, and the great landlords continued to improve their economic position: in 1700 peers owned about 15 to 20 per cent of England's landed wealth, and by 1800 they owned between 20 and 25 per cent. In some cases they could increase their wealth too, from coal and iron royalties, from canals and, above all, from urban properties – with the Bedfords and the Grosvenors leading the way in London. It was their country seats, however, which were both symbols and centres of display and of hospitality. 'Banishment alone will force the French to execute what the English do for pleasure,' Arthur Young was to write. 'Reside and adorn their estates.'

Below the aristocracy the landed gentry, with diverse properties and varying fortunes, were in a strong position in an age of 'improving agriculture' to increase their wealth, and a few of them, like Thomas Coke of Holkham, were to improve their status too and become peers. Whatever their titles, their social role as squires was the key one in local society. They determined its patterns of power as Justices of the Peace, backed by Clerks of the Peace and unpaid parish officers, churchwardens, overseers and constables. There was no money in such activities, only burdens, yet because of local and national influence they were in a position as a group to maintain corn laws and game laws. They also often had substantial patronage at their disposal.

Their composition and wealth might be reinforced through links with London and with overseas trade, for in the City there were 'merchant princes' who, as one foreign visitor observed in 1727, were 'far wealthier than many sovereign princes of Germany or Italy'. In the same decade one Lord Mayor of London held £122,000 in South Sea stock and £118,000 in Bank of England stock. The mixture – or 'confusion' – of the nobility and the 'mercantile part of the nation,' wrote P. J. Grosley in his *Tour to London* in 1772, 'is an inexhaustible source of wealth to the state.

The nobility having acquired an accession of wealth by marriage, the tradesmen make up for their loss by eager endeavours to make a fortune, and the gentry conspire to the same end by their efforts to raise such an estate as shall procure a peerage for themselves or their children.'

This was an ideal picture, and it has been suggested recently that the entry to the peerage, in particular, was far more restricted than contemporaries like Grosley (or earlier and later writers) claimed. Nonetheless, it is beyond doubt that marriage remained a main way to wealth: the father of Lord North, for example, married three heiresses. (It should be added that his brother was in turn Bishop of Lichfield, Worcester and Winchester, the last the richest of all the sees.) Neither the aristocracy nor the gentry constituted closed orders of society, and although the former may have been more closed than in most other periods of English social history, contemporaries took pride in what was called in 1757 'gradual and easy transition from rank to rank'. 'Merchants are commonly ambitious of becoming country gentlemen,' observed Adam Smith along with many others, including Daniel Defoe; his character Robinson Crusoe bought land in Bedfordshire when he returned from his island solitude. Similarly, Pinney, a member of the family which acquired a West Indian fortune, wrote in 1778 that his 'greatest pride is to be considered as a private country gentleman, therefore I am resolved to content myself with a title and shall avoid even the name of a West Indian.'

A 'title' was perhaps too modest. Land values almost doubled between 1700 and 1790 as more land, approximately a further 4,000,000 acres, was brought into cultivation and as agriculture became more productive. At no point did the growth of industry imply that farming languished: 'while manufacturers are flourishing and increasing,' wrote the Reverend John Howlett in 1772, 'agriculture will flourish with them.' There was no spectacular agricultural revolution, and some of the corn-growing areas even faced depression during the 1730s and 1740s, but there were so many changes over the country as a whole, most with their origins in the seventeenth century, that they have been compared to the movement of a tide. 'Move your eyes which side you will,' wrote Arthur Young, eloquent advocate of agricultural improvement, 'you behold nothing but great riches and yet greater resources.' One economic historian has calculated that in 1700 each person engaged in farming fed 1·7 persons, whereas in 1800 each fed 2·5 persons, an increase of 47 per cent. Even so, England ceased to be a regular net exporter of wheat and wheaten flour in 1750 (the peak year for exports) and there were net imports in 1757 and 1758, and regularly after 1767, due to the rise in population which can be traced back to the mid-1730s.

The merits of improved farming – better use of soil, crops, cattle, tools (like Jethro Tull's famous drill) and farm layout – were much publicized, notably by Arthur Young, who himself was a failure as a farmer; his *Six Weeks' Tour through the Southern Counties of England* appeared in 1768, eight years after the accession of George III (1760–1820), who liked to consider himself a farmer king. Livestock and potatoes were sources of lively controversy. Oil paintings of the bulls and, of course, the horses of the period hung alongside portraits and landscapes in large numbers of new eighteenth-century houses, gems of the landscape, many of which began as farmhouses.

The geographical area most publicized by Young, who began to publish his *Annals of Agriculture* in 1784, was the county of Norfolk. It was there that experimenters in crop rotation developed the so-called 'new husbandry', which enabled fields to be cultivated continuously with no years in fallow. They were able to provide hay and winter feeding stock for sheep and cattle, making possible an increase in the numbers of livestock and thereby in the quantity of manure. 'Half the county of Norfolk within the memory of man had yielded nothing but sheep feed,' but now, it was claimed, 'those very tracts of land are covered with as fine barley and rye as any in the world and great quantities of wheat besides.' Thomas Coke, later Earl of Leicester, the great improver who enjoyed such financial success that under his management the value of produce from his estate increased fourfold within fifteen years, was the name chiefly associated with the changes in Norfolk, but he had his predecessors, notably 'Turnip Townshend' and the Prime Minister Robert Walpole. There were some counties, like Gloucestershire, where Coke could not persuade farmers to change their ways, or Hertfordshire, where as late as 1804 Young travelled 'near one hundred miles' without seeing 'drilled crops'. Even as late as the 1840s there were as many acres under fallow as under turnips.

Leicestershire was publicized for its agricultural change at least as much as Norfolk, and visitors from all over Europe visited Robert Bakewell's farm at Dishley Grange, near Loughborough, to admire his horses, cattle and sheep, which he considered as 'machines for turning grass into mutton', although they were dismissed by his critics as 'too dear to buy and too fat to eat'. It was not always big farmers or those who were most publicity-conscious, who succeeded in the long run: Bakewell's hospitality was too lavish and he bankrupted himself. Meanwhile, the spread of what became great English breeds, like Herefordshire cattle or Southdown sheep, went on successfully without being a matter of controversy. While counties like Norfolk and Gloucestershire turned increasingly to arable farming, those like Leicestershire were turning increasingly to livestock. Indeed, in 1790 William Marshall could describe Leicestershire as 'a continuous sheet of greensward'. The most flexible system was mixed farming, which had the extra advantage of maintaining soil fertility.

Continuing enclosure was a necessary part of the process of agricultural 'improvement', and following the enclosure of the clay fields of the Midland counties in the earlier part of the century, between 2,000,000 and 3,000,000 acres of open fields and waste lands in the Midlands, south and east, were enclosed between 1760 and 1799. The procedure used was usually enclosure by act of parliament rather than by voluntary agreement or pressure. A successful Enclosure Act did not require local unanimity but it did require enough money to pay for the lawyers' and surveyors' fees and for fences, hedges, roads and drainage after the bill had been passed. This was largely a formality since the Enclosure Commissioners appointed to survey the land invariably favoured the parties wishing to enclose, and so too did Parliament, which passed a general Enclosure Act in 1801 simplifying future procedures. By then more than 1,300 Enclosure Acts had been passed since 1760. Almost 1,000 more were to come between 1800 and 1820.

Contemporaries thought that farmers who favoured enclosure were 'new men in point of knowledge and ideas' (a description suggested by the physical appearance of farmers at Banbury market), while Young believed that enclosure itself quickened enterprise: it 'changed the man as much as it has improved the country'. Inevitably, big men led the way. 'It will at once be apparent,' Young wrote, 'that no small farmers could effect such great things as have been done in Norfolk. Great farms are the soul of Norfolk culture; split them into tenures of an hundred pounds a year, and you will find nothing but beggars and weeds in the whole county.' However, the demand for enclosure came from their tenant farmers – about three-quarters of English land was cultivated by them at the end of the century – and from small landlords too: there was a drive to consolidate holdings and to eliminate waste. Yeomen who could be tempted to augment their capital by selling their freeholds and go on to become tenant farmers were another category again.

Enclosure and agricultural change transformed the appearance of the rural environment. Even by the 1760s Smollett described it as 'smiling with cultivation . . . parcelled out into beautiful enclosures'. As the fields were enclosed, woodlands and wastes disappeared and a new pattern of hedges, walls, fences and roads took shape. 'I admit I was often amazed,' wrote a German visitor who returned to England in the early nineteenth century, 'to see great uncultivated areas made productive as though through magic and transformed into fine, corn-bearing fields.' Not until the late twentieth century was there to be such a drastic transformation in the appearance of the countryside.

There was certainly wealth to be made out of enclosure: rent rolls rose, farm profits were boosted and styles of life changed. Yet some of the big men were attacked, as their ancestors had been in previous centuries, as oppressors of the 'indignant many', and even of lesser men Cobbett could write that 'when farmers become gentlemen their labourers become slaves.' Young himself, often inconsistent, came to feel that enclosure led to human suffering. While he believed that labourers in parishes without enclosure worked 'like negroes and did not live so well as the inhabitants of the poor house', he admitted that, 'by nineteen enclosure bills in twenty, the poor are injured, and in some cases grossly injured.'

Enclosure threatened the independence of a number of people who had previously felt themselves to be independent. Nor did it help when they were told by Sir Frederick Eden, author of an invaluable late eighteenth-century book on the state of the poor, that 'it is one of the natural consequences of freedom that those who are left to shift for themselves must sometimes be reduced to want.' Just as 'independence' was later prized by craftsmen in the age of the machine, so too it was prized by cultivators whose holdings were so small that access to common land was of vital importance to them: they had no capital at their disposal to build fences, drains or barns. Squatters on common land were, of course, those who suffered the most: they had no legal rights and they were often evicted without ceremony. For a time the actual process of enclosure itself might provide them with work, but in the long run it left many of them paupers. Not surprisingly, therefore, they might become disaffected.

> They hang the man and flog the woman
> That steals a goose from off the common
> But leave the greater criminal loose
> That steals the common from the goose.

Political discontent might accompany demoralization. 'The poor . . . may say, and with truth, Parliament may be tender of property; all I know is, I had a cow and an Act of Parliament has taken it from me.' Enclosure turned land into absolute private property and quickened suspicion both of the law which enshrined that process and of the justices of the peace who administered it; it was one more demonstration of Oliver Goldsmith's dictum that 'laws grind the poor and rich men grind the law.' And although what was happening seemed irrevocable, poor men in the nineteenth century might still dream of repossessing the land, and even seek actively to repossess it long after the process of enclosure had been completed.

There had been strains in the village community long before eighteenth-century enclosure and deserted villages long before Oliver Goldsmith wrote about them. But there could now be a sense of crisis. Thus the village of Wigston Magna in Leicestershire, the population of which had tripled between 1524 and 1765, was completely transformed by an enclosure of 1765. The small owner–occupiers (two-thirds of the population owned less than fifty acres) virtually disappeared as a group within sixty or seventy years, becoming instead rural labourers, framework knitters or paupers. In 1754 local poor rate expenditures amounted to £95; in 1802 they amounted to £1,776.

In many parts of the country local magistrates decided to grant outdoor relief allowances to the poor when bad harvests led to soaring wheat prices, and went on to prepare formal scales of wage support even when such peak points of distress were passed. The best-known example was that of Speenhamland, a village in Berkshire which gave its name to such a system of allowances; yet the 'system' was never universally or consistently applied, and it is wrong to divide England into 'Speenhamland' and 'non-Speenhamland' counties. The number of workhouses enforcing labour on the able-bodied poor also increased between 1776 and 1801. A General Workhouse Act which enabled parishes to build a workhouse if they wished had existed since 1723, and by 1776 there were almost 2,000 such places, usually with twenty-five to thirty inmates, while a further Act of 1782, Gilbert's Act, permitted parishes to combine into unions to deal with their poor law problems. Such changes, often supported by humanitarians, ushered in the last stage in the history of the 'old poor law'.

It was to become increasingly expensive to operate in the early nineteenth century and increasingly irrelevant to the needs of a more industrialized society. The origins of that society lay in the eighteenth century. It ended with two decades of spectacular industrial advance, but already by the beginning of the century, when the word 'industry' still designated a quality of human beings not a sector of the economy, Defoe had observed that 'an estate is but a pond, but trade is a spring'. His successors might have added that 'industry' could be a fountain. By the end of the century the word was already beginning to suggest fire and smoke.

The Quaker Ambrose Crowley, Tyneside ironmaster, made a fortune out of his great works. By 1760 Ben Truman had a brewing plant valued at £30,000 and a floating capital of over £100,000. Abraham Darby, another Quaker, was the first man to smelt iron with coke, in 1709; he transformed Coalbrookdale in Shropshire. Matthew Boulton, who started business as a button maker, was dealing successfully in all kinds of metal enterprises before he met James Watt in 1769, and his great works at Soho, near Birmingham, were described by a local poet as 'Europe's Wonder and Britannia's pride'. Richard Arkwright, who had opened his first factory at Nottingham in 1768, built a handsome new factory at Cromford in Derbyshire three years later, and when he died in 1792 he left many factories the income of which was greater than that of most German principalities. Josiah Wedgwood, the potter, who had founded the Wedgwood Potteries in 1759, the 'year of victories', was clever enough to be made a Fellow of the Royal Society in 1783, and left a fortune of £500,000.

The politician Edmund Burke, who after the French Revolution was to lambast popular English radicals and in turn be lambasted by them, suggested that there was another side to the picture, as there was in the village. Indeed, he did not hesitate to draw comparison between English slaves and slaves overseas.

> I suppose that there are in Great Britain upwards of a hundred thousand people employed in lead, tin, iron, copper and coal mines . . . An hundred thousand more at least are tortured without remission by the suffocating smoke, intense fires and constant drudgery necessary in refining and managing the production of those mines.

In fact, conditions varied. Crowley's men were ordered to work; those to whom he gave poor relief – and he believed both in that and in health care – had to wear a badge inscribed 'Crowley's Poor'. Arkwright's men were attracted to work at Cromford by good conditions, but they were also expected to sing:

> Come let us all here join in one,
> And thank him for all favours done;
> Let's thank him for all favours still
> Which he hath done beside the mill.

A significant proportion of the new labour force consisted of child pauper apprentices brought in from London parishes; they had no choice in the matter.

The eighteenth century did not create contrasts, but it added to them. There were child chimney sweeps before there were factory children and disgruntled and unevenly employed craftsmen before there were discontented and unemployed factory workers. It was a tile hewer who complained:

> My trade and occupation
> Was ground for lamentation,
> Which makes me curse my station
> And wish I'd ne'er been born.
> I ne'er can save one shilling
> And must – which is killing
> A pauper die when old.

Any picture of the eighteenth century that focused exclusively on poverty would be completely misleading as far as both structures and motives were concerned. Between the aristocracy, the gentry, the yeomen, the tenant farmers and the landless labourers on the one hand and the employers, industrial workmen and craftsmen on the other, there were extremely large numbers of 'middling folk', who increased in numbers and income during the eighteenth century, and growing groups of professional people. Below them, as always, there was an 'underground' – vagrants, sharpers, cheats, thieves, the 'upside-down world' of John Gay's *The Beggar's Opera* (1728). There could be heroes in the underground, among poachers and highwaymen in particular. There were few heroes among the rest, except the heroes of the Services. Indeed, the eighteenth century – after Marlborough – is more remembered for its clubs than for its heroes.

The role of the 'middling folk' in work and leisure – with their own gradations of status – has long been recognized; indeed, it was fully recognized at the time. They were involved in a wide variety of occupations, respectable or otherwise, rural or urban (the two were never completely set apart), and all of them 'bearing', in the words of one contemporary, 'the heat of the day'. They had more opportunities of making money than ever before, and like the rich, whom they were often accused of imitating, they had more opportunities of spending it.

So too had lawyers, who benefited directly from the growing volume of legal business. Their professional income came from fees, not from trade, and for this reason, and because many of them came from 'good families', they were clearly distinguished from 'middling folk'. There was no doubt that they, like physicians (if not apothecaries) and army officers, were 'gentlemen', a word much used in the eighteenth century. So too were clergymen, though there were considerable nuances of status in their case. 'Men of letters', artists and musicians were whole spectra in themselves, fashionable or 'Bohemian' (the use of the word had not been coined), independent or servile. Samuel Johnson, best remembered of them, knew well the variety of possible conditions.

Women, however, have left only a limited record of their own condition. As to male thoughts on women, for Lord Chesterfield they were 'children of a larger growth' and 'a man of sense only trifles with them.' For Johnson himself 'the chastity of women' was of 'all importance since property depends on it'. There were contradictions in male views. Some women were associated with pleasure; married women were associated with property; and respectable unmarried women – the word 'spinster' was used to describe them in 1719 – were associated with charity. It was enough for the great lawyer Blackstone that 'in marriage husband and wife are one person, and that person is the husband.'

Spending was in vogue and could benefit artists, men of letters and musicians along with those engaged in service trades of every kind. This was an age when fashion counted, when tastes were becoming more sophisticated and when considerable effort was being made – successfully – to satisfy them. Arthur Young, who objected to 'the poor' treating tea as a 'necessary' and to farmers or farmers' wives buying pianos, could talk in 1771, the year of the first coloured fashion-plate (in *The Lady Magazine*), of 'universal luxury'. Handbags had only been introduced during the previous decade, but by the end of the century they were to be called 'indispensables'. So too were umbrellas. By 1800 there were 153 shops in Oxford Street in London, catering for the 'whim-whams and fribble-frabble of fashion'. London was unique – in its growth as well as in its variety: to be 'tired of London' for Johnson was to be 'tired of life'. There was manifest pride in this, and pride too that London novelties, and the 'civilization' which went with them, could be shared by the middle ranks of society in the provinces as well as in London.

Bath, called by Defoe 'the resort of the sound rather than the sick', grew rapidly during the century, from a population of 2,000 in 1700 to 34,000 in 1800, and as it did so an old town gave way to a sparkling new one. Near by, Bristol prided itself not only on its trade but on the fact that its 'theatrical performances are little inferior (if any) to those in London'. Liverpool, a northern port which was to grow at the expense of Bristol and in 1800 was the second largest city in the kingdom, prided itself not only on its 'elegant houses' but on its imposing public buildings. And even in Leeds an inhabitant noted soon after the beginning of the nineteenth century that whereas he could remember a time when 'there were not seven carriages' kept in the city, 'now there are a hundred'. A subscription library, still in existence, was opened in 1768. Birmingham, like many other towns, had its Assembly Rooms: they were dignified with the French name of *Hôtel*. It too had its own theatre by 1774 and a subscription library had been opened six years earlier.

By then local urban amenities were as much in demand as new country houses with engaging 'prospects' (and new stables and gardens); and in both town and country there were the same aspirations to acquire elegant mahogany furniture made by Chippendale, Sheraton and Hepplewhite, Adam brothers decorations, silver tableware, porcelain teasets and chinoiserie. For the wealthy who looked further afield it was also the great age of the Grand Tour through France, Italy and Germany, which was thought of by landlords and squires as not the least important stage in education for living, more important perhaps than the university stage, which was for the very few:

> His honour posts o'er Italy and France,
> Measures St Peter's dome, and learns to dance

returning home

> Half atheist, papist, forester, bubble, rook,
> Half fiddler, coachman, dancer, groom and cook.

Public school education provided for those who had access to it –
and in this period they were not only the very rich – a necessary
classical preparation. It was left to dissenting academies to pursue
scientific education with a practical bent: they catered intelligently
for Congregationalists, Unitarians and others, offering a
challenging as well as a useful curriculum.

To know the rules of polite taste did not need too much formal
education. Richard Steele and Joseph Addison had pointed the
way to their definition early in the century in essays in *The Tatler*
(1709–11) and *The Spectator* (1711–12), and as the century went by
(with, it should be added, significant changes of taste and fashion)
the rules were clearly defined, as in the work of the painter Sir
Joshua Reynolds, the first President of the Royal Academy,
founded in 1768; in the design and layout of rural and urban
buildings and gardens (the great Capability Brown, redesigner of
nature, was the son of a tradesman); in the framing of heroic
couplets in 'poetic diction'; in the oratorios of the German-born
composer Handel, who arrived from Hanover in 1710 and
composed his *Messiah* in 1741; in the formal dance steps of the
great ball; in spelling books and dictionaries, which increasingly
standardized the language.

Yet it was a sign of the vitality of the period that none of the
rules was universally accepted and that neither exuberance nor
prophecy could be completely constrained within set limits. The
great poet William Blake, a man of genius, hated Reynolds and all
that he stood for. Ordering nature (like philosophizing about it)
was followed by, sometimes accompanied by, newly discovered
delight in 'the picturesque' – including moors and mountains and
sentimental musing about landscapes and ruins. Gothic buildings
were built, sometimes near Palladian buildings. There were early
stirrings of 'romanticism', which was to blossom in the romantic
poetry of Byron, Wordsworth and Keats. 'Enthusiasm' always
had its devotees, despite Johnson's definition of it as the 'heat of

imagination' and 'violence of passion' in his great *Dictionary* of 1755.

The ordered novels of Jane Austen, who was born in 1775, were admired by the Prince Regent (they did include one gentle satire of a horror tale), but in her own time they never attracted the kind of admiration reserved for men of letters of the early eighteenth century. Yet even then 'Grub Street' had been a subject of satire; and the appeal of the novel itself as a new form was itself a matter of controversy. There were, indeed, as many shifts of approval and disapproval in the eighteenth century as in the nineteenth, so that the detailed story of eighteenth-century enjoyment and enrichment demands a carefully compiled chronology which takes account of literary and aesthetic currents and their eddies at every stage. It must take account also of new economic circumstances affecting patronage and the public, including the rise of publishing and the growth of a feminine readership. Goldsmith was only one of several writers who objected to 'writing being converted into a mechanic trade' and to booksellers 'instead of the great' becoming 'the patrons and paymasters of men of genius'.

One reason why sophistication was so much accented throughout the century was that eighteenth-century life could be extremely raw. There was a place in it for roughnecks alongside rakes, buffoons alongside *savants*. Nor were the boundaries always easy to define in practice. Elegance and squalor coexisted. Far more people died young than old, and if there was no plague there was still fever. Similarly, one reason why order was so much accented was that eighteenth-century life could be extremely violent – verbally in the pamphlet and the broadsheet; physically in the ring, and in the street – and the boundaries between political demonstration and crime were not always easy to define either. Henry Fielding, author of *Tom Jones*, who was a magistrate as well as a novelist, had strong views about both.

The principles of authority and hierarchy were frequently challenged, not as the result of any faltering of purpose on the part of government, which set out to uphold them with the full force of law (especially during the French Revolution and the long struggles with Napoleonic France which began in 1793), but by political, religious and economic discontent. In an attempt to deal with crime, rural and urban, the Waltham Black Act of 1724 created no less than fifty new capital offences, most of them concerned with attacks on property. Yet although there were now nearly a hundred capital offences on the Statute Book, no more than two hundred people a year were actually hanged. One effective statutory intervention was the Gin Act of 1751, which, through heavy taxation, brought to an end a 'gin era' which had begun in 1720 and which inspired Hogarth to present his contrast between what happened in Gin Lane and Beer Lane.

In the countryside a 'moral economy' was acknowledged which in practice allowed for the expression of discontent through ritualized behaviour (including tolerated but circumscribed violence) when food prices were high; the crowd assumed that their views of what was right would be appreciated if not shared. In the cities, however, there was already more uncertainty about both motivation and behaviour. London, in particular, was a frequent scene of unritualized rioting, most notably in the Wilkes Riots of 1763 and the Gordon Riots of 1780. Indeed, it has been claimed that in financial terms ten times as much damage was done to London property during the week of the Gordon Riots as was done to Paris throughout the French Revolution. The riots, provoked by the repeal of some of the Penal Laws against Roman Catholics (notably concerning the right to acquire and inherit property), began with cries of 'No Popery', but as they went on targets included rich men's houses. Everything was out of control. Nor was there any police force to attempt to control it.

The circulation of radical ideas during the French Revolution further inflamed passions: Thomas Paine's *Rights of Man* was the most disturbing book, which led to fierce controversy: it stirred into action what Burke called contemptuously 'the swinish multitude', while at the same time encouraging supporters of 'King, Constitution and Country' to create their own organizations. It was in Birmingham, not London, that Paine was burned in effigy in 1793 and a hostile crowd provoked not by radicals but by conservatives attacked the house of Joseph Priestley, the non-conformist preacher, writer and scientist.

Priestley was a product of the dissenting academies. John Wesley, whose 'enthusiastic' religion was very different from Priestley's 'enlightened' Unitarianism, was a product of Oxford. Priestley seemed far removed from the poor, although he recognized their rights; Wesley appealed to them, although he stressed their duties. In 1738 Wesley had been 'converted' to a 'religion of the heart', open to all, rich or poor, and he preached it fearlessly. The Church of England was dominated at that time by bishops and clergymen who thought of Christianity in terms of virtue and prudence rather than in terms of salvation and judgement. In consequence, Wesley, who remained a member of the Church to his death, was often treated as fiercely as any Unitarian as he travelled 25,000 miles from parish to parish, claiming the whole world as his own parish. With his own history of personal redemption he made many converts, 'the people called Methodists', who eventually were to form a Church of their own and to spawn sects: one of them, the 'Primitives', was to produce not only preachers but future radical and labour leaders.

Evangelicalism inside the established Church was a more powerful force even than Methodism, for there were still less than 100,000 Methodists at the end of the eighteenth century at a time when the so-called 'Saints', with William Wilberforce, a friend of William Pitt, prominent among them, were demanding from places of power a wholesale 'reformation of manners'. Bitterly opposed to the French Revolution, they were concerned at this time too with the struggle to free the slaves overseas, a successful struggle, strongly supported by the Quakers: the trade, with all its entrenched interests, was abolished by Act of Parliament in 1807 in the middle of the wars against Napoleon. Already, by the beginning of the nineteenth century, as G. M. Young has written, 'virtue was advancing on a broad invincible front,' and when Napoleon was defeated in 1815 the Evangelicals were to claim a share in the victory on the grounds that they had provided a moral armour for the nation.

Moral armour would not have been enough. The expensive wars against Napoleon could not have been won had England not been a far richer country at the end of the century than it was at the beginning, and the riches were now coming increasingly from the growth of industry. With that growth, the moral economy of the crowd was to give way to the political economy of the market place and of the factory; and within this new and never static context what was cheap was to matter more in practice than what was elegant or what was fair. At the same time, the fact that England's revolution, unlike the French Revolution of 1789, was industrial not political meant that there was less emphasis on equality than on development. In such a society the pursuit of pleasure, while it continued, became suspect to the 'industrious'. There was little place for it among the smoke.

8

THE EXPERIENCE OF
INDUSTRIALIZATION

Were we required to characterize this age of ours by any single
epithet, we should be tempted to call it . . . the Mechanical Age.
                              Thomas Carlyle, *Signs of the Times*, 1829

Whilst the engine runs, the people must work – men, women and
children are yoked together with iron and steam. The animal
machine – breakable in the best case . . . is chained fast to the iron
machine, which knows no suffering and no weariness.
              J. P. Kay, *Moral and Physical Conditions of the Operatives
              Employed in the Cotton Manufacture in Manchester*, 1832

It is a historic irony that the nation that gave birth to the industrial
revolution, and exported it throughout the world, should have
become embarrassed at the measure of its success.
                         M. J. Wiener, *English Culture and the Decline
                                        of the Industrial Spirit*, 1981

THERE was a time when the study of the English industrial
revolution, the first of its kind in the world, was left almost
entirely to social historians. They sympathized deeply with the
poor, usually considered the beneficiaries of revolution, who
were felt to be its victims in this case. 'The English people never,
by any plague, or famine, or war,' wrote the Oxford historian
Frederick York Powell in 1901, 'suffered such a deadly blow at its
vitality as by the establishment of the factory system without the
proper safeguards.'

Values were more prominent than facts in such studies. Thus, when in the 1880s Arnold Toynbee argued that more had been destroyed than created through the smoke of the industrial revolution, he had long historical perspectives in view. For him the essence of the revolution was neither the spectacular transformation of the coal, iron and textile industries nor the development of steam power, but 'the substitution of competition for the medieval regulations which had previously controlled the production and distribution of wealth'. However, although many of these regulations, including those relating to wages and employment, continued to be invoked, they had in fact ceased to be effective *before* the industrial revolution.

The same inadequacies of general explanation are obvious also in a number of more recent interpretations by economic historians, some of whom have been tempted to treat the industrial revolution as a simple success story, others to eliminate altogether the sense of a break, even of revolution. They have been right, of course, to point out that mechanization and power production were not triumphant until the middle of the nineteenth century and to insist that cumulative economic processes led up to the changes a century earlier. They have also been right to take other factors into account: England's (and Britain's) intricate overseas trade connections before the industrial revolution; the large numbers of middlemen; the existence of rural industries before the rise of factories; the developed mechanical skills of many Englishmen as water power was harnessed before the coming of the steam engine; the increase in population; and the growing demand for a wide range of products, including simple products which could be made cheaper by new forms of processing. Daniel Defoe had noted most of these aspects of the English economy early in the eighteenth century, and when William Hutton went to busy Birmingham in 1741 he found there a 'vivacity' which he had never seen before. 'I had been among dreamers, but now I saw men awake.'

Nonetheless, there was the sense of a leap forward in the late eighteenth century. Human and animal strength were replaced, or supplemented, by machines and inanimate power; output figures soared. Coal production doubled between 1750 and 1800, then increased twenty-fold in the nineteenth century; within that sequence it was to double between 1800 and 1830 and again between 1830 and 1845. Pig-iron production rose four times between 1740 and 1788 and quadrupled again during the next twenty years; it was to increase more than thirty fold in the nineteenth century. Raw cotton imports quintupled between 1780 and 1800 and rose thirty-fold during the nineteenth century, as cotton supplanted wool as England's main textile. Many other indices, notably those relating to the falling proportion of the population involved in agriculture, tell the same story. Neither these quantitative changes, nor the paths of growth themselves, were smooth or continuous, and business rhythms led sometimes to 'boom', sometimes to 'crisis', yet it was as a result of this massive, if jerky, capitalist development, still related to the fortunes of the harvest, that England produced the kind of society that is only now, belatedly, beginning to seem obsolete. It did not spring into existence fully formed, and it incorporated many elements from the past, but for most people this is 'where we came in'.

One necessary lever of change, often feared then as it is today, was invention, without which it would have been impossible to achieve such huge increases in output. As D. N. McCloskey has put it, 'ingenuity rather than abstention' was what counted. Nonetheless, more than half the achieved technical progress between 1780 and 1860, measured in terms of the contribution made to aggregate economic growth, lay with a few sectors of the economy. It owed little directly to science and much to empirical efforts, including rule of thumb, although an interest in science inspired some of the inventors and led them to believe that nothing was impossible. Moreover, bodies like the Royal Society for the Encouragement of Arts, Manufacture and Commerce in Great Britain, founded in 1754, directed the spirit of inventiveness into *useful* channels. Ingenuity by itself was not enough.

The success of the inventors themselves, who came from varying social backgrounds and ranged from millwrights to clergymen, required qualities other than inventiveness. Business acumen was one of those. The Scotsman James Watt, who revolutionized the use of steam power and died a national hero, found a perfect partner in 1773 in Birmingham's Matthew

Boulton. Meanwhile, Henry Cort, the inventor of a crucial puddling and rolling process (1781) that made possible a huge increase in the production of wrought iron, was 'treated shamelessly by the business people, who are ignorant asses one and all,' as Watt himself observed. Other inventors fell foul of their fellow workmen: thus, John Kay, inventor of the flying shuttle (1733), had his home attacked and had to flee to France.

Some of the inventors worked in solitude behind the scenes; others, like the businessmen with whom they had to cooperate unless they became businessmen themselves, were publicity-minded, and their skills, like those of the great potter Josiah Wedgwood, turned to marketing and the exploitation of fashion. The enthusiastic foundry-owner John Wilkinson, who helped to make England iron-conscious, had an iron boat, which was as well known as his iron coffin. After Wilkinson's death the story spread that he would rise out of the coffin and visit his blast furnaces seven years later, and a large crowd gathered for the resurrection.

It is as much the adoption of technological innovation as the innovation itself that constitutes the social history of the industrial revolution. The dynamics of adoption were relatively simple in general terms if complex in detail. There had to be willingness to take risks, although it appears that economic growth may have tended to produce entrepreneurs rather than vice versa, and there had to be capital. Rags to riches was not the usual story. Legal barriers, notably the patent law, might stand in the way of change; conversely, holding a patent could be a spur to effort and there was frequently an articulate demand for a particular invention. 'We want as many spotted Muslins and Fancy Muslins as you can make,' a northern cotton spinner was informed by his London agent in 1786. 'You must look to Invention, Industry you have in abundance . . . As the sun shines let us make Hay.' More often, one successful invention led to a demand for a complementary invention (in cotton spinning and cotton weaving, for example): thus, so long as business and consumer expectations were high, one technological change generated another.

Yet there were many economic activities that by 1860 were still relatively little touched by invention: in a labour force which was more specialized than that which had existed in 1780, only three out of ten people were employed in activities that had been radically transformed in technique since 1780. Nor was human strength completely obsolete, as boilermakers (or dockers) of later generations would testify. There were also large numbers of out-workers, sub-contractors and, at the base, casual workers, including 'wandering tribes' of migrant labourers; and there were more domestic servants than operatives in the textile industry, more males engaged in building and construction than in mining and quarrying and more still engaged in agriculture, horticulture and fishing than in construction and mining combined.

The numbers of miners were increasing, however: there were 216,000 of them in 1851 and 495,000 thirty years later. Coal was the fuel of the industrial revolution, both metaphorically and literally. There was a sufficiently wide new repertoire of skills, particularly following the development of machine tools and precision engineering, to produce what Sir Robert Peel, Prime Minister and son of a cotton manufacturer, called 'an additional race of men'. He should have added women and, in the first stages of industrialization, children.

The main new unit of production in the most advanced sectors of the economy was the factory, which concentrated production in one place and imposed a new discipline on the workforce, where women and children were prominent, and by the 1820s and 1830s observers and workers alike knew that the 'factory system' had come to stay. Its defenders took pride in the claim that it was a revolutionary system opening up future possibilities of complete automation, 'the great minister of civilization to the terraqueous globe,' as Andrew Ure called it in his *Philosophy of Manufacture* (1834). Its critics saw it as an agency of social (particularly family) disorganization.

It was success in the 'dynamic' sectors of the economy which made possible a substantial growth of *per capita* income between the 1780s and the 1860s, despite a three-fold increase in population that was related to the economic growth in complex and con- troversial ways. Whereas previously larger numbers had pressed hard on the means of subsistence during periods of population growth – and during the sixteenth and seventeenth centuries may have halved the incomes of the poor – average incomes now rose. Phyllis Deane has calculated that the average *per capita* income of the total population, which had been around £8–9 a year in 1700 and £12–13 fifty years later, rose to £22 by 1800 and doubled again by 1860. Behind this rise in incomes was an increase in capital, although the proportion of national investment to national income was stable at around 13–14 per cent during most decades between 1780 and 1860. On the eve of the industrial revolution, durable national assets other than land, the oldest asset, accounted for less than one-third of the national capital of Great Britain; by 1860 their share had increased to a half.

Not all these relevant statistics of economic growth were known to contemporaries, but those that were known fascinated them as much as they have fascinated recent economic historians; the successive editions of the statistician G. R. Porter's *Progress of the Nation*, which first appeared in 1836, recorded such rapid change that they were said 'to partake of the nature of a periodical'. They were a matter of widespread (though not universal) pride, particularly when placed in their international context. In 1780 the national output of iron was smaller than that of France; by 1848 it was greater than that of the rest of the world. By then, also, coal output was two-thirds, and cotton cloth more than half, of total world output. In 1851, when a Great Exhibition of the products of all the Nations was held in the Crystal Palace, over half the 14,000 exhibitors represented Great Britain and her colonies. In the 'age of the machine' Britain stood out as 'the workshop of the world'.

Yet the qualitative changes impressed the Victorians most. 'The Crystal Palace,' wrote one of them, 'is an outstanding sign of the mind of the age. It could not have taken place half a generation back . . . It could not have been imagined by the chivalry of the middle ages.' The new glass building designed by the Duke of Devonshire's gardener, Joseph Paxton – who was extolled, not surprisingly, as a model of self-help – was often compared with a temple; its length was, indeed, three times that of St Paul's Cathedral. And the objects exhibited inside conveyed the message of visible 'progress' more eloquently than statistics. A contemporary writer drew the proper lesson – that 'Englishmen employ their capital, but are ever seeking for mechanical means to work it.' It was right and proper too that there should be an enormous block of coal, weighing twenty-four tons, at the entrance to the Exhibition (although it was placed next to a statue of Richard Coeur de Lion), and that many of the objects on display inside came from distant countries. 'The products of all quarters of the globe are placed at our disposal,' wrote Albert, Victoria's Prince Consort, who had much to do with the success of the Exhibition, 'and we have only to choose that which is best and cheapest for our purposes, and the powers of production are entrusted to the stimulus of competition and capital.' Free trade and free competition were already gospel.

Yet this was only part of the story. The object of both free trade and free competition, it was claimed, was to lower prices. 'It is very odd,' wrote a French visitor enviously in 1851. 'An aristocratic country like England is successful at supplying the people, whereas France, a democratic country, is only good at producing goods for the aristocracy.' There was certainly a wide repertoire of consumer goods, including matches, steel pens and envelopes, in use and on display at the Exhibition. And the postage stamp too was a Victorian invention, started by the beautiful Penny Black of 1840. Later in the century there was to be a striking expansion of mass markets, with new kinds of shops offering a perpetual display: William Whitely, 'the Universal Provider', opened a great department store in London in 1863, while one enterprising retailer in Liverpool, David Lewis, described himself and his staff as 'Friends of the People'. By the end of the century there were also many chains of shops: Jesse Boot, the Nottingham chemist, owned 181 local shops, Thomas Lipton, the grocer, had more than sixty in London alone, and Michael Marks and Tom Spencer had launched their business from a stall in Leeds Market.

Optimistic Victorians believed, therefore, that the industrial revolution had made possible for the first time not only 'the conquest of Nature' but also 'the betterment of the species'. In the enthusiastic language of Samuel Smiles, who more than any other nineteenth-century writer popularized the heroes of the industrial revolution and proclaimed their values, there was 'a harvest of wealth and prosperity'. 'We are an old people,' he added, 'but a young nation . . . The civilization of what we call "the masses" has scarcely begun.' Smiles's sense of newness had been anticipated by an earlier writer in 1843 who stressed that steam power had no precedent and the spinning jenny no ancestry: 'the mule and the power loom entered into no prepared heritage: they sprang into sudden existence like Minerva from the brains of Jupiter.' And the editor of the new periodical *Engineering* wrote in a similar tone in 1866:

> Engineering has done more than war and diplomacy; it has done more than the Church and the Universities; it has done more than abstract philosophy and literature. It has done . . . more than our laws have done . . . to change society. We have . . . reached an age of luxury, but without effeminacy. Few of our middle class . . . could be induced to exchange their homes and appliances for comfort for the noblest villas of ancient Rome.

Smiles, as much interested in civil as in mechanical engineering, was most interested of all in 'the civilization of what we call "the masses"'. So too was William Whewell, Master of Trinity College, Cambridge, who thought 'useful application' was 'the name of the great engine working on the railway of civilization'. This conception of industrialization was taken up in the late twentieth century by Charles Snow. With the Northern and Midlands machine breakers of 1812 in mind, he argued that only 'Luddites, including intellectual Luddites' could condemn it. Yet his view was over-simplified. The impact of the industrial revolution on the way people lived, thought and felt was greater than that of most political revolutions, and there never was – nor could have been – one single response to it.

There are two main reasons why the Smiles thesis did not command universal assent at the time and why it has been possible for historians, interpreting it from different vantage points in time, to resist its logic. First, although *per capita* incomes increased so substantially, the rich benefited more than the poor. Indeed, there was a contemporary debate, which has been taken up again this century, as to whether the poor benefited at all in the crucial period of early industrialization. And the poor themselves took part in the debate with a new voice.

Critics of industrialization, like the poet Robert Southey, were particularly disturbed by the situation of those workers who were obviously not better-off, like the handloom weavers, who had prospered during the early years of the Napoleonic Wars but who later saw both wages and opportunities for employment fall drastically. There was no question that they were victims of the power loom: the only question was how long it would take them to wither away. In 1820 there were 240,000 of them, nearly half of whom were in Lancashire; there were 123,000 by 1840, and 23,000 by 1856. 'We are shunned by the remainder of society and branded as rogues because we are unable to pay our way,' a weaver in Bury, Lancashire, wrote as early as 1818. Ten years later, one-third of the inhabitants of Colne in the same county were subsisting on twopence a day: their main fare was meal, buttermilk and potatoes with a few gills of ale on Saturday nights. Yet the position of the handloom weavers was exceptional. Real wages, which declined between the end of the Napoleonic Wars in 1815 and 1820, seem to have increased every decade until the Great Exhibition of 1851. It seems also that the earning power of women and children, who were a main source of labour in the factories, kept pace with the increase in the earnings of men. These were years of volatile local prices, however, and of severe unemployment, and the most striking gains to the poor accrued later in the century as prices fell sharply – by 40 per cent between 1875 and 1900.

Much of the early critique of industrialization was moral and sociological rather than economic, although Karl Marx, who lived in England for thirty-four years, tried to discover 'laws of development' and to present a scientific analysis. Thus, Southey compared the rhythms of the seasons with the tempo of the factory, villages with cities, cathedrals with cotton mills and factory children with Negro slaves. There was a romantic element in this response. By the end of the century, however, industry had settled down into routines, and while socialists had systematized their analysis, other new critics of machines and the steam that drove them, like D. H. Lawrence, complained of the deadening effects of industrialization on the sensibilities and on the imagination.*

The second attack on Smiles's interpretation of industrialization came from critics like John Ruskin, who felt that industry not only disturbed human relations but led inevitably to the deterioration of the physical environment. Ruskin foresaw the possibility of twentieth-century England 'set as thick with chimneys as the masts stand in the docks of Liverpool,' with 'no meadows . . . no trees, no gardens'; 'no acre of English ground shall be without its shaft and its engine'. William Morris, convert to socialism, asked bitterly whether all was 'to end in a counting house on the top of a cinder heap, with the pleasures of the eyes having gone from the world'.

Ruskin, with his theory of 'illth' and wealth, was certainly not alone in his response to the industrial landscape. One German visitor, J. G. Kohl, caught the essence of the new environment after a visit to England as early as 1844:

> Imagine black roads winding through verdant fields, the long trains of waggons heavily laden with black treasures . . . burning mounds of coal scattered over the plain, black pit mouths, and here and there an unadorned Methodist chapel or school house, and you will have a tolerable idea of what the English delight to call their 'Black Indies'.

And this picture left out the large industrial towns and cities. In the view of the critics, signs of 'degradation' were never compensated for by canals or railways. 'Here civilization makes its miracles, and civilized man is turned back almost into a savage,' wrote de Tocqueville of Manchester. 'From this foul drain the greatest stream of human industry flows out to fertilize the whole world. From this filthy sewer pure gold flows. Here humanity attains its most complete development and its most brutish.'

During the 1830s and 1840s Manchester was a Mecca for everyone who wished to understand what was happening to society and what would happen to it in the future. Its distinctive characteristics fascinated Marx's friend Friedrich Engels, who lived there as a businessman and wrote his *Condition of the Working Class in England* from a Manchester vantage point. In it he relied heavily on official Blue Books, the famous reports of parliamentary committees of inquiry, a uniquely valuable if often loaded source, and on earlier writers like Peter Gaskell, who regretted the decay of 'community' and the values that went with it, claiming that 'the domestic manufacturer, as a moral and social being, was infinitely superior to the manufacturer of a later date'. Yet Engels himself drew different conclusions from the same data, for while Gaskell perceived the rise of organized labour as the rise of a dangerous *imperium in imperio*, Engels welcomed it as an inevitable agent of revolution – and therefore of salvation. Moreover, like Marx, he enthused about the increase in output in a way that Gaskell would not have done.

Neither Gaskell nor Engels had grasped the whole truth, for there were more modes of social adaptation at both the local and parliamentary levels than simplified diagnoses of society suggested. Community, however strained it might be, did not always lose its integrity, and paternalism could exist, even flourish, in an industrial setting. Workmen, who had more often been attracted into the factories and towns by higher wages and greater social opportunities than coerced into them, were more quickly adapted to the new industrial environment than was often thought at the time, while employers were not all ruthless exploiters. It was said, for example, of one Lancashire employer, Hugh Mason of Ashton, that 'it would be impossible for him to buy the labour of his workpeople and for the workpeople to sell him that labour the same as an ordinary commodity over the counter of a shopkeeper. He felt a deep interest in the welfare of his workpeople.'

England was not reduced to a society of 'two camps', with the 'millionaire commanding whole industrial armies and the wage-slave living only from hand to mouth', as a contemporary socialist put it. There was still a governing class as well as an employing class and large sections of it continued to draw their incomes not from industry but from the land; squires and aristocrats could sometimes sympathize with industrial workers more than with their employers (and vice versa), while some industrial employers were willing to turn the spotlight on bad living and working conditions in the countryside. A model of social action which leaves out these diagonal links (or the ideals of conduct which influenced behaviour) is misleading rather than inadequate.

Religion also retained its force – often divisive and cutting across other social divisions – even though many working men never went to church or chapel. Methodism, particularly Primitive Methodism, could either push working men into, or provide a substitute for, politics.

The new industrial town and city were not the insensate places that some social historians, drawing mainly on secondary evidence, have suggested they were. There was a deep concern about the implications of a huge new population being 'herded' there, but there was city pride too: in freedom from aristocratic influence; in a greater diversity of opinion; in the remarkable range and vitality of voluntary organizations; and, finally, in the belief that the city itself was the 'nidus of a new commonwealth', a phrase coined by a Leeds Nonconformist minister who welcomed the rise of the operatives, whom, he believed, it was completely wrong to categorize as 'masses', a term which displayed ignorance of real people.

'Murky Leeds' itself was a lively place, one of the new breed of industrial cities which, in Yorkshire alone, included nearby and rival Bradford and Sheffield, large numbers of smaller industrial towns like Huddersfield and Rotherham, and industrial villages like Denholme. There were also mining villages and one mining town, Barnsley. At the first census of 1801 (a landmark in social history) there had been only fifteen towns with a population of over 20,000 inhabitants; by 1891 there were sixty-three. Leeds, along with Manchester, Sheffield and Birmingham, experienced a growth rate of over 40 per cent between 1820 and 1830, the decade of most rapid growth, and Manchester's population almost doubled (and that of adjacent Salford almost trebled) again between 1851 and 1901. Meanwhile, the old towns grew far more slowly, though there was growth there too, at differing rates. The population of Oxford, for example, more than doubled between 1801 and 1851, from 12,000 to 28,000, while Winchester increased only from 8,171 (which included nearly 2,000 soldiers) to 13,706. York, now a railway centre, increased from 17,000 to 36,000.

Like old towns, industrial towns had different profiles and were not, as Lewis Mumford was to claim, the same place, Coketown, with different aliases. In particular, there were marked differences in the industrial and social structures of Manchester and Birmingham: in the first there were many great 'capitalists' (the term was beginning to be used), some of them in Richard Cobden's phrase 'sturdy veterans with £100,000 in each pocket', in the second, there were large numbers of small employers. Mercantile Liverpool was different again: here there was a huge floating population of casual workers and of migrants hoping to find their futures abroad. Among the smaller towns, there were marked differences between Oldham, Northampton, Barrow-in-Furness and Middlesbrough, 'the youngest child of England's enterprise'. Old landlords, among them the Duke of Devonshire, might own new streets. So too could new industrialists in model towns like Owen's New Lanark or Titus Salt's Saltaire.

At the same time, there were many common features of cities at this stage of their development. Working-class housing with its long rows of terraces, the Coronation Streets of the future, often looked very similar, particularly when they were built in brick. Railway stations, institutes and public houses – even churches and chapels – might resemble each other too. The key problems of public health and public order faced all towns and cities, old as well as new, as did those of urban transport. The patterns of local government, reformed by the Municipal Corporations Act of 1835, which transferred power to ratepayers, were tested severely in the process. Eventually, late nineteenth-century legislation provided a common framework to deal with these problems, although the drive behind local politics varied, so that municipal development in fact followed different courses and chronologies, with London, the wonder and horror of the age, the exception to most rules in both government and scale of development.

The degree of local determination of policy was substantial enough to persuade city and town councillors that initiative lay with them and not with Parliament in Westminster. 'We have little independent "local authorities", little centres of outlying authority,' wrote Walter Bagehot in 1867. 'When the metropolitan executive most wishes to act, it cannot act effectively because these lesser bodies hesitate, deliberate, or even disobey.' Bagehot was writing at a time when the London vestries were strong and the recently founded Metropolitan Board of Works weak. Yet it was on the eve of a dramatic demonstration of positive and effective local politics in Birmingham. 'Our Corporation,' the local Liberal leader Joseph Chamberlain argued forcefully, 'represents the authority of the people,' and another local advocate of a 'civil gospel' claimed that 'a town is a solemn organism through which shall flow, and in which shall be shaped, all the highest, loftiest and truest ends of man's moral nature.' Under the direction of such men Birmingham municipalized gas and water supplies and carried out a huge scheme of urban improvement. A new Corporation Street was the visible result.

Chamberlain, who was a screw manufacturer before he became a politician, was typical of most early entrepreneurs in that he was associated with a small business. Individual ownership or partnership was the key to the manufacturing system, and businesses were passed on from one generation to the next as if they were landed estates. There was much intermarriage amongst business families too, particularly but not exclusively when the families were Quaker or Unitarian. The great company growth in manufacturing industry, with steel, shipbuilding and chemicals leading the way, came later. There had been important limited liability acts in 1856 and in 1862, consolidating rules relating to the business company, but as late as the 1880s there were, for example, only four limited liability companies in Birmingham. The separation of ownership from control and the development of increasingly specialized management were features of the later, not of the early, industrial revolution, except in banking, a necessary and increasingly institutionalized service in the new industrial society, and in transport. As late as 1882, the paid-up capital of all the companies quoted on the London Stock Exchange was only £64 million out of a total of £5,800 million. Moreover, there was only one significant large-scale amalgamation in England before the 1890s – the Nobel Dynamite Trust of 1886.

In the later industrial revolution Britain's lead was cut as other countries, notably Germany and the United States, the latter with far greater natural resources, themselves experienced industrial revolutions, so that by 1913 Germany was producing 13,500,000 tons of steel, the key new material, and the United States

The growth of London

London at the end of the eighteenth century

London in the 1830s

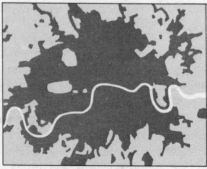

London in the 1870s

31,000,000 as against Britain's 8,000,000 tons. Textiles also faced increasing competition: although there was heavy investment in Lancashire between 1895 and 1914, it was largely in what was by then traditional technology. Coal output rose to a peak of over 270,000,000 tons in the years 1910–14 (as against 66,700,000 tons in the years 1855–60) and coal exports to a peak of 62,700,000 tons. Yet productivity was falling in mining, and in newer industries like chemicals and electrical engineering, industries with a scientific base, other countries were ahead from the start.

It has been claimed recently that the Great Exhibition marked the peak of English confidence in the industrial economy and in the technology which made it possible, and that soon afterwards there was a 'decline of the industrial spirit'. Yet during the thirty years between 1851 and 1881 the national product rose from £523 million (£25 per capita) to £1,051 million (£75 per capita). And exports, on which Britain's international strength depended, rose too, from £100 million in the decade 1850–59 to £160 million in the following decade and £218 million in the next. The tonnage of British shipping rose from 3,600,000 tons in 1850 to 6,600,000 in 1880 and the production of cast iron increased three-fold between 1850 and 1875. Industry itself was certainly not in decline. The greatest Victorian boom had ended by 1875, but while it lasted it was striking enough for Benjamin Disraeli, the Conservative Prime Minister, to describe it as a 'convulsion of prosperity'.

There was ample evidence too of both technical and entre-preneurial ability later in the century and in the years before 1914, and one important new invention, Charles Parsons's steam tur-bine of 1884, which pointed to the future. William Lever's soap enterprise led him to the jungles of West Africa and his successors joined hands with the Dutch in the huge Unilever concern of 1929, the first great European multinational. Ludwig Mond, whose chemical business was eventually to become a key com-ponent in the Imperial Chemical Industries, was another tycoon, and William Armstrong, later of Vickers Armstrong, who vied with Krupps in the world's armament business, was a third. It was through enterprise as well as hard work that in 1913 Britain still accounted for a quarter of the world's trade in manufactured goods (as against 37 per cent in the early 1880s). Its share of the world's industrial production had fallen from over 30 per cent to 13 per cent, yet the rate of growth of the national income (2·3 per cent) was not very different from that of the mid-Victorian years.

Nonetheless, while these years cannot be labelled as years of a 'great depression', as they used to be, they were years of increasing uncertainty. The Cambridge economist Alfred Marshall caught the mood when he wrote in 1908 that while it had been 'inevitable' that the United States and Germany should oust England from its leadership of many industries in the sixty years before, it had not been inevitable 'that she lose so much of it as she has done'. Five points were made in relation to this 'decline'.

First, the financial power of the City of London conveyed more status than the skills and resources of industrial England, and capital which might have been used in England was diverted abroad to countries of formal and informal empire: by 1914 total investment abroad was £4,000,000,000, a far larger figure than that of any other country. It was, and is, a matter of argument whether home industry was inadequately re-equipped in consequence and whether new industries developed as quickly as they might or should have done. 'Plutocrats' who made their money from South African diamonds or Argentina were certainly richer than English industrialists, and, according to one estimate, *rentier* (that is, primarily unearned) incomes in 1913 surpassed the whole budgetary revenue of France, where the term *rentier* had originated.

Second, Britain was said to be lagging behind in the 'new industrial revolution', which called for more research, demanded more standardized equipment and product specification and required a more adaptable labour-force, able and willing to cope with increases in the operating speeds of machinery.

Third, statistics demonstrated the greater productivity of industry in other countries. One estimate for the period from 1870–1907 suggested that the annual average rate of increase of productivity in the United States was over twice that of Britain, and the German rate was even greater.

Fourth, there were vociferous complaints about management, trade unions and education as agents of retardation. Marshall traced a decline in entrepreneurial vigour (sons were not as good as their fathers), while other critics complained that 'the Gospel of Ease' had 'permeated the nation', employers and workers alike. The latter had been hard worked during the early industrial revolution. Now they did not work hard. 'England shows traces of American enterprise and German order,' wrote Arthur Shadwell in 1906, 'but the enterprise is faded and the order muddled.' Employers blamed trade unions for restrictive practices and trade unions blamed employers for not installing up-to-date machinery, while a few foreign critics, notably the French historian Elie Halévy, blamed a tacit collusion between the 'two sides' of industry for a lack of clarity and drive. The inadequacy of technical education and the future of the apprenticeship system had been matters of concern since the 1850s, and the Education Act of 1870 introducing primary schools, provided for out of local rates, came late in the story of industrialization. When the Education Act of 1870 was passed, W. E. Forster, its proposer, told the House of Commons:

> We must not delay. Upon the speedy provision of elementary education depends our industrial prosperity . . . If we are to hold our position among . . . the nations of the world, we must make up the smallness of our numbers by increasing the intellectual force of the individual.

By the end of the century a whole generation had passed through the primary schools, but by then there were additional complaints, to be echoed throughout the twentieth century, not only about inadequate secondary education, substantially expanded only after a further Act of 1902, but about the classical bias of the public schools, their 'neglect of science' and 'hostility to business'. How could the owners or managers of the future be given the right start there? Meanwhile grammar schools, it was said, were producing people who did not know how to use their hands.

Fifth, the 'decline' was blamed on a lack of incentives to workers to become 'American-minded'; wages were low and expectations were low too. Good layout of plant, reasonable conditions of work and managerial efficacy were deemed necessary to encourage individual operatives to work hard and earn as much as they could. Yet English and American circumstances were different, and American trade unions in particular were very different from their English equivalents in terms of both leadership and objectives. Above all, there was an exceptionally strong sense of class in England, affecting daily relationships more than ideology.

It is to the later years of the nineteenth century and the first decade of the twentieth that we should turn for the making or remaking of 'the English working class'. The language of class was a product of early industrialization when, in the words of a contemporary, 'operative workmen, being thrown together in great numbers, had their faculties sharpened and improved by constant communication.' It was then that 'movements' were formed from below, some dedicated to reform, a few to revolution, all to 'union'. It was after 1870, however, that a new working-class culture with a distinct way of life took shape, the product essentially of segregation. Involvement in politics was not general, although there had long been a working-class version of political economy, pivoting not on competition but on cooperation, not on mobility but on solidarity, not on 'a reserve army of unemployed' but on 'the abolition of poverty'. Chartism had been the first independent working-class movement in the world, a snowball movement of social protest drawing in elements which were to prove incompatible but which were united on the six points of a political programme which included universal male suffrage set out in the People's Charter of 1838. There was a marked difference, however, between the late-nineteenth-century years, when labour had its own set of institutions, and the years of fluctuating discontent from 1820–50, which reached their climax in the rise and fall of Chartism.

The complexities of the emerging English class structure were revealed during the Chartist period, particularly in 1842, one of the most difficult 'crisis' years of the early nineteenth century. It was the fourth year in a run of bad harvests and a year of heavy unemployment when, in the words of Thomas Hood's poem *The Song of the Shirt*, 'bread was dear and flesh and blood were cheap'. A three-fold division of classes (upper, middle and working) is not adequate to assist in the analysis of the disturbances of that year; nor, indeed, is a two-fold division into rich and poor, or a five-fold division of a more intricate kind as historians critical of Marx have proposed. There were too many variables and too many differences of both interest and outlook.

There were, indeed, at least as many differences of fortune and outlook within the middle classes (one-sixth of the population) as there were within the working classes, for while the gulf between skilled and unskilled workers was so great that one acute observer spoke of them as two separate races, there was just as wide a gulf between rich merchants and small shopkeepers. There were also increasing numbers of professional people, including doctors, clergymen, schoolmasters and engineers, although they remained a minute proportion of the population. Some depended on fees and others on salaries, while the industrialists, who were vulnerable to the movement of the trade cycle, depended on profit. Even 'below' the working classes there were wide differences in fortune and outlook among the 'casual' workers and the marginal workers brilliantly described by Henry Mayhew in his *Life and Labour of the London Poor* in 1861. This was one of the main points he made about them.

The limits to class-consciousness, which was neither the only nor necessarily the main influence on thinking and behaviour in many parts of the country, were also revealed during labour struggles. Old notions of hierarchy and deference survived even the deepest crises of early industrialization, and for all the growing sense of middle-class and working-class consciousness, the latter carefully charted by E. P. Thompson, it was probably the aristocracy and the gentry who in both good and bad times felt the strongest sense of identity: 'a common blood, a common condition, common pursuits, common ideas, a common dialect, a common religion and . . . a common prestige, a prestige growled at occasionally, but on the whole conceded and even, it must be owned, secretly liked by the country at large,' as one contemporary put it in 1867. Thus, while there was plenty of self-conscious middle-class pressure during the struggle for the Reform Act of 1832 and during the fight for the repeal of the Corn Laws from 1838 to 1846, there was also plenty of aristocratic calculation, not least concerning what and when to yield. The repeal was eventually secured in 1846, carried through Parliament not by radicals but by a Conservative Prime Minister, Sir Robert Peel, who believed in public service not in party, and who had persuaded himself that the measure was intellectually and morally right. Peel wanted to keep a balance between agriculture, which interested him personally as well as politically, and industry, the source of his own wealth, and he wanted to contribute to the solution of the much debated 'condition of England question' by reducing the price of bread, England's basic food. Once the crucial decision had been made in Parliament, however, Peel was very soon sacrificed by his party and the prime ministership passed to a Whig aristocrat, Lord John Russell, member of the well-established Bedford family with immense properties – and traditions.

It was while Russell was Prime Minister, though not at his instigation, that Parliament, after furious agitation from outside, passed the Ten Hours Act of 1847 restricting the working hours of women and children in textile factories, a sign that the powers of the state could be used to regulate aspects of the new industrial system. Already, indeed, an earlier act of 1833 had introduced the machinery of inspection. The first four factory inspectors, appointed by the end of the year 1833, were at first viewed with suspicion by masters and workers alike, but as they were drawn into the tasks of enforcement they devoted themselves with remarkable energy and dedication to the task of what one of them described as 'correcting the great moral evils that had taken root and extensively spread in . . . industry'. As the century went by, further factory acts, involving more systematic state intervention in a widening range of industries, were passed, culminating in the consolidated Factory Act of 1901: its 'fine-meshed, wide-cast, "bureaucratic" net,' Sir John Clapham has written, was what the men of that day 'were learning to use or tolerate, if not always approve'.

The most important countervailing element in nineteenth-century industrial development was not, however, the regulation of hours by the state, which severely restricted its range of interventions, both on financial grounds and on grounds of principle, but the development of collective bargaining by the trade unions. By the end of the century they were a force in society despite fluctuating numbers. In the early 1890s there were about 1·5 million trade unionists, over 300,000 of them miners, another 300,000 in the retail trade, with some also in new 'unskilled' unions.

There had been trade clubs, different in character from the old journeymen's guilds, under the old domestic system. Printers' chapels (the term had no religious significance and was borrowed from France) were in existence in the seventeenth century, and as early as 1696 journeymen feltmakers in London were involved in a 'combination' to fix wages. In industrial Lancashire machine spinners' unions were organized in the 1790s, and there was even an attempt at federation in 1792. A general Spinners' Union organized unsuccessful major 'turn-outs' (strikes) in 1808 and 1810 for 'equalization' to Manchester rates while Preston weavers struck for higher wages in 1808, 1818 and 1821. New laws against such combination had been passed in 1799 and 1800, but they did not stop such action.

The social implications of trade unions inspired as much comment on both sides as did their economic implications. By 1824, the year when the combination laws were repealed, the Manchester Chamber of Commerce was not alone in maintaining that 'combinations, whether of masters or workmen, produced a hostile feeling . . . directly opposed to the best interests of society.' Those who supported repeal believed that if the restrictive laws were to go, trade unions would disappear, but in fact the unions went on to gain both in strength and in ambition, and attempts were made to achieve local, sectional or 'general' unions of workers. Indeed, there was more faith at first in 'general union' than in sectionalism. John Doherty, a young Irishman living in Manchester, where, as in Liverpool, there were many Irish settlers, created a Grand National Union of the Operative Spinners of Great Britain and Ireland and later a National Association for the Protection of Labour. In 1833, Bronterre O'Brien wrote eloquently that

a spirit of combination had grown up among the working classes of which there has been no example in former times . . . The object . . . is the sublimest that can be conceived, namely . . . to establish for the productive classes a complete domination over the fruits of their own industry . . . They aspire to be at the top instead of at the bottom of society – or rather that there should be no bottom or top at all.

It was in 1834, before the rise of Chartism, that early trade unionism reached its peak, supported by the ideas of Robert Owen. It was then too that the movement found its first martyrs – not in an industrial town or district, but in rural Dorset. Six trade unionists from the village of Tolpuddle, Methodists by religion, were accused and convicted of administering unlawful oaths under the Mutiny Act of 1797 while their 'combination' held abortive discussions with their employers, who had cut their miserably low wages from nine to six shillings. Their sentence to transportation to Australia, to which convicts of every kind had been sent since the 1780s, provoked large-scale demonstrations in London and other cities. While the judge who sentenced them pointed out that part of the 'object of all legal punishment' was to 'offer an example and a warning', the real significance of Tolpuddle was the public warning to society that trade unionism was here to stay. It was as much a by-product of England's industrial experience as smoky towns and polluted rivers, the new financial and service infrastructure, and the limitless hopes of universal free trade among Manchester businessmen.

It has often been pointed out that in its early stages trade unionism was most successful (as in 1834) when business was prosperous and there was a good harvest, and weakest when times were bad, as they were to be in the depression of unprecedented depths which began in 1837. Political action, therefore, was related to 'distress'. 'You cannot agitate a man on a full stomach,' declared William Cobbett, in his lifetime one of the most influential of radicals, although he had a tory frame of mind and looked back to a golden age more than to a new kind of society in the future.

Yet during the last years of the nineteenth century, the state of the home harvest, which had directly influenced the whole level of economic activity during the 1830s and 1840s, began to count for less than it ever had done before; more food was imported from overseas, and bread itself was less the staple of life than it had been for centuries. But this was not all. The forms of capitalism were changing too, as employers as well as workers began to organize collectively and there was a far bigger group of professional people, including 'experts', inside and outside business. Politics also took on a new shape. In the early years of the century political agitation had moved from one platform demonstration to another, with landmark dates like the 'Peterloo massacre', when the Yeomanry charged the crowds in Manchester in 1819, and years of lull between. Now more organized political parties kept politics constantly in movement, particularly after the extension of the suffrage to large numbers of working men in the towns in 1867. And behind the parties were well organized pressure groups, many of them also operating continuously as part of a rich social and cultural infrastructure.

Within this context, the trade unions became a part of the economic and political system, with a distinctive English style, expressed in well-drafted books of rules, carefully kept minute books and audited sets of accounts. In 1868, when the newly formed Trades Union Congress held its first annual meeting, a small affair with only thirty-four delegates present, at Manchester, the new unions, which drew their first main support from relatively well-paid workers, like engineers, carpenters and builders, had only 250,000 members, but within five years (of economic boom) their number had trebled. In fact, the number was to drop again soon afterwards when economic conditions deteriorated. Some agricultural workers had joined the unions during the boom, but the main union strength was in the cities, in some of which there were Trades Councils, like the London Trades Council, founded in 1860.

Mid-Victorian trade unionists have often been described as an 'aristocracy of labour', and even at the time they were accused by other workers of running mere benefit societies (like the other 'friendly societies' which flourished during the period). Yet they were willing to strike when occasion seemed to demand it, and the number of strikes did not diminish between 1850 and 1880. They took part in political movements, including the renewed struggle for the suffrage during the 1860s, and were often active in the cooperative movement, the origins of which were older than the store in Toad Lane opened by twenty-eight Rochdale workers who raised an initial capital of £28 in 1844. By the early 1870s the cooperators had 927 branches and 300,000 members.

It was the skilled trade unionists who, through their organizational strength, secured increased recognition for trade unions under the law during the middle years of the nineteenth century. They gave evidence to a Royal Commission of 1867 and thereafter served as a pressure group to secure the Trade Union Act of 1871, sometimes called the Trade Unionists' Charter, which provided that the purposes of a union should not be regarded as criminal merely because they were in restraint of trade. Trade unions were to be protected by the law, but were to be free from the interference of the law in their own internal affairs. This act, passed by a Liberal government, was followed by a still more favourable act introduced by Disraeli's Conservative government in 1875. Breach of contract was no longer to be a criminal offence and peaceful picketing was legalized. The legal position of the trade unions was to be challenged in the early twentieth century when a court decision of 1901 in the Taff Vale case – involving a railway worker – laid down that unions were liable to actions for damages by employers for civil wrongs payable by union funds. But this was not the end of the story. The trade unions were determined to redress the law.

Meanwhile, general labourers also had been drawn increasingly into trade unions, pressing for further claims like the eight-hour day (King Alfred, they said, was the first to divide the day into three parts – work, sleep and recreation). Some of them were willing to turn not to liberal but to socialist politicians: many of them pinned their hopes on legislation rather than on collective bargaining. The numbers of trade unionists increased from 800,000 to 1,500,000 between 1888 and 1891. Two years later Keir Hardie, the Scots socialist in a cloth cap, symbol of the new working class which was being formed in the last years of the century, became leader of the new Independent Labour Party, which was brought into existence in industrial Bradford in 1893. This party joined with other socialist groups, including the Fabian Society, whose famous book of essays appeared in the same year

as the great dock strike of 1889, to form the Labour Representation Committee, which, under the new name of the Labour
Party, won twenty-nine seats at the general election of 1906. It had
solid trade-union support from the start, and its long-term life
was guaranteed as the number of unionists in the country rose to
four million by 1914. Hardie talked often of green fields and quiet
streams, but when he looked into the future, he drew on a
metaphor from the recent industrial past. Within the Labour
Party the ILP would be, he claimed, 'what steam is to machinery,
the motive power which keeps all going'.

9

WEBS OF COMMUNICATION

'Only fancy, Aunt Helen, that Uncle Henry was in Paris yesterday
and will be at home today. Is it not wonderful? What did men do
before there were railroads and steamboats?'

Anon, *The Triumph of Steam*, 1859

We have been considering the cases in which independent persons
run motor-car services along the roads to our railway stations. We
do not see why we should not fuel our own railways ourselves by
means of motor cars.

The Chairman of the Great Western Railway Company, 1903

When flying machines begin to fly
We shall never stay at home,
Away we'll skip on a half-day trip
To Paris, perhaps, or Rome.

The Musical Comedy, *The Bride of Bath*, 1906

THE TRANSFORMATION of England from an agricultural and
mercantile society to an industrial society would have been
impossible without the development of an improved communications system: the more efficient transport of both raw
materials and finished products – including heavy goods of low
and high value – to extended markets and at lower costs, was as
basic an activity as production itself. And just as industrialization
was not an entirely new phenomenon which began with the
industrial revolution, so the transformation of transport was
preceded by steady, if patchy, improvement.

Canal building seemed a natural rather than a revolutionary development, for England's inland transport system had for centuries depended more on water than on land. Inland waterways had been improved more or less continuously from the second half of the sixteenth century, during which there was one unique development, the Exeter Lighter Canal, paid for and built by the Exeter Corporation in 1564–6. But the rivers, particularly the Severn and the Mersey, which were said to carry more traffic than any other rivers in Europe, remained the main arteries in the seventeenth century.

The main age of canal building did not begin until the early eighteenth century, and it did not reach its peak until the canal 'rage' of the 1790s, during which a total of forty-two new canals, requiring a capital outlay of £6,500,000, were projected. Indeed, the year 1792 was described by contemporaries as a year of 'canal mania', with 'the passion of speculation spreading like an epidemical disease'. Canal shares, usually in large units, were not quoted on the Stock Exchange until 1811, but they were taken up eagerly then by local merchants, manufacturers and landowners.

It was men from the last of these broad groups who had done much to pioneer canals. Thus in 1761 the young Duke of Bridgewater, working with an able, and entirely self-educated engineer named James Brindley, opened a 10·5 mile stretch of canal linking his coal mines at Worsley in Lancashire to the outskirts of Manchester; with its impressive aqueduct and its underground canals tunnelled into coal measures it was described at the time as 'perhaps the greatest artificial curiosity in the world'. Merseyside, where Liverpool was beginning to forge ahead as an ocean port, was already a main area of development, and an even earlier stretch of artificial canal, the Sankey Cut, had been built by a Liverpool engineer in 1759.

The canal system – and it deserved to be called a system – was concerned first with linking the great rivers and then with providing facilities for places that had none. The rivers had many disadvantages for the transport of industrial goods: in 1796, for example, the level of the Severn, which, unlike the Dee, never silted up, was so low that the river was navigable for only two months. A developing industrial area like Coalbrookdale in

Shropshire, where Abraham Darby first smelted iron with coke in 1709 and where Thomas Telford built the world's first iron bridge over the Severn in 1779, could not operate successfully in such conditions, and there were other industrial areas far less favoured by nature, notably the West Midlands, which lay on the great watershed of central England; traffic to and from there had to use a combination of land and water. There were many other places which were completely landlocked.

James Brindley had dreams of creating a great silver cross of over 260 miles of canal to join up the rivers Mersey, Severn, Thames and Trent. In fact, from 1772 the Severn was linked with the Mersey through Stourport, which eclipsed the old river town of Bewdley, and there was a further link with the Thames in 1790, when the first boatload of coal despatched from Coventry reached Oxford. Other land barriers were pierced later. The Leeds and Liverpool Canal, the most important water route across the Pennines, was begun in 1770 but was not completed until 1816, by which time there were already many other canal links, among them John Rennie's Rochdale Canal with its impressive but expensive locks. The system was, however, never completed. There was never any direct canal link between Manchester and Sheffield, and when the Manchester to Liverpool Ship Canal was completed in 1893 the age of canals was long past.

At the peak of the canal enterprise there were 4,000 miles of inland waterways, often built on local initiatives (with some London backing) and they had immediate effects on employment and distribution. 'A good canal,' said Bridgewater, 'should have coals at the heels of it'; in fact, corn and all kinds of agricultural and industrial products were carried as well as coal. People could be carried too, in 'passage' or 'packet' boats, with travellers enjoying the sensation of gliding 'tranquilly onwards through a continuous panorama of cows, cottages and green fields,' as one nineteenth-century traveller described it. The first boats, like the first barges, were often highly decorated, and there were agreeable canal inns with names like The Anchor or The Navigation along the tow paths.

The canal and the machine were to produce quite different responses during the industrial revolution: while the machine inspired or disturbed, the new waterway with its tow paths, locks and bridges satisfied men and seemed even to complement nature. Mechanical engineering carried with it the idea of conquering nature; civil engineering moulded an environment which already existed. There was one handicap, however. Canal water was usually as 'black as the Styx and absolutely pestiferous'.

The early days of the canal coincided with the great days of coaches. 'Door to door' traffic was still dependent on eighteenth-century English rutted roads, which had a bad reputation with many travellers. Arthur Young, in characteristic vein, described the main road between Preston and Wigan as 'infernal' and to 'be avoided by travellers as they would the Devil'. In London itself the Edgware Road was often deep in sludge, and one irate resident complained that the road from Kensington to Westminster had 'grown so infamously bad that we live here in the same solitude as we would do if stranded on a rock in the middle of the ocean'.

Nonetheless, there were many eighteenth-century improvements in both the roads themselves and the vehicles that carried passengers and other traffic along them. Turnpike roads, not all of them of high quality, had begun to be built from 1706 onwards, not by parishes, on which the maintenance of roads had previously depended, but by business trusts, supported by local interests, which were individually authorized to borrow money and levy tolls by act of parliament. (The first Turnpike Act had actually been passed in 1663.) During the second half of the eighteenth century the number of turnpikes increased rapidly (452 Acts were passed between 1760 and 1774 – Horace Walpole claimed that they were the main business of Parliament – and a General Turnpike Act became law in 1773) so that there were 1,600 of them in existence by 1800. There was a further substantial increase in mileage throughout the golden age of coaching which lasted until the 1830s. Great surveyors and engineers, like blind 'Jack' Metcalf of Knaresborough in Yorkshire, who tapped his way along the roads, Thomas Telford, more famous still as a bridge builder, and John Loudon McAdam, who gave his name to a modern road surface, not only improved individual roads but planned, usually abortively, almost on Roman lines, great road systems into which parish roads would serve as feeders.

The number and spread of coaches increased and journey time was cut drastically. In 1754 there were six firms operating wagons from Manchester to London. 'However incredible it may appear,' a newspaper advertisement boasted, 'this coach will actually arrive in London four days after leaving Manchester,' yet thirty years later travel time had been cut by a half. By 1816 there were as many as 200 land carriers transporting goods to and from Manchester in 'wagons or carts', and by 1830 there were fifty-four passenger coaches per day travelling each way. All in all, the number of stage coach services provided in major urban centres multiplied eightfold between 1790 and 1836, when 700 mail coaches and 3,300 stage coaches were in regular operation.

Some of the coaches were already beginning to deliver 'royal mail' as well as people. As early as 1784 John Palmer of Bristol had introduced lighter springed vehicles and a combination of relays and stage points on the journey. Very quickly government as well as passengers saw advantages in such improvement, both for the postal services and for the transport of people; coaches were licensed, and mileage was taxed – at increasing rates in 1783 and in 1815. Innkeepers, of course, profited directly from the traffic, and one of them, W. J. Chaplin, manager of The Swan with Two Necks in London, owned no fewer than sixty-eight coaches and 1,800 horses in 1838. Yet there were risks in the business just as there were hazards for the traveller – even after highwaymen, a notorious menace in the eighteenth century, had been brought under control. Meanwhile, the early rioting against turnpike tolls – some of it, like disturbances in 1753 near Leeds and Bradford, so fierce that it amounted almost to 'rebellion' – had passed into legend.

Far more daring ways of conveying people and goods were also contemplated during the early canal and great coaching age. Indeed, there was as much talk about improvements as there was about the construction of new kinds of machines in the century after 1750: 'rowing barges against the stream', 'propelling carriages without horses', balloons (there was a balloon craze in the 1780s) and even 'conveying Letters and Goods with Great Certainty and Rapidity by Air' were all discussed. Erasmus Darwin was daring enough to contemplate carrying people by air in steam-driven 'fiery Chariots'. Nevertheless, the fastest form of travel was still by horse, and the eighteenth century was a great age of the horse. The Jockey Club dates back to 1752, the St Leger to 1777, and the Derby to 1780.

The first great new development came with the successful introduction of 'iron horses', the railways, which from the start carried far more passengers than had been predicted. The development of the railway was a protracted process, with a long prehistory for each of its different features: the rail track, the locomotive and its engines, the movement of goods by rail and, not least, the movement of passengers. It is not surprising that the mining areas were centres of innovation, as they were in the development of pre-Watt Newcomen steam engines, used not for transport but for pumping.

The name of George Stephenson, a self-made Northumberland engineer who started as a brakesman in a pit and whose engine *The Rocket* won the railway trials between Liverpool and Manchester in 1830, is usually associated with the creation of the railway. Certainly, for Smiles, Stephenson was 'the father of the locomotive'. Yet George Stephenson was only one man out of many; indeed, the engineering contributions of his son Robert were greater than those of his father. The most remarkable of the earlier railway pioneers was a Cornishman, Richard Trevithick, who (against the advice of James Watt) began working successfully with noncondensing high-pressure steam engines, known as 'puffers', in the very early nineteenth century. Trevithick took out his first patent in 1802, and six years later he was tempting Londoners to pay to see his mechanical engine, the 'Catch-me-who-catch-can', outstrip the 'animal speed' of a horse. Already it was being predicted that the number of horses in England would be considerably reduced in the steam-driven future, and already, too, power was being measured in terms of 'horse power' as it was to be in the age of the motor car.

It was not only inventors who were enthusiastic or foresaw future developments. One of the most eloquent assessments of future possibilities was a book with the formidable title *Observations on a General Iron Railway or Land Steam Conveyance; to supersede the Necessity of Horses in all Public Vehicles; showing its vast*

Superiority in every Respect, over all the Pitiful Methods of Conveyance by Turnpike Roads, Canal and Coasting Traders, Containing every Species of Invention relative to Railroads and Locomotive Engines, by Thomas Gray, published in 1821. In it Gray predicted many future features of the railway. So too did the Quaker Edward Pease, a Darlington manufacturer and one of Stephenson's backers, who took as the motto of his railway 'At private risk for public service'.

During the years between 1825 and 1835 fifty-four Railway Acts permitting railway building were passed, resulting by the end of 1838 in 500 miles of track, but it was in 1836 and 1837, when forty-four companies concerned with 1,498 miles of track were sanctioned, that there was the first sense of a railway 'boom'. By 1843 there were 2,036 miles in actual use. And the 1830s boom was to be far eclipsed by the feverish 'railway mania' of 1845–7, when 576 companies and a further 8,731 miles of track were sanctioned.

The dimensions of the 'mania' exceeded those of the canal 'rage' of the 1790s, and although there is scanty evidence to suggest that it 'infected all classes from peer to peasant', as one historian has suggested, there is no doubt about the intensity of the urge to buy shares in railway companies. The promoters were quick to seize on it, knowing that behind steam power there had to be money power. It is true that English railways were far more costly to build and more wasteful in their duplication than most later systems, but much of the private money that was lost disappeared in speculation – and in peculation. Thus George Hudson, 'the railway king', who started as a draper in York and whose statue still stands there, had one of the dizziest of all business careers which led him first to Westminster and then to gaol. The greatest of the railway contractors at home and abroad, Thomas Brassey, who had strong views on labour and the economy, left a fortune of £3,200,000 on his death in 1870.

Brassey, like his fellow contractors, learned how to manage a large, mixed and, at times, awkward labour-force, dismissed by contemporary moralists as 'impetuous, impulsive and brute-like . . . owning no moral law and feeling no social tie'. This was too comprehensive an indictment: once the railways began to work there was ample evidence of discipline in the uniformed railway staff with its carefully built-in differences of status and authority. In the new railway towns like Crewe (which had not even figured as a place name in the 1841 census) and Swindon there were new social ties as well. The paternalistic community building provided by the London and North Western Railway Directors who acquired Crewe in 1840 was said to prove that even a railway company, which some critics described as a 'feudal organization with modifications', had 'bowels of compassion', although it was added that they were not 'on public exhibition'. In Swindon (where the first small 'lock-up' had proved too small to contain railway labourers who were drunk or disorderly) it was claimed with exaggeration in the 1870s that 'whatever is good for the company is good for New Swindon.'

Whatever the perils of entrepreneurship or investment, by 1855 there were over 8,000 miles of track, managed by fewer companies than a decade earlier, and all the great cities had long been linked, with Birmingham the first to get two lines to London. In 1845 a Clearing House scheme came into existence, a benefit that the canal companies, now in decline and subject to relentless competition or railway take-over, had never been able to achieve. One of the railway gauges – that of the Great Western, designed by the great engineer Isambard Kingdom Brunel – was broader than the rest, inhibiting the creation of a unified system, but conversion started in the west, was widespread by the later 1860s and was completed by 1892 at the company's own cost. Financiers might come and go, but the engineers, contractors and navvies stuck to their tasks and it was soon difficult to remember what the country had looked like and been like before their advent. 'We who lived before railways and survive out of the ancient world,' wrote the novelist William Thackeray, 'are like Father Noah and his family out of the Ark'. As one excited journalist had commented on the triumph of The Rocket in the 1830 trials, 'The victory has established principles which will give a greater impulse to civilization than it has ever received from any single source since the Press first opened the gates of knowledge of the human species at large.' No journalist could have said more. Yet even he did not know how much the future development of the

Press, described in the 1850s as a 'Fourth Estate', would depend on railway transport.

By the 1850s railways were no longer thought of as a novelty and had ceased to capture the imagination of the public. They were taken for granted, not just because what they carried was now deemed commonplace (they quickly revolutionized the distribution of consumer goods, perishable, bulky and fragile, from milk to mail), but because passengers no longer felt that great excitement in speed of movement which the first travellers had done. There had been a time, before time itself was speeded up, when a traveller by rail had noted with pride that 'had the double tailed comet passed that way, the country people could scarcely have been more interested by the spectacle'. He continued

> the men at work in the fields and quarries stood like statues, their pick axes in their hands, in attitudes of fixed attention . . . and women . . . in their best gowns and bonnets fled from the villages and congregated at the corner of every intersecting lane. Neither were the brute creations less animated . . . Every horse was on the alert, viewing the huge moving body as it approached with a mixture of fear and surprise.

Some of the first travellers by rail did not stop at the plain metaphor of the iron horse: they elaborated it. Thus, for the actress Fanny Kemble,

> she goes along wheels which are her feet and are moved by bright steel legs called pistons; these are propelled by steam . . . The reins, bit and bridle of this wonderful beast is a small steel handle, which applies or withdraws the steam from its legs or pistons, so that a child might manage it. This snorting little animal . . . I feel rather inclined to pat.

Given that horses had figured so prominently in English life, the arrival of the 'iron horse' was, indeed, a moment of truth. It has been estimated that to keep a single horse on the road for a year in the great coaching age required five acres of hay and oats, not to speak of an army of blacksmiths. Coal, carried everywhere by rail, was a cheaper source of power, although it needed miners (women included among them until 1842) still working in difficult (and often dangerous) conditions underground to produce it.

Such exhilaration was only part of the early story. For many nineteenth-century English men and women the railway was controversial, and locomotives, in the words of the Tory diarist Thomas Creevey, were 'monsters navigated by a tail of smoke and sulphur'. Railway accidents, even those that occurred at the building stage – like the terrible story of death in the construction of the Woodhead Tunnel not far from Sheffield between 1839 and 1845, when at least thirty-two men were killed and many injured – were man-made horrors on a huge and unprecedented scale. 'A railway is long, but life is short,' wrote a critic in *Punch* – 'and generally the longer the railway, the shorter your life.' Other critics were ambivalent in their attitudes, complaining, as modern critics of motorways do, about the displacement of families and the bisection of communities on the two sides of the track. Even those critics who believed that railways might indirectly favour sanitary reform by carving their way through densely packed and unhealthy working-class districts admitted that while the locomotive had 'a giant's strength', he was no better than 'a blind and undistinguishing Polyphemus when he is called in as a sanitary reformer'.

The impact of the railways on Victorian cities, many of them cities of the railway age, was enormous. By 1890 railway companies owned up to 8–10 per cent of central land in the cities and influenced the use made of another 20 per cent, although they did not achieve their ambition of completing a central link through London (there were instead many complex outer links). It was London from which all main lines radiated: there were very few cross-country lines.

The railway could have as marked an effect on smaller communities as on large ones. Thus, Teddington, described in 1837 as a 'quiet rural village, with its "grove", its "Manor", its little waterside church, and its broad expanse of open meadows', was completely transformed by 1884. 'Rows of spruce villas and neat terraces' had appeared along with 'grand hotels' and 'magnificent stores' that drove out other hostelries and alarmed small traders.

Even when there were no social displacements or accidents,

railway travel was felt by its critics to be breaking the established rhythms of life and challenging accepted social relationships. It seemed to be too 'democratic', as Dr Arnold, Headmaster of Rugby School, put it, 'destroying feudalism for ever'. Some landowners feared its intrusion into their estates and kept it as far as they could from their property. So too did the Provost of Eton and the Vice-Chancellor of the University of Oxford. Yet the railway could rarely be resisted; even Oxford got its miserable station. A stilted dialogue between two aristocrats in Disraeli's novel *Sybil* (1845) caught contemporaries' fears and entanglements.

> *Lord de Mowbray:* You came by railroad?
> *Lady Marney:* From Marham, about ten miles from us.
> *De M:* A great revolution.
> *M:* Isn't it?
> *De M:* I fear it has a dangerous tendency to equality. I suppose your husband gives them all the opposition in his power.
> *M:* There is nobody so violent against the railroads as George . . . He organized the whole of the district against our Marham line.
> *De M:* I rather counted on him to assist me in resisting this joint branch line here, but I was surprised to learn that he had consented.
> *M:* Not until the compensation was settled. George never opposed them after that. He gave up all opposition to the Marham line when they agreed to his terms.

That was the view from above.

From below, many people, particularly businessmen seeking to enlarge their markets, immediately found railways useful, and by 1870 were finding them indispensable. Mass distribution, particularly of perishables, depended on the railway which carried, for example, beer from Burton-on-Trent or fish from Grimsby, Hull, Lowestoft and Yarmouth, ports which acquired new significance. Between 1849 and 1870, while track doubled, the number of first-class and second-class passengers increased four times and the number of third-class passengers six times. An act of parliament of 1844 obliged railway companies to run at least one train every weekday, except Christmas Day and Good Friday, at fares not exceeding one penny a mile for adults and a

Railways in 1870

100-400 metres above sea level

over 400 metres above sea level

halfpenny for children between three and twelve years of age, and although this did not immediately produce a nation of commuters, middle-class or working-class, it opened up the new system to everyone in the community. The first *Bradshaw* of 1839 presented regular timetables, and as the century went by other new ideas, including that of specifically suburban routes, made their way into the railway guides along with the appropriate guidance. For many people railways quickly became essential in the journey to work.

Just as important was the recognition, quick to take shape, that railways could lead not only to the factory or to the office but also to the seaside and the country. As early as 1839, a special train on the Whitby and Pickering Railway in North Yorkshire had carried visitors to a church bazaar, and in 1841 Thomas Cook, founder of the huge travel agency, persuaded the Midland Counties Railway to issue cheap tickets to 510 Leicester temperance workers to attend a quarterly delegates' meeting in Loughborough. 'We must have RAILWAYS FOR THE MILLIONS' was Cook's cry. And he got them. The aristocratic image of Brighton was dented in 1844 by the first day excursion train from London, and the proletarian image of Blackpool was built up from the time the railway arrived there two years later; before that it had been 'the sweet little village by the sea'. Cook himself became 'so thoroughly imbued with the tourist spirit' that he began to contemplate 'Foreign Trips, including the Continent of Europe, the United States and the Eastern lands of the Bible'.

It took more than a century for the English to follow Cook outside the island in their millions, but already, by the end of the nineteenth century, they were pouring out along the English coast. The Bank Holiday Act of 1871 laid down that certain days in the year should be official holidays, very different in motivation from the old holy days of the Christian calendar, which ensured not only crowded trains but crowded beaches: the picture postcard, a late-nineteenth- and early-twentieth-century innovation, helps us to recapture the mood. And it was the railways that determined the pattern of holiday geography: the old inland spas declined in importance while the new seaside resorts rose. Morecambe was nicknamed Bradford-by-the-Sea. From

London there was a choice of Brighton, Eastbourne, Worthing or Southend. Each resort had its own history and its own tone.

It took time, however, for railway directors and managers to free themselves fully from the view from above when they considered future prospects. At first, they had been far more concerned with freight than with people and were content, as a Great Western Railway director put it bleakly in 1839, to contemplate for the 'accommodation' of third-class passengers only 'carriages of an inferior description at very slow speed'. One early traveller wrote of third-class carriages that

> there was a general feeling of bare boards and cheerlessness as you entered them . . . Even the windows were but small apertures [and] the seats were cushionless . . . Trains stopped at every little place on the way; you were shunted here and shunted there, or found yourself resting in some lonely siding for what seemed an age.

However, standards of third-class service improved as the nineteenth century went by and 9,000 stations, big and small, were built. The second class disappeared, and even third-class carriages (unlike most of those across the Channel) had padded seats. Coaches with separate corridors and lavatories had been introduced in 1881 and de luxe Pullman coaches even earlier on some lines.

The opening of Victoria Station in 1860 was of great importance in relation both to the journey to work and the escape from it. It had no spectacular Doric arch like Euston, nor was it housed in a great Gothic building like St Pancras. Yet it pointed resolutely to the commuter age and it opened up a great new 'gateway to the Continent'. Three years later, London's first underground railway, the Metropolitan, was opened; it ran between Paddington and Farringdon Street, a distance of nearly four miles, and was supported both by the City of London and by the Great Western Railway. The District Railway brought Victoria into this system in 1871, and in 1884 the Inner Circle was completed. The underground opened up whole new housing areas in South London and in 'Metroland', which led in turn to early morning and late evening travel rushes.

The late nineteenth century was, for the social historian, the real 'railway age', but the term has also been used in relation to an earlier age of economic individualism and competition, when railway construction brought England out of deep economic depression, mobilizing new capital if diverting some of it from activities like housing. 'For the first time in history, an economy was devoting a net tenth or more of its total income to capital accumulation.'

Very soon, however, old questions of monopoly reappeared in a new industrial context. A few people favoured either public ownership of railways or a substantial degree of public control. Yet the weight of official opinion continued to recommend private enterprise and limited government guidelines. Of course, the framework of private enterprise itself changed: it would have been difficult in the case of railways to allow the market to operate completely freely. Governments were forced to accept company 'deals' rather than unlimited competition, and amalgamations (which were to last until 1923) were sanctioned during the 1860s. While in some European countries the railways were nationalized in the nineteenth century, in Britain they were not nationalized until after the Labour victory of 1945.

The next major development in communication – the rise of the automobile – was very different in character. For the well-off traveller it had been a major weakness of the railroad that 'you were shunted here and there' along fixed tracks. You did not know, moreover, whom you would meet when you entered a railway carriage. By contrast, if you had the money, a motor car was your own, and subject to the conditions of the highway you could do what you liked with it. You had 'the freedom of the road'. You would also, it was claimed, find an automobile easy to maintain. 'Looking after a motor car,' a speaker told a London audience in 1897, 'is child's play compared to attending to a horse. If you do not use your carriage for a month, it does not cost you anything: there is no horse eating his head off in the stable.' Moreover, 'what pair of horses could carry a load, as my Daimler has done, of 250 pounds of baggage, myself and my man?'

The internal combustion engine, which supplanted the steam carriage that had for more than a century seemed to offer the best prospect for 'self-propulsion', was developed not in England but in France and Germany. It was not until 1888 that Edward Butler, son of a West Country farmer, produced the first petrol driven engine capable of being attached to a moving vehicle; three years earlier he had taken out a patent, and six years later the first Benz car was imported. (The importer of the first Benz, who collected it himself at the docks, was stopped by the police as he crossed London.) There had actually been an increase in the amount of traffic on the roads between 1878 and 1890, but it was horse-driven traffic, mainly 'short-stage'. It was in 1895 that Frederick Lanchester produced the first English four-wheeler car and Herbert Austin designed a car that was built (this was real continuity) by the Wolseley Sheep Shearing Machine Company in Birmingham. At nearby Coventry, an old city which had switched profitably from silk and watch-making to sewing machines and bicycles, the Daimler Company soon began to manufacture cars in a disused silk factory.

Butler's first design for a vehicle, however, had been not for an automobile but for a bicycle. The age of the bicycle (with or without petrol) preceded the age of the automobile. There was a social as well as a technical contrast here alongside the historical continuity. Bicycles were relatively cheap, and the people who bought them, both in their early 'boneshaker' phase and later, came from different sections of society, with a large proportion of young purchasers who were enthusiastic not only about self-propulsion but about the 'open air'. There were many 'bicycle cultures', some of them dominated by women. (The bicycle did more to encourage 'rational' women's dress than generations of dress reformers.) As early as 1878, a Bicycle Touring Club was founded, to be renamed the Cyclists' Touring Club five years later, when the National Cyclists' Union was founded. By the 1890s there were also Clarion socialist cycling clubs, dedicated to the creation or recreation of a 'merrie England'.

By contrast, the first motor car owners were plutocratic. Early motor cars were superb hand-made vehicles which retained a luxury image down to 1914, inspiring lavish advertisements, friendly and unfriendly jokes, occasional physical assaults and numerous witty verses, like Hilaire Belloc's well-known lines:

> The rich arrived in pairs
> And also in Rolls-Royces;
> They talked of their affairs
> In loud and strident voices.

Nonetheless, by the time Belloc wrote, there were motor cars of a different kind and price in active use across the Atlantic, where the utility of the automobile in a continent of huge distances was immediately recognized. Henry Ford was at work to lower their costs, and Belloc could add a further verse to his poem:

> The poor arrived in Fords
> Whose features they resembled;
> They laughed to see so many lords
> And ladies all assembled.

6,000 Ford Model Ts were being produced in Manchester in 1913.

If the 'railway age' had seen a diversion of social capital from such activity as housing to transport, the 'automobile age' saw a diversion of private capital, and incomes, away from necessities to diversion itself. Although the internal combustion engine was introduced 'hesitantly' in London for public buses in 1907, following the earlier introduction of electric trams in the 1890s and the metered motor taxi for the better-off in 1905, the private motor car continued to draw most attention. 'Wandering machines, travelling with an incredible rate of speed,' a socially-minded Liberal politician called them in 1909. 'You can see them on a Sunday afternoon, piled twenty or thirty deep outside the new popular inns, while their occupants regale themselves within.' Not all the hostile comment was equally polite. 'Your birthright is being taken from you by reckless motorists,' warned a Fulham handbill of 1908. 'Men of England . . . rise up, join together and bring pressure on your representatives in Parliament.' Such opponents of motoring were far less influential, however, than the (Royal) Automobile Club, founded in 1897, and the Automobile Association, established in 1905 after a merger of earlier bodies.

Nevertheless, there were social problems that could not be solved by lobbying. Thus the number of fatal car accidents increased from 373 in 1909 to 1,328 in 1914, by which time there were 132,015 licensed private cars on the roads of Britain, nearly three times as many as in 1909. Of course, at first the roads had been inadequate for motor traffic: the age of the turnpikes was past (22,000 miles of road had been turnpiked by 1838, but by 1890 there were only two turnpike trusts left in existence). There were also restrictions on the freedom of the motorist: the Red Flag Act of 1865, extended with limited amendments in 1878, restricted speeds to four miles an hour in the country and two miles an hour in the towns and required every 'road locomotive' to have three attendants, one to walk not less than six yards in front carrying a red flag. Local authorities could even regulate the hours of travel. These irksome restrictions, which were introduced to deal not with motor cars but with older and heavier types of road vehicle, were repealed by the Light Locomotives on Highways Act of 1896, and different motoring controls later took their place: licensing, introduced in 1904 along with number plates, specific motor taxes, first levied in 1909, and speed limits, to be followed decades later by beacons, traffic lights and white lines in the road. These were the product of a new age, not the epilogue of an old one. In 1896, the year in which the magazine The Autocar, 'published in the interests of the mechanically propelled carriage', was founded, Harry J. Lawson, patentee of the safety bicycle, organized the first London to Brighton motor race, with the Earl of Winchelsea ceremonially tearing up a red flag to celebrate the occasion.

It would have been difficult to predict in 1896 and 1897 just how popular motor cars were to become in England in the late twentieth century. And this was true also of the cluster of new communication developments (some of them English) that followed on the advent of the telephone, which had been patented by Alexander Graham Bell in 1876, and the phonograph, which had been patented by Thomas Edison in 1877, but was to be much 'improved', mass-produced and given a new trade name, 'the gramophone', by Emile Berliner just twenty years later. In 1896 the word 'record' had just come into use, although two-sided records were not to be manufactured until 1904.

The development of the telephone was not greatly influenced by the British Post Office. This was partly because in 1868 it won an entrenched interest in the exploitation of this earlier invention of the 1840s which had achieved as much for the Press as railways and penny postage. The Post Office had taken over private telegraphic undertakings and in 1885 it had almost halved the rate for internal telegraphs to sixpence for twelve words, leaving the first exploitation of the telephone under Post Office licence to private enterprise. A near monopolistic National Telephone Company was formed in 1890–91, however, and a year later the Post Office acquired the trunk line system and in 1911 the provincial system too. The English were as slow to learn how to use the telephone as they were to learn how to mass-produce the motor car. Nonetheless, there was as much excitement about some of these 'consumer inventions' as there had been about 'factory inventions' a century earlier. The aged Queen Victoria, who had sent messages by telegraph at the Great Exhibition and was quick to have a telephone installed, shared the enthusiasm. At the time of her Diamond Jubilee in 1897 she sent out a Jubilee message by telegraph to her 'beloved people' all over the world.

The previous year, 1896, was even more of a landmark year in social communications: alongside the developments in motoring, there were significant interrelated developments in the Press and in new forms of communications which were to culminate in what has been called 'the mass producing of the moment'. That year Alfred Harmsworth, later Lord Northcliffe, himself an early motorist and future editor of a volume on *Motors and Motor Driving* (1902), founded the halfpenny *Daily Mail*, a popular newspaper to which the label of the 'new journalism' was attached, in which he promised his readers that 'four leading articles, a page of Parliament, and columns of speeches will N O T be found'. Lord Salisbury, England's Conservative Prime Minister at the end of the century, might dismiss the *Daily Mail* as 'a journal produced by office boys for office boys', but nearly a million copies of it were selling, and within the next decade Harmsworth was to take control of *The Times*, England's supreme 'quality newspaper', as well: it had first appeared more than a hundred years earlier.

The first regular cinema shows, which also made their

appearance in 1896, in London's Leicester Square, did not seem revolutionary at the time and certainly no one anticipated the huge size of mid-twentieth-century cinema attendances. The entry of a new technology of pictures into society and culture had begun in 1839 with the daguerreotype; and the much advertised trademark Kodak for what George Eastman, its American inventor, called a 'detective camera' was registered in 1888. The moving film, however, was quickly to become a form of 'mass entertainment' rather than a private diversion: it rapidly supplanted older technologies like the magic lantern and very soon it was to challenge the theatre.

It was in 1896 also that a young Italian inventor, Guglielmo Marconi, arrived in England to demonstrate for the benefit of the British Post Office a bundle of wireless gadgets which he kept in a black box. In Marconi's case, neither the inventor himself nor the Post Office engineers thought of 'wireless' as an instrument of broadcasting; indeed, it needed further technical invention to make possible 'wireless telephony', communication by voice rather than by signals. They thought of radio telegraphy as a substitute for line-to-line communication by wire, and were fascinated in this context by its naval and military possibilities. Neither Marconi nor Edison could foresee the time when George V (1910–36) would talk to his subjects throughout the Empire by radio. In Edwardian times radio attracted attention when it helped to catch a criminal (the famous Dr Crippen) or to save liners in distress.

Thirty years later (much in the history of communications seems to move in thirty-year generational cycles) wireless was to become the country's main story-teller. Then it was to have unanticipated economic, social and cultural consequences, serving a great audience and levelling time and place. A British broadcasting handbook was to stress that

> till the advent of this universal and extraordinary cheap medium of communication, a very large proportion of people were shut off from first-hand knowledge of the events which make history . . . Today he who has something to tell his countrymen can command an audience of millions ready to hand.

The 'communications revolution', as it came to take shape in retrospect, was by its nature an international revolution, crossing frontiers. It had a common technology, which was not distinctively English. Yet the institutional shell devised to handle the technology in Britain was very specifically British, if not English. Broadcasting was driven by a sense of service rather than the profit motive, and the programming for which the BBC was given a monopoly was to reflect this. This was not true, however, of either the cinema (although British film-making was to be subsidized) or the Press, both of which were developed by businessmen interested in profits.

No account of the communications revolution before 1914 would be complete without reference to both shipping and the aeroplane. Shipping was thought of as a 'traditional' activity throughout the period, although it was in fact transformed as profoundly as land transport during the steam revolution of the nineteenth century. The facilities and services accompanying it underwent the same transformation. The first modern dock, the West India Dock in London, was sanctioned by Parliament in 1799 (and opened in 1802), and the Warehousing Act was passed in 1803, in what was still an age of sail; by the time of the foundation of the Port of London Authority in 1908, however, the London shipping world had completely changed. So too had other shipping centres, such as the port of Southampton, which, with the acquisition of its dock estate by the London and South Western Railway in 1892, passed into a new phase of its history as a rival to London. At that time Britain had more registered tonnage than the rest of the world put together.

Transatlantic crossings were the first ocean traffic to be influenced by steam: the *Sirius*, the first British ship to cover the whole journey by steam, crossed from London to New York in 1838, one day ahead of, but three and a half days more slowly than, Brunel's *Great Western*, which had made the journey from Bristol. A year later Samuel Cunard secured the valuable North Atlantic mail contract and the Cunard line was born. It took time and effort, first for the steam-powered iron ship to supplant the wooden ship under sail and then for the steel ship to take the place of the iron ship during the 1880s.

By the end of the century, however, things had changed. Crowded cargo ships, small or big, were plying the oceans from the Arctic to the South Pacific, so that Rudyard Kipling could ask in one of his frequently recited poems:

> 'Oh, where are you going to, all you Big Steamers,
> With England's own coal up and down the salt seas?'
> 'We are going to fetch you your bread and your butter,
> Your beef, pork and mutton, eggs, apples and cheese.'

Not all the ships were going to the ports Kipling listed, like Melbourne, Quebec, Hong Kong or Bombay, over which the Union Jack flew; some went to Buenos Aires, Bangkok, Baltimore and San Francisco, and to more remote harbours in what historians have identified as 'informal' empire. There were also passenger boats with, at one end of the scale, luxury liners complete with brightly lit salons and richly furnished cabins, and at the other, ships with much lower standards (though these too were improving) in which large numbers of emigrants travelled to lands of imperial settlement, like New Zealand or Canada, or crossed the Atlantic to find a new life in America. In fact, as many as two-thirds of the three million people who left to form a new life overseas between 1850 and 1880 went to the United States.

The emigrants' motives were as mixed as their backgrounds. Some were pushed out of England in hard times; many hoped for a better life and were attracted by opportunities not be found in their own country. The first settlers in Australia had been convicts, but transportation was brought to an end in 1849. Meanwhile, New Zealand and South Australia were settled from the start by free men on 'principles calculated to promote the earliest and greatest prosperity'. 'Impossible to describe their energy, their ardour, their decisiveness,' wrote the French observer Taine of two young people, born into a family of twelve, who were about to leave for New Zealand in the 1850s: 'one feels a superabundance of energy and activity, an overthrow of animal spirits.' And for almost all the emigrants there was no return: Ford Madox Brown chose the right title for his famous painting 'The Last of England'.

Colonial society was very different from that at home. A

fashionable Englishman in Adelaide in 1854 was appalled when a wharf hand, refusing to carry his carpet bag or to be lectured on deference to his superiors, retorted, 'You may keep your dignity and I will keep my blue shirt and we shall see who will wear the best and longest in this country.' A great imperial city like Melbourne might think of itself as a Victorian city like Birmingham or Leeds, and might celebrate Queen Victoria's Jubilee of 1887 'with an enthusiasm that was not excelled in any part of the Empire', but only thirty years earlier the colony of Victoria had been turned topsy-turvy by the great gold rush of the 1850s. The values not of the city but of the outback came to be appreciated late in the century and were ultimately to shape a distinctive 'Australian' legend. In 1823 a young Australian at Cambridge University, who came second in the competition for the Chancellor's medal, yearned for an 'Austral Milton', even an 'Austral Shakespeare', but seventy years later there was a very different strain in verses called 'Old Australian Ways':

> The narrow ways of English folk
> Are not for such as we:
> They bear the long-accustomed yoke
> Of staid conservancy:
> But all our roads are new and strange,
> And through our blood there runs
> The vagabonding love of change
> That drove us westward of the range
> And westward of the suns.

By the final decades of the century, however, the greatest imperial expansion came not through settlement but through conquest and rule, reaching its zenith between the 1880s and 1914 when over 4,500,000 square miles were added to the areas of the world printed red on maps. There were many different versions of the imperial mission, presented by missionaries, traders, industrialists, politicians, poets and professors, and their arguments for colonization ranged from 'carrying light and civilization to the dark places of the world' to the expansion of British trade and support for British industry (and British working men) and to the search for adventure and romance. But whatever the motives behind formal and informal empire, there was one necessary condition of their existence, the *Pax Britannica*, and that in turn relied on a command of the oceans. Ships were essential not only for defence, but for all links between the Empire and the mother country.

If ships were ubiquitous, aeroplanes were rare. As late as 1901 H. G. Wells, prophet of 'the shape of things to come', stated that he did not think it at all probable that aeronautics would 'ever come into play as a serious modification of transport and communications', although he conceded generously that 'very probably by 1950 a successful aeroplane will have soared and come home safely'. In fact, Orville and Wilbur Wright made the first powered flight in December 1903, not in an airship but in an aeroplane, and in 1909 Louis Blériot was to fly across the Channel from France to England in forty minutes. Although it was not until around 1950 that civil aviation became a major form of transport, already, while England was in command of the world's oceans, it had lost its secure island status. 'Aeroplanes actually in stock,' read an advertisement in *Aero* magazine in the year Blériot crossed the Channel. 'Prices from £200 . . . FREE TUITION given with all aeroplanes and one mile guaranteed flight on delivery.' Five years later a German aeroplane was to drop a bomb on English soil for the first time.

10

VICTORIANISM:
PRELUDE, EXPRESSION, AFTERMATH

The middle third of the nineteenth century does not, I acknowledge, appeal to me. It is probably due to the natural ingratitude which we are apt to feel towards our immediate predecessors.

A. J. Balfour, *University Address*, 1905

People don't realize that the Victorian age was simply an interruption in Britain's history.

Harold Macmillan, quoted by Anthony Sampson, 1981

Victorian values were the values when our country became great.

Margaret Thatcher, in a television interview with
Brian Walden, 1983

SOME of the most eminent Victorians, conscious of the fact that they belonged to a new and *parvenu* civilization, sharply questioned the triumphs of communication and the industrialization with which it was associated. Matthew Arnold, for example, complained of 'this strange disease of modern life with its sick hurry, its divided aims'. England was always something more than an industrial society. And older influences, notably the survival of pre-industrial forms of social hierarchy and their accompanying values, prevailed until the last decades of Victoria's long reign (1837–1901) and often impressed themselves upon visitors more strongly than what was new.

'Palaces, halls, villas, walled parks all over England, rival the splendour of royal seats,' wrote R. W. Emerson, who visited England in 1833 and 1847. 'Primogeniture built those sumptuous piles.' The so-called New Domesday survey of English land showed that in 1873 four-fifths of the land was held by 7,000 individuals, peers prominent amongst them. Nor was it only the great owners who commanded deference through their titles as well as through their possessions. For the Reverend John Hamilton Gray in the preface to the fourth edition of Burke's *Landed Gentry* published in 1862, the year after Mayhew's *London Labour and the London Poor* appeared, some peers were 'mere mushrooms when compared with a large proportion of our country gentry . . . whose families were established as a county aristocracy at a date when their lordships' ancestry did not possess an acre of land'. Bagehot suggested three years later in his brilliant essay on the English constitution that even the insolvent squire 'will get five times as much respect from the common peasantry as the newly-made rich man'. The whole of society, including, to the horror of Richard Cobden, industrialists, continued to give precedence to status that was transmitted rather than acquired.

Bagehot was at pains to insist, as many earlier social commentators had done, that Queen Victoria reigned over a society dominated by contrasts. On one side were men of ideas and men of power who had made their way to success or inherited it; on the other side were 'ignorant' Dorset labourers, who would pelt 'agitators' rather than listen to them. The 'characteristics of the lower regions' of society resembled 'the life of old times rather than the present life of the higher regions'. An American visitor to England in the same decade discovered 'queer little villages' in Wiltshire 'which looked as if the cottages were built by the immediate followers of Hengist and Horsa'. Despite the rise of 'public opinion' (and its organ, the Press), there were limits to effective social communication, even in the cities. One writer in Liverpool claimed, for instance, that 'two communities dwell side by side as within sound of the same bells and under the same chief magistrate . . . practically as wide apart as if they lived in separate quarters of the world.'

And according to Bagehot, there were large numbers of Englishmen who believed that the Queen, and not Parliament, governed the country. The civil servants most Englishmen knew were, first, tax collectors and, second, inspectors of various kinds whose activities, like those of the police (another largely Victorian invention), were often resented. In reality, the civil service, which doubled in size between 1854 and 1900, was playing an increasingly important part – along with local government officials – in the task of governing the country. An uncorrupt civil service, chosen after 1870 not by patronage but by open competitive examination, has been rightly described as 'the one great political invention in Victorian England'; and its role in shaping the course of legislation has been carefully analysed. Another distinctive feature of Victorian England was the low level of direct taxation. Although income tax was introduced in 1842 by Peel, who reduced or abolished a whole cluster of indirect taxes, it was still possible for Gladstone, who hated all taxation, to contemplate getting rid of it in 1873. Meanwhile, from 1866 the Select Committee on Public Accounts, serviced by a Comptroller and Auditor-General, was supervising government spending and at the same time safeguarding institutional morality.

The adjective 'Victorian', which first came into use in 1851, the year of the Great Exhibition, is a more fitting label to apply to a highly distinctive age than labels like 'industrial society'. It carries with it all the conflicts and compromises of the times, and all their self-consciousness and pride. But there were many changes in attitudes and styles during Victoria's long reign. The notion of a single, shared moral code, to which the label 'Victorianism' has been attached, becomes absurd when one places Florence Nightingale, the 'lady with the lamp', a woman of spirit with the highest sense of service, alongside the Earl of Cardigan, Crimean War commander, who fought a duel as late as 1840, was accused of adultery and spiriting away the chief witness in 1843, and once ordered his men to wear 'cherry-coloured pants', which, according to *The Times*, were 'as utterly unfit for war service as the garb of the female hussars in the ballet of *Gustavus*'. Eccentricity was an important part of the Victorian pattern.

Victoria's sixty-three-year reign, with all its light and shade, can most usefully be divided into early, middle and late periods. It is the middle period, which was a time of economic progress, social stability and cultural diversity – punctuated by the Crimean War, which is often left out of the reckoning – that has been allowed to colour too strongly the interpretation of the whole, but in fact the early years, which came to an end with the Great Exhibition, have more in common with the late Victorian years that began with the 'watershed' of the 1870s. Then, as the young Liberal John Morley put it brilliantly, 'Those who dwell in the tower of ancient faiths look about them in constant apprehension, misgiving and wonder . . . [for] the air seems to their alarm to be full of missiles, and all is doubt, hesitation and shivering expectancy.' During the middle years there was a balance of interests; during the early and late years there was a divergence of interests, even a sense of rebellion.

During the 1840s the voice of prophets, notably Thomas Carlyle, could always be heard, and the language of both working-class Chartists and middle-class anti-Corn Law Leaguers was often violent and their rhetoric romantic. Landlords were 'a breadtaxing oligarchy', 'unprincipled', 'unfeeling' and 'rapacious'. At the same time, Lord Melbourne, Victoria's first Prime Minister, could call the League 'the wildest, maddest scheme that has ever entered into the imagination of man to conceive,' and he had even less sympathy with its leaders than with 'the fustian jackets and unshorn chins of England'. A survivor from the eighteenth century, he was not alone in contemplating the possibility of revolution. Although in 1828 the Metropolitan Police Force had been founded by Peel, Melbourne's successor as Prime Minister, there was no adequate provincial police force to control the situation until the County and Borough Police Act of 1856 made obligatory the maintenance of local police forces. It was the army (and special constables) who had had to be called upon to deal with the threat of physical force which Chartism seemed to carry with it.

During the middle years of 'equipoise' many of the fires of discontent burnt out and the contemporary emphasis was on interlocking interests and on specific and limited pieces of improvement, local as well as national, the need for which was usually forced on the attention of the public by a particular mid-Victorian scandal. There were still storms, but many of them were storms in teacups. Palmerston, 'Lord Evergreen', the leading politician of the age, was very different from Peel. In the words of Bagehot, he was a statesman of the moment who managed to reconcile 'self-help', the ideal which lay at the heart of mid-Victorian thought and behaviour, with the older ideal of 'the gentleman'. In a speech on foreign policy in 1850, he told the House of Commons, still elected on a strictly limited franchise:

> We have shown the example of a nation in which every class of society accepts with cheerfulness that lot which Providence has assigned to it, while at the same time each individual of each class is constantly trying to raise himself in the social scale not by injustices and wrong, not by violence and illegality, but by persevering good conduct and by the steady and energetic exertion of the moral and intellectual faculties with which the Creator has endowed him.

Foreigners could not easily translate either 'self-help' or 'the gentleman' into their own languages, but there were many English people who were as well aware as Palmerston was of how to reconcile the two ideals in practice. Thus the hero of Mrs Craik's much-read *John Halifax, Gentleman* (1854), the story of an orphan who made a fortune, built a house and bought a carriage (the most important Victorian status symbol), was told by his son, 'We are gentle folks now.' 'We always were, my son,' was the father's reply.

Much that is thought of as characteristically Victorian belongs to this middle period of the reign, when no single political party dominated the scene. Although a new Liberal Party was in the course of formation, the idea of a highly organized national political party with a constituency base was new. Progress did not seem to depend on the state: it was the product of society. The favourite mid-Victorian historian, the Whig Macaulay, whose unfinished *History of England*, published in several volumes, was extremely popular with his own contemporaries, extolled not only past triumphs, notably the constitutional settlement of 1688, but also, with a touch of complacency, the current burst of economic, technical and scientific progress. Recent scientific progress, he claimed, had

> lengthened life . . . mitigated pain . . . extinguished diseases . . . increased the fertility of the soil . . . given new securities to the mariner . . . furnished new arms to the warrior . . . spanned great

rivers and estuaries with bridges of form unknown to our forefathers . . . lightened up the night with the splendour of the day
. . . extended the range of human vision . . . multiplied the power
of human muscles . . . accelerated motion, annihilated distance
. . . facilitated intercourse, correspondence, all friendly offices, all
dispatch of business; and enabled man to descend the depths of the
sea, to soar into the air.

At the time that Macaulay was writing, England was the richest
country in the world, with a per capita income 50 per cent higher
than that of France and almost three times that of Germany in
1860. Moreover, all sections of society, except the poorest,
seemed to be benefiting from prosperity. Prices were rising, but
not sharply, and money wages were rising faster, particularly for
skilled workers. (One-seventh of the workers, according to the
mid-Victorian statistician Dudley Baxter, took up one-quarter of
the total remuneration.) Profits were rising too, as were rents and
farm incomes, a fact of equal importance in ensuring harmony.
The repeal of the Corn Laws had not taken the prosperity out of
the land; the mid-Victorian years, indeed, were a golden age of
high-profit farming.

There was a place in these years, however, for argument and
even for doubt and pessimism. In the remarkable year 1859, the
year in which Darwin's *The Origin of Species* was published, along
with Fitzgerald's *The Rubaiyat of Omar Khayyam*, and Smiles's
Self-Help (which admitted that 'prodigality is more natural to
man than thrift'), John Stuart Mill's *Essay on Liberty*, which
attacked social conformity and pleaded for full play to be allowed
to man's individuality, also appeared. The most controversial of
these books was undoubtedly *The Origin of Species*, which reinforced religious doubts that already existed and which shocked
not only religious fundamentalists and Evangelicals but also
leading figures within the scientific community. But it was Mill's
Essay on Liberty that raised most questions about the pattern of
contemporary society. Mill's father had been a close friend of
Jeremy Bentham, whose insistence that government should seek
to realize 'the greatest happiness of the greatest number' pointed
towards both more responsible and more efficient government.
John Stuart Mill had been brought up as a Benthamite utilitarian,

but now he was primarily concerned with the quality of society and with the character of individuality.

There was always scope for criticism in mid-Victorian England, both of loose thinking and of dubious practice. 'Cant', in particular, was much under attack by essayists and poets, among them Matthew Arnold, spokesman of 'sweetness and light', and Arthur Hugh Clough, a close friend – he was also a close friend of Bagehot's – who commented in his famous *New Decalogue*:

> Thou shalt not steal: an empty feat
> When it's so lucrative to cheat.
> Thou shalt not covet, but tradition
> Approves all forms of competition.

The critique could be broader. Following a murder trial at Aylesbury in 1857, for example, the *Saturday Review*, a sharp-edged periodical, summed up the difference between fact and fancy in the often sentimentalized countryside:

> Fornication and adultery, incest and murder, abortion and poison-ing – all the tangled annals of the poor – this is 'Our Village' at work – this is Christian and happy England.

In the less sentimentalized town Emerson saw childhood 'oftenest in the state of absolute beggery' and women as 'cheap'.

Nonetheless, the critics were never in the majority. The *Saturday Review* was an edgy voice, and only one of a wide range of periodicals which, along with novels, reflected or shaped minority opinion. Carlyle's prophecies had been most welcomed when they were in harmony with existing prejudices. Emerson, who went with him on a visit to Stonehenge, choosing the company of the 'latest thinker' in the oldest place, was convinced that England had produced 'more great men than any other actual nation'. The cult of greatness was always strong, turning natur-ally into hero worship.

Charles Dickens, the most popular member of a great galaxy of Victorian novelists, who reserved his own life from his readers, knew that there was much in mid-Victorian society that many mid-nineteenth-century readers (and most writers) believed had to be kept out of view because it was 'debasing' and not 'elevat-ing', a favourite Victorian adjective. Melbourne had dismissed Dickens's *Oliver Twist* as 'all about Workhouses, and Coffin Makers, and Pickpockets'. 'I don't like that low and debasing view of mankind.' And now a new generation was shocked by everything that did not fit into the accepted pattern, sharing the pontificating Mr Podsnap's prejudice, 'I don't want to know about it; I don't want to discuss it; I won't admit it.'

During the early years of the reign there had been sharp conflicts of style – above all between revived and revered Gothic, style among styles, and disparaged but not discarded classical – and argument continued between those who favoured 'old' styles and those who pressed for a 'new' style appropriate for a 'new age'. There were, in fact, many would-be taste-makers in this changing society, a society which was influenced both by fashion and by some 'elevated' taste-makers who wanted to stay above it. During the eclectic mid-Victorian years, however, there were so many combinations and compromises that historians of the arts and crafts, and of design and architecture, have written of an unprecedented bastardization of tastes. You could choose any-thing from Ancient Egyptian or Norman to Moorish-Spanish and Chinese, not to speak of 'French Renaissance freely treated'. There were new materials too, like gutta-percha, brought in from Malaya in 1842 and 1843, and 'silver electroplate', made by a process discovered one year before Victoria came to the throne and commercialized in 1840.

Another new process was invented by William Baxter and used in his widely distributed Baxter prints. These could fill every inch of wall space. Indeed, within the mid-Victorian home – and often outside it – there was little free space. Most of the surfaces were decorated; curves were generous; nothing, least of all the table leg, was allowed to be bare; and the anecdotal pictures on the wall usually carried with them messages. Churches and chapels too – and many new ones were built – had their texts.

The collapse of the great Victorian boom of the late 1860s and the early 1870s was one of the breaks between the middle and later Victorian years. So too was the collapse of high farming during the late-1870s, which produced not only a marked drop in the incomes of farmers and landlords but a change in the appearance of the countryside – far more pasture and far fewer fields of wheat, 'from corn to horn', as the saying went, with more market gardens, orchards and hopfields during the 1880s. And while foreign competition was driving some farmers to demand a return to protection, industrialists were also complaining of the threat from abroad. Nonetheless, the countryside was becoming an increasingly desirable place of retreat for businessmen, and working men were enjoying a wider range of cheap consumer goods than they had done earlier in the century.

There were other themes in the period too: the growth of the professions in terms of numbers, organization and influence, which brought with it more specialized knowledge, set out in textbooks and assessed in examinations; the rise of unskilled labour, most obvious in London and the big cities; the new demand not for limited but for organic reform; the impact on English politics of Irish home rule, which split Gladstone's Liberal Party and left the Conservatives in power for the better part of two decades; local government reorganization, which led to the setting up of elected county councils in 1888 – and a new London County Council; changes in taxation, notably death duties in 1889; the extension of the franchise to many working men in the towns and in 1884 to village labourers. 'A country of respectful poor, though far less happy than where there are no poor to be respectful,' Bagehot had written, 'is nevertheless far more fitted for the best government.' But there was trouble in the streets as well as in the mind – demonstrations of the unemployed, rioting in Trafalgar Square. The extension of school education was almost inevitable in such circumstances – and Morley thought it the most important national question – but cultural anxieties persisted. George Gissing and Thomas Hardy were two novelists who expressed them. What was the difference between a 'market' and a 'public'? Was quality being debased? Were traditional values adequate? Elizabeth Chapman could write in 1888 of a 'general revolt against authority in all departments of life which is the note of an unsettled, transitional, above all democratic age,' while the anatomist of his time, T. H. S. Escott, perceived 'old lines of demarcation' being obliterated, 'ancient landmarks of thought and faith removed . . . The idols which we revered but a little time ago have been destroyed.'

The Victorian critics of 'Victorian*ism*' were more determined and audible during the late Victorian years than they had been at the beginning. It was not only that 'self-help', 'character' and 'respectability', essential elements of Victorianism, began to be questioned, or that manifestations of these Victorian qualities in action, such as industry, abstinence and thrift, were also under attack, but that the tone in which the qualities were discussed was very different from before. Thus 'earnestness' was completely out of fashion during the early 1890s. Oscar Wilde could play with all its dubious associations in *The Importance of Being Earnest*, subtitled 'a trivial comedy for serious people', and the novelist Samuel Butler could treat the Christian name Ernest more ironically still in *The Way of All Flesh*. 'The virtues of the poor may be readily admitted,' Wilde and the socialist playwright George Bernard Shaw explained, 'and are much to be regretted. The best among the poor are never grateful. They are ungrateful, discontented and rebellious. They are quite right to be so.'

During the last decades of the century there was also a general 'reaction' against mid-Victorian styles when the designers of more simple 'Arts and Crafts' objects (the term 'Arts and Crafts' was coined in 1888), including furniture, tried to get rid of Victorian 'clutter' and 'jumble'. It was then also that a new generation of Victorian 'domestic' architects built homes in styles, including 'Queen Anne', into which older mid-Victorian objects just would not fit. These were the bridge years in the making of the 'modern movement', although at the same time there was as much talk of *fin de siècle* as of *art nouveau* and all the other so-called 'new' phenomena, from the 'new woman' to the 'new unionism'. It was not, however, that luxury disappeared from the world, for if the landed interest was facing increasing financial problems, a new 'plutocracy' was coming into its own. 'The great advantage and charm of the Morrisian method,' wrote Walter Crane, a socialist disciple of William Morris, 'is that it lends itself to either simplicity or splendour.' You might have an oak trestle table and rush-bottomed chairs and a piece of matting or 'golds and lustre . . . jewelled light and walls hung with rich tapestry'. The reaction was possibly not as general, however, as the earlier reaction against the taste of the eighteenth century, when Bath began to look dull and Chippendale chairs were relegated to the attics.

The reign of Edward VII (1901–10) was to provide many further contrasts. Not only were many Victorian restraints removed but increasing recognition of the inequalities of society produced sharper feelings of guilt and more organized forms of protest. After statisticians had probed poverty and popular newspapers had publicized their conclusions, Liberal politicians, returned to power with a huge majority in 1906, turned to social reform as an issue. The franchise question had dominated reform politics in the nineteenth century; now the time seemed ripe to make England, in the words of the new Liberal Prime Minister, Campbell-Bannerman, 'less of a pleasure ground for the rich and more of a treasure house for the nation'. Yet in some respects social contrasts became more picturesque. This was the golden age of the country weekend, of the London season, of the new business tycoon, of the Gaiety Girls (who sometimes married not tycoons but aristocrats), of the bustle and of the top hat, and, above all, of the golden sovereign. It was also an age, however, when real wages were falling and when farm labourers were worse off than many of the casual labourers in the docks. Maud Pember Reeves was the author of a much publicized book of 1913, *Round About a Pound a Week*. Nearly eight million people were living on incomes of less than twenty-five shillings a week, 'underhoused, underfed, and insufficiently clothed'.

It is the first age in history for which we have ample surviving oral evidence, following Paul Thompson's tape-recorded interviews with 500 surviving Edwardians, but other kinds of evidence are relevant too. 'To an American democrat,' the American ambassador wrote in 1913 – in a year when there were many signs of protest on the part of working men and, above all, of militant Suffragettes – 'the sad thing is the servile class.' Some historians have been impressed by the fierceness of social conflict in the years between Lloyd George's radical budget of 1909, which produced a constitutional crisis when it was thrown out by the Lords, and the outbreak of the First World War. Trust in the law seemed to be giving way to intransigent assertion of the will. 'They place the golden age behind them,' *The Times* wrote of many of its readers in 1909. For the ambassador, however, it was the 'abjectness' of the servile class which stood out. 'It does not occur to them that they . . . or their descendents . . . might ever become ladies and gentlemen.'

What, in retrospect, had been most remarkable through the breaks of Victoria's reign was a shared continuity of experience, finally to be broken in 1914. It was landmarked experience too, stretching back self-consciously to the Great Exhibition of 1851, the symbol of the beginning of the mid-Victorian years, and reaching later climaxes in the two great Jubilees of 1887 and 1897. By that time the weekly magazine *Punch*, which since its first publication in 1841 had often caught the middle-class mood, at least in London, was in no doubt that the Queen herself, more than any other person, represented continuity in a changing society and culture. No monarch after Elizabeth I left quite such a powerful impression on contemporaries and posterity.

'We have come to regard the Crown as the head of our morality,' wrote Bagehot. 'We have come to believe that it is natural to have a virtuous sovereign.' But this was a new belief; during the Regency and the reign of George IV (1820–30) almost the opposite had been taken for granted. George's memorial was the Brighton Pavilion, a magnificent building, dismissed though it was by the Reverend Sydney Smith as 'the dome of St Paul's . . . come down to Brighton and pupped.' George IV's zest for the arts – and knowledge of them – has recommended him more to posterity than to his contemporaries, who were already beginning to be shocked by his rakishness and debauchery. There were, in fact, several signs of 'Victorianism before Victoria', like Dr Bowdler's carefully tidied 'family version' of Shakespeare, published in 1818, by which time Evangelical influences were already strong, but it was Queen Victoria herself who, probably uniquely among monarchs, gave her name to a new 'ism', and, despite rare signs of active republicanism during the 1870s, by the time of her death in 1901 the editorial of a popular newspaper could read:

> The Queen is dead. No language can express the sense of personal
> loss . . . Few of us, perhaps, have realized till now how large a part
> she had in the life of everyone of us; how the thread of her life, in
> binding and strengthening, like a golden weft, the warp of the
> nation's progress, has touched and brightened the life of each and
> all her subjects.

The *Annual Register*, searching for precedents for such reactions,
had to look as far back as Alfred.

At the core of Victorianism there had been what Gladstone, the
popular Liberal leader who had started as a Conservative before
the Reform Bill of 1832, called 'the rule of ought'. He introduced
the twenty-ninth volume of his remarkable *Diary*, a key document for an understanding both of the private man and of the
public figure, with the two compelling lines:

> He spoke no word, he thought no thought
> Save by the steadfast rule of Ought.

For many Victorians duty took precedence over inclination, and
the moral law over the pursuit of pleasure or of power. Gladstone, like many of his eminent contemporaries, was a convinced
Christian. He found the 'rule of ought' difficult to follow himself, and in trying to do so, or in pointing out to the public that
his rival Disraeli did not, he neither neglected the opportunities
nor avoided the perils of politics. Indeed, he became a popular
politician who bridged the transition to democracy and lived
long enough (1809–98) to become 'a Grand Old Man', lampooned as well as worshipped. Many of his most devoted supporters were Noncomformist chapelgoers who, in supporting
public 'causes' like the campaign against 'Turkish atrocities'
which gripped Gladstone, demonstrated the operation of
what was known at the time and since as 'the nonconformist
conscience'.

The motive of public service, local or national, was as active a
force in Victorian society as the profit motive, and although it had
not been absent in previous periods of history, many of its
features were unmistakably Victorian. It not only guided individuals like Florence Nightingale, who set out to reform nursing,
but mobilized voluntary organizations and pressure groups of

every kind, like the Royal Society for the Prevention of Cruelty to Animals, for foreigners a characteristic English institution, itself founded before Victoria came to the throne. 'In England,' one of Wilde's characters was to exclaim, 'a man who can't talk morality twice a week to a large, popular, immoral audience is quite over as a serious politician.' Yet moral reform cut across the increasingly sharp dividing lines of party and could cross social and religious barriers also. The best-known of all social reformers was the Conservative seventh Earl of Shaftesbury, an Evangelical who was inspired by his religion to take up such causes as that of the factory workers battling for the Ten Hour Day and that of the chimney sweeps who were too young and weak to battle for themselves. He was also a prominent supporter of public health reform and of strict Sabbath observance. At his funeral in 1885 large numbers of the working men whom he had tried to help were in attendance.

If moral reform often united, religion often divided, and although judges insisted that Christianity was 'part and parcel of the law of the land', there were sharp divisions within the Church of England itself from the 1830s onwards between the Evangelicals, who had done much to shape 'Victorianism', and the high church Tractarians, some of whom, like John Henry Newman, moved 'over to Rome', to the alarm of their contemporaries. A debate on the nature of religious authority, which divided Evangelicals and Tractarians from the beginning of the reign, was extended in later years into dispute about styles of worship in the Church, plain or colourful, Protestant or Catholic. Both 'parties', however, shared a fear of developing nineteenth-century science, which challenged most current versions of Christian orthodoxy, and it was left to a third 'Broad Church' party, neither Tractarian nor Evangelical, to seek to align itself with the liberal forces of the century. What is remarkable is that religious 'agnostics' – a new term – could share Victorian moral values and rules of conduct while doubting Christian beliefs. Thus the great non-Christian novelist George Eliot believed fervently that it was necessary to be good for the sake of good, not for God. She once deeply impressed a Cambridge don by telling him 'with terrible earnestness' in the evening light of a college garden that whenever she

heard talk of the three powerful Victorian words 'God, Immortality and Duty', she felt that the first was inconceivable, the second
unbelievable and the third peremptory and absolute. The moral
law spoke from inside: it was not imposed. Those Victorians who
felt its demands were 'inner-directed' people, and the demands
lost their absolute quality only when indifference took the place of
opposition or when relativism became fashionable. It was recognized, of course, that there were always perils of indifference,
particularly in the cities and among the working classes. In the
new diocese of Manchester alone £1,500,000 might be spent
between 1840 and 1876 to create parishes and build new churches,
but as the one national religious census of the nineteenth century,
that of 1851, showed, there were large numbers of people outside
the influence both of Church and Chapel.

Gospelling seemed a duty in such circumstances, and this was
not an activity confined to religion alone. If Gladstone and
Shaftesbury could turn liberalism and conservatism into gospels,
T. H. Huxley, taking up Darwin's cause, could do the same with
science. And so also, late in the century, could many socialists with
politics. They thought of themselves as belonging to a 'movement' that drew its strength from below, from failure as much as
success, and dreamed of a transformed society based not on
privilege and power but on the acceptance of fundamental human
principles of equality and justice. Indeed, for many years they
were less inhibited than other politicians in their gospelling by
reason of the fact that they were not associated with one single
party. They were not forced, therefore, either to make compromises, as the Liberals were, or to depend on support from the vested
interests of property, as the Conservatives did. The ethical note of
socialism, its appeal to 'truth and righteousness', was usually
strong. 'The meaningless drivel of the ordinary politician,' Keir
Hardie wrote in 1888, 'must now give place to the burning words
of earnest men whose hearts are on fire with love of their kind.'
The new society was to be characterized by solidarity (or
'brotherhood'), but within it all individuals would be able to
realize their full individuality.

Even during the 'naughty 1890s', the years of the late Victorian
rebellion, the 'rule of ought' held sway. In the very year when *The*

Importance of Being Earnest was produced, Wilde's trial, the *cause célèbre* of the century, which centred on his homosexuality, not only destroyed him personally but broke the spell of other rebel influences: after the trial all forms of 'decadence' and all attacks on 'respectability' were pilloried. There was a huge gulf between the *Yellow Book*, the creation of the avant-garde, and the new popular 'Yellow Press', as its critics called it. The weekly magazine *Punch* wrote definitively after the trial:

> Reaction's the reverse of retrograde,
> If we recede from dominant excesses,
> And beat retreat from novelists who trade
> On 'sex', from artists whose *chefs d'oeuvres* are messes,
> 'Tis time indeed such minor plagues were stayed.
> Then here's for cricket in this year of Grace,
> Fair play all round, straight hitting and straight dealing
> In letters, morals, arts, and commonplace
> Reversion into type in deed and feeling
> A path of true Reaction to retrace.

The sense that cricket, represented in these lines by W. G. Grace, was quintessentially English was well brought out eight years later when G. K. Chesterton wrote that 'we have a much greater love of cricket than of politics' and 'C. B. Fry [another great cricketer] represents us better than Mr Chamberlain.' 'It isn't cricket' became a catch phrase.

If the intricate conventions of the playing field were linked in some sense with the 'rule of ought', the home was its shrine. 'The possession of an entire house,' the author of the introduction to the 1851 census had remarked, 'is strongly desired by every Englishman, for it throws a sharp, well-defined circle round his family and hearth – the shrine of his sorrows, joys and meditations.' The special place of the home, 'Home! Sweet Home!', was a continuing theme of the period. 'The Englishman's home' was 'his castle'. This was the first generation, G. K. Chesterton also wrote, 'that ever asked its children to worship the hearth without the altar'. The hearth featured prominently not only in cottage parlours and in the back rooms of palaces but in brand new, sometimes turreted, Gothic Victorian villas, where the new middle classes lived in privacy and detachment. It was John

Ruskin, whose 'family life' was far odder and sadder than that of Queen Victoria, who described the family, with a note of longing, as 'the place of Peace; the shelter, not only from all injury but from all terror, doubt and division'. It was hailed as a refuge too from the often fierce competitiveness of business life.

What many Victorians *wanted* the home to be was in fact very different from the 'lodgings' in which many of them lived for part, at least, of their lives. 'Household happiness, gracious children, debtless competence, golden mean', sang the modern poet of the age, Alfred, Lord Tennyson, but in practice there was often a huge gap between ideal and reality, the kind of gap which was to make 'Victorianism' suspect as a code. The game of happy families was only a spectator game for some of the most eminent Victorians, and the kind of reverence that ran through Coventry Patmore's poem *The Angel of the House*, a hymn to conjugal love, was out of fashion by the end of the century. Family values within the working-class home are still largely hidden from the historian's view: there was a contrast there, however, between the 'respectable and the rowdy', the latter drawn from childhood into the life of the streets.

The biggest city homes were detached villas, complete with lawns, shrubberies and, in the richest homes, conservatories, sometimes with pineapples growing in them. There were even bigger Victorian country houses, of course, most of them used now for other purposes or already pulled down, ornate piles, draughty and often uncomfortable as well as imposing. In the towns, semi-detached houses (an invention of the nineteenth century) were commonplace, but so too were standard terraced houses and, in a few places, 'back-to-backs'. The smallest city and village homes were 'cruel habitations' packed into limited space, cramped as well as cluttered. Sir John Simon, a pioneer of public health, pointed out in his *Report on Sanitary Conditions of the City of London* in 1854 that 'it was no uncommon thing, in a room of twelve foot square or less, to find three or five families styed together . . . in the promiscuous intimacy of cattle.' The terms 'overcrowding' and 'slum' were new in the early nineteenth century, and there was increasing awareness of their reality towards the end of it.

Contrasts were evident at every point within the 'domestic economy'. The biggest divide was between those who employed domestic servants and those who did not; during the twenty years following the Great Exhibition the number of domestic servants increased by 60 per cent, twice the rate of increase of the population. Not all the families who did employ servants were rich by the standards of the day, but those who did not employ them were indubitably poor. The pattern varied. Great households employed elaborate hierarchies of servants, while upper- and middle-class families had their own different versions of the upstairs/downstairs divide. Lower-middle-class families, dependent on one or two servants, had to make do within small space. There were similar variations in patterns of manners, food and dress, though belief in the 'roast beef of old England', if not the ale that accompanied it, was shared across the social divides. In her successful, often reprinted and rewritten *Book of Household Management* (1861), Mrs Isabella Beeton included dishes which depended not only on lavish ingredients but also on servants for their preparation (and sometimes, given their scale, for their consumption). Yet although there was a vaunted increase in working-class consumption of foodstuffs, particularly during the mid- and late-Victorian years, the adulteration even of relatively cheap food, including bread and milk, was a serious and much publicized problem, and popular addiction to pickles and to beer has also been attributed – too easily perhaps – to decaying food and filthy water. Annual tobacco consumption, the social costs of which, unlike those of beer and of spirits, were not measured, had already risen from 14 oz. to 1·5 lb. per capita between the 1830s and the late 1870s.

It is necessary to probe more deeply behind the tobacco smoke into the demography of the Victorian period before taking Victorian sermons on the family and home, or books and novels about them, at their face value. Yet the hidden features of Victorian family patterns became the subject of a considerable literature for the Victorians themselves, more extensive and searching from the 1870s onwards. One particularly illuminating mid-Victorian book on sex, the first edition of which appeared in 1857, was Dr Acton's *Functions and Disorders of the Reproductive Organs in Youth, in Adult Age, and in Advanced Life, Considered in their Physiological, Social and Psychological Relations*. Acton, who has been described as the Samuel Smiles of continence, stated categorically – and he was not alone in this appraisal – that 'intellectual qualities are usually in an inverse ratio to the sexual appetites. It would almost seem as if the two were incompatible; the exercise of the one annihilating the other.' His choice of the adjective 'intellectual' was too restricted, for his prized quality of 'abstinence' was closely related to foresight, self-control and thrift, the qualities demanded not of the thinker but of the businessman. And there was a widespread opinion among Victorian – and Edwardian – middle-class observers that it was lack of foresight that most distinguished the working classes.

Leaving on one side questions of social circumstance, a moralizing attitude to sex was inevitable in an age when there was a moral colouring to all social argument. Yet as the nineteenth century went by, sexuality, even when repressed, emerged from a conspiracy of silence and became a part of social consciousness. The late Victorian revolt concerned itself with sex as well as with class (and with the relation between the two). It also seemed bound up with the national destiny, so that Havelock Ellis, born in 1859, who wrote profusely about sex, could argue that it was 'not merely the instrument by which race is maintained and built up' but 'the foundation on which all dreams of the future must be erected'.

It is not easy to relate either mid-Victorian ideals or late-Victorian criticisms of these ideals to practice. While the woman was apparently 'venerated' within the mid-Victorian home, at least as much as the Queen was in the nation as a whole, the pedestal on which she was placed was a false one. Women had to be 'pure': chaste before marriage and 'modest' after marriage. Their sexuality was explicitly denied, and annual pregnancies (along with limited employment opportunities outside the home) guaranteed their dependence.

> Man for the field, woman for the hearth,
> Man for the sword and for the needle she:
> Man with the head and woman with the heart,
> Man to command and woman to obey.

The father who expressed these thoroughly pre-industrial sentiments in Tennyson's *The Princess* was a good Victorian. Yet the influence of prostitution, which was acknowledged as 'the great social evil' in the mid-Victorian years (estimates of the number of prostitutes then varied widely between 30,000 to 368,000), derived not from a different but from the same male moral code. There were many 'secret lives', some of the most active of which often crossed class lines. While bachelors who married late might turn to a prostitute, married men with enough money might take a mistress. 'Fallen women' were the 'victims'. Rebel voices openly attacked this double standard of morality in the late nineteenth century, and a 'social purity alliance', led by Josephine Butler, was formed to campaign against the Contagious Diseases Acts. Their suspension in 1883 (three years later they were repealed) was followed by a Criminal Law Amendment Act in 1884 which set out to suppress brothels, raised the age of consent for girls to sixteen, and introduced eleven new penalties against male homosexual behaviour. There was to be further tightening-up of legislation in a Vagrancy Act of 1898 and a second Criminal Law Amendment Act in 1912.

In marriage, the dominating position of the husband was still buttressed by the law, and it was not until 1870 and 1882 that Married Women's Property Acts were passed, granting women rights to property whether secured before marriage or after. (Political rights were not to come until after the suffragette agitation.) The first of a chain of divorce acts, the Matrimonial Causes Act of 1857, which set up secular divorce courts, had authorized divorce on different terms for those few men and women who could afford it. A husband needed only to show evidence of his wife's adultery; a wife had to show evidence of other marital failings too, like cruelty or desertion. For social and economic reasons, as well as religious ones, the number of divorces remained low throughout the Victorian years, affecting only 0·2 per cent of all marriages at the end of the century.

There was clearly a great variety of relationships between husbands and wives. In particular, there were significant class and local differences; and there may well have been less restrictive attitudes to pleasure or enjoyment in working-class than in middle-class (if not in aristocratic) families by the end of the century. Nevertheless, artisans were marrying later, illegitimacy rates had fallen since the mid-nineteenth century and rates of first pregnancy conceived before marriage dropped from 40 per cent to 20 per cent between the early nineteenth and early twentieth centuries.

In general, Victorian families were big. In 1851 their average size was 4·7, roughly the same as it had been in the seventeenth century, but the 1·5 million couples who married during the 1860s, which the historian G. M. Young described as the best decade in English history to have been brought up in, raised the figure to 6·2. Only one out of eight families had one or two children, while one in six had ten or more, so that the counsel 'little children should be seen and not heard' was prudent rather than simply authoritarian advice.

The most obvious of the many new 'facts' that stood out in nineteenth-century England was the growth of population and its concentration in increasingly segregated districts. The decennial statistics are almost as compelling as the imposing set-piece photographs of family groups and crowded shopping streets, another new kind of evidence for the social historian. Total population rose from 16·9 million in 1851 to 30·8 million in 1901, increasing at a faster rate than that of Germany, Italy or Russia, and at a far faster rate than that of France. Families might have been larger still had not infant mortality remained high, although, as it was, one out of two Englishmen in 1871 was under the age of twenty-one and four out of five under forty-five. The aged Victorians with their great beards were a small minority, though these mid-Victorian years were undoubtedly peak years for the *pater familias*, years of potency and fecundity, years of pride more than of fear.

At the beginning of the century there had been national fears of over-population, and Thomas Malthus, clergyman, political economist and moralist, who believed fervently that social measures like outdoor relief for the poor or indiscriminate alms-giving added to the demographic – and human – problems, was widely quoted in early-Victorian England. The tough new Poor Law of 1834 was not directly inspired by him, but many of its defenders were 'Malthusians' who wanted restraint on family size to be enforced in workhouses, the often terrifying places which the Victorians described simply as 'institutions' and to which all types of poor were confined. By the middle of the nineteenth century, however, in defiance of Malthus, family size had reached its peak, and by the late-Victorian period there were already scattered fears of under-population which were to grow during the twentieth century.

We know little, nonetheless, about the changes in demography which were associated with a fall in the birth rate during the 1870s, the decade of Victorian uncertainty. The rate, which had been nearly stable for half a century at around thirty-five per 1,000, fell between 1875 and 1880 – without any obvious new display of what Malthus called 'moral restraint' – before falling more sharply still to around twenty-four per 1,000 in the years before 1914. By the last decade of the nineteenth century, average family size had fallen to 4·3 and by the outbreak of the First World War to 2·3. There was talk of a 'twilight of parenthood'.

What kept total population up was an equally remarkable phenomenon, a steady fall in the death rate from 1875 onwards. By the end of the century it had dropped from around twenty-two per 1,000 to fourteen per 1,000, while life expectancy had risen from forty to forty-four for men and forty-two to forty-eight for women. There was no Malthusian explanation for this phenomenon either, since it clearly reflected a measure of social if not individual control which was no more envisaged by Malthus than the great increase in economic productivity achieved in the nineteenth century. Other factors were clearly at work in the change of attitudes to family size from the 1870s onwards. Improved living standards and rising material expectations seem to be among them, and family budgets reveal some of the underlying economics.

Nutritionists as well as economists and sociologists have interpreted both what the Victorians ate and how much of it. From the late 1870s onwards, cheap American corn began to arrive in the country in large quantities, along with refrigerated meat and fruit from Australia and New Zealand, and in a period when both

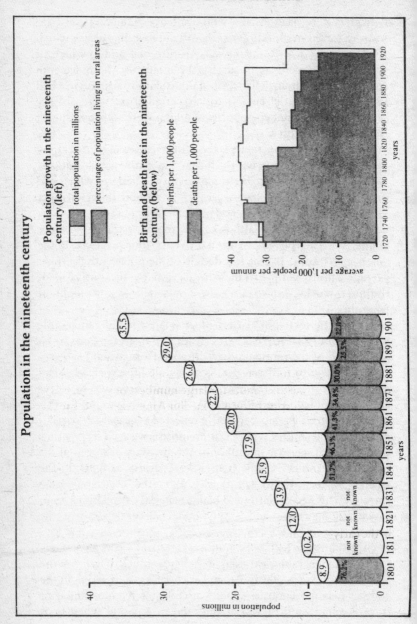

Population in the nineteenth century

farmers and businessmen were complaining of depression, standards of living rose higher than they had ever done. The change began, as Victorian writers frequently pointed out, with the daily 'hearty' breakfast table – porridge, eggs and bacon were staple fare for the middle classes – and went on through tea, high or low, to multi-course dinners or fish-and-chip suppers. The poor were eating better as well as the rich. The annual per capita consumption of sugar, which had increased from 18 lb. to 35 lb. between the Queen's accession and 1870, rose to 54 lb. in 1870–99 and 85 lb. in 1900–10; consumption of tea, which, along with beer, had now become a national drink, went up from 1·5, first to 4·25 lb. and then to 6 lb. For the middle classes, sugar tongs went with the sugar and table covers with breakfast, lunch, tea and dinner.

Yet the key to the explanation of change in family size is not hidden in piles of family bills nor, in the case of working-class families, in lost calculations about how much children cost (from 1876 they were compelled to go to school) and how much they could earn. More important was the growing sense that children were not just 'sent by God' and that the number of children within each family could be 'controlled' in relation to circumstance. Work and leisure patterns and considerations concerning the upbringing and care of the individual child were part of these circumstances. So too was religion, although it was no longer the determining guide to conduct for large numbers of people.

The term 'birth control' was coined in America just before the First World War, before Marie Stopes, who did not like the term, drew public attention to it. Death control had come earlier as a response, in part at least, to the terrifying statistics of differential mortality in the 1830s and 1840s. Given that people in different areas and social groups had such enormous differences in their chances of death, could not the gap between their fortunes be narrowed? The 'sanitary idea' and improvements in public health in the early- and mid-Victorian period, like the Public Health Acts of 1848 and 1869, had a moral dimension: you could get behind Fate and manage your own destiny. In retrospect, the quest for 'birth control' seems complementary, although it involved hidden decisions in the home rather than public decisions in the open by parliament or by the local authority. There were links, of course, between the two, as doctors concerned with public health exposed the conditions in which poorer people lived.

Given the multiplicity of family decisions, the fall in birth rate was bound to be differential. Figures of family size by social group reveal different chronological patterns of development, with the upper and professional middle classes apparently leading the way in contraception. The trial in 1876 of Charles Bradlaugh, spokesman for the secularists, and Annie Besant for republishing Charles Knowlton's tract on the subject had drawn public attention to the issue, and over 200,000 copies of the Knowlton tract had been sold within five years. For couples married between 1890 and 1899 the average number of children was 2·8 in a professional family, 3·04 in a white-collar worker's family, 4·85 in a skilled manual worker's family and 5·11 in an unskilled labourer's family. During the following decade the comparable figures were 2·05, 1·95, 3·24 and 4·09.

It was during this period that compulsory schooling introduced a set of influences that were to become as significant as any from within the family. Indeed, the tasks of the new Board Schools, set up after 1870, were conceived of as social even more than educational: pupils were to be disciplined to accept their place in society. In the wide range of working-class private schools in existence before 1870, where the teachers were not formally qualified, there had been little emphasis on the regulation of conduct, but in the schools controlled by religious or other voluntary bodies before 1870 and in the new Board Schools, 'proper conduct' was instilled in a disciplined manner and 'street culture' was as far as possible controlled. So too were manners and morals. 'Found boys and girls playing in the same playground,' a Rotherham school log book recorded in 1890. 'Witnessed much indecent behaviour.'

Secondary and higher education, reorganized though it was in the important new Education Act of 1902 which abolished the School Boards and handed education over to the local authorities, remained socially stratified. The grammar schools, given new scope by the Act, took in a limited number of local boys, some of ability demonstrated in scholarship examination, some as fee-payers; and there were girls' schools too, some with remarkable headmistresses, dealing with a smaller section of the population. The 'public schools', many of them explicitly high church or Evangelical, educated a segregated section of the community along lines designed to assure that those leaving them would be 'gentlemen'. Their tasks too were pre-eminently social. As a writer in the *Athenaeum* put it in 1860, they were in harmony

> with a certain rude, vague, yet quite intelligible something, which may be called the English Scheme of Life. The Great Endowed Schools are less to be considered as educational agencies, in the intellectual sense, than as social agencies.

By the end of the century the public schools had produced many Flashmans, the bully described in *Tom Brown's Schooldays*, Thomas Hughes's gripping novel set at Rugby School, alongside the kind of spiritual leaders Dr Arnold, its headmaster, had set out to produce and the middle-of-the-way boys like Tom Brown himself; and, following Rugby, which had invented that supremely English game, they turned increasingly to the ethos of team games. All three types found opportunities for themselves on the frontiers of empire as well as in the City and in the professions at home. For all the insularities of Mr Podsnap, Victorianism was never a completely insular phenomenon.

11

THE DIVIDES OF WAR

War is everywhere, and is more and more conceived as an end in itself.

The Nation, 7 October 1916

I am not getting any new flags though, only using an old one I had left over from the last war.

Woman overheard in a bus, *Mass-Observation*, 1945

Never such innocence again.

Philip Larkin, 'MCMXIV' in *The Whitsun Weddings*, 1964

'THE STORY of the human race,' wrote Winston Churchill, 'is War' – and he was writing before the Second World War, during which he emerged as one of the greatest twentieth-century war leaders. Yet in 1900, even though English troops were fighting in South Africa, only a few people in England could have forecast that war and peace would be a main theme in twentieth-century world history. Bagehot had represented the views of many nineteenth-century Englishmen when he had argued earlier in the century that modern society had moved from the 'fighting age', a relic of feudalism, into the 'age of discussion'.

There was not much English experience to suggest otherwise. The great European wars of the twentieth century, both of which became world wars, were very different in scale and character from the 'little wars' of the nineteenth century, in some of which Churchill had been personally involved as a young man. The latter had been fought along the lines of many of the wars of the

Roman Empire, by small numbers of regular soldiers against hostile forces on distant frontiers (Sikhs, Afghans, Ashanti, Zulus and Sudanese); sometimes they were punitive expeditions to enforce law and order, sometimes they were more ambitious campaigns to annexe territory. As little theory was applied to warfare as to industry, and the armed forces themselves underwent only very limited changes until the last decades of the century. At the close of the protracted Napoleonic Wars, the last great struggle, there had been 220,000 men in the regular army. By 1840 the number had fallen to just over 100,000, although it climbed back to 200,000 during the last decades of the century following major War Office reforms carried out by Edward Cardwell, a staunch supporter of Gladstone, between 1868 and 1874. The purchase of commissions was abolished, short service enlistment was introduced and the War Office itself was reorganized. Nevertheless, the emphasis was still placed on traditional continuities: 'Great Britain has produced a race of heroes who, in moments of danger and terror, have stood as "firm as the rocks of their native shores",' wrote 'A Voice from the Ranks' in the popular book *A Soldier's Experience* at the end of the century.

The Royal Navy remained the senior service and the guardian of the *Pax Britannica*. Tennyson described its importance for England:

> Her dauntless army scattered, and small,
> Her island – myriads fed from alien lands –
> The fleet of England is her all-in-all.

Yet it had changed little more than the merchant navy, the indispensable instrument of the country's wealth. Nor had strategy been re-examined during the 1860s and 1870s in the light either of new technology or of the fact that the country was more vulnerable to blockade than ever before. It was only during Gladstone's period as Prime Minister in 1884, immediately following the widening of the franchise, that a supplementary naval appropriations bill was passed. This introduced a five-year plan of naval build-ups, the prelude to the Naval Defence Act of 1889 which authorized the building of eight large and two small battleships and heralded an age of naval expansion.

By then there had been war between France and Germany in 1870. Britain remained neutral, but by the end of the century there had been a significant growth in both war expenditure and the appeal of militarism. At the end of the century 'soldiers of the Queen' were engaged in the most protracted and controversial of the colonial wars, not against 'native tribes' but against white Boers in South Africa. And this war pointed to general questions which were to be posed by the 'Great War' of 1914–18 – the physical fitness and educational standards of the recruits, links between war and social policy, the need for 'efficiency', the role of public opinion and of propaganda, the horror rather than the glory of battle, and the awareness that war could not be won quickly or easily despite preponderant British strength. 'Our days are spent with reading our papers ever clamouring for more action,' wrote an English friend of Alfred (later Viscount) Milner, Britain's leading representative in South Africa, in November 1899, 'our nights in dreaming of all that is and to be . . . The war affects all, rich and poor alike. All have friends and relations in it.' A few months later, however, another knowledgeable correspondent was suggesting that the 'English public' was war-weary: 'the heroics are over'. The war did not end in 'unconditional surrender'. Nor did it provide the basis for a settlement of the problems that were to force South Africa into English newspaper headlines in the 1980s.

There was a growing sense during the Boer War that 'the Empire's destinies for good and evil' were 'in the hands of the masses of the people'. Yet crucial decisions relating to war and peace between 1902 and 1914 were taken behind the scenes, many of them inside the newly established Committee of Imperial Defence, which was described by Asquith, the Liberal Prime Minister, in 1909 as a 'useful, indeed an invaluable addition to our constitutional machinery'. The origins of the Great War were located in Europe; the public was not aware of the implications of an evolving network of diplomatic alignments which guaranteed that if war did break out it would not be restricted war, as it had been in 1870. Yet the naval race between Britain and Germany often hit the headlines in the popular press, and the word 'crisis' acquired a new meaning.

Opinions about international issues were as divided as they were about empire. The Nonconformist conscience was strong, but so too were undercurrents of jingoism. And there was an increasing literature of violence, including a popular invasion and resistance literature, which, looked at in retrospect, helped to prepare opinion for war. As Bertrand Russell put it, 'the barbaric substratum of human nature' was tapped. There was flirtation with violence too in domestic and Irish politics between 1910 and 1914, so that it has been possible to interpret the arrival of war not as a surprise but as a consummation.

The small regular army with which Britain entered the war, supported by a large contingent of reservists brought back to the colours who constituted 60 per cent of the first Expeditionary Force, was quite inadequate, and although a 'New Army' created during the first fourteen months of the war – in response to the appeals of a charismatic Secretary for War, Lord Kitchener – eventually attracted over 2,250,000 volunteers, it was still not big enough. And it was losing its officers. By the end of 1914 the dead included six peers, sixteen baronets, six knights, eighty-five sons of peers, eighty-two sons of baronets and eighty-four sons of knights. After a series of compromises general compulsion was accepted in the early summer of 1916 and by 1918, when the war ended, the army's ration strength, which had been 164,000 in August 1914, had risen to a remarkable peak of 5,363,352; indeed, there were far more men in the newly formed Royal Air Force alone (30,127 officers and 263,410 other ranks) than there had been soldiers in 1914. The men were backed with animals and internal combustion engines; the animal ration strength rose from 27,500 in 1914 to 895,770 in 1918, while petrol consumption in France alone rose during the same period from 250,000 gallons a month in 1914 to 10,500,000. 'This has been called an engineers' war,' wrote the 'Temporary Lieutenant' author of *The Motor Bus in War* in 1918, 'and petrol is the key to it.'

The relentless demand for munitions as well as for men, animals and machinery forced government to intervene increasingly in the management of the economy. The taking over of the railways in 1914, to be administered 'not by government but for the government', was the first of many limitations on private enterprise, and by the end of the war large new government departments, like shipping and food, had been set up, some of them almost overnight. What has been called 'a command spiral' took the place of the laws of supply and demand, leading inevitably from one government intervention to another. The result was a great increase in the number of civil servants, though power at the top, particularly after 1917, was often in the hands of businessmen turned politicians.

Attempts were made to control the land as well as industry, and Milner of South Africa was appointed Chairman of the Committee on Agriculture in the summer of 1915. In practice, County War Agricultural Committees were not very effective, although one war-time change, the introduction of 'summer time' in May 1916, met with both farmers' and industrial workers' protests. By 1917, when there was only about three weeks' food supply in the country and the Women's Land Army was set up, two-thirds of the industrial workforce were subject to governmental regulations. There was also a system of rationing, limited in scope but bureaucratic in organization. A *Punch* cartoon of 1918 with the caption *David in Rhonddaland* showed Lloyd George arguing with Lord Rhondda, businessman turned Minister of Food. 'I'm often away from home,' says David (Lloyd George). 'How do I get sugar?' 'You don't,' replies the Mad Grocer (Lord Rhondda). 'You fill up a form.' 'But I *have* filled up a form,' David insists. 'Then you fill up another form,' the Mad Grocer tells him.

Lloyd George was the second war-time Prime Minister, appointed in 1916 after Asquith's government collapsed, and it was he more than any other politician who drew businessmen into government. It was he who had been in charge of also munitions, the sinews of war, and he who had been taken up by the Press. Both he and Asquith were Liberals, although from 1915 onwards the governments they headed were coalition governments, and liberalism, in fact, was one of the casualties of the war. 'War is not conducted according to the rules of liberty,' wrote one well-known Liberal in 1918, 'although the war has been the only means by which liberty can be preserved.' The Defence of the Realm Acts (DORA) of 1914, extended in 1915 and 1916, involved a degree of government interference with individual freedoms which would have been thought intolerable a year earlier, and military conscription was a particularly difficult issue for the Liberals. So too were war-time economic controls, bringing to an end decades of free trade and high direct taxation. In 1914 the highest rate of income tax had been 1s. 2d. in the pound, so that even the richest taxpayer was not called upon to pay more than one-seventeenth of his income to the State; by 1918 the standard rate of income tax was 5s. in the pound, and there were now six times as many taxpayers. Even then heavy borrowing was necessary, and Liberals were not alone in expressing profound anxiety about the post-war burdens this would carry with it. 'We have started this war,' Charles Trevelyan (brother of the historian) said in a speech of 1915, 'on the assumption that our resources are so vast that we can do anything that occurs to us.' And by 1918 the national debt was four times the 1914 figure. Indeed, as late as 1932 the burden of debt was twelve times greater than it had been when war started.

It would have been no consolation to most staunch pre-1914 Liberals that one of General Haig's officers could write in 1916:

> Here at GHQ . . . nearly every one of the ramifications of civil law and life has its counterpart in the administrative departments . . . Food supply, road and rail transport, law and order, engineering, medical work, the Church, education, postal service, even agriculture, and for a population bigger than any single unit of control (except London) in England.

Indeed, one prominent left-wing Liberal economist, J. A. Hobson, whose writings on imperialism had influenced the exiled Lenin, believed that militarism would remain an enemy in the peace-time future. It was at the centre, he claimed, of a 'vicious circle of Improperty' along with 'Imperialism, Protectionism, Legalism, Distractions and Emollients (Charity, Sport and Drink etc.), Regulative Socialism, Conservatism, State Absolutism, Authoritarianism (Church, School, Press etc.) and Bureaucracy.' Not many Englishmen, however, thought in such terms. In fact, there were soldiers and civilians who wanted more 'Distraction and Emollients' rather than less. All the great hotels and restaurants were thronged 'for feasting and dancing'. So too were night clubs. 'Every girl has her man in khaki,' a Cambridge professor of economics wrote to the editor of the *Economist*.

The craving for 'Distractions and Emollients' was an inevitable by-product of the kind of war which was waged. Many soldiers had gone to war eagerly in 1914 to the sound of cheering crowds; some were romantic about it. 'Now God be thanked who has matched us with this hour.' Yet the reality of war in the trenches soon dispelled all hints of romance. For years there was stalemate since neither side, hard though it tried (and with appalling losses), had sufficient force to break through. There were 6,000 miles of trenches, numbered by sections, given names like Piccadilly, Hyde Park Corner and Marble Arch by the soldiers serving in them, not only to distinguish them but to try to 'humanize' them. The confined horizons of the trenches enclosed a world of mud and barbed wire, and it seemed sinister when map references were exchanged for names. When Wyndham Lewis first heard the name Passchendaele, where there were to be 144,000 casualties in 1917, he felt from its suggestions of 'splashiness' and 'passion' that it was 'pre-ordained' that 'nonsense' would come to its full flower there. 'Evil and incarnate fiend alone can be the master of this war,' the painter Paul Nash had written in 1915. 'No glimmer of God's hand is seen anywhere.' 'Everywhere the work of God is spoiled by the hand of man,' wrote young Second Lieutenant William Ratcliffe, who was killed in 1916.

Nash's war-torn landscapes contrast sharply with his paintings of the peaceful English countryside. Only the poppies were common to both, but in Flanders fields, where they grew prolifically, 'sunset and sunrise' were 'blasphemies'. In his verses the war poet Isaac Rosenberg huddled together the men in the Flanders fields, as post-war cemetery keepers were to place crosses over their graves neatly, side by side, in rows:

> Iron are our lives
> Molten right through our youth
> A burnt space through ripe fields
> A fair mouth's broken tooth.

THE DIVIDES OF WAR

Slaughter was, in fact, appalling, though the English lost far fewer than the French. While it is true that war deaths among the troops – it has been estimated that some 850,000 soldiers were killed – were fewer than the number of emigrants from the British Isles in the years just before the war, such a statistic did not matter. In time, it was said, people began to get used to the deaths, a terrifying form of adaptation. Yet as families were broken up and communities ravaged, a pall of grief hung over all sections of society. Asquith himself lost a brilliant son killed in the Somme; almost one in five Oxford students were killed. Wives lost their husbands, sweethearts their fiancés; some women were never to marry. Personal relationships were irretrievably affected – not always, of course, for ill – and there were breaks in the continuity of management in nearly every local and national institution. These were the great divides of the twentieth century: one writer has compared them to the Grand Canyon.

Death, which was a matter of luck, was not the only human sacrifice to a new Moloch. Injured, gassed, shell-shocked, blinded men staggered back from the wars to a life that would never be the same again. Of the 8,000,000 men who were mobilized, some 2,000,000 were wounded and in 1922 more than 900,000 war pensions were being paid out. In 1928 forty-eight special mental hospitals were still catering for over 60,000 victims of shell shock. The most popular poem of the First World War during the 1920s and 1930s, Laurence Binyon's *For the Fallen*, repeated annually in the shadows of the new local 'war memorials', linked memories and realities:

> They shall not grow old, as we that are left grow old:
> Age shall not weary them, nor the years condemn
> At the going down of the sun and in the morning
> We will remember them.

It was written only seven weeks after the beginning of the war, before the extent of the sacrifice was appreciated. A still more forceful reminder of the level of sacrifice are the far later lines by Henry Reed:

When war is spoken of
I find
The war that was called Great
Invades the Mind.

'Cheerful' letters from the front, duly censored, deliberately concealed the truths of the war, although some soldiers must have revealed them privately on leave in 'dear old Blighty'. The historian R. H. Tawney, then Sergeant Tawney, who took part in the assault on the Somme in July 1916, complained of the popular stereotype of 'the Tommy' as 'a merry assassin, invariably cheerful, revelling in the excitement of war, rejoicing in the opportunity of a scrap'. The full truth – a cluster of individual truths – was revealed in public only after the war ended, in books like *Her Privates We*, whose author concealed his identity, putting only his number on the title page, 'Private 19022'.

This was lyric, not epic, war, although Haig and the generals would obviously have preferred the latter. The most they could achieve was a kind of stoical silence, while Wilfred Owen's deeply felt poems, such as the *Anthem for Doomed Youth*, can still speak across the divides of time and place:

What passing bells for those who die as cattle?
Only the monstrous anger of the guns,
Only the stuttering rifle's rapid rattle
Can patter out their hasty orisons.

Primitive horror was bursting through disciplined routines and the sardonic soldiers' war-songs like *The Bells of Hell* are very different from *Tipperary*, which was written just before the war.

Human sacrifice was more real than technical advance during the war. Zeppelins were used by Germans and not by the British – there were around forty raids – and it was the Germans also who in 1917 began to launch aeroplane attacks on London, producing a feeling that 'the raiders have London at their mercy'. At the front, tanks (another new weapon) were used in numbers by the British only in 1917 after the church bells were rung (prematurely) to celebrate their effectiveness at Cambrai. Lord Northcliffe's claim that the men of the tank crews were 'dare devils' entering upon their task 'in a sporting spirit with the same cheerful enthusiasm as they would show for football' is best forgotten. Yet one of the most memorable – and powerful – images left over from the war remains that of Siegfried Sassoon's tank rolling down the stalls of a theatre in London:

> I'd like to see a tank come down the stalls
> Lurching to rag-time tunes or Home Sweet Home
> And there'd be no more jokes in music halls
> To mock the riddled corpses round Bapaume.

Rag-time rhythms had come in before the war, along with those of the tango – a hundred years before there had been the waltz – but it needed the war itself to create a sense of black comedy.

Many civilians were anxious to share the burden of war, and voluntary organizations contributed substantially to the war effort, handing over to the soldiers 1,742,947 mufflers, 1,574,155 pairs of mittens, 6,145,673 hospital bags, 12,258,536 bandages, 16,000,000 books and 232,599,191 cigarettes. The cheap cigarettes ('fags') they supplied were as much a part of the life of the trenches as the barbed wire, and one of the main army chaplains was named 'Woodbine Willie' after a cigarette. The Salvation Army, a product of the 'darkest England' of the 1880s, was as active a social agency among the troops as it had been in city slums before 1914. But the psychological gap between 'civvy street' and the soldiers' war was far wider between 1914 and 1918 than it was to be during the 'people's war' from 1939 (or at least from 1940) to 1945.

Just as big a psychological gap bedevilled relations between politicians and generals. 'Politicians gave no credit to the Generals,' wrote Lord Beaverbrook, owner of the *Daily Express* and sharpest of all writers on the political scene of that time. 'The Generals denounced the politicians. Soldiers and sailors serving in the Forces had little confidence in either. The public had no heroes.' In 1917 and 1918 there were many signs of war weariness, for it proved difficult to discern, amid what a liberal periodical called 'the stormy welter of waste and woe', any 'stream of cause and effect' pointing the war effort towards 'a determinate conclusion'. The entry of the Americans into the war brought with it, however, new talk of war aims as well as indispensable human reinforcement; and revolution in Russia, culminating in the Bolshevik victory of October 1917, directed attention to fundamental social issues. It was in such circumstances that politicians began to talk more and more of 'reconstruction', changing society after the war. 'No such opportunity has ever been given to any nation before – not even by the French Revolution,' Lloyd George proclaimed. 'The nation is now in molten state . . . We cannot return to the old ways, the old abuses, the old stupidities.'

Already, however, through war experience itself – welfare in the munitions factories, for example, and the extension of pension schemes – issues of social policy had been raised, and trade unionists in particular had urged the need to deal sensibly with social discontent if war production were to be maximized. In 1914 their leaders had urged both employees and their own rank and file to make a serious attempt . . . to reach an amicable settlement before resorting to a strike or lock-out, but as the war effort intensified, such a self-denying ordinance was difficult to maintain, at least at the shop-floor level. Shop stewards were a new force, forging links across the country, and unrest was not stilled when Lloyd George included Labour ministers in his government. One of them, George Barnes, enumerated the reasons for continuing unrest: 'the feeling that there has been inequality of sacrifice, that the government has broken solemn pledges, that the trade union officials are no longer to be relied upon, and that there is a woeful uncertainty as to the industrial future'.

The War Emergency Workers' National Committee of 1914, designed 'to protect working-class interests during the war', was by 1917 waging a 'conscription of riches' campaign, which culminated in the insertion in the new Labour Party constitution, adopted in February 1918, of the unequivocally socialist Clause 4:

> to secure for the producers by hand and brain the full fruits of their industry and the most equitable distribution thereof that may be possible upon the basis of the common ownership of the means of production and the best obtainable system of popular administration and control of each industry or service.

Arthur Henderson, the busy Secretary of the Labour Party, had left Lloyd George's cabinet in August 1917 after sharp differences on foreign policy (in particular, in relation to international labour solidarity and attitudes to post-revolutionary Russia) and the break was to have even longer-term implications than Clause 4. As A. J. P. Taylor has argued, it represented 'the real parting of the ways between Lloyd George and "the people"'. Labour gave notice to quit. And although the reconstructed Labour Party (now with individual as well as corporate members and with a firm constituency base) won only fifty-seven seats when Lloyd George was swept back to power in the General Election of 1918, its electoral position was far stronger than it had been in 1914 – indeed, within a few years it was to take the place of the Liberal Party as the second party in the State.

Labour's position was stronger in other ways also. The Representation of the People Act of 1918 guaranteed for the first time in history a genuinely democratic franchise, and an increase in trade union membership to a peak of more than six million provided the reconstituted party with a corresponding increase of funds. Moreover, in the long run there was no disadvantage in the fact that the party leadership included men who had opposed war in 1914 and had been counted among the much pilloried conscientious objectors when 'super-patriotism' was at its height, since during the 1920s there was to be a sharp revulsion against 'super-patriotism'.

It was possible by then to see many of the other war-time social changes in perspective. One of them was the changing role of women, some of whom benefited from the 1918 extension of the franchise, which gave the vote to women householders and wives of householders over the age of thirty. This cautious reform opened the gates, and nine years later, when it had been demonstrated that the peace-time female electorate was not going to subvert the constitution, women secured the vote on the same terms as men. Most pre-war Suffragettes had responded at once in 1914 to the call of the 'war effort': 'this great war,' Christabel Pankhurst had written, 'is God's vengeance on the people who held women in subjection.' And by 1917 the influential journalist J. L. Garvin could write, 'Time was when I thought men alone maintained the State. Now I know that the modern State must be dependent on women and men alike.' In the same year it was

Asquith, pre-war English enemy and target of the Suffragettes, who moved a parliamentary motion calling for an early bill to effect a recommendation of a recent all-party conference 'to confer some measure of woman suffrage'. The role of women had been greatly extended during the war: some had worked as nurses at the front, far more at the bench in munitions factories, and many others in offices and in occupations hitherto closed to them. Yet by 1921 they constituted exactly the 29 per cent of the workforce that they had done ten years before, and they were not to transform politics.

Perhaps the biggest changes in the role of women were evident in the home rather than the factory or the office, for the struggle for food could be as relentless as the struggle in the trenches. Two weeks before Christmas 1917, *The Times* reported long rows of women queueing for margarine outside multiple-shops in London, some with infants in their arms and many with children at their skirts. Bread and potatoes were never rationed, but staple prices had to be subsidized in 1917, and potatoes were often in short supply. The first commodity to be rationed was sugar in January 1918, after *Punch* had invoked a highbrow nineteenth-century ghost:

> O Matthew Arnold! You were right:
> We need more Sweetness and more light;
> For till we break the brutal foe
> Our sugar's short, our lights are low.

Weekly per capita consumption of sugar fell between 1914 and 1918 from 1·49 to 0·93 lb. and of 'butchers' meat', which was rationed by coupon later in 1918, from 2·36 to 1·53 lb. Yet despite the grumbles about short supplies and increase in prices – and they were not confined to the middle classes – the calorie intake almost kept up to the pre-1914 level, and Englishmen ate much better than their opponents. Indeed, some working-class English women and children were better fed than they had been before 1914 due to improved employment, canteen meals and easier access to the weekly pay packet. An official report of 1918 noted that School Medical Officers in London had observed that 'the percentage of children found in a poorly nourished condition is less than half the percentage in 1913'.

A social policy spiral directed government inexorably from one kind of intervention to another, just as the command economy did in relation to economic policy. Lord Rhondda insisted that there should be a new post-war ministry before he took up the controversial post of Minister of Food, and when in 1919 Christopher Addison, Lloyd George's aide-de-camp in the 'reconstruction' campaign and one of a group of Liberals who later joined the Labour Party, introduced the bill creating the new Ministry of Health, he glanced sideways at education and drew special attention to physically unfit children in the elementary schools: 'We have them in every age and in every year, not a company or a brigade, but an army.'

By 1918 it was recognized that children as well as women were in need of increased attention on the part of the State as a result of both the effects and experience of war. It may well be that their war-time role changed even more than that of women as the number of children of fourteen or under at work quadrupled. In March 1917, an official demanded the substitution for the conception of the juvenile as primarily 'a little wage earner' by that of the juvenile as primarily a 'workman and citizen in training', and when five months later the Minister of Education, H. A. L. Fisher, introduced the first major Education Act since 1902, he justified the raising of the school-leaving age to fourteen on the grounds that 'industrial pressure on the child' should cease. Fisher, who believed in wider opportunities for 'advanced instruction' as well as primary education, pressed for continuing education after school and defended the abolition of all fees in public elementary schools for the same reasons – that talent should not be wasted. He appealed also to the 'increased feeling of social solidarity' generated by the war and argued that conscription, which had caused so much liberal concern, implied that 'the boundaries of citizenship are not determined by wealth'. J. A. Hobson, whose diagnosis of the effects of war (and conscription) was so different, was in complete agreement with this particular conclusion.

Addison also introduced the crucially important and far-reaching Housing Act of 1919, which was to influence future shapes of family life and the whole appearance of the environment (not to speak of party politics). The act laid on local authorities the duty of surveying the housing needs of their areas and submitting plans for building houses to be subsidised from State funds. Although subsidy arrangements varied significantly during the post-war years, it was this legislation which provided the basis on which local authorities, assisted by the State, went into the business of providing council houses, often in new housing estates. Both women and children were to be given a new home environment.

There were moral issues here as well as social ones. The war had broken up families and 'keeping the home fires burning' was never an easy task. Nor did earlier marriage – one of the effects of war – make for stability. Children's futures were being plotted by politicians at a time when they had often been left to themselves more than ever before. 'Discipline' had slackened as juvenile wages increased and religious restraints were further weakened. 'Nonconformity' in particular began to look old-fashioned: its canons of behaviour were difficult to follow, let alone enforce, in war-time conditions. Sexual *mores* were changing too. Illegitimacy rates increased and contraceptives were increasingly taken for granted: according to one witness, by 1919 'every village chemist was selling them'. The Registrar-General accounted for an upsurge in the illegitimacy rate in 1916 in terms of 'the exceptional circumstances of the year, including the freedom from home restraints of large numbers of young persons of both sexes'.

There was a flood of moral criticism both during and after the war, ranging widely (usually over other people's changing life styles) from dress (short skirts, for example) to drinking (notably by women in pubs). Much of the criticism was class-biased and much of it was anti-urban in tone. And it did not take account of awkward facts like a fall of illegitimacy rates in the 1920s to figures below those of 1914 or the marked decline in drunkenness (convictions had fallen to a fifth during the war-time years). Obviously, however, many surviving Victorian certainties had gone. Contemporaries themselves collected whole anthologies of social comment. 'Everything now being relative,' wrote the novelist John Galsworthy, who had once been a critic of

Edwardian society, 'there is no absolute dependence to be placed on Free Trade, Marriage, Consuls, Coal or Caste.' In the equally eloquent words of a woman graduate, the war shattered 'that sense of security which brooded over Victorian homes and made men buy estates and lay cellars against their old age and for the benefit of their sons'.

Economic changes led to further disruption and anxieties. 'England is changing hands' was a stock remark of 1919, when over a million acres of land were sold. The Marquess of Lansdowne, who had favoured a negotiated peace, used to show visitors a large map of England with the parts belonging to country squires marked in green, exclaiming 'practically all those are doomed to disappear.' In the background was a short-lived post-war boom, but for the government it sometimes seemed that a revolution was in the offing. During both 1919 and 1920 there was a dramatic wave of strikes, with even the police joining in. The boom was followed by what the *Economist* in 1921 called 'one of the worst years of depression since the industrial revolution'. The peace-time temper of organized labour could be as militant as that of the troops in war-time, though the difficulties of bringing different sections of the trade union movement together were well illustrated on 'Black Friday', 15 April 1921, when the railway and transport unions, bound in 'triple alliance' with miners, called off a joint strike a few hours before it was due to begin. The most frequent response of Lloyd George's coalition government to pressure was not to redress injustices – indeed, it drastically disbanded war-time controls (except for those on rents) – but to temporize while its intelligence service investigated 'subversive' activities. It knew that it was backed by a majority in Parliament and by middle-class opinion, with *The Times* proclaiming, for example, that 'the domestic economic war, like the war with Germany, must be fought to a finish'.

Unlike the Great War, however, the domestic war was not fought to a finish because, in the last resort, there was not the same degree of determination on either 'side'. The fall of the coalition government in 1922 and the return to power of the Conservatives gave the Labour Party the opening it needed; in 1924 it came to power for the first time as a minority government. Yet events thereafter showed that there was little pressure inside England for revolutionary change: the Labour government itself did nothing to suggest that it wished to carry through even a far-reaching radical programme. Nor did a second minority Labour government, in office from 1929 to 1931. Indeed, faced with financial crises Labour's Prime Minister Ramsay MacDonald, who had been a pacifist during the war, chose (without a general election) to head a 'national' government consisting predominantly of Conservatives. Clearly, the social framework of the country, by then tested by severe economic depression, had not changed as much as many of the commentators of 1919 and 1920 had suggested.

Nor should the General Strike called on 3 May 1926 in support of the miners, a unique event in English history, be considered evidence to the contrary. The response was total, and practically no trade union members in any occupation returned to work until the strike was called off, but the Conservative government, returned to power in 1924, was able to keep sufficient services running to maintain supplies – and order – and to avoid breakdown, largely as a result of voluntary support. And despite propaganda from both sides, there was relatively little social tension. It has been suggested by one historian that 'though each side attributed extremist policies to each other, neither meant it seriously.' Despite rank and file commitment, the trade-union leaders at the centre, who had been reluctant to embark on the strike, were lacking in the will-power to continue it, while the Prime Minister Stanley Baldwin, who believed in seeking consensus, was more anxious to encourage reconciliation than to impose unconditional surrender. The General Strike was called off on 12 May with no assurances to the miners, who were left to fight alone at heavy cost – including the further decline of their industry.

In 1927 the government passed a new Trade Disputes Act, which sought to ensure that there would be no doubt in the future as to the illegality of a general strike, and the trade unionists were insistent that they would repeal it as soon as possible. Nevertheless, some of their most important leaders took part a year later in talks with employers about the future of industry which were arranged by Sir Alfred Mond, head of the massive Imperial Chemicals Industries, an example of the increasing scale and concentration of post-war industry. There were so many forces making for collaboration rather than for confrontation that the General Strike has been seen in retrospect not as the high-water mark of class warfare but as the moment when the class war ceased to shape the pattern of British industrial relations – until the 1970s. At the time the General Strike ended, the editor of the Labour newspaper the *Daily Herald*, first launched in 1911, detected 'a feeling of intense relief everywhere'. 'I saw just now a placard in a shop window, "Peace with Honour",' he went on. 'I hope it is.' The point was as much debated as 'peace with honour' in Europe was twelve years later after Neville Chamberlain, who succeeded Baldwin as Prime Minister in 1937, returned from Munich waving in his hand an agreement with Hitler. The novelist E. M. Forster summed up the mood of the intervening years when he wrote, 'the twenties react after the war and recede from it; the thirties are apprehensive of war and are carried towards it.'

Baldwin himself was strongly aware of the shadow of the last war as the shadow of a new war approached. 'Its memory still sickens us,' he explained in 1935, when he stressed the necessity to preserve 'the lives of our children and grandchildren, the familiar sites and institutions of our own land and all the boundary stones of our spiritual estate'. This was the language Baldwin always liked to use. England was neither fascist nor communist, he insisted, by reason of the history of its people. It was too late by then to pass from history to economics and to count the cost of the great war, for already rearmament, designed not to prepare Britain for a new war but to save it from one, was about to stimulate the economy. In fact, Britain had never fully returned to 'normalcy': 40 per cent of its merchant fleet had been lost and foreign investments drastically cut, and while British manufacturing production had fallen during the war, that of the United States had increased by 22 per cent and that of Japan (a formidable rival in the post-war textiles industry) had risen by 76 per cent between 1913 and 1920. Markets abroad were lost while new competitors industrialized. In 1932, on the eve of Hitler's rise to power in Germany, 2,750,000 people in Britain, including large numbers of uninsured black-coated workers, were unemployed, and the structural problems of the economy were to persist in the 1930s.

Baldwin left it to Chamberlain to try in vain – although with the backing of a sizeable proportion of the electorate – to 'appease' Hitler. Yet Hitler could not be appeased, and when war did come it was to be even longer than the 'Great War'. On this occasion there was none of the remarkable enthusiasm of 1914. Nor did the news of its beginning break upon the country by surprise; a significant proportion of the electorate opposed 'appeasement' and believed that Hitler should have been 'stopped' sooner. Conscription had already been introduced and 'air raid precautions' organized on a limited scale.

At first, however, the struggle against Hitler was perceived rather as a 'phoney' war, called by one Mass-Observation correspondent the 'rummest war I ever knew'. There was little excitement to stir a public which had been led to expect a quite different kind of struggle – experts had predicted that 600,000 people would be killed and the same number injured in the first air attacks, which would last 60 days. When the first air raid siren sounded on Sunday 3 September 1939 one woman not untypically 'clasped' her baby, 'sent aloft a prayer and waited for the worst'. Characteristically, however, that warning was a false alarm. The worst did not come, and soon, amid the 'blackout', there was a sense of anti-climax. The number of children evacuated from their homes was ten times the size of the Expeditionary Force sent to France, but the serious psychological and social problems spotlighted by the evacuation had more to do with pre-war deficiencies than wartime exigencies. Closing cinemas, now a leisure mainstay, and theatres and putting the BBC into a straitjacket did not help, although the former soon reopened (and prospered) and broadcasting rapidly became an indispensable agency both to inform and to sustain. Meanwhile, it did not help that in order to foster a mood of confidence, the Ministry of Information, an unpopular wartime innovation, was making a conscious appeal to history and that one official's suggestions for the Ministry's first poster had been a picture of a long bowman from the Hundred Years War, standing with his feet outspread (to represent steadiness) and drawing his bow (to denote vigour). Behind him there would be a silhouette of England (in green): one of the man's feet might be in Devon, the other in Kent . . .

It was not until the hot summer of 1940, following the German Blitzkrieg in the West, that the country experienced what Winston Churchill – who in May 1940 had replaced Chamberlain and formed a coalition government including Labour – proudly called its 'finest hour'. British troops – 225,585 of them – were forced to leave the European mainland and escape in an improvised fleet of small boats from Dunkirk between 26 May and 4 June, and for a time the island seemed to be in danger of invasion. 'Be ye men of valour,' Churchill commanded as there were signs of pride in standing 'alone' against Hitler. The threat of invasion ('careless talk costs lives') led to the mobilization of a 'Home Guard', which has passed into legend, but very soon air raid wardens were to be more in demand than platoons of soldiers as the German Air Force attacked the island in strength. It was fortunate that barrage-balloon Britain was supported by the Empire, by allied governments in exile and quietly, behind the scenes, by the President of the United States and large numbers of its people.

A fascinating picture of life in bombed London has been reconstructed from contemporary accounts collected by Mass-Observation, which had been set up in 1937 'to supply accurate observations of everyday life and *real* public moods'. It was one of the most interesting new ventures of the 1930s, started by Tom Harrisson, who watched human beings in the same way as he watched birds; and during the war some of its scattered surveyors were drawn into public reporting. There was, in fact, no single response to the protracted German attack in either London or the provinces, where there was massive destruction in towns like Coventry and Hull, but in general the blitz brought people closer together to share their burdens.

This was the 'people's war', when J. B. Priestley's Yorkshire voice so proclaiming it was almost as influential as that of Churchill. And while he sought consolation in English history and the countryside, as Churchill did, he demanded with equal firmness equality of sacrifice and a new and more equal deal when the war was over. 'We're not fighting to restore the past,' he exclaimed. 'We must plan and create a noble future.' Churchill's 'unknown warriors' were to be not merely allowed but encouraged to win both the war and the peace. This was the message too of the lively illustrated magazine *Picture Post*, which had been launched in 1938, although for the cinema's British Movietone News it was usually enough that 'we live in the presence of history'.

One point was certain. The wartime experience itself remained very different from that of the First World War, particularly after the entry into it of the Soviet Union and the United States in 1941. Although, therefore, the First and Second World Wars were separated by less than twenty-one years, often described as the inter-war years, it would be completely misleading to telescope them together as if they were one. As Vera Brittain wrote, 'to look upon it this way would not only be to get the two wars wrong, but to drastically simplify twenty years of lost history.'

The differences between the two wars were striking. First, there were few trenches and fewer horses. ('Horses have ration books,' a Mass Observer noted in 1942. 'I wonder when they'll issue them for cats.') Second, there were many tanks. Third, there was more science, including radar, primitive computers and atomic power. Fourth, there were many fronts, and much of the war was fought in strange places, including deserts and jungles which contrasted sharply with the English countryside. Much of it too was fought on the 'cruel sea'. In the early and middle months of 1940 it was airmen and, above all, sailors who bore the brunt of the German attack. Literature reflected this, as did films and art: in this war Paul Nash painted not barbed wire fences but wrecked aircraft. 'In the Spitfire,' wrote Richard Hillary, who was the 'type of a new generation' just as the Spitfire was the type of a new breed of fighter aircraft, 'we're back to war as it ought to be. Back to the individual combat, to self-reliance, total responsibility for one's fate.'

The most important difference, however, was the participation of civilians; children were encouraged to do their best 'to help to win the war' and women played an active part on many fronts. By

1944 there were almost 500,000 women in the forces, another 200,000 in the Women's Land Army and well over 300,000 (48 per cent of the total labour force) in the civil service. Garvin's 'dependence' had become greater than even he could have foreseen.

As the war proceeded more and more people were involved in it and the human toll of civilians in the front line was often heavy. During the four months from 7 September 1940 to 1 January 1941, for example, 13,339 people in London were killed and 17,937 severely injured, with the worst still to come – on 10–11 May 1941, 1,436 people were killed and 1,752 injured. In such circumstances courage became a necessary civilian quality. 'My landlady in Pimlico was as brave as a lion,' says a character in Charles Snow's novel *The Light and the Dark* (1947). By the end of the war 60,000 civilians and 35,000 merchant seamen had been killed, while combatant casualties, 300,000, were less than half those of 1914–18. The front line ran through Hull, Bristol, Southampton, Plymouth, Coventry and, in London itself, deep below ground, in the 'good old London tube'. The sculptor Henry Moore's superb shelter drawings catch the flavour; they were given top priority printing in July 1941, when four times as many were printed as a year earlier. And occasionally phrases in the most private diaries catch the flavour too. One civilian wrote:

> When the bombing first started, people were rather nervous, and they didn't know what to do, but after a few days they soon got accustomed to this. When they came along to the shelter in the evenings, they fetched their belongings, insurance cards, the cash, the jewellery, if they had any, a flask of tea, milk for the kiddies, boiled sweets, and the Council started dancing in the parks.

Popular entertainment was increasingly necessary as material austerity had to be enforced. By May 1943, four million workers in nearly 7,000 factories were listening to 'Music While You Work' and to 'Workers' Playtime', given the blessing of Ernest Bevin, the powerful trade unionist whom Churchill chose as his able and effective Minister of Labour. The Council for the Enjoyment of Music and the Arts, known as C E M A – one of the many familiar sets of wartime names based on acronyms – was almost as well known as ENSA, the Entertainments National Service Association, although Bevin thought it 'too highbrow'. When the government gave its first grant to CEMA late in 1939, a popular newspaper described the grant as 'madness' on the grounds that 'there is no such thing as culture in wartime . . . and cultural activities . . . must now be set aside.' But there were far broader cultural aspirations during the Second World War than during the First: Myra Hess's wartime concerts in the National Gallery, for example, were deeply appreciated by a cross-section of Londoners and so too were Sadler's Wells Opera performances in the provinces. Only cultural minorities were involved – the other side of the picture was the Hammersmith Palais de Danse – but minorities were important in the switch from patronage and voluntary organization in the arts to increased state encouragement: the post-war Arts Council was a child of CEMA.

If all this was in some sense the 'superstructure' of war, the material austerity was far more evenly shared than it had been from 1914–18 and a higher proportion of its long-term burdens were borne by taxation rather than by borrowing. Rationing, plans for which were worked out before the war started, was tightly enforced, but it was sufficiently imaginatively handled to allow for an element of choice through 'the points system', introduced at the end of 1941 for non-basic items. Ration levels were related also to nutritional requirements, neglected or misunderstood a quarter of a century before, so that many people were better fed in nutritional terms than they had ever been before. In 1944, total protein intake was higher than it had been in 1939, and the only possible deficiency was in vitamin A. Bread and potatoes were never rationed, and a 'dig for victory' campaign allowed for a regular, if not always plentiful, supply of vegetables in many homes. Communal feeding was encouraged in canteens as well as in schools and in 'British Restaurants' (Churchill coined the term). The Ministry of Food, headed for much of the war by the former general manager of David Lewis's retail store, Lord Woolton – an avuncular politician, new to politics and later to be given charge of 'reconstruction' – was well organized, and its propaganda, though often lampooned and in retrospect dated, was not ineffective. Bread, eggs, meat and cheese were all subsidized and the food prices index at the end of 1944 stood only 20 per cent higher than in 1939. Whatever the privations of war – from censorship to black-out – food controls, coupled with full employment (never achieved during the 1930s) and steadily rising real wages, ensured a relative improvement in the economic position of the lower third of the population.

Warfare and welfare seemed to go together. The number of school meals doubled in 1940–41, as their provision ceased to be a relief measure and became instead a social service. Likewise, more attention was paid to post-natal care, 'putting milk and orange juice into babies', while the Emergency Hospital Service was extended 'so that by the end of the war it provided a solid basis upon which a National Health Service could be built'. In 1944 future social policy was forecast when the Disabled Persons Act made it possible to force employers to take a prescribed quota of rehabilitated workers.

Soldiers, sailors and airmen were as concerned as civilians for their future after the war was over. And so also were the many other people who had either volunteered for, or had been conscripted into, the war effort. 'They don't expect the millennium,' Howard Marshall, skilled pre-war broadcaster, said of the troops; 'They do expect a fair deal.' The pre-war experience of the 'bitter society', as Arthur Marwick has called it, was turning people towards the vision of a better society.

It seemed necessary, therefore, as the war went on, to follow Priestley's approach and not only talk about the future but plan for it. Churchill, preoccupied with 'winning the war', remained reluctant to do so, but it was impossible for him to ignore the immense popular interest generated by Sir William (later Lord) Beveridge's Report on Social Security, published late in 1942, which became a 'symbol of the new Britain', not least for servicemen, who read about it in one of the most discussed pamphlets of the Army Bureau of Current Affairs, ABCA. Beveridge favoured not only a comprehensive social insurance system but economic policies designed to maintain full employment, a national health service, child allowances and a 'new deal' in housing and education. By 1945 most of these matters had either been discussed (often at length) in other official reports, in a 'white paper' chase, or had become objectives of the government. Critics behind the scenes might complain of the cost, but there was little public awareness either of the economic problems of the future or of Britain's wartime economic dependence on the United States. All aspects of social policy from insurance to town planning were explored. Of around 400 memoranda submitted to the principal War Cabinet committees on 'reconstruction' between 1941 and 1945, only sixty-four dealt with Britain's economic future.

In relation to education, action which had a direct bearing on that future came in wartime itself. Ironically, the day that had been set for the raising of the compulsory school leaving age to fifteen in 1939 had been the very day war broke out, but R. A. Butler's Education Act of 1944, the culmination of an insistent demand for educational reform and much backstairs negotiation, more than compensated, it seemed, for the delay. The Act went much further in its proposals than the Education Act of 1918: its object was 'free secondary education for all'. 'War woke people up to the fact that the nation possessed a supply of ability never ordinarily used to the full.' The act provided a framework within which educational change could continue in the classroom 'according to the age, ability and aptitude of the pupils', but it went further in envisaging compulsory part-time education in County Colleges for all persons under eighteen not receiving other kinds of education. The society of the future was to be a better educated society than ever before, although what kind of education there should be was thought out far less carefully.

The two words 'for all' were the clue words to most wartime proposals relating to social policy. Thus, Beveridge insisted on 'universality' in his social security proposals, referring back to the 'solidarity' of the nation in wartime: 'in a matter so fundamental it is so right for all citizens to stand together without exclusions based upon differences of status, function or wealth.' Thus, proposals for housing and planning stressed the need both to build homes and to plan communities. 'Bombs,' wrote the editor of the monthly journal of the Federation of British Industries in October 1940, 'have made builders of us all.' In the wartime film *Dawn Patrol* (1941) one home guard told another, 'We found out in this war how we're all neighbours, and we aren't going to forget it when it's all over.'

12

POVERTY AND PROGRESS

Freedom from want cannot be forced on a democracy or given to a democracy. It must be won by them.

W. H. Beveridge, *Social Insurance and Allied Services*, 1942

Affairs are conducted in a manner at once more just and more humane; and the angry clamour of past struggles is now heavily muffled.

C. A. R. Crosland, *The Future of Socialism*, 1956

Despite the growth in national wealth the age-old inequalities remain. The position of the poor has improved. But so too has that of the rich.

Frank Field, *Unequal Britain*, 1973

THREE years after the end of the Second World War Ernest Watkins set out to write a book for an American audience which would describe clearly and simply 'what life was like for the people of Britain after 1945'. He had been prompted to write by an American friend who asked him a number of leading questions:

Has it all been one long crisis or not? . . . What is this 'socialism' that you English seem to like and we don't? . . . Are candies still rationed? . . . Why don't your trade unions like high wages and high production? And what does it feel like to lose an Empire almost overnight?

Watkins, like other authors before him, began by setting the English scene in terms of a play. The stage directions were plain.

'The curtain rises on a partially wrecked factory. The floor is littered with unfinished shell cases. From the skylights in the roof the blackout material has been roughly torn away.'

His answer to the first American question was that it had not 'all been one long crisis', although there had been a frightening fuel crisis in 1947, when Englishmen shivered in front of their almost empty grates, and an alarming currency crisis two years later when the dollar deficit doubled and Sir Stafford Cripps, the country's austere Chancellor of the Exchequer, devalued the pound drastically (lowering the exchange rate from \$4·04 to \$2·80). His answer to the third question was yes: candies were still rationed and remained so until 1954. There was, indeed, a worsening of the situation for domestic consumers after 1945: bread, which had never been rationed even in the darkest years of the war, was rationed between July 1946 and July 1948 and potatoes at the end of 1947.

The answers to the second, fourth and fifth questions, about socialism, the trade unions and the loss of the Empire, were more complicated. The Labour government of 1945, led by Clement Attlee, had been returned with a huge majority (393:213) and had carried through a testing programme of nationalization of industry while at the same time reorganizing social policy. Yet Labour was to be returned with only a small majority (315:298) in 1950, the year of the outbreak of the Korean War. While the austerity measures were necessary, and while that necessity was expressed in very strong moral terms (particularly by Cripps), they proved increasingly depressing as victory in war receded. Indeed, their unacceptability eventually came to outweigh the popularity of the government's welfare measures.

Churchill, whose anti-socialist slogans had lost votes in 1945, found a winning one in 1951 when he told the electorate that they could choose between ladders (on which everyone could rise) and queues (in which everyone waited for his fair share). Socialism, he claimed, made men equal only by making them equally miserable. The Labour leadership was divided about what strategies to follow, as was the rank and file, and conceded defeat (321:295) to Churchill's Conservatives, although with 48·8 per cent of the votes the Labour Party had more support at the poll than the

Conservatives. It was not to regain office for thirteen years: 'thirteen wasted years', as a future Labour Party slogan was to put it.

Meanwhile, in answer to the fourth American question, the trade unions, now over nine million strong, continued firmly to back the Labour Party and its leadership without succeeding in converting most of their rank-and-file members to a recognition of the need for an end to restrictive practices. When challenged, they usually pointed to the weaknesses of management. There were, in fact, such sharp differences in conditions of work for managers and for workers on the shop floor that dispassionate European observers were often convinced that this was the main reason for Britain's serious industrial problems. Lack of adequate investment and physical and fiscal controls which limited it received less attention.

As for the loss of Empire, there was little popular reaction in England itself, either for or against. As H. G. Wells had once pointed out, the public knew too little about the Empire – 'as little as they know about the Argentine Republic or the Italian Renaissance' – really to care about it. As early as 1948 an American scholar estimated that Britain's strength was one-seventh that of the United States, and much later, in 1962, Dean Acheson, from a position of relative comfort across the Atlantic, made his much quoted judgement that Britain had lost an empire and not yet found a role. In fact, America, which had supported Britain so substantially during the war, had itself contributed greatly to Britain's immediate post-war difficulties by failing – and failing abruptly – to renew Lend-Lease in 1945 and by imposing stringent terms for a post-war loan, negotiated on Britain's behalf by J. M. Keynes. The conditions of the loan, including the convertibility of the pound by July 1947, were impossible to meet. What had been impossible became absurd when prices in the United States rose by 40 per cent between the time when the loan was negotiated and mid-1947. The imaginative if belated attempt in the Marshall Aid programme of 1946 to rescue Britain and its future European rivals (and after 1973, even more belatedly, partners) came only just in time.

Labour's Colonial Secretary, Arthur Creech-Jones, had wanted to carry the benefits of Labour's welfare policies into the remaining colonies, ensuring their peoples 'a fair standard of living and freedom from oppression from any quarter'. But as the histories of the colonies diverged, his – and many of the colonies' – hopes for 'welfare states' were soon to be dashed. Churchill, who was a spectator when India secured its independence in 1947, still preferred the term 'Empire' to 'Commonwealth' in 1951, but it continued to diminish in extent during the next thirteen years.

Watkins by-passed many of these big questions. What seemed to stand out most clearly to him in the immediate perspectives of the late 1940s were the *favourable* contrasts between past and present in Britain, at least as far as 'ordinary people' were concerned. 'The pattern of life for a great many people in Britain between 1945 and 1950 has been different from that which they led ten years previously. More people have a larger income and fewer people have very large incomes.' The same point was made in many of the statistical surveys of this period, which ranged from party political brochures to thick volumes of tables.

Nonetheless, such a sense of material improvement had been obvious in and before 1945. Indeed, it was there even in 1938 and 1939 at the end of what some people called the 'devil's decade', which began in slump, was dominated by unemployment, the main theme of Walter Greenwood's *Love on the Dole* (1932), and the Hunger Marches, and ended in the disaster of war. George Orwell's *Road to Wigan Pier* (1937) catches that mood. Yet already in 1937 a thoroughly revised *Handbook of Suggestions* for elementary school teachers described how 'the general standard of life' had improved and how life itself was being lived 'at a faster rate':

> The universality of motor-transport, of broadcasting, and of . . . cinemas presents new features in the common life, while better housing, the increasing use of electrical and other mechanical devices, the possibility of increased leisure and wider social contacts for all, with their increased opportunities for the enrichment of experience, make it necessary for those engaged in education to review their task afresh.

There was no pessimism there, and nor was there any in the schools themselves, most of which had left the days of drill behind.

Economic historians have subsequently pointed to other signs of 'progress' in the decade before the war, even though the official unemployment rate never fell below 10 per cent and at its peak in 1932 reached 22·5 per cent. In particular, they have offset the development of 'new' industries (and of new industrial areas) against the doldrums of old industries (and of the grim 'depressed areas'), and have pointed away from the images of closed shipyards and derelict mills and mines to the images of brightly lit shops, many of them in new premises. Thus employment in the electrical industry more than doubled between 1924 and 1938, while that in the distributive trades went up from 1,661,000 in 1920–22 to 2,436,000 in 1937–8. Turnover in Marks and Spencer's stores, defying depression, multiplied nearly ten-fold between 1929 and 1939. The index of industrial production stood 75 per cent higher in 1935–8 than it had in 1910–13.

Since there were considerable fluctuations in production from year to year, interpretations of long-term trends often rest too heavily on the year chosen as the base line. Nevertheless, between 1913 and 1938 – and the latter year was a year of recession – real wages had increased by 50 per cent and the working week had decreased by 10–14 per cent. Expenditure on food had fallen from 60 per cent to 35 per cent and on rent from 16 per cent to 9 per cent while weekly expenditure on so-called 'other items' in the housekeeping of the average working-class family had risen from a negligible sum to almost 16s. 'State insurance' was at the top of this revealing list of other items, followed by voluntary insurance and 'medical fees, drugs and hospitals'; equal fourth were trade-union subscriptions and expenditure on 'cinemas, theatres, football matches, etc.' and below that came 'postage, telegrams, stationery, pens, etc.', 'licences for dogs and wireless, food for pets, etc.', hairdressing, laundry and domestic help, and holidays. Reading materials of various kinds do not figure on the list, although with the Penguin paperbacks appearing in 1935 they might well have done.

The last item on the list, holidays, is one of the most interesting.

It would not have been there without a reduction in working hours and a more enlightened pay policy. During the 1920s, 1,500,000 wage earners were entitled to a holiday with pay; by 1938 the figure was 3,000,000 and, as a result of the Holidays with Pay Act passed in that year, the figure rose to 11,000,000 in 1939. Holiday camps, the best known of them Billy Butlin's super-organized camp at 'sunny Skegness', opened in 1937, were widely advertised and on the August Bank Holiday of the same year over half a million visitors arrived in Blackpool. Leisure was increasingly commercialized. Meanwhile, trade unionists – and there were then almost five million of them – were pressing with few signs of militancy and 'not very hopefully' for the forty-hour week, which the French and American workers had to a large extent already secured.

Patterns of demand had also changed significantly before 1945. In nutritional terms, the proportion of income devoted to carbohydrates was now far less than it had been. The consumption of fruit had increased by 88 per cent, but that of potatoes by only 1 per cent; twice as much was now spent on fruit as on bread. Net imports of butter had doubled and those of meat had risen by 50 per cent (the figure had been higher still between 1925 and 1929 before the great depression). While the consumption of brilliantly advertised Guinness had gone up, that of beer had declined dramatically. Tobacco had won, however, where alcohol had lost: from 1913–38 and 1929–40, per capita consumption of tobacco and cigarettes practically doubled.

The continuing decline in drunkenness as a social problem, in the home and on the street, had been brought about neither by the power of the State (although the number of licensed premises fell), nor by the vigour of organized teetotallers, but by changes in education and manners and the diversification of social activities, some of which met with strong, if minority, disapproval. The £5,500,000 spent in 1914 on gambling (which included small-scale betting on football as well as highly organized betting on horse racing), to the horror of Seebohm Rowntree and the Anti-Gambling League among others, was dwarfed by the £40,000,000 spent in 1938 on football pools, a creation of the 1930s. Two years earlier the *Economist* had described gambling, which had a turnover of £200,000,000, as Britain's second biggest industry.

Frequent doubts were expressed also by observers about the mass appeal of spectator sports (including new sports like greyhound racing, initiated at Belle Vue, Manchester, and 'speed-way', started in 1926) and there were complaints about cinema 'addiction' and the inability of audiences to discriminate. Football also came under attack. As early as 1898 a worried observer had noted how, on a night walk around an industrial town, almost every fragment of overheard conversation was a 'piece of football criticism or prophecy'.

There was often a wide gap, of course, between the value judgements of observers and the attitudes of the observed, as only sensitive psychologists recognized. The cinema, for example, provided warmth as well as glamour – and the chance of cuddling in the back row. Gambling, like drinking, which remained an upper-class as well as a working-class pursuit, was more than diversion: the football pools, at least, opened up prospects of fortune to millions of people. There was escapism in all this. And football significantly thrived most in some of the most economi-cally depressed areas: it had deep social roots. Cricket was popular in some of these areas too, notably Yorkshire and Lancashire, where the annual 'Roses Match' was a grimmer struggle than any Cup Final, although the 'culture' of cricket, with its county associations, its 'amateur' leadership and its Test Matches, con-trasted sharply with that of football, then an essentially insular game. One of the 'sayings of the year' in 1933, when sharp national feeling was created by the 'body line bowling' con-troversy, was 'I am not one of those who believe that England is degenerate if it has lost the Test Match.'

There were, in fact, many different 'Englands' in the 1930s, well described by J. B. Priestley in his book *English Journey*, published in 1934, in which he drew all the necessary contrasts, setting the England of factories against that of cathedrals, the England of long back-streets against that of semi-detached houses and often immaculate suburban gardens, the England of scrap-iron against that of aluminium and bakelite. There was still an upper-class England too, which he did not describe, brought back to life in the diaries of Chips Channon. London had its three month season, shorter than before the war, when balls were held and debutantes were presented at Court. This was an England of diamonds and champagne.

The coexistence of these different Englands means that interpretations of its moods depend on whether 'the spotlight' is turned on Skegness or Oldham, Slough or Jarrow, Birkenhead or Oxford, Aston Villa or Ascot. All such disparities went together with class disparities, for there was evidence in relation to every social indicator of profound differences between the social classes, as they had been defined by the Registrar-General in the 1911 census. The definitions, used in all subsequent surveys, were determined by occupation: Class I, 'Professional' (wholly non-manual); Class II, 'Intermediate Income Groups'; Class III, 'Skilled Occupations'; Class IV, 'Partly Skilled Occupations'; Class V, 'Unskilled Occupations' (wholly manual). Occupational differences determined incomes (barring unemployment) and class differences began with them and the structure of property.

The social indicators of class began with infant mortality. Everywhere during the 1930s it was higher in Class V than in Class I, although the actual differentials varied substantially from region to region according to levels of employment and the range of community services and amenities. Even during periods of 'trade boom', and however 'sensibly' they disposed of their incomes, at least 15–20 per cent of all working-class people were unable to afford a 1933 basic British Medical Association diet to ensure 'health and working capacity'. One-third of this primary poverty was attributable to inadequate unemployment benefits, one-third to old age (pensions did not meet minimum needs) and one-third to earnings below the minimum subsistence line.

Patterns of deprivation and expectation did not coincide: it has been claimed since, indeed, that it was 'not feasible' for a working-class family to aspire to 'anything approaching the standards of the family of the middle-class wage earner' and that, in so far as the expectations of manual workers were rising during the late 1930s, they were rising only 'in terms of limited reference groups'. Class I was so far removed from Class V, which had its own differences of status and income, that it inhabited a different world with lifestyles which were too exotic to provoke envy. Moreover, there was less consciousness of property differences than of differences of income. In fact, one in a hundred adults who died left over half the total property passed on to the next generation, while two-thirds of the adults who died left less than £100 of possessions. Between these sharp extremes there was scope for comparison – and for envy – though there appears to have been far less envy within the society than there had been twenty years before and was to be forty years later. 'It occurred to me today as I sat stirring my third cup of tea,' wrote Margaret Halsey, an American visitor who complained of 'the relentless subservience of the working classes', that a 'relaxed, late after-noon atmosphere extends over a good deal of English life.' This was the England of Barbara Pym's novels, not those of Evelyn Waugh.

The marked contrasts between limited reference groups were revealed in a detailed survey of 1937 by G. D. H. Cole, who along with R. H. Tawney and Harold Laski was England's leading academic socialist. Comparing the diet of a family of five earning the average industrial wage with a middle-class family of the same size earning £500 to £600 a year, he noted how the richer family consumed on average 12 per cent less bread and flour and 16 per cent less potatoes than the poorer family, but ate nearly 36 per cent more meat, more than twice as much fish and fresh milk, 68 per cent more eggs, 56 per cent more butter and only half the quantity of margarine. Inter-war 'repeats' of two of the most famous of all Victorian poverty surveys enable statistical com-parisons to be drawn within a longer perspective. In 1928 a 'New Survey of London Life and Labour', following in the footsteps of the great investigator Charles Booth, showed that 13 per cent of London's children and 22 per cent of those over sixty-four years of age in working-class families were still living in primary poverty, while in 1936 Rowntree, who had first surveyed York at the end of the nineteenth century, found that 31 per cent of its working-class families were still living in primary poverty. Moreover, unemployment there, which had accounted for only 2·31 per cent of primary poverty at the end of the nineteenth century, now accounted for 44·5 per cent.

However, Rowntree's method of computing the minimum sum necessary to keep families above the poverty line had changed significantly. His concern to avoid any possible charges of 'sentimentality' in 1901 had led him even to exclude fresh meat from his subsistence diet. 'I didn't want people to say,' he explained defensively, 'that Rowntree's "crying for the moon"'; and he went on, in an eloquent but extraordinary passage, to explain that a family living at his £1 1s. 8d. level

> must never spend a penny on railway fare or omnibus. They must never go into the country unless they walk. They must never purchase a half-penny newspaper or spend a penny to buy a ticket for a popular concert. They must write no letters to absent children . . . They must never contribute anything to their church or chapel, or give any help to a neighbour which costs them money. They cannot save, nor can they join a sick club or Trade Union . . . Children must have no pocket money for dolls, marbles or sweets. The father must smoke no tobacco and must drink no beer. The mother must never buy any pretty clothes for herself or for her children, the character of the family wardrobe as for the family diet being governed by the regulation. Nothing must be bought but that which is absolutely necessary for the maintenance of physical health, and what must be bought must be of the plainest description. Should a child fall ill, it must be attended by the parish doctor; should it die, it must be buried by the parish. Finally, the wage earner must never be absent from his work for a single day.

After applying this grim test, Rowntree had revealed in 1901 that 1,465 families in York were living in primary poverty. By 1936, however, he had decided that what he had offered his readers in 1901 was 'a standard of bare *subsistence* rather than *living*,' and as a result he incorporated in his new figure of £2 3s. 6d. nine shillings for 'other expenses'. These included one shilling for travelling to and from work, sevenpence for a daily newspaper and sixpence for 'wireless'.

Seen within this longer-term perspective, working-class expectations and aspirations had changed significantly by the 1930s, even if they were still bounded by a refusal to compare lots with people very different from themselves and by what Bevin called 'poverty of desire'. Whereas in 1901 it was Lloyd George and the 'new Liberals' who waved Rowntree's book on political platforms, by 1936 working-class voices were highly critical of his 'fodder standard', as they dubbed it. They were not prepared simply to accept a sociologist's version of what they needed as a minimum. And Rowntree himself expressed sympathy with their aspirations. 'If instead of looking backward we look forward, then we see how far the standard of living of many workers falls short of any standard which would be regarded, even for the time being, as satisfactory.'

Ten years later, in 1951, Rowntree published a third and final survey dealing with the immediate post-war period, the years which had stood out to Ernest Watkins as a time of marked material improvement for 'ordinary people'. He concluded that as a result of 'welfare measures' introduced since 1936, along with full employment, which by then was being taken for granted, there were now only 846 families in York (1·66 per cent of the total population and 2·77 per cent of the working class) in primary poverty, and that in no single such case was unemployment of an able-bodied wage earner the cause. The proportion of people over sixty-five in the population had risen from 5 per cent to 11 per cent between 1901 and 1951, and old age had become the primary cause of poverty.

The nine shillings Rowntree had allowed for other expenses in 1936 had become 11s. 6d. by 1951, and the allowance for 'stamps, writing paper, etc.' had doubled. The exercise was becoming more artificial, or arbitrary, however, since Rowntree and his co-surveyor admitted that a doubled sum, now fixed at 6s. 8d. for 'all else' ('beer, tobacco, presents, holidays, books, travelling, etc.') 'would not buy anything like as much as 3s. 4d. did in 1936'. Nevertheless, in retrospect, the relative stability of the price levels stands out in Rowntree's surveys. It was possible to compare budgets with relatively minor adjustments and one item, 'travelling to work', actually stayed at the same level in the account – at one shilling – in 1936 and in 1951. There was one statistic, however, about which Rowntree said little. There was relatively little violence in this society, but in 1951 the number of indictable criminal offences, which had risen by a half during the Second World War, reached a new peak: in 1938 one in a hundred of the age group fourteen to seventeen committed such an offence, but in 1951, the figure was one in fifty. There was little public criticism of the police: more attention was focused on prisons and probation.

It became fashionable after 1945 to trace connections across the great twentieth-century divides in relation not only to the economics of improvement but to the policies designed to secure it. A new version of an older Whig interpretation of history became common, therefore, during the late 1940s and early 1950s, with the welfare state, rather than constitutional monarchy or representative government, standing out as the distinctively English culmination of centuries of history. According to this new version of social history, the seventeenth and eighteenth centuries had seen the successful assertion of English civil rights and the nineteenth century the successful realization of English political rights, while it had been left to the twentieth century to implement 'social rights'.

The theme had been anticipated in an E. H. Carr editorial in *The Times* in 1940, the year of Britain's greatest physical danger, before the term 'welfare state' (a term apparently and, if so, not inappropriately invented by an Archbishop of Canterbury, William Temple) had passed into common parlance:

> If we speak of democracy we do not mean a democracy which maintains the right to vote but forgets the right to work and the right to live. If we speak of freedom, we do not mean a rugged individualism which excluded social organization and economic planning. If we speak of equality, we do not mean a political equality nullified by social and economic privilege. If we speak of economic reconstruction, we think less of maximum production, though this too will be required, than of equitable distribution.

Carr, who compared the 'night watchman state' of the nineteenth century with the welfare state of the twentieth, not only underestimated the need for 'maximum production' – in post-war circumstances this was to be essential – but expressed no reservations about the increase in the power of the State. Indeed, most makers and defenders of the 'welfare state' of all political parties underestimated the costs and preferred to talk of citizenship rather than state machinery. 'Homes, health, education and social security, these are your birthright,' Aneurin Bevan, Labour's thrustful Minister of Health, told the electorate, while the members of a Conservative Reform Group insisted in 1948 that the social services were designed to give to all 'the basic minimum of security, of housing, of opportunity, of employment and of living standards below which our duty to one another forbids us to permit anyone to fall'. They were anxious to destroy the stigmas of the Victorian poor law.

The welfare state may have been thought of, even attacked, as a characteristic expression of socialism – many Americans for whom Watkins was writing thought of it in this way – yet it was, in fact, the product of many different minds and hands, and it reflected many motives and many compromises. They were all employed, however, in an effort to realize a different kind of society from that which would have existed had economic forces been allowed free play.

Given such a perspective, the origins of the 'welfare state' of the twentieth century have often been pushed back before the 'reconstruction' politics of two world wars to the Edwardian period or even to the nineteenth century, when the first steps were taken to control industry (through factory acts), to regulate health (through investigation and inspection), to expand education (first on a voluntary basis and then through public machinery) and to promote 'social justice'. The way had thus been prepared, it has been argued, for twentieth-century 'transformation' through the 'natural growth' of 'social responsibility'. Conservatives had become increasingly concerned with health and housing, while Liberals had moved from *laissez-faire* individualism, expressed in extreme form in the idea of '*Man* versus the *State*', to a recognition of the need to introduce collectivist policies 'to equalize freedom'. And the Fabian socialists, under the guidance of Sidney and Beatrice Webb, had been the natural successors to the Benthamites.

But there was a major break to be made, as the Fabians realized: the 1834 Poor Law with all its penalties and stigmas had to go. This was the message of the 1909 minority report of the Royal Commission on the Poor Laws (set up by a Conservative

Government and with Beatrice Webb as a member), and there was a considerable measure of agreement between the minority, strongly influenced by the Fabians, and the majority. In fact, a different route was followed by the reforming Liberals. Following a series of welfare measures, among them the first School Meals Act of 1906, the Old Age Pensions Act of 1908 and the setting up of Labour Exchanges in 1909, they introduced national insurance in 1911 on a limited scale and on a contributory basis. Hitherto, whatever social insurance existed had been provided through an extensive network of friendly societies (which by then had 14,000,000 members), trade unions and commercial companies. Now the State stepped in with 'aids to thrift', aimed at protecting the free citizen from social contingencies outside his control. 'We seek to substitute for the pressure of the forces of nature operating by chance on individuals,' wrote Winston Churchill, then Lloyd George's chief ally, 'the pressures of the laws of insurance, operating through averages with modifying and mitigating effects in individual cases.' Lloyd George, who had defended old age pensions as morally right against critics who claimed that they were 'largesse' or even 'a mortal blow to the Empire', went further. He jotted down a note, 'Insurance necessarily temporary expedient. At not distant date State will acknowledge full responsibility in the matter of making provision for sickness, breakdown and unemployment.'

Responsibility was taken further in 1920, but 'full responsibility' not until 1946, when the post-war Labour government carried a National Insurance Act and a National Health Service Act. The National Insurance Act was comprehensive, with flat-rate individual contributions (one stamp, one card) and benefits covering sickness, old age, unemployment and industrial injury: it provided 'a shield for every man, woman and child . . . against the ravages of poverty and adversity'. The National Health Service Act, more controversial and more bitterly contested at the time than the National Insurance Act, created a completely free and universal health service, financed not out of personal insurance contributions but out of taxes, and voluntary and municipal hospitals were nationalized and grouped geographically under Regional Boards. Consultants gained in power, however, and individuals retained the right to choose their own family general practitioner. The 'appointed day' for implementation, 5 July 1948, was a kind of D-Day for welfare. Meanwhile, a third piece of welfare legislation, the National Assistance Act, designed simply to provide a safety net, began with the dramatic words 'the existing poor law shall cease to have effect.' The discontinuity was deliberate. Relief was now to be paid through a National Assistance Board and to be financed not out of rates but out of taxes. This was a break, therefore, not only with the 1834 Poor Law (the Boards of Guardians had gone in 1929) but with the 'old Poor Law' of 1601. Neighbours were no longer to be directly responsible for their poor. There was a strong feeling in 1948, indeed, not only that the old laws had at last gone but that in future 'the poor would no longer be with us'.

Within five years of D-Day, however, Beveridge himself was accusing the government of undermining his scheme. He had insisted that the flat-rate benefits payable under the National Insurance Act should genuinely cover subsistence, but in 1954 the Minister of Pensions and National Insurance formally abandoned that principle. And even before the Conservatives came into power, the principle of a completely free National Health Service was abandoned when the Labour government decided for financial reasons to charge individuals for medical prescriptions and later for false teeth and spectacles. Aneurin Bevan, the architect of the National Health Service, was reluctantly prepared to accept the necessity of prescription charges but resigned when the second series of charges were introduced, on the grounds that it marked the 'beginning of the destruction of those social services in which Labour had taken a special pride and which were giving to Britain the moral leadership of the world'.

The danger of a clash between the ideals of welfare policy and the facts of economic life had existed since the 1920s. Indeed, there had been bitter arguments about a new Unemployment Insurance Act reducing benefits in 1921, and ten years later MacDonald's Labour government, facing a financial crisis, split on the details of an 'economy' programme which would have cut insurance benefits by 10 per cent, half the figure recommended by the recently appointed May Committee on national expenditure. The clash

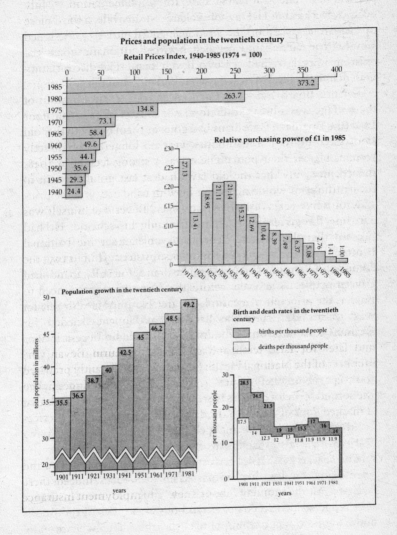

Prices and population in the twentieth century

Retail Prices Index, 1940-1985 (1974 = 100)

Year	Value
1985	373.2
1980	263.7
1975	134.8
1970	73.1
1965	58.4
1960	49.6
1955	44.1
1950	35.6
1945	29.3
1940	24.4

Relative purchasing power of £1 in 1985

Year	Value
1915	27.13
1920	13.41
1925	18.95
1930	21.11
1935	21.14
1940	15.23
1945	12.69
1950	10.44
1955	8.39
1960	7.49
1965	6.37
1970	5.08
1975	2.76
1980	1.41
1985	1.00

Population growth in the twentieth century

total population in millions

Year	Value
1901	35.5
1911	36.5
1921	38.7
1931	40
1941	42.5
1951	45
1961	46.2
1971	48.5
1981	49.2

years

Birth and death rates in the twentieth century

■ births per thousand people
□ deaths per thousand people

per thousand people

Year	Births	Deaths
1901	28.5	17.5
1911	24.5	14
1921	21.5	12.3
1931	19	12
1941	15	13
1951	15.5	11.8
1961	17	11.9
1971	16	11.9
1981	14	11.9

years

between ideals and economics was always there after 1945. While pre-war gaps in social services were being filled in and welfare policies were being elaborated, posters on the walls read, 'We're up against it' and 'Work or Want'. Financial outlay on the social services had already quadrupled between 1938 and 1949 and criticism was restrained or silenced only because of the reduction of demands on the Exchequer due to full employment.

The principle of offering to *all* the optimum social service, not the average, was always difficult to implement: 'it brought to the surface fundamental problems,' wrote *The Times* in 1952 (in an article significantly headed 'Crisis in the Welfare State'), 'which were less obvious when the services were fewer and far less comprehensive.' The fact that services were used by all sections of the community – keeping up the spirit of solidarity and the principle of universality established during the Second World War – increased costs and raised complaints when the promised 'best' was not offered. At the same time, it diminished the redistributive effects of social service expenditure financed from taxation, favouring Classes I, II and III more than IV and V. So too did government food subsidies, which had first been introduced in 1940 as an emergency measure designed to impose restraint on wage claims. By 1949 it was obvious that they were subsidizing the food consumption of the millionaire with no dependants as much as that of the poorest wage-earner with a large family to support and a ceiling was placed on them before they were abolished. Nonetheless, few voices seriously questioned the 'welfare state' before the early 1950s. It was in a period of relative 'affluence', not of austerity, that both the ideals and the practices of the welfare state came under closer scrutiny.

It was then also that more attention began to be paid to the relative effects of market forces and of state intervention on the 'well-being', a by then more acceptable general term than 'welfare', of the individual and of the family. This was a subject which had tended to be neglected both in surveys of the Booth and Rowntree type and in political speeches. The 'welfare state' was intended to compensate for the vagaries, inadequacies and inefficiencies of the market and, if necessary, to guarantee individuals and families a minimum income irrespective of the market value of their work and property. What, however, of the beneficial influence of expanding markets not only on those below the poverty line but on those above it?

Even when austerity became unpopular, many of Labour's supporters were suspicious of what Priestley called 'admass', the 'creation' by advertising and other means of new consumer demands and the encouragement of the view that enjoyment springs from more spending. They retained a puritanical distaste not only for conspicuous consumption but also for working-class 'materialism'. They were horrified at the thought that advertising expenditures, which, according to the Advertising Association, had stood at £58,800,000 a year in 1938, stood at £79,000,000 in 1948 and almost doubled to £157,000,000 in 1954. Mark Abrams, who spanned the worlds of the social survey and of 'market research', pointed out less critically that the generation of new demand went back long before 1938. Indeed, the pattern of demand had changed significantly since the early century.

The increase in advertising had undoubtedly attracted the attention of the public to a far wider range of branded goods, tinned (or canned) and packaged, than had ever been available before. The 1930s were the decade of Quaker Oats, of Kellogg's corn flakes, Horlicks and Ovaltine, tins of John West salmon and Del Monte peaches, Birds' custard powder, Crosse and Blackwell soup and Heinz (57 Varieties) baked beans. The consumer had benefited strikingly from increased foreign trade in food products and from a revolution in retail distribution, the success of which still depended as much on the railways as on the growth of motorized transport facilities. Chain stores with many branches proliferated – those with twenty-five branches or more increased from 20,602 to 39,013 between 1920 and 1939, and bigger chains with 200 branches or more increased from 10,942 to 21,283. Montagu Burton and Sainsbury became household names. The appearance of the high streets of the country was changing, although not as radically as it was to do later, with supermarkets and building societies. Single unit retailers still accounted for 88 per cent (657,000) of the total retail establishments in 1938, though for only 66 per cent of the trade, with cooperative stores accounting for another 10 per cent. Meanwhile, resale price maintenance, which in 1900 had covered only 3 per cent of domestic consumers' expenditure, covered 38 per cent by 1938.

Such development, unplanned though it was, had a levelling effect on material well-being. Yet one disturbing by-product of unplanned change was an unplanned environment. 'Ribbon development' along the roads was one messy feature, 'conurbations' and the congestion of city centres another, the invasion of villages a third. In the background was an almost twenty-fold expansion in the number of cars on the roads between 1919 and 1939, with the millionth Morris car leaving the Cowley works at Oxford – by now a transformed city – four months before the outbreak of the Second World War. Although Second World War restrictions, including petrol rationing, held back further developments, by 1950 the output of motor vehicles, including vans and tractors – agriculture was becoming mechanized – had reached over 900,000 as compared with 526,000 in the pre-war peak year. While use of the motor car was not a mass phenomenon in England, as the development of public road transport reveals, a distinctive car culture, centred on the Motor Show held at Earls Court for the first time in 1937, had clearly emerged before 1939.

Efforts to control, if not completely to plan, the environment had been made since the first decade of the twentieth century, when the first 'Housing, Town Planning, etc. Act' of 1909 empowered, but did not require, local authorities to control the growth of towns and cities. And five years later the newly founded Town Planning Institute demanded 'the emancipation of all communities from the beast of ugliness'. The difficult struggle to tame 'the beast', if not to dispose of him entirely, quickened during the 1930s, when an important new Town and Country Planning Act was passed in 1932, and while by 1938 only ninety-two approved urban – and rural – schemes were in operation under the terms of the Act, London, in particular, had made an energetic start, with its 'Green Belt' policy. The Barlow Commission, appointed in 1937 to consider the distribution of the industrial population in 1937, faced difficulties when it turned to its final task, that of suggesting 'remedial measures', but its Report, which appeared in 1940, was a landmark in that it recommended the setting up of a Central Planning Board, 'national in scope and character'.

The Second World War gave a further impetus to the planning movement at every level: the Uthwatt Committee was appointed in 1941 to consider 'Congestion and Betterment' and the Scott Committee the future of the countryside, while Patrick Abercrombie's *County of London Plan* appeared in 1943. When the Labour government came into power in 1945 the Uthwatt proposals became the basis of compensation policy. A Distribution of Industry Act was passed also in 1945, which remained the basis of all later regional planning, a 'New Towns Act' followed in 1946, and when, a year later, a new Town and Country Planning Act became law, it suggested to one enthusiast that Englishmen were at last 'enlarging our family souls and suiting them to the bigger compass of a nation'. The 'new towns', a bold idea with antecedents in the Garden Cities movement of the past – Stevenage was the first of them – represented the main hopes of the future. Yet progress was slow, and at the end of 1950 only 451 new houses had been completed in the new towns around London. Nor was slow progress in housing the only problem. It was the psychology behind the idea of new towns, as much as the logistics, which was in question. 'Must utopia always disappoint?' asked Harold Orlans in his study of Stevenage, published in 1952.

The story of housing, planned or unplanned, raised similar but even more extended issues, for throughout the twentieth century housing differences – inside as well as outside – were, like differences in education, major social and cultural indicators. That there had been a general improvement during the inter-war years had been suggested by Rowntree, who found that whereas 5·7 per cent of the working-class population of York lived in over-crowded houses and 26 per cent lived in slums in 1900, the comparable figures for 1936 were only 1·7 per cent and 11·7 per cent.

But the 'housing problem' still persisted. Indeed, it had become more serious during the war since the building of all houses – private or council-controlled – had ceased. Aneurin Bevan started explicitly from the premise that 'the housing problem for the middle classes had been roughly solved before the Second World War, but for the lower income groups it had not been solved since the industrial revolution.' Although five million new houses had been built between 1911 and 1939 and 350,000 slum properties had been demolished, four million people were still living in largely 'unmodernized' nineteenth-century houses, and it was left to Bevan's successors to deal with the large-scale demolitions of the 1950s – concrete and 'high rise'. There was a social as well as a physical transformation, for each 'slum' had its own social identity and there were evident continuities in ways of thinking, feeling and behaving in slums across the divides of time, continuities which have been well brought out in books like Robert Roberts's fascinating description of 'classic' Salford slum life in the first quarter of the twentieth century, Michael Young and Peter Willmott's study of Bethnal Green and Richard Hoggart's account of Hunslet in Leeds.

There was a marked contrast in the 1930s not only between slums and suburban housing estates but between private and public housing estates. Sometimes, indeed, as in Oxford, physical barriers were placed between them. Some of the new estates of both kinds were lifeless, silent, dull and anonymous, although there were impressive new public estates in Manchester and Birmingham, while in the heart of Leeds, against the national pattern, a huge new block of flats was built at Quarry Hill (now destroyed) which admirers – and they were in a minority – compared with Vienna.

Working-class houses outside the estates were usually rented, and until the Housing Act of 1949 introduced subsidies to landlords to improve such property, the system of rent control and subsidy – plus high building costs – held back progress. Improvement remained slow, and the fact that Labour governments after 1945 never reached their annual target of 247,000 houses gave an incentive to the Conservatives to give housing a high priority in 1951. Indeed, the pledge to build 300,000 houses a year – with a further target of 400,000 – was one of the most appealing items in their programme in 1951. The fact too that they had proposed to remove controls had an appeal of its own. Licences for private building were duly abolished in 1954, with the effect that private builders, who had built only 18 per cent of new houses under Labour, very soon doubled their proportion. The concomitant building boom was directly related, therefore, to a boom in consumer expenditure which characterized the late 1950s. The sale of 'durable use consumer goods', an ugly but necessary term invented by economists, had already been facilitated by hire purchase, which multiplied twenty times in value in the two decades between 1918 and 1938.

The importance of suburban housing estates to the social historian of the twentieth century is at least as great as that of the country house to the social historian of the eighteenth century. They brought greater light and space to new council tenants and they influenced the shape and content of municipal politics, but they did not convert a proletariat into a bourgeoisie, as was often claimed. The real bourgeoisie – and for the first time in England, perhaps, it was possible to speak of one – looked for support to the building societies. Already by 1913, building societies had total assets of £65,000,000 and in that year they were already advancing £9,000,000 in mortgages. By 1940, however, the total amount outstanding on mortgages had risen to £678,000,000. By then they had made advances to over 1,500,000 borrowers, one in eight of all families in Britain. Abrams compared them in 1945 not with a continental bourgeoisie but with a continental peasantry, their way of life governed not by an attachment to the soil but by an investment in suburban bricks.

Changes in the middle-class home reflected a continuing fall in family size and a dramatic decline in domestic service as well as shifts of taste and fashion. The result, once wartime 'utility' disappeared, was 'no parlours, no dedicated rooms . . . And our colours? Mushroom and primrose, cream and dove grey.' Yet as the *Daily Mail Ideal Home Book* put it in 1950, 'where money is no object good taste is often the first casualty.' As far as the aesthetics of the working-class home were concerned, Richard Hoggart was less sure. Indeed, he detected not progress but decline. 'Chain store modernism, all veneer and varnish stain, is replacing the old mahogany; multi-coloured plastic and chrome biscuit barrels and bird-cages have come in.'

The fact that most of the new private housing developments

and the local authority housing estates (before and after 1945) were alike built on the edge of towns or beyond their limits, and sometimes swallowed up old villages, further altered the relationship between home, work and community. Their development would have been impossible, indeed, without important changes in private and public transport. The late-Victorians had developed trams – the year of their peak mileage was 1924 – and their successors developed motor buses and, in London, new lines of underground. Indeed, the biggest of all the transport schemes was the creation by the London Passenger Transport Act of 1933 of a new London Passenger Transport Board with a monopoly of all transport within an area of 2,000 square miles. By then there were 4,656 buses on the roads with a seating capacity of 237,618, and there were also many completely modernized and well-designed underground stations.

Public transport, like the railway before it and like private transport, could be either an occupational necessity or a medium of leisure, and by the late 1930s leisure was beginning to feature as prominently as work in all the accounts of twentieth-century 'progress'. A detailed study of 'contemporary influences on urban life' in one English industrial town, Derby, published in 1954, not only included chapters on education, clubs and associations, sports and hobbies, public houses, the cinema and religious activities, but also examined the impact of national newspapers, radio, television, sports and hobbies, public houses, the cinema and religious activities on the local community. Its underlying historical assumption was that while local differences persisted in England the differences had become 'far less marked' than they had been a hundred or even fifty years before. Yet local and regional differences continued to persist. Different towns with apparently similar economic and social characteristics could generate if not completely different cultural patterns at least different styles of leadership and different degrees of participation.

The Derby study revealed, as other local studies would have done, a complex network of clubs and societies, many of them with nineteenth- or early-twentieth-century origins. They had many different pedigrees and contacts. Thus, professional football clubs might have originated as school teams, church teams or factory teams, and philanthropic associations might have been founded in the local church, chapel hall or public house. More-over, those charitable associations among them had often been the product of different impulses, drawing in both those who wished to serve and those who wished to reform (sometimes, of course, they were the same people). All of them depended, as hospitals had done before 1947, on mobilizing private funds. The 'flag day', therefore, was as regular a feature of a changing society as the football coupon. Yet they were part of a national pattern of voluntary effort, represented in bodies like the Family Welfare Association and the National Council of Social Service, formed in 1919, which Beveridge considered essential in a 'welfare state'. The Workers' Education Association, founded in 1903, had its branches. So too did the Townswomen's Guilds and the Women's Institutes.

Two of the main institutions throughout the country were still supremely local – the public house and the church or chapel, with the husband often supporting the first and the wife the second. During the week of the Derby survey more people visited the public house than the cinema, although only one-third of Derby's women, compared with three-quarters of its men, had been out for a drink. All in all, 30 per cent of the population were going to the cinema at least once a week as against 12 per cent who had been to church or chapel on the previous Sunday. But very few people admitted to not having a religion in the late 1940s, and on the basis of the Derby survey only one home in ten did not possess a copy of the Bible.

There was a marked difference in Derby (and elsewhere) between home-centred leisure activities and those activities which drew members of the family outside the home. The home, indeed, stripped of its Victorian halo, became more of a centre of private relaxation during the 1920s and 1930s, even if relaxation (and information) were now shared with people everywhere through radio programmes. Most homes had a wireless set; many had gardens. These were the years of the floribunda rose, the crossword puzzle, the detective novel and the 'hobby', very much an 'individual thing', although the experience could be shared – as in the case of stamp collecting – by hundreds of thousands of people and sustained by commercial interests. 'Outside activities', like going to the cinema or sport, supplemented home life. By 1945 there were over 4,500 cinemas in the country, 70 per cent of the largest of them controlled by large circuit business concerns, some with other financial stakes in leisure, and the new social phenomena of stars and fans were here to stay. Some were to become bingo halls in time, but in the 1930s the new gamble was the football pool.

Differences of social class were usually the most important factor in determining leisure patterns. Public houses were as different from each other in 'tone' as the holiday resorts, and they were split in the middle between the 'lounge' and the 'public bar'. The dance hall was far removed from the hunt ball. Horse racing was supported by a wide range of the population, including thousands of gamblers who never went to a race course, but greyhound racing was not. Yet social processes were more complex than this. Football, which had moved from field and alley to the public schools in the middle years of the nineteenth century, had become plebeian by the end of the century. Football crowds were peaceful, however; as late as 1955 Geoffrey Gorer in his *Exploring English Character* called them as 'orderly as church meetings'. Cinema attendance was highest among the least well-off, for whom the (sometimes) glamorous cinema was a place of physical escape as well as of diversion, yet the appeal of the cinema cut across all social classes and the art of the film fascinated a cultural minority.

Age and sex differences also, of course, determined leisure patterns, particularly sports. The number of Cubs and Boy Scouts rose from 152,000 in 1913 to 438,000 in 1938, and the name of Baden-Powell was one of the best known in the country. Bowls already made its appeal as a sport of the old – for men first, but soon for women. Only tennis – almost from the beginning – had been a game for women as much as for men. Wimbledon was one of the characteristically English cultural products listed by T. S. Eliot in his *Notes Towards the Definition of Culture* in 1948, along with Derby Day, Henley Regatta, the twelfth of August, a Cup Final, the dog races, the pin table, the dart board, Wensleydale cheese, boiled cabbage cut into sections, beetroot in vinegar, nineteenth-century Gothic churches and the music of Elgar.

For Eliot, however, culture was not progressing but was in decline. He found little consolation in the growth of education, which by 1948 was beginning to produce what another writer, Michael Young, looking to the future not to the past, was to call 'the rise of the meritocracy', or the increasing strength of the professions, which he believed caused people to think and move in grooves. There were many other serious critics of society, not all of them as conservative as Eliot, most of whom concentrated on the relationship between education, work and leisure. Indeed, one of the most vocal groups during the 1930s and after 1945 were the teachers, who complained persistently that what their pupils did after school nullified their activities in school. The view was widespread that leisure, unplanned though it might be, was not strictly 'a matter of private tastes like the colour of the hearthrug or the pattern on the pottery'.

The policies of the British Broadcasting Corporation during the 1930s, 1940s and early 1950s reinforced such views, and its first Director-General, John (later Lord) Reith, argued from the start that 'to have exploited so great a scientific invention [as radio] for the purpose and pursuit of entertainment alone would have been a prostitution of its powers'. The programmes of the Corporation were not influenced, therefore, as in the United States, by the pressure to sell goods. They emphasized the need to treat people as an audience not as a market, and to give them not 'what they wanted' but what they might 'come to want' given the opportunity. This included classical music, the taste for which the BBC did much to encourage, and serious drama. The same policies were followed after 1945, although they were to be eroded in the age of television.

The symbolic climax of fifty years of disputed progress was the Festival of Britain in 1951, unlike 1851 a specifically British occasion. It was the brainchild of the Labour politician Herbert Morrison, who had risen to power through London politics; he thought of it as 'the people giving themselves a pat on the back'. It has been described in retrospect by Michael Frayn, however, as 'the last, and virtually the posthumous, work of the Herbivore

Britain of the BBC news, the Crown Film Unit, the sweet ration, the Ealing [film] comedies . . .' The verdict is eloquent but incomplete. The Festival, which brought 'fun, fantasy and colour', was a far bigger popular success than its critics prophesied, and by harnessing new creative talent it helped to set standards of design which persist today, even after the drastic changes of the last thirty years. 'One can doubt whether such a thing as happiness is possible without steadily changing conditions involving enlarging and exhilarating opportunities,' H. G. Wells had written in 1905. The changes that took place between 1955 and the 1980s were to put his proposition to the test.

13

ENDS AND BEGINNINGS

We may our ends by our beginnings know.
Sir John Denham, Of Prudence, 1668

You're hurt because everything's changed. Jimmy's hurt because everything's the same. And neither of you can face it.
Alison in John Osborne, Look Back in Anger, 1956

The best is yet to come.
William Davis, writing in Highlife, 1982

THE CLOSER social historians get to their own times, the more difficult it is for them to be sure that they have grasped what is essential about their period. This is largely a matter of vantage point. Some features of the pattern may not yet even be clearly visible.

It is partly in order to achieve an interim perspective that much writing about recent social history has taken the decade as the unit of account. The labelling adjectives differ, however: the 1960s, zestfully described at the time as 'swinging', are now often dismissed as 'overheated', the 1950s have been called on the one hand 'an age of illusions' and on the other an 'age of fear', while the crisis-ridden 1970s, it was remarked as they came to a close, had a less distinctively recognizable character than almost any other decade in the twentieth century. 'We survived,' wrote the Economist. 'That was all that could be said economically of the 1970s.' The 1980s have still not been given a name.

Economic problems, however, cannot be explained in terms of

decades taken by themselves, whether they be the problems of oil prices or of unemployment; nor can social (or political) reactions to them. Longer-term 'social trends', as they were called in a new statistical publication with that name which appeared in 1970, can also be identified. At first there was optimism. 'There is a growing awareness,' wrote its editor, 'that the first fruits of economic progress can only be fully appreciated by looking at the total social effort.' And the effort might even look impressive. By the middle of the 1970s, however, when prices were rising faster than at any time since the war, when unemployment topped the million mark and when the value of money was not much more than one-fifth of what it had been in 1945, pessimistic editorials were stressing not progress but crisis. And politics had to be brought into the picture at every point, for in 1974 Edward Heath's Conservative government, beset by the unfamiliar phenomenon of 'stagflation' – inflation *and* unemployment at the same time – fell from office after a bitter confrontation with the trade unions. Heath's government was brought down by militant action on the part of the miners, but from the very start it had met union hostility, because of its determination to pass an Industrial Relations Act designed to strengthen legal restraints on trade union activity. (In the end the measure was kept largely in cold storage.)

The editor of *Social Trends* would probably have insisted that what appeared on the surface as economic patterns had deep psychological and social roots, in attitudes to work and to management, modes of education and the continuing sense of class. Indeed, much unofficial English social commentary of the years since 1955 has been concerned with *die Englische Krankheit*, 'the English disease', which Anthony Sampson, anatomist of contemporary society, compared with the decline of Spain in the seventeenth century. It might have been true, as Rebecca West remarked in 1980 in a review of an American volume of essays *Is Britain Dying?*, that:

> A suspicion must form in the minds of all readers of this volume that perhaps our plight may be due to sheer misfortune; and we must not forget Joseph Conrad's remark that it is the mark of an inexperienced man not to believe in ill luck.

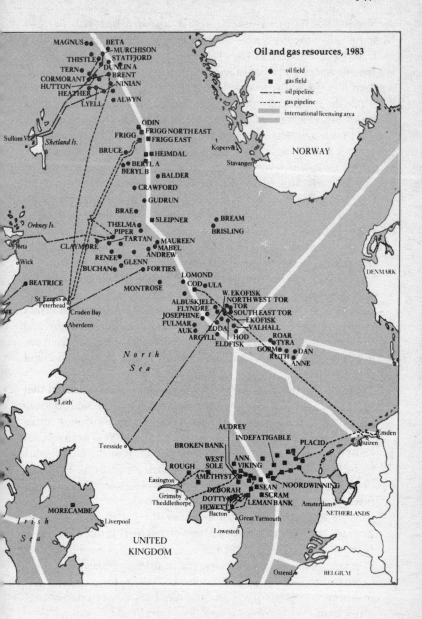

Oil and gas resources, 1983

● oil field
■ gas field
– – – oil pipeline
- - - gas pipeline
▨ international licensing area

NORWAY

MAGNUS ● BETA
● MURCHISON
THISTLE ● STATFJORD
TERN ● DUNLIN A
● BRENT
CORMORANT ● NINIAN
HUTTON
HEATHER ● ALWYN
LYELL

ODIN ●
FRIGG ● FRIGG NORTH EAST
● FRIGG EAST
BRUCE ● ■ HEIMDAL
Koperv●
BERYL A
BERYL B
● BALDER
Stavanger
● CRAWFORD
● GUDRUN
BRAE ●
THELMA ■ SLEIPNER ● BREAM
PIPER ● BRISLING
TARTAN
● MAUREEN
CLAYMORE ● MABEL
RENEE ● ANDREW
BUCHAN ● GLENN
● FORTIES
LOMOND ●
COD ● ULA
MONTROSE ● W. EKOFISK
NORTH WEST TOR
ALBUSKJELL ● TOR
FLYNDRE ● SOUTH EAST TOR
JOSEPHINE ● ● EKOFISK
FULMAR ● VALHALL
AUK ● EDDA ●
ARGYLL ● HOD ROAR
ELDFISK TYRA
GORM ● DAN
RUTH
ANNE

Sullom Vo●
Shetland Is.

Orkney Is.

Flotta
Wick
BEATRICE ●
St Fergus
Peterhead
Cruden Bay
● Aberdeen

North
Sea

● Leith

DENMARK

AUDREY ●
INDEFATIGABLE ●
BROKEN BANK ● PLACID ●
Emden
huizen
WEST ● ANN
Teesside ● SOLE VIKING
ROUGH ● NOORDWINNING
AMETHYST ●
Easington
DEBORAH ● SEAN
Grimsby DOTTY ● SCRAM
Theddlethorpe HEWETT ● LEMAN BANK
Bacton Amsterdam
MORECAMBE ● NETHERLANDS
Liverpool ● Great Yarmouth

Irish
Sea

Lowestoft

UNITED
KINGDOM

Ostend
BELGIUM

Yet neither Sampson nor Corelli Barnett, a historian of contemporary society, would have agreed. Barnett, indeed, has traced symptoms the disease to the Second World War, when Britain was most proud of its achievements. The industrial record then was riddled with problems.

Much publicized comparisons between Britain and almost every other 'advanced' country were obviously disturbing from the 1950s onwards following the disturbed immediate aftermath of war. Despite several changes of approach and policy, Britain's rate of economic growth between 1950 and 1970 remained only one-half to three-fifths that of other industrialized countries. Growth had been faster in these years than in any other comparable period in this or previous centuries, but other countries' growth had been faster still. Nor were comparisons of productivity or investment in industry, on which Britain's industrial competitiveness depended, any more encouraging than they had been in the past: investment in England was said to have risen by only 30 per cent between 1960 and 1974 in comparison with 90 per cent in Germany. When the European Economic Community was formed in 1958, British gross domestic product per head had been a third higher than it was in the Community of Six; by 1974 it was 27 per cent less and, according to one calculation, lower than that of Italy.

Britain joined the European Economic Community under Heath in 1973 – 'a journey to an unknown destination' as Andrew Shonfield called it, the ticket for which was confirmed by an unprecedented national referendum under Harold Wilson in 1975 – but there were to be no huge economic gains of the kind the Six had secured during the early years of their association. Hopes of untapped markets across the Channel were counterbalanced by fears of an 'import invasion'.

More important in economic terms than the decision to 'enter Europe' was the discovery of North Sea natural gas in 1965 and of North Sea oil in 1970. Industrial investment ratios might be lower in England than in other European countries, but geology now came to the aid of economics. Once, in prehistoric times, there had been no North Sea; now, the tilted sea bed came to matter more than ever before. Natural gas was already meeting half of

Britain's demand for gas before oil was discovered. And oil itself began to flow in 1975, the year of the European referendum. It was capable of tranforming the balance of payments position, but neither oil nor gas could relieve the country either of short-term inflation nor of long-term unemployment, and when world oil prices fell sharply during the 1980s there were to be new and all too familiar pressures on the pound.

The long-term social trends began not with economics but with demography. The total population of England rose slowly from 41,000,000 in 1951 to 46,000,000 in 1971, and between then and 1981 by only 200,000. But there were important changes in its structure as the expectation of life was lengthened; by 1981 those aged sixty-five and over made up 17 per cent of the population (compared with 15 per cent in 1961 and 5 per cent in 1901), and for every twenty people of working age there were thirteen who were either over retirement age or under sixteen years of age. The crude birth-rate rose to a peak of 17·8 in 1966, compared with 16 in 1956, but fell to a low point of 11·6 in 1977. The social consequences of these demographic changes were related primarily to forward projections, particularly the likely costs of pensions and the numbers of children in schools.

Educational change has been a major social trend of the last three decades, with debates about both theory and policy reflecting sharp differences of values and objectives, and also with a growing sense of 'crisis' in this key area of national life. The first comprehensive schools, challenging both traditional and meritocratic theories of education, opened soon after Butler's Education Act of 1944, but their most rapid growth followed the Labour Party's commitment to comprehensive education after the 1964 General Election. In 1971 34 per cent of English secondary school children were attending comprehensive schools, but by 1980 that proportion had risen to 80 per cent. The educational and social consequences of the change were, and still are, a matter of debate. So too is the examination system and the curricula which lie behind it. Meanwhile, the role of the fee-paying public schools, which are often condemned as divisive, not only by the Left, remains important. Indeed, these schools have increased in numbers as some parents have reacted against tendencies and, most recently, events, such as teachers' strikes within the state system.

Numbers in higher education doubled during the 1960s, encouraged by the optimistic mood of expansion expressed in the Robbins Report of 1963. This was a real breakthrough. But even before that date, the opening of new universities – Sussex was the first, in 1961, and ancient cities like York, Canterbury and Colchester would soon acquire universities too – reflected an increasing sense that access to higher education was too restricted and total numbers too small. The increase in the number of students in higher education continued in the 1970s, but the rate of growth was to slow down in a period of serious cuts, the most alarming of them during the 1980s. The cuts affected not only universities but also polytechnics, new institutions first developed, usually from older institutions, during the 1960s as the other side of a so-called binary system. They also hit the most important new educational institution of the 1970s, the Open University – a child of the 1960s, with its headquarters in a new town, Milton Keynes, which catered not for school leavers but for adults. The development of continuing education and part-time education was restricted and there were few new approaches to technical education before 1985 and 1986.

The case for educational expansion (and, more recently, continuing education) was often argued in terms of national need, since it was widely recognized that the changing structure of the labour force constituted another major social trend. The size of the male workforce in England reached its peak in 1955, a higher peak than in most European countries, even though young workers were entering employment later and men in their sixties were retiring earlier than in the past. The main reason for an increase of over two million workers between 1961 and 1980 was a 70 per cent rise in the number of employed married women. In a society based on smaller families and delayed child-raising, women were at last offered the possibility not only of finding employment when young but of returning to work after a time devoted to the home. The range of jobs available was wider too. It was not surprising, therefore, though individual motives were mixed, that the number of female students in higher education rose even during the 1970s by 10 per cent, with Oxford and Cambridge colleges vying with each other to attract them, and that the Open University appealed strongly to women outside. Men too found that higher education offered often essential job qualifications, and in the late 1970s and 1980s there was a tendency towards securing places in science, technology and vocationally orientated subjects. Meanwhile, professional groups, including accountants – an increasingly important group in society – and surveyors, were revising their own entrance requirements and in many cases remoulding their structures and procedures.

The most important change in the British labour force, as in other countries, was the continuing decline in the numbers employed in industry – they fell by 12 per cent between 1965 and 1975 – and although as a corollary there was a marked swing towards the service trades, even the numbers employed there had fallen by 1980. Unemployment which became a major problem in the 1970s, tended to be accepted as a bleak fact of life in the 1980s, largely because unemployment benefits were just enough to provide basic livelihood, but also because in some – but not all – parts of the country there were opportunities of supplementing them through the operations of a flourishing 'dual economy'. Large numbers of people have evaded the tax system altogether as the moonlighter has become as publicized a figure in the 1980s as the spiv, the man who got round shortages, was after 1945.

During the 1950s and early 1960s it was often argued that unemployment had been exorcized from the economic system, despite 'stops' and 'gos', by Keynesian management of demand. In fact, however, it had no more been exorcized than poverty had, as a new generation of statisticians explained. Indeed, although unemployment fell to as low a point as 1 per cent in 1955, there was an ominous increase thereafter in the numbers of unemployed from the trough of one trade cycle to the next. During the early 1980s it reached new proportions, with many old industries, like steel, and some newer industries, like motor car manufacture, going through protracted crises involving the closure of plant, heavy redundancies, and survival thanks only to substantial injections from public funds. In 1982 more people than ever before, over three million, were 'on the dole'. And in the same year, for the first time ever, there was a net loss on trade with the rest of the world in manufactured goods, for which profits from North Sea oil were no substitute. For Paul Theroux in his *Kingdom by the Sea* (1983) the 'nightmare of the North' was not blackened factory chimneys and smoke and slag-heaps but empty chimneys and clean air and grass growing on slag-heaps. For the London evening newspaper the *Standard*, which had survived 'crises' in the newspaper industry itself, 'the great Victorian engine of Britain's prosperity had finally run out of steam'.

All these economic trends were closely related, of course, to the development of technology, which has been discussed with varying degrees of optimism and pessimism, not least in relation to the newspaper industry itself, more than any other topic during the period and which has had an enormous and clearly visible effect on people's everyday lives. The Second World War had left Britain with an advanced military-based production system centred on aviation, electronics and nuclear power, even if this system, as Barnett has shown, had its weaknesses. However, despite heavy post-war national expenditure on research and development, it proved difficult to exploit to the full commercially these technologies – and British inventions related to them. The failure of the Comet aircraft in 1954 was a serious blow to designers and to engineers, and the collapse of the Blue Streak ballistic missile system in 1961, by which time the use of nuclear power had become highly controversial, was a second blow. Fifteen years later, the first prototype supersonic Concorde, long in preparation and far more costly than had been projected, took to the skies, but there was no business breakthrough there. The growing number of British tourists flying abroad, most of them in packaged tours to find the sun, were flying mainly in American-built aeroplanes.

And there was always an undercurrent of fear and suspicion. Although Englishmen had pioneered first-generation computers, already by the late 1950s more attention was being focused on the problematic human effects of automation than on its economic advantages, and during the 1960s and 1970s the rapid development of the microchip was mainly achieved elsewhere. Harold Wilson promised a 'white-hot technological revolution' before he was returned to power as Labour Prime Minister in 1964, but the kind of excitement that ran through Alvin Toffler's American study, *Future Shock*, was shared by only a minority in England. By the late 1970s and early 1980s there was gloomy apprehension that unemployment in England was not only cyclical but structural – and that, whatever promises politicians might make, enhanced scientific and technical development would actually increase it.

Even medical science and technology, which had launched a wide range of new pharmaceutical products (among them antibiotics, coagulants and contraceptives) and introduced innovative techniques of surgery (among them transplants), met not with rapture but with criticism. Their effects on ways of life (and death) were undoubtedly controversial, and there was protracted if intermittent debate on abortion, the effects of chemistry on ecology, and the ethics and economics of bio-engineering. It is too early, however, to draw up a balance sheet, for a new generation is emerging which takes for granted computers (work on them in schools is highly advanced), word processors (which are revolutionizing all forms of paperwork) and video-recorders (which have achieved record sales in England and, along with cable and satellites, represent a new phase in a continuing communications revolution). Some change, therefore, is welcomed, but the best-known robot in England is still television's Dalek from the popular science fiction series 'Doctor Who'.

Technology is one of several challenges which have forced the institutionally entrenched trade-union movement to concern itself, often reluctantly, with a wider range of issues than wages. Rank-and-file trade unionists – and there were eleven million of them in 469 different unions in 1970 (as against less than ten million in 1960) – often felt threatened by 'revolutionary' labour-saving technologies. Nor were employers, not all of whom were represented in the Confederation of British Industries (CBI), set up in 1965, necessarily enthusiastic. They were themselves operating within difficult conditions as interest rates rose during the 1970s and foreign markets became more competitive. Moreover, industrial structures were also changing. There was a long-term trend, which is still continuing, towards business mergers: it attracted widespread attention during 'take-over' disputes of the 1950s and 1960s, the creation of a number of new giant concerns between 1967 and 1973, and most recently during a phase of 'hostile' take-over bidding, often more concerned with quick financial gains than with long-term economic efficiency. In consequence, the form of English capitalism is now very different from that even of the late nineteenth century, so that the argument that 'small is beautiful' has appealed to both conservatives and radicals without making life much easier for small businessmen.

In an age of greater scale, unprecedented inflation and increasing unemployment, even so-called traditional wages questions proved difficult to handle, particularly during the 1970s. Between 1754 and 1954 prices had risen six times; between 1956 and 1976 they trebled. And different groups of workers were bound to be affected in different ways. Increased scale meant more managerial delegation and less intimate human relations. Inflation, which was to fall sharply after 1980, was a disturbing force affecting different groups of workers in different ways but always raising complex questions of differentials. Unemployment tilted bargaining power back towards the employer and reduced the propensity to strike, but fear of redundancy, even in the period of high unemployment after 1983, provoked particularly militant strikes, the most bitter of them in the coal industry in 1984–5.

By then the trade-union movement, still basically unreformed in its internal structures and processes and finding it difficult to deal with demarcation disputes and sectional pressures inside particular unions, was operating within a new statutory context. A Labour government plan to limit trade-union power by law, *In Place of Strife* (1969), never had a chance of success and was soon withdrawn, and legislation favourable to the unions carried through Parliament in 1975 as part of a so-called social contract proved unacceptable to the Conservative Party and those articulate sections of the community and press which argued that the unions were abusing their power, seeking indeed to 'take over the kingdom'.

It was under a Conservative government that new legislation was devised deliberately in 1983 to curb the strength of the unions at a time when the numbers of trade unionists had fallen; and its effects have subsequently been seen in a series of anti-union decisions in the Courts.

The legislation was passed in the second of two Conservative governments headed by Mrs Thatcher, who was first chosen as Prime Minister in 1979 following a 'winter of discontent', bitter industrial unrest, under her Labour predecessor James Callaghan, who had succeeded Wilson in 1976. Her advent to power marked a decisive break with earlier attempts by Wilson, Heath, Callaghan (and earlier Prime Ministers) to implement a wages and incomes policy and to bring trade unionists and business-men closer together. In theory, at least, market forces were now to prevail, with the government indirectly 'controlling' incomes in the large 'public sector'. In fact, there has been strong if divided opposition to the post-1983 approach, with no agreement that the pre-1983 approaches were any more sensible. Proposals on industrial democracy put forward by the Bullock Committee in 1976 had met with criticism from the trade unions themselves, who were nervous of their members 'joining management', and the only surviving product of the mid-1970s is an Advisory, Con-ciliation and Arbitration Service (ACAS), the only obligatory characteristic of which is patience.

The Thatcher governments have not sought consensus. Ac-cused of polarizing the country, they have been prepared both to alienate members of their own party and to face social and political confrontation, not only with other parties but with extra-parliamentary groups and with other institutions. They have not dismantled the 'welfare state', but they have challenged its premises and carried measures which have deliberately reversed the trend of nearly twenty years of what they themselves describe pejoratively as 'consensus' politics and the 'wasteful' expenditures that have gone with it. They have advocated lower direct taxation, even though this has meant ceilings on or cuts in most public spending except defence; 'privatization'; getting rid of inflation, although this has meant increasing unemployment; the sale of council houses; concentration in social matters on crime and 'law and order', although in 1986 violence was to extend to the prisons as prison officers went on strike; and economic individualism, even in the name of restored Victorian values.

Inevitably the prosecution of such policies, backed since the general election of 1983 by a large majority in Parliament, has provoked extra-parliamentary opposition. In social terms it has meant also that the power of 'class' has continued to remain strong – despite or because of stress on economic individualism and attempts to challenge it or to erode it. In such a climate 'class' continues to shape many people's perceptions of themselves and others. Moreover, all measurable social indicators demonstrate its continuing power to influence the whole pattern of society as it is. Ivan Reid set them out carefully in his strictly empirical study *Social Class in Britain* (1977), published before the Thatcher governments, in which he considered not only conditions of work but all aspects of circumstance and behaviour, from birth and death, health, family, education, politics, religion, law and financial services to leisure activities, sex and opinion. And for all the changes in English society since the 1930s he still found it appropriate to use as the motto for one of his chapters words written by Orwell in 1937: 'whatever way you turn, this curse of class difference confronts you like a wall of stone. Or rather it is not so much like a wall of stone as the plate glass pane of an aquarium.' Since Reid wrote in 1977 many stones have been thrown at the glass, but the sense of an aquarium persists. The film-maker Lindsay Anderson, who played a creative part in the 'free cinema' movement of the 1950s, has preferred a different metaphor – Britannia Hospital.

Orwell was to be widely quoted in 1984, the title of one of his most generally read books. But his prediction that there would be one single 'Newspeak' never came about. Different regions still have different accents and different class structures. And if there are different strains within each region, there are different strains also in each class, as Nancy Mitford and others showed for the 'upper class' in studies of 'U' and 'non-U' language. Age has been a dividing factor in society also. During the 1960s in particular, the decade most frequently discussed in terms of its own distinctive idiom and momentum, the so-called 'generation gap' was apparent in language as much as in behaviour. Talk of a 'youth culture' and even a 'youth cult' had already become increasingly common in the late 1950s, when the sixteen to twenty-one-year-old age group had more disposable income than ever before and when the small minority of delinquents seemed to be increasing in size and increasingly 'ganging' together. And in both decades, the words and music of 'pop songs' (big bands and general ballad singers had given way to 'groups') often capture moods better than literature or statistics, not just for historians or for sociologists – themselves a conspicuous phenomenon of the 1960s – but for the people they were writing about.

> People try to put us down.
> Talking about my generation,
> Just because we get around.

There was, in fact, no sharp break between the 1950s and the 1960s, and 'Fifties Children: Sixties People' was a fitting title for the last chapter of *The Age of Affluence* by Robert Skidelsky and Vernon Bogdanor. The real break had come during and after the middle years of the 1950s, when, with increased prosperity, educational opportunity and social and physical mobility, society seemed to be more fluid and less willing to accept old ways. There were new supermarkets with self-service, new urban shopping centres in place of old markets, more television – including commercial televison – taking the place of what was now called 'steam radio' with remarkable speed, and credit cards. Mary Quant's first shop, harbinger of the new fashions and 'boutiques' of the 1960s (Carnaby Street style), was an indication of future changes in style and preoccupations.

This was also a time when so-called 'angry young men', many of whom spoke in provincial accents, challenged the 'Establishment'. Nuclear disarmament, an issue which has not disappeared since, was already a central topic, for seven years after atomic bombs were dropped on Hiroshima and Nagasaki the first British hydrogen bomb was tested in 1954. For Jeff Nuttall, writing in retrospect in *Bomb Culture* (1968), as for many people since, this was *the* issue of post-war years. The real break therefore had come in 1945. 'VE Night [the end of the European war] took place in one world and VJ Night [the end of the Japanese war] in another.' It was at that point that 'the generations became divided in a crucial way'.

But for most observers at or near the time, the year 1956 seemed a more symbolic break. This was the year of John Osborne's play *Look Back in Anger*, of James Dean's *Rebel Without a Cause*, of Elvis Presley's *Heartbreak Hotel*, of Bill Haley and the Comets' *Rock around the Clock*, and of the first premium bond (which the Archbishop of Canterbury feared might debauch the country). It was the year also of two separate and deeply disturbing international crises, which forced people to talk and argue: the Russian invasion of Hungary, which divided England's small Communist Party and led to the emergence of a 'New Left', and British armed intervention of Suez, which sharply divided the country (more than the Falklands campaign of 1982 was to do), starkly revealing to all that Britain was no longer the great power that Englishmen – and others – had felt it was during the Second World War. As the country moved from (relative) austerity to affluence, it was forced also to exchange illusions of world power for a blunted recognition of its limitations.

Less dramatic long-term changes altered perceptions in equally significant ways. In particular, the BBC lost its monopoly in 1955, after some of the most bitter Parliamentary debates of the post-war years, and between 1956 and 1960 the number of television licences doubled. As 'instant pictures' came into the home they speeded up reactions and gave a new significance to the day and its events. Some accused television of stimulating violence, as they continue to do; others talked of 'opening a window on the world'. There was also an unparalleled consumer boom between 1955 and 1960 which recalled rates of economic change during the 1780s: the proportion of the population using refrigerators rose from 6 to 16 per cent, washing machines from 25 to 44 per cent, and those owning a motor car from 18 to 32 per cent. Significantly, total advertising expenditure rose to an all-time peak of 1·91 per cent of consumer expenditure and 1·42 per cent of gross national product in 1960.

These were the years when the sociologist Ferdinand Zweig discerned 'a deep transformation of values', 'the development of other ways of thinking and feeling, a new ethos, new aspirations and cravings', and when the *Economist* saluted the liberating effects of the new cluster of domestic inventions. 'Ten years ago the ordinary working woman – nearly one-half the nation – was a slave in an antiquated kitchen; today mechanical slaves on hire purchase have sprung up around her as she works in the non-telly hours.' This was 'the revolution of the de-proletarianized consumer'. And, according to the *Economist*, it was affecting politics as much as everyday life, and Conservatives more than radicals. The working class, it argued, was ceasing to be working class and Conservatives were ceasing to be conservative. London was the centre of a new melting pot, although life in the provincial cities, like lively Liverpool, and once remote villages in Shropshire or Sussex was also being transformed. All subsequent changes in ethos and styles, not least in Liverpool, must be related to this initial 'deep transformation', however it is interpreted: it has recently been reassessed by Trevor Blackwell and Jeremy Seabrook in their 'reconstruction of the post-war working class'.

The *Economist*'s line of argument was strongly challenged at the time, for it had deliberately not focused attention on continuing inequalities of circumstances – in hours and conditions of work, for example, or in housing – and sociologists, notably John Goldthorpe and David Lockwood, were able to show then that so-called 'affluent' workers, even in pre-militant times, were not unlike their predecessors. The *Economist* did concede, however, with Conservatives in mind, that when 'de-proletarianized societies' developed they would not necessarily become 'more discriminate, more moral and more self-reliant'.

This appeared to be proven when changes of style in the 1960s – the advent of the mini-skirt, tights, jeans and the pill – were accompanied by a challenge to many established institutions – business, the State, the Church and the university, although there were to be reactions later. The most obvious proof, it seemed, was that in 1960 the BBC, near to its thirtieth birthday, with an annual revenue only half that of the new commercial companies, appointed a 'reforming' Director-General who wished to push the BBC 'right into the centre of the swirling forces that were changing life in Britain'. 'That Was The Week That Was' introduced barbed satire, moral as well as political, into the home in November 1962; it was taken off the screens in November 1963, but *Private Eye*, founded in 1962, was to extend the scope of satire far beyond BBC bounds. Nor did satire slacken when Harold Macmillan's Conservative government, damaged by scandals in the long and difficult winter of 1962–3, was succeeded in 1964 by Harold Wilson's Labour government.

'Permissiveness' remained a major theme of the 1960s until it gave way in 1968 and 1969 to the 'student rebellion' with which it was often associated. 'Permissiveness', however, was always a metaphor; and particularly when associated exclusively with a 'youth sub-culture' or with 'counter-culture', it obscured under-lying forces more than it illuminated cultural changes. Advertis-ing had been more sexually explicit than the cinema long before the generation gap was exposed; the pill, brought in from the United States in 1960 and made commercially available in January 1961, was widely distributed before there was talk of radical and militant 'women's lib'. The very intensity of political and moral argument centring on youth revealed that any consensus among older generations had already broken down before the argument really started.

There was an economic dimension to the 'breakdown' too. The consumer boom undermined surviving Puritan values in most sections of society as spending, not saving, became the order of the day and as hire purchase, and later the credit card, introduced from America – relieved the obligations of thrift. Houses became warmer inside as a result of the development of central heating; leisure clothes began to cost more than working clothes; garden centres multiplied. And food habits began to change more than in any period since the industrial revolution, with the revolu-tionary development of refrigeration, the popularity of 'new' fruit like avocados, the widespread distribution of 'fast-foods', the increasing appeal of foreign cuisines – including the Chinese and Indian, each with its 'take-aways' – and the adoption of vegetarianism, health-foods and low-calorie slimming diets. Colour supplements of Sunday newspapers, the first of which appeared in 1962, were as active as television in pushing forward changes in values in both their editorial content and their advertisements.

Within the context of the 1960s themselves, all these develop-ments were to persist after the social and economic changes of the

1970s and 1980s. After the avocado came the kiwi. And parallel to the food boom came the wine boom. In dress, after jeans came sneakers and trainers, a revolution in footwear. Many young people were always less permissive than the media suggested or the more credulous among their elders believed. Indeed, when the Latey Committee on the Age of Majority recommended in 1967 that the voting age should be reduced from twenty-one to eighteen (the recommendation was implemented in the Law Reform Act of 1969), its authors pointed to the conformity of the younger generation. In the same year, after a member of the Rolling Stones was sentenced to imprisonment for drug offences, a national opinion poll concluded that 85 per cent of teenagers either agreed with the sentence or thought it too lenient. The 'hippies' and 'flower people', who turned to a psychedelic counter-culture in the late 1960s, were a small minority, drawn mainly from the middle class, smaller probably than 'mods and rockers' and at a later date 'skinheads' or 'punks', drawn mainly from the working class; the important point about all such groups is that they were minorities.

Meanwhile, through the 1960s Parliament initiated a number of measures, sometimes across party lines and usually in the face of opposition, which marked a significant change in attitudes to morality. Several of them drew a crucial distinction between 'the realm of private morality', which 'was not the law's business', in the simple words of the Wolfenden Committee on Homosexual Offences and Prostitution, and 'the realm of the law'. In 1959 Macmillan's government had carried a Suicide Act which removed the penalties of the criminal law from a practice which had consistently (and almost universally) been condemned by Christian morality and which had hitherto been punishable by law. It was left to a private MP, Leo Abse, to introduce and carry eight years later an act permitting homosexual acts between consenting adult males in private. The Abortion Act (introduced by the Liberal MP David Steel), which laid down that an abortion could be carried out if two doctors were satisfied that the operation was necessary on medical or psychological grounds, and the National Health Service (Family Planning Act), which made it possible for local authorities to provide contraceptives, were carried in the same year. Two years later, the Divorce Reform Act of 1969 affirmed that the irretrievable breakdown of marriage was the only grounds on which a petition for divorce should be presented to the courts by either party in the marriage, but it also laid down that if separation had lasted for more than five years either party was entitled to a divorce whether or not the other partner agreed.

Other important legislative changes in the 1960s were the Betting and Gambling Act of 1960, which legalized gambling clubs and – far more important for the majority – betting shops, and a 1968 act redefining theatrical censorship. There was a mixture of motives behind such legislation. One was a conservative motive, apparent in the Betting and Gambling Act, of making the law credible and enforceable. A second was a liberal motive – that of freeing people from imposed restraints: it had been prominent in 1960, when the right to print a paperback edition of D. H. Lawrence's novel *Lady Chatterley's Lover*, hitherto banned, was granted after a test case in the courts. A third was humanitarianism, most strongly expressed in the abolition of the death penalty in 1965: nine years earlier a private member's bill proposing this had been carried in the House of Commons but thrown out in the House of Lords. A fourth was the egalitarian desire to deal with all sections of society in the same way: abortion had been available to the rich (at risk) before 1967; now it was to be available to all. The same motive lay behind the introduction of far-reaching legal aid schemes in 1964. A fifth motive was the principle of treating men and women on the same terms, which was apparent in the Divorce Act – although one woman Labour politician called it a 'Casanova's Charter' – and which lay directly behind both the Matrimonial Property Act of 1970, by which it was established that a wife's work as either a housewife or wage-earner should be considered as an equal contribution towards the creation of the family home, and the Equal Pay Act of 1970. This, however, did not come into force (and even then with qualifications) until 1975, the year in which the Sex Discrimination Act was passed. The position of women in society – and their own image of themselves – was changing more as a result of what happened outside Parliament than inside it.

Due to qualifications and limitations in practice, the social legislation of the 1960s increasingly failed to satisfy militant minorities who wanted to press their claims further, usually by demonstration in the streets (and ultimately in Trafalgar Square), to bring about greater, and more controversial, changes. And the minorities remained active too – in many cases becoming even more active – when there were increasing signs during the 1970s of a swing away from 'permissiveness' – an even more inadequate term in this new context than in that of youth culture in the 1960s. There was talk at this time not only of the disintegration of English society but of the twilight of the 'British state', even of its breakdown into different national components and, at a different level of argument, highly publicized anxieties about football hooliganism, mugging in the streets, the sophistication of organized crime and vandalism. The early 1970s, before the fall of Heath and the unprecedented rise in oil prices in 1974, revealed how complex society had become. A spending spree with new pennies and pounds (decimal coinage was introduced in 1971) was associated with a hectic property boom, but the miners were prepared to bring a government down. There were power cuts and short working days on the eve of the first of two elections in 1974, both lost by the Conservatives.

Characteristically, the Annan Committee on the Future of Broadcasting, appointed in 1974, pointed to the increasing difficulty of holding together English society and culture. The 'new vision of life' as presented by television, Annan wrote, inevitably reflected every kind of social division, between classes, generations and sexes, between North and South, the provinces and London, pragmatism and ideology. Some had existed before but were now given new publicity; sometimes 'they were postulated and they were brought about'. Yet there was something supremely English about such a judgement, just as there was something supremely English about the institutional continuities on which the Committee insisted, including the continuity of the BBC. Annan had no sympathy with Jeff Nuttall's 1968 view that 'culture, being the broad effect of art, is rootedly irrational and as such is perpetually operating against the economic workaday structure of society'. Nor did many providers of culture. It is significant that one of the most effective new organizations of the 1970s was the Society for Business Sponsorship of the Arts.

In such a context, the Church of England, the dissenting Churches, the Roman Catholics and the Jews could seek to dispose of their old animosities, while, in fact, religion was as much under pressure as politics. Even at the beginning of the 1950s, before significant changes in ways of thinking and feeling were apparent, only 10 per cent of the population were regular churchgoers. Now, in the late 1950s and early 1960s, there was a sharp decline, particularly among the Nonconformist sects. The power of the chapel, particularly the inner city chapel, already in decline, declined further, and many of the great Victorian chapels were pulled down or used for other purposes, even as bingo halls. Members of the Roman Catholic Church continued to increase, at least until the early 1970s, and the Church of England, in which there was a very wide range of opinions even on basic questions of liturgy, theology and ethics, suffered less than the old sects until it was subjected to attack in Press and Parliament in the 1980s. New fundamentalist or fringe sects gained, perhaps precisely because they made no compromises with secular society and showed no interest in ecumenicism.

Patterns of authority in society were changing – in schools and universities (where pupils and students asserted their claims), in hospitals and on the railways (where matrons and stationmasters no longer ran their little empires), in the factories (where shop stewards addressed, but did not always convince, mass meetings), and on the football ground and tennis court (where referees and umpires became suspect). So too did the Police.

There was one unprecedented change in English society. Until 1948 there had been only a trickle of black and coloured immigrants into England, and it was in the 1950s that they first became 'visible' ethnic minorities. Travel agencies, backed by advertising, actively developed the traffic, particularly from the West Indies. Low wages and heavy unemployment there were one spur; relative prosperity in Britain was another. In 1948, 547 immigrants arrived from Jamaica alone; by 1955 this figure had risen to a peak of 18,561 and three years later it stood at 1,992. Before 1957 the majority of migrants were adult males, but in that

Transport in England, 1986

100-400 metres above sea level

over 400 metres above sea level

main line railway

motorway

airport

year there were as many women and children for the first time, and during the next two years they outnumbered men. There were signs, therefore, of settlement. The new immigrants took up many occupations and industries, though men concentrated on railways and women on hospitals. In a so-called age of affluence, when there were serious labour shortages, they were often prepared to accept jobs and terms of work which did not appeal to English-born workers. They had to face persistent discrimination, and they were often forced to find flats or houses (often large Victorian houses with basements, built for middle-class families) in so-called 'zones of transition' within the great cities.

In 1958, when an estimated 210,000 people from 'coloured minorities' were living in Britain, there were serious disturbances in Nottingham and Notting Hill, started not by black new-comers but by 'nigger-hunting' youths, still vaguely known as 'teddy boys'. According to the judge who sentenced nine white youths after Notting Hill, 'it was you men who started the whole of this violence in Notting Hill. You are a minute and insignificant section of the population . . . and you have filled the whole nation with horror, indignation and disgust.'

It was within a context of prejudice and conflict that the issues of racial discrimination, immigration control and police conduct began to be debated for the first time, although the word 'debated' is too polite in relation to much that happened. There was little general knowledge among English people of the different backgrounds from which the newcomers came or of their way of life, even though, unlike Turkish, Spanish and Portuguese migrant workers in the German and Swiss workforce, all of them came from former colonial backgrounds with varying kinds of cultural contact with England. Despite the slogans of 'Keep Britain White' agitators, there was little sense at the end of the 1950s that many of the minorities would either deliberately seek or be driven by circumstances to settle together in relatively segregated areas. Indeed, it could still be pointed out in 1958 that 'despite some concentrations' the minorities were 'dispersed throughout the country' and that the majority of English people hoped that there would be full 'assimilation'.

During the early 1960s one experienced observer noted social tensions in areas where there was coexistence rather than segregation, and suggested that in Brixton in South London, for example, 'coloured people had become an accepted part of the British urban landscape, if not yet of the community'. Yet as numbers increased, so did tensions, particularly after an influx of Kenyan Asians with British passports in 1967. The much-publicized speech of an able and prominent Conservative politician, Enoch Powell, who described his foreboding in the dramatic terms that 'like the Romans, I seem to see the River Tiber foaming with much blood', further heightened tensions. There was a later influx in 1972, this time of Ugandan Asians.

Meanwhile, immigration controls had been introduced in Parliament to 'regulate the migrant flow', the first put into force in 1962 under a Conservative government, the second in 1968 under a Labour government. A further more restrictive Immigration Act of 1982, the British Nationality Act, ended 'seven centuries of traditions' and replaced a single, unified citizenship of the United Kingdom and Colonies by three separate citizenships – British citizenship, British Dependent Territories citizenship and British Overseas citizenship.

By then, largely because of changed economic circumstances in Britain, the flow of new immigrants had returned to a trickle. By then too, however, there were big Asian concentrations in Leicester (16·5 per cent), Wolverhampton, Powell's old constituency (8·8 per cent), and Bradford (7·8 per cent), with large West Indian communities in London and the Midlands. Moreover, there had been serious rioting with a racial element in Southall and Brixton in London and Toxteth in Liverpool. The Scarman Report sought to present a lawyer's analysis of the causes. There was more than one, and their relative significance remained a matter of dispute: black youth unemployment; the plight of the inner city, the subject of a controversial report by the Church of England in 1986; the still more controversial role of the Police. Whatever the relative significance of the causes, English social history had clearly taken a new turn when the children of people from very different ethnic and cultural backgrounds were living in England in large enough numbers for their presence to be felt.

With immigration, membership of the European Community

and increasing American influence through the media, identifying what was peculiarly English became an increasing national preoccupation. It was intensified too by the violence provoked by the Irish Republican Army, including acts of terrorism in English cities in the 1970s and 1980s. What had the country come to?

Even in the most peaceful parts of England there could be a different sense of threat. Symbolically, the twentieth century began with a violent gale which blew down one of the upright stones at Stonehenge. At the time it did not seem like an omen; nor was there then any sharply articulated concern about the future appearance of the countryside: the main anxieties were about agricultural depression. It is only in recent years of agricultural prosperity that deep fears have begun to be expressed about the future of the English countryside. 'Our surroundings are part of what we are,' the sculptor Henry Moore wrote in 1980, when he felt that they were in danger. 'And the special quality of the English countryside has helped shape the English character.' His own sculptures would have been different, he added, had not the shapes of the Yorkshire landscape existed first.

The growing threat to the countryside has been felt to come not so much from land speculators and industrialists as from farmers, whose incomes, supported by an agricultural price policy determined not in London but in Brussels, rose in 1982 more than those of any other social group. Modes of farming – and with them the appearance of the farm landscape and buildings – have changed more during the last quarter of a century than they did in the eighteenth century, disturbing the traditional variety of landscape, wild life and buildings. Different parts of the country, like different parts of the city, have begun to look the same.

Thousands of acres of down and heath have already disappeared with the spread of battery farming, cereal growing controlled by chemical fertilizers and a grass monoculture supporting intensive stock-rearing. Barley has taken the place of scrub on the chalk hills of Dorset, conifers have been planted on the heath, barbed wire has supplanted hawthorn – 125,000 miles of hedgerow have been lost since 1945 – and pylons stretch across the plains, corrugated iron barns and silos have appeared in

well-drained farmyards, and everywhere there are chemical fertilizers and pesticides. (There was an eight-fold increase in the use
of nitrogen-based fertilizers between 1953 and 1976.) Both
animals and men have been giving way to machines for decades.
In 1950 there were still 300,000 horses working on farms; in
1979 there were 3,575. In 1945 there were 563,000 regular full-
time farm workers; in 1980 there were 133,000.

This was a new 'agricultural revolution', comparable with the
neolithic breakthrough and with the changes of the eighteenth
century in terms both of greater agricultural yields and environmental implications. And it was significantly speeded up by the
actions of the State, which have been more effective in supporting
English farmers (though not hill farmers) than the protective
fiscal policies of the past. A 1947 Agricultural Act designed to
save the farmer from the insecurities of pre-war farming, passed
by a Labour government, laid the foundation. By 1973, when
Britain entered the Common Market, it had been extended by
capital grants, tax concessions and price supports which served
not as a support but as a generous subsidy. While farmers were
organized in a powerful lobby, the National Farmers' Union,
founded in 1908, have been at pains to deny that they are
over-subsidized and to challenge the view that they are destroying the countryside. Meanwhile, governments have professed
themselves concerned with long-term planning for the countryside. The Countryside Act of 1968 charged the Minister of
Agriculture to pay attention to 'the desirability of conserving the
natural beauty and amenity of the countryside' and the Wildlife
and Countryside Act was passed in 1982. It put its main trust in
voluntarily arranged local management agreements backed with
limited powers of compulsion and with no provision for binding
arbitration. During the same period the National Trust did much
as a voluntary body to save houses, estates and landscapes of
special historic interest, while local government boundaries – and
powers – were radically and controversially 'reformed'.

If the countryside has been under threat and the inner cities have
faced what often seem to be insoluble problems, social, financial
and political – with Liverpool under the spotlight – England's
small towns, the 'Banburys of England', as Alan Everitt has

described them, have not been left untouched. It is in them that both the continuities and changes of English social history are most faithfully recorded today. Their long-term future, like that of the country as a whole, depends on the stimulation of both economic and community enterprise. While the differences between England's small towns, expressed in their carefully designated conservation areas, are the source of their charm, the bigger differences between the regions of the country, above all, North and South, can be disturbing, and they have been further accentuated during the 1980s. The electoral map reflects those differences. So too does the incidence of unemployment and the distribution of social amenities. Some of the oldest industrial areas now seem some of the oldest parts of the country. Yet there can be no completely local – or national – answers to their problems. In the late twentieth century the parish cannot easily be set against the world: the local and the global, both in ecology and in history, are now two dimensions of the same set of problems and opportunities.

Nor can the old be kept safely intact. One of the most sympathetic and knowledgeable of foreign observers to write recently about England, Ralf Dahrendorf, is refreshed by much that he sees in England, but confesses that he finds few things more bewildering than the extent to which current public debate is preoccupied with yesterday's world. It is not likely that this world will survive for long, or that a Conservative government will be primarily concerned any longer with conserving it. Yet as Winston Churchill wrote: 'The longer you look back, the farther you can look forward.' All history is unfinished history, and just as we have had more than one yesterday, so we can, if we choose, have more than one future.

FURTHER READING

This is a highly selective guide to further reading which includes major books and more detailed studies at very different levels of information and interpretation. The major books often include fuller bibliographies. Some of the most interesting and up-to-date reading is to be found in periodicals, although I shall not cite individual articles in them here. The most relevant periodicals include *History*, *History Today*, *Antiquity*, *The Economic History Review*, *Social History*, *Past and Present*, *History Workshop*, *Oral History* and the *Journal of Social History*, but there are good reasons also for reading periodicals concerned with local and regional history.

CHAPTER I
UNWRITTEN HISTORY

I. H. Longworth, *Prehistoric Britain* (1985) provides an excellent brief introduction. Invaluable general surveys include C. Renfrew (ed.), *British Prehistory – A New Outline* (1974) and J. V. S. Megaw and D. D. Simpson, *Introduction to British Prehistory* (1979). There are 320 excellent photographs in S. Thomas, *Pre-Roman Britain* (1965).

For the history of prehistory see T. Kendrick, *British Antiquity* (1950); Glyn Daniel, *A Hundred and Fifty Years of Archaeology* (1981 edn); and K. Hudson, *A Social History of Archaeology* (1981). See also Glyn Daniel, *The Idea of Prehistory* (1962). For method and debate see, *inter alia*, the fascinating collection of articles edited by C. Renfrew, *The Explanation of Culture Change: Models in Prehistory* (1973). There is a very different angle in S. Piggott, *Ruins in a Landscape* (1976) and R. Jessup, *Curiosities of British Archaeology* (1974). All these books reveal how difficult it is to keep up to date with prehistory.

For the changing face of England see Sir Cyril Fox, *Personality of Britain* (1932); W. G. Hoskins, *The Making of the English Landscape* (1955), necessary reading for many chapters of this book; E. Hyams, *The Changing Face of Britain* (1977); the authoritative and stimulating study by J. G. Evans, *The Environment of Early Man in the British Isles* (1975); and I. Sissons and M. Tooley (eds.), *The Environment in British Prehistory* (1982).

R. Bradley, *The Social Foundations of Prehistoric Britain* (1984) deals, *inter alia*, with inference in archaeology and with much else, including the time sequence. For the beginnings see J. M. Coles and E. S. Higgs, *The Archaeology of Early Man* (1975); J. B. Campbell, *The Upper Palaeolithic Age of Britain* (1977) and *The Prehistoric Settlement of Britain* (1978); J. J. Wymer, *The Palaeolithic Age* (1986); and P. J. Fowler, *The Forming of Prehistoric Britain* (1983). J. G. D. Clark, *Star Carr* (1974) deals with a classic excavation.

S. Piggott's *Neolithic Cultures of the British Isles* (1954) is valuable, but dated. There is no general survey of the Bronze Ages, but see D. D. A. Simpson (ed.), *Economy and Settlement in Neolithic and Early Bronze Age Britain and Europe* (1971) and F. Ashbee, *The Bronze Age Round Barrow in Britain* (1960). For the Iron Ages see B. W. Cunliffe, *Iron Age Communities in Great Britain* (2nd edn, 1978); D. W. Harding, *The Iron Age in Lowland Britain* (1974); and, at an introductory level, W. Laing, *Celtic Britain* (1981).

For Stonehenge and other places to visit see R. J. C. Atkinson, *Stonehenge* (1979 edn); J. Fowles and B. Brukoff, *The Enigma of Stonehenge* (1980); and, adding to the mysteries, G. S. Hawkins and J. B. White, *Stonehenge Decoded* (1966). N. Thomas, *A Guide to Prehistoric England* (1976) does exactly what it sets out to do, as do J. Dyer's *Southern England, an Archaeological Guide* (1973) and *The Penguin Guide to Prehistoric England and Wales* (1981). See also G. E. Daniel, *Megaliths in History* (1972), and for arguments about megaliths C. Renfrew's *Before Civilisation* (1972) and E. Mackie, *The Megalith Builders* (1977). J. R. L. Anderson and F. Godwin, *The Oldest Road* (1975) and A. Burl, *Prehistoric Avebury* (1980) are interesting specific studies. More comprehensive scholarly works include A. Burl, *The Stone Circles in the British Isles* (1976); B. W. Cunliffe and T. Rowley, *Oppida in Barbarian Europe* (1976); and M. Jesson and D. Hill (eds.), *The Iron Age and its Hill Forts* (1971).

For art see I. M. Stead, *Celtic Art* (1985); I. Finlay, *Celtic Art* (1973); P. Jacobsthal and E. M. Jope, *Early Celtic Art in Britain* (1977); and D. L. Clarke's highly specialized *The Beaker Pottery of Great Britain and Ireland* (1969).

For religion see A. Ross, *Pagan Celtic Britain* (1967); S. Piggott, *The Druids* (1967); and T. Kendrick's classic study *The Druids: A Study in Celtic Prehistory* (1927), one of a number of older and now dated books which deserve to be read even after new evidence has been collected. Others include V. G. Childe, *Prehistoric Communities of the British Isles* (1940) and M. Dillon and N. Chadwick, *The Celtic Realms* (2nd edn, 1972).

For the general context, see B. G. D. Clark, *World Prehistory: A New Outline* (1977). For further mystery, much of it treated as such, as it so often is, see J. and C. Bord, *The Secret Country* (1976) and W. Johnson, *Folk Memory or the Continuity of British Archaeology* (1908).

CHAPTER 2
INVASION, RESISTANCE, SETTLEMENT AND CONQUEST

It is interesting to compare the two major Oxford histories of Roman Britain, R. G. Collingwood and J. N. L. Myres, *Roman Britain and the English Settlements* (1934) and P. Salway, *Roman Britain* (1981), for changes in perspectives as well as in scholarship. Shorter studies include M. Todd, *Roman Britain* (1981) and J. Wacher, *Roman Britain* (1978). See also S. Frere's impressive *Britannia: A History of Roman Britain* (2nd edn, 1978); S. Johnson, *Later Roman Britain* (1980); and P. J. Casey (ed.), *The End of Roman Britain* (1979).

Aspects of economic history are examined by B. W. Cunliffe (ed.), *Coinage and Society in Britain*; D. E. Strong and D. Brown, *Roman Crafts* (1976); A. D. McWhirr, *Roman Crafts and Industries* (1978); and J. du Plat Taylor and H. Cleere (eds.), *Roman Shipping and Trade: Britain and the Rhine Provinces* (1978).

For aspects of social history see A. R. Birley's indispensable *The People of Roman Britain* (1979); D. Miles (ed.), *Countryside Studies in Rural Settlement and Economy* (1982); A. L. F. Rivet, *Town and Country in Roman Britain* (1958); J. Wacher, *The Towns of Roman Britain* (1975); M. Todd, *Studies in the Romano-British Villa* (1978); and B. W. Cunliffe, *Fishbourne, A Roman Palace and its Garden* (1971). See also D. J. Breeze and B. Dobson, *Hadrian's Wall* (1978 edn) and P. Marsden, *Roman London* (1980).

The most comprehensive study of culture is J. Munby and M. Henig (eds.), *Roman Art and Life in Britain* (1977). Religion is explored in W. Radwell (ed.) *Temples, Churches and Religion: Recent Research in Roman Britain* (1980) and in C. Thomas, *Christianity in Roman Britain to A.D. 500* (1981). See also A. L. F. Rivet and C. Smith, *The Place Names of Roman*

Britain (1979) and the Ordnance Map of Roman Britain (4th edn, 1978). D. E. Johnston (ed.), *Discovering Roman Britain* (1983) is a useful guide to sites.

There are several good introductions to Anglo–Saxon history, the most recent of them being J. Campbell (ed.), *The Anglo Saxons* (1982): it is beautifully illustrated and has a full bibliography. See also P. Hunter Blair, *An Introduction to Anglo-Saxon England* (2nd edn, 1977); P. A. Sawyer, *From Roman Britain to Norman England* (1978); and H. R. Loyn, *Anglo-Saxon England and the Norman Conquest* (1962). Sir Frank Stenton's *Anglo-Saxon England* (1943; 3rd edn, 1973) remains one of the best of the Oxford Histories. A shorter history is D. J. V. Fisher, *The Anglo-Saxon Age*, c. *400–1042* (1973). D. M. Wilson, *The Anglo-Saxons* (3rd edn, 1981) is clear and straightforward. See also *The Archaeology of Anglo-Saxon England* (1976), which he has edited.

L. Alcock's *Arthur's Britain* (1953) provides a fascinating epilogue and prelude and should be compared with J. Morris, *The Age of Arthur* (1973). D. Whitelock's *The Beginnings of English Society* (1952) is a sensible introduction to social history. She has also edited *English Historical Documents: Vol. I* (2nd edn, 1979).

Among detailed monographs see E. John, *Land Tenure in Early England* (1960); E. C. Dyer, *Lords and Peasants in Changing Society* (1981); and C. W. Hollister, *Anglo-Saxon Military Institutions* (1962). P. H. Sawyer (ed.), *Medieval Settlement* (1976) presents recent scholarship on a subject of increasing interest to social historians, not only medieval historians. Return to the source with M. Winterbottom (ed. and tr.), *Gildas, The Ruin of Britain and other Works* (1978); J. Campbell, *Bede* (1968); D. Wright (tr.), *Beowulf* (1957); J. C. Pope (ed.), *Homilies of Aelfric* (1967; 1968); G. M. Garmondsway (ed.) *The Anglo-Saxon Chronicle* (1953); and R. T. Farrell (ed.), *Bede and Anglo-Saxon England* (1968). Classic studies of more recent times which almost have the air of primary sources include F. W. Maitland, *Domesday Book and Beyond* (1897); H. M. Chadwick, *The Origin of the English Nation* (1907); and M. Bloch, *Feudal Society* (1961). See also K. J. Jackson's, *Language and History in Early Britain* (1960) and O. G. S. Crawford, *Archaeology in the Field* (1953), a view from the air.

For the Vikings see P. H. Sawyer, *The Age of the Vikings* (1971 edn,); J. Bransted, *The Vikings* (1965); P. G. Foote and D. M. Wilson, *The Viking Achievement* (1970); J. Graham-Campbell, *The Viking World* (1980); and R. T. Farrell (ed.), *Viking Civilisation* (1982).

For Christianity see H. Mayr-Harting, *The Coming of Christianity to Anglo-Saxon England* (1972); M. W. Barley and R. P. C. Hanson (eds.), *Christianity in Britain, 300–700* (1968); M. Deanesly, *The Pre-Conquest*

Church in England (2nd edn, 1962); E. S. Duckett, *Anglo-Saxon Saints and Scholars* (1947) and *St Dunstan of Canterbury* (1955); F. Barlow, *The English Church 1000–1066* (1943); and J. Godfrey, *The Church in Anglo-Saxon England* (1962). C. F. Battison (ed.), *The Relics of St.Cuthbert* (1956) pushes from Saxon present into medieval future.

For art and architecture see J. H. L. Myres, *Anglo-Saxon Pottery and the Settlement of England* (1969); T. D. Hendrick, *Anglo-Saxon Art to 900* (1938) and *Late Saxon and Viking Art* (1949); D. Talbot Rice, *English Art, 871–1100* (1952); C. R. Dodwell, *Anglo-Saxon Art* (1982); and H. M. and J. Taylor, *Anglo-Saxon Architecture* (3 vols, the last appearing in 1978). See also J. Beckhouse, *The Lindisfarne Gospels* (1981).

For particular places and sites see R. L. S. Bruce-Mitford's *The Sutton Hoo Burial, A Handbook* (3rd edn, 1979); C. Green, *Sutton Hoo* (1968); P. Rahtz, *The Saxon and Medieval Palaces at Cheddar* (1979); C. Fox, *Offas's Dyke* (1955); and B. Hope-Taylor, *Yeavering* (1977).

For a special angle on the period see W. Bonser, *The Medieval Background of Anglo-Saxon England* (1963).

For 1066 see D. C. Douglas, *William the Conqueror* (1964); F. Barlow, *William I and the Norman Conquest* (1965); D. J. A. Matthew, *The Norman Conquest* (1966); and F. M. Stenton, *The Bayeux Tapestry* (1957). F. Barlow's *The Feudal Kingdom of England 1042–1216* (1972 edn) is a comprehensive survey, looking backwards as well as forwards. See also R. A. Brown, *The Normans and the Norman Conquest* (1969) and *Origins of English Feudalism* (1973).

CHAPTER 3
DEPENDENCE, EXPANSION AND CULTURE

The best general introduction to the economic and social history of the period is J. Hatcher and E. Miller, *Medieval England: Rural Society and Economic Change, 1083–1348* (1978). It can be supplemented by other studies, among them R. V. Lennard, *Rural England, 1086–1135* (1959); J. L. Bolton, *The Medieval English Economy, 1150–1500* (1980); M. M. Postan, *The Medieval Economy and Society* (1957 edn); and J. Z. Titow, *English Rural Society, 1200–1350* (1969).

An indispensable book for the geography behind this and later chapters is H. C. Darby (ed.), *A New Historical Geography of England* (1973). For general background see F. Heer, *The Medieval World* (Eng. tr., 1963); R. W. Southern, *The Making of the Middle Ages* (1953); G. Duby, *The Chivalrous Society* (1977); J. Evans, *The Flowering of the Middle Ages* (1966); and N. F. Cantor, *The English* (1968).

Much of the detailed research on which general studies are based is local. Indeed, some general studies concentrate on evidence derived from particular researched localities, and the representativeness of the evidence can lead to debate. Among further books of economic and social interest see E. King, *Peterborough Abbey, 1086–1310* (1973), which precisely covers the years described in this chapter; Z. Razi, *Life, Marriage and Death in a Medieval Parish: Economy, Society and Demography in Halesowen, 1270–1400* (1980), a fascinating study which should be read for this and the next chapter; P. R. Hyams, *King, Lords and Peasants in Medieval England: The Common Law of Villeinage in the Twelfth and Thirteenth Centuries* (1980); and J. Raftis, *Tenure and Mobility: Studies in the Social History of the Medieval English Village* (1964). A pioneering Russian study, translated into English in 1956, was E. A. Kosminsky, *Studies in the Agrarian History of England in the Thirteenth Century*.

Older studies often deal vividly with the experience of daily life. See in particular H. S. Bennett, *Life on the English Manor* (1956) and W. G. Hoskins, *The Midland Peasant* (1957), the latter covering a broad span of history. C. S. Orwin's *The Open Fields* (1938) is still readable. A recent non-specialist study of a household is M. W. Labarge, *A Baronial Household of the Thirteenth Century* (1980). Compare M. Altschul, *A Baronial Family in Medieval England: the Clares, 1217–1314* (1965). J. E. T. Rogers, *Six Centuries of Work and Wages* (1891) has not been entirely superseded, and G. C. Homans, *English Villagers of the Thirteenth Century* (1940) remains a lively pioneering study of the past by an American sociologist. See also W. J. Ashley, *Bread of our Forefathers* (1928).

G. C. Coulton, *A Medieval Panorama* (2 vols, 1961) is vivid but in places controversial, as its author always chose to be. See also his *The Medieval Village* (1931). R. H. Hilton, *Bond Men Made Free* (1973), also controversial in a different vein, is relevant to this and the next chapter; see also his *A Medieval Society: The West Midlands at the End of the Thirteenth Century* (1966). A. MacFarlane, *The Origins of English Individualism* (1978) is a stimulating and equally controversial study which takes a very different point of view. The latter should be related also to K. Thomas, *Religion and the Decline of Magic* (1971), a seminal work which should be read for all the pre-industrial chapters in this History. Peasants are dealt with generally in T. Shanin (ed.), *Peasants and Peasant Societies* (1971), a book which brings out indirectly the distinctiveness of much English experience. See also D. Oshinsky, *Walter of Henley* (1971).

On towns see J. Tait, *The Medieval English Borough* (1936); S. Reynolds, *The Town* (1961); C. Platt, *The English Medieval Town* (1976); M. W. Beresford, *New Towns of the Middle Ages* (1967); and S. Thrupp,

The Merchant Class of Medieval London (1948). An older descriptive work by L. F. Saltzman, *English Trade in the Middle Ages* (1931) provides useful detail. See also D. Knoop and G. P. Jones, *The Medieval Mason* (1933).

F. Pollock and F. W. Maitland, *History of English Law Before the Time of Edward I* (1968 edn) is a great basic work, originally published in 1898. See also J. C. Holt, *Magna Carta* (1965) and A. Harding, *Law Courts of Medieval England* (1973).

Castles are dealt with generally in W. Anderson, *Castles of Europe* (1970). F. Wilkinson, *The Castles of England* (1973) is a useful guide. Along with other buildings they are discussed in the well illustrated volume by C. Platt, *Medieval England: A Social History and Archaeology from the Conquest to A.D.1600* (1978). For cathedrals see A. Clifton-Taylor, *The Cathedrals of England* (1967). See also A. Martindale, *Gothic Art* (1967). For what remains of Norman England see T. Rowley, *A Traveller's Guide to Norman Britain* (1986): it contains a useful glossary.

Monasteries are studied at length in massive volumes by M. D. Knowles, *The Monastic Orders in England, 943–1216* (1940) and *The Religious Orders in England* (3 vols., 1949–59). See also for religious history his *Saints and Scholars* (1962); J. R. H. Moorman, *The Franciscan Order to 1517* (1968); and G. R. Owst, *Preaching in Medieval England* (1961). For the Jews see J. Parkes, *The Jew in the Medieval Community* (1938) and H. G. Richardson, *English Jewry under the Angevin Kings* (1960). F. W. Powicke and A. B. Emden's edition of H. Rashdall, *Universities of Europe in the Middle Ages*, Vol. III (1976), is also useful on religious history in its institutional setting.

I have also quoted in my chapter J. Fortescue's *History of the British Army*, Vol. I (1899), and I owe much to J. Thornton, *The Habit of Authority* (1974), a suggestive and original Canadian study of 'paternalism in British history' which is relevant also to later chapters. See also M. R. Powicke, *Military Obligation in Medieval England* (1962).

For this and the next chapter see also E. Prestage (ed.), *Chivalry* (1928) and R. Barber, *The Knight and Chivalry* (1970). I have written an introduction to Henry Adams's classic essay *Mont St. Michel and Chartres* (1980); and for a further study of past and present – or rather, two pasts – see A. Chandler, *A Dream of Order: The Medieval Ideal in Nineteenth-Century Literature* (1971).

There is scope for far more work on themes identified by D. M. Stenton in her *The English Woman in History* (1957) and for new themes identified by more recent writers on women's history. See, however, D. Baker (ed.), *Medieval Women* (1978) for a series of profiles.

CHAPTER 4
ORDER AND CONFLICT

The best general introduction is M. H. Keen, *England in the Later Middle Ages* (1973). See also the Oxford History by M. McKisack, *The Fourteenth Century, 1307–1399* (1959) and, in briefer compass, A. R. Myers, *A History of England in the Later Middle Ages* (1965) and G. Holmes, *The Later Middle Ages* (1962). Barbara Tuchman, *A Distant Mirror* (1978) presents a very different kind of brilliant panoramic interpretation. Compare F. R. H. Du Boulay, *An Age of Ambition: English Society in the Later Middle Ages* (1970) and J. R. Hale, R. L. L. Highfield and B. Smalley (eds.), *Europe in the Later Middle Ages* (1965). See also J. Hatcher, *Plague, Population and the British Economy, 1348–1530* (1977), which includes a useful reading list; P. Ziegler, *The Black Death* (1969); P. Slack (ed.), *The Plague Reconsidered* (1977) and B. R. Dobson (ed.), *The Peasants' Revolt of 1381* (1970).

There is a short narrative history of the wars with France, D. Seward, *The Hundred Years War* (1978). See also K. Fowler (ed.), *The Hundred Years War* (1971); C. T. Allmand (ed.), *Society at War: The Experience of England and France During the Hundred Years War* (1973); and, with the same editor, *War, Literature and Politics in the late Middle Ages* (1976).

The Oxford History *The Fifteenth Century* (1961) is by E. Jacob. See also J. R. Lander, *Government and Community, England, 1450–1509* (1980) and *The Wars of the Roses* (1965). C. D. Ross, *The Wars of the Roses* (1976) is a readable account. See also C. L. Kingsford, *Prejudice and Promise* (1925) and *Historical Literature in the Fifteenth Century* (1913). J. Huizinga, *The Waning of the Middle Ages* (1924) is a European classic.

K. B. Mcfarlane's posthumously published studies *The Nobility of Later Medieval England* (1973) deal with basic themes. See also for aspects of economic history A. R. Bridbury, *Economic Growth, England in the Later Middle Ages* (1921).

A. Wagner's *English Genealogy* (1960), *Heredity and Heraldry in the Middle Ages* (1956) and *Heredity and Ancestry* (1978) are all useful.

More specialized studies include E. Searle, *Lordship and Community* (1974); N. Saul, *Knights and Esquires: The Gloucestershire Gentry in the Fourteenth Century* (1981); F. R. H. Du Boulay, *The Lordship of Canterbury* (1966); B. P. Wolffe, *The Crown Lands, 1461–1536* (1970); and, from a more distant time, C. Oman, *A History of the Art of War in the Middle Ages, 1278–1485* (1924). Compare H. J. Hewitt, *The Organisation of War under Edward III* (1966). There is much of interest in M. W. Beresford and J. G. Hurst, *Deserted Medieval Villages* (1971), like all Beresford's work, an invitation to research through exploration. See also W. Minchinton (ed.), *Essays in Agrarian History* (1963).

For wool see E. Power, *The Wool Trade in English Medieval History* (1941) and for trade E. Power and M. Postan (eds.), *Studies in English Trade in the Fifteenth Century* (1933) and E. Carus Wilson and D. Coleman, *England's Export Trade, 1275–1547* (1963). C. Gross, *The Gild Merchant* (1890) is still useful: the subject has recently been neglected. See also S. Kramer, *The English Craft Gilds* (1927); G. Unwin, *The Guilds and Companies of London* (1925); and T. Baker, *Medieval London* (1970).

There is much of intellectual interest in J. T. Norman, *The Scholastic Analysis of Usury* (1957), which should be studied as a learned postscript to R. H. Tawney's *Religion and the Rise of Capitalism* (1926). There is a different note in W. E. Meade, *The English Medieval Feast* (1971).

For religion see, *inter alia*, W. A. Pantin, *The English Church in the Fourteenth Century* (1955); K. B. McFarlane, *John Wycliffe and the Beginnings of English Non-Conformity* (1952); P. Heath, *English Parish Clergy on the Eve of the Reformation* (1969); and D. J. Hall, *English Medieval Pilgrimage* (1966). For education see N. I. Orme, *English Schools in the Middle Ages* (1973).

Printing is dealt with in its general European context in E. Eisenstein, *The Printing Press as an Agent of Change* (2 vols., 1979). See also the older study by H. S. Bennett, *Books and Readers, 1475–1557* (1969 edn.) and G. D. Painter, *William Caxton* (1976).

M. H. Keen, *The Outlaws of Medieval Legend* (1961) should be studied within the context of R. H. Hilton (ed.), *Peasants, Knights and Heretics: Studies in Medieval English Social History* (1976); E. J. Hobsbawm, *Bandits* (1969); J. G. Bellamy, *Crime and Public Order in England in the Later Middle Ages* (1979); and A. McCall's colourful *The Medieval Underworld* (1979). See also J. C. Holt, *Robin Hood* (1982); J. J. Jusserand, *English Wayfaring Life in the Middle Ages* (1889); and G. T. Salisbury Jones, *Street Life in Medieval England* (1939).

CHAPTER 5

PROBLEMS, OPPORTUNITIES AND ACHIEVEMENTS

D. M. Palliser, *The Age of Elizabeth: England under the Later Tudors, 1547–1603* (1983) is a thorough and well-documented general introduction to the social and economic history of the later period. W. G. Hoskins, *The Age of Plunder: The England of Henry VIII* (1976), the previous volume in the same series, is more personal in its interpretations. For an excellent survey and analysis see D. C. Coleman, *The Economy of England, 1450–1570* (1977). P. Ramsey, *Tudor Economic Problems* (1963) is succinct and selective. J. Youings, *Sixteenth-Century*

England (1984) is the most recent study. See also W. B. Rye, *England As Seen by Foreigners in the Days of Elizabeth and James* (1965).

It is impossible to separate out distinctly social, even economic, history from political and administrative history. For this reason, G. R. Elton's *England Under the Tudors* (2nd edn, 1974) and A. L. Rowse's *The England of Elizabeth* (1950), important books by two very different historians, are indispensable reading. See also L. Stone, *The Crisis of the Aristocracy, 1558–1641*, (1965). More recent studies include P. Williams, *Life in Tudor England* (1964) and *The Tudor Regime* (1979); J. L. Hurstfield, *Freedom, Government and Corruption in Elizabethan England (1973)*; J. R. Lander, *Government and Community: England, 1450–1509* (1977); A. Fletcher, *Tudor Rebellions* (1973), a good short survey; W. T. MacCaffrey, *The Shaping of the Elizabethan Regime* (1968); and C. Haigh (ed.), *The Reign of Elizabeth* (1984). K. Wrightson, *English Society, 1580–1680* (1982), useful for this and the next chapter, discusses issues which do not figure in most other books.

For agrarian England, see J. Thirsk (ed.), *The Agrarian History of England and Wales*, Vol. IV (1967), which covers this and parts of the next chapter; R. H. Tawney, *The Agrarian Problem in the Sixteenth Century* (1912); E. Kerridge, *Agrarian Problems in the Sixteenth Century and After* (1969), a shorter work which should be compared with it. For examples of the history of an estate see J. M. W. Bean, *The Estates of the Percy Family* (1958) and F. G. Davenport, *The Economic Development of a Norfolk Manor* (1906). A readable work on one element in rural society is M. Campbell, *The English Yeoman under Elizabeth and the Early Stuarts* (1942).

For industry see D. C. Coleman, *Industry in Tudor and Stuart England* (1975); W. English, *The Textile Industry* (1969); and the older study by G. Unwin, *Industrial Organisation in the Sixteenth and Seventeenth Centuries* (1904). G. D. Ramsay's *Wiltshire Woollen Industry in the Sixteenth and Seventeenth Centuries* (1965 edn) is a valuable local study. J. O. Nef, *The Rise of the British Coal Industry* (2 vols., 1932) introduced the idea of an early industrial revolution.

The economy as a whole is examined for this and the period covered in the next chapter in J. D. Chambers, *Population, Economy and Society in Pre-Industrial England* (1972); L. A. Clarkson, *The Pre-Industrial Economy in England, 1500–1750* (1971); and R. O'Day, *Economy and Community: Economic and Social History of Pre-Industrial England 1500–1700* (1975). See also N. B. Harte *et al.*, (eds.), *Trade, Government and Economy in Pre-Industrial England* (1976).

Town life is dealt with in P. Clark and P. Slack, *Crisis and Order in*

English Towns, 1500–1750 (1972) and *English Towns in Transition, 1500 –1700* (1976), which started a controversy set out as it then was in P. Clark (ed.), *Country Towns in Pre-Industrial England* (1981). See also W. G. Hoskins, *Provincial England* (1964) and T. Baker, *Medieval London* (1970).

For riches and poverty and charity and poor relief see J. Pound, *Poverty and Vagrancy in Tudor England* (1971); A. L. Beier, *The Problem of the Poor in Tudor and Early Stuart England* (1983); J. Loach and R. Tittler (eds.), *The Mid-Tudor Polity* (1980); E. M. Leonard, *The Early History of English Poor Relief* (1900); and W. K. Jordan, *Philanthropy in England 1480–1660* (1959).

For education see J. Simon, *Education and Society in Tudor England* (1967), which has a good bibliography. For this and the next chapter D. Cressy's *Literacy and the Social Order: Reading and Writing in Tudor and Stuart England* (1980) is stimulating. See also the second volume of H. S. Bennett, *Books and Readers* (1965), which covers the period from 1558 to 1603; K. Charlton, *Education in Renaissance England* (1965); and L. Stone (ed.), *The University in Society*, Vol. I (1974).

The changes associated with the Reformation are dealt with very clearly and in balanced fashion in A. G. Dickens, *The English Reformation* (1964). See also for continuities and discontinuities his *Lollards and Protestants in the Diocese of York, 1509–1558* (1959) and M. Aston, *Lollards and Reformers* (1983). G. W. O. Woodward's *The Dissolution of the Monasteries* (1966) is useful, but see also A. Savine, *English Monasteries on the Eve of the Dissolution* (1909). C. Cross, *Church and People 1450–1660* (1976) should be supplemented by R. O'Day and F. Heal, *Church and Society in England, Henry VIII to James I* (1977) and *Princes and Paupers in the English Church, 1500–1800* (1981). R. O'Day, *The English Clergy, 1558–1642* (1979) is a valuable additional study. For Puritanism see P. Collinson, *The Elizabethan Puritan Movement* (2nd edn, 1982) and J. Phillips, *The Reformation of Images: The Destruction of Art in England, 1535–1660* (1973). P. McGrath, *Papists and Puritans under Elizabeth I* (1967) brings two sides together.

A reading of K. Thomas's *Religion and the Decline of Magic* (1971), cited before, should be followed by A. Macfarlane, *Witchcraft in Tudor and Stuart England, 1560–1680* (1970). See also C. Phythian-Adams, *Local History and Folklore: A New Framework* (1975); V. L. Neuberg, *Popular Literature: A History and Guide* (1977); and B. Capp, *Astrology and the Popular Press* (1979).

For law and administration see J. S. Cockburn (ed.), *Crime in England* (1977); A. Fletcher and J. Stevenson (eds), *Order and Disorder in Early Modern England* (1985); G. Scott Thomson, *Lords Lieutenant in the Sixteenth Century* (1923); J. H. Gleason, *The Justices of the Peace in England,*

1558–1640 (1969); L. Boynton, *The Elizabethan Militia, 1558–1638* (1967); and G. R. Elton, *Policy and Police* (1972). For finance see F. C. Dietz, *English Public Finance, 1558–1642* (1932).

For housing see M. W. Barley, *The English Farmhouse and Cottage* (1961); N. Pevsner, *The Planning of the English Country House* (1961); and M. Girouard, *Robert Smythson and the Architecture of the Elizabethan Era* (1966).

As in previous chapters, some of the most interesting studies can still be found only in the form of articles, some of them dealing with particular localities, some based on the work of the Cambridge Group for the History of Population and Social Structure. See P. Laslett, *The World We Have Lost* (2nd edn, 1971). Yet there are now nearly a dozen books on Tudor and Stuart Essex alone. Useful studies include M. E. James, *Family, Lineage and Civil Society: A Study of the Durham Region, 1500–1640* (1974); P. Clark, *English Provincial Society from the Reformation to the Revolution: Religion, Politics and Society in Kent, 1500–1640* (1977); K. Wrightson and D. Levine, *Poverty and Piety in an English Village: Terling, 1525–1720* (1979); and M. Spufford, *Contrasting Communities: English Villagers in the Sixteenth and Seventeenth Centuries* (1974), which deals with three Cambridgeshire villages.

For the demographic frame see E. A. Wrigley and R. S. Schofield, *The Population History of England, 1541–1871* (1981). Compare it with the first publication of the Cambridge group, E. A. Wrigley's *An Introduction to English Historical Demography* (1966). See also C. Webster (ed.), *Health, Medicine and Mortality in the Sixteenth Century* (1979) and L. A. Clarkson, *Death, Disease and Famine in Pre-Industrial England* (1975). For the view, often challenged, that 'affective individualism' was a later phenomenon than the Tudors, see L. Stone, *The Family, Sex and Marriage in England, 1500–1800* (1977). Other family studies include M. Anderson, *Approaches to the History of the Western Family* (1980) and R. B. Outhwaite (ed.), *Marriage and Society: Studies in the Social History of Marriage* (1981).

Contemporary texts, most easily read in modern editions, include *The Itinerary of John Leland* (1535–43); William Harrison's *The Description of England* (1587) and Thomas Wilson's *The State of England* (1601). See also M. St Clare Byrne's edition of the Lisle letters in six volumes (1981), which reveals in detail the life of an aristocratic family between 1533 and 1540. The old three-volume collection of *Tudor Economic Documents* edited by R. H. Tawney and E. Power in 1924 is still useful.

Statistics figure prominently in J. Burnett's *A History of The Cost of Living* (1969), useful for this and other chapters of the book. See also both for reference and for browsing the classic study by J. E. Thorold Rogers,

History of Agriculture and Prices in England, (7 vols., 1866–1902). R. N. Outhwaite provides an excellent modern introduction in *Inflation in Tudor and Early Stuart England* (1969).

CHAPTER 6

REVOLUTION, RESTORATION AND SETTLEMENT

The most widely read books on the seventeenth century are those by Christopher Hill. They include *Puritanism and Revolution* (1958); *Society and Puritanism in Pre-Revolutionary England* (1964); *From Reformation to Industrial Revolution* (1967); *The World Turned Upside Down* (1972); *God's Englishman: Oliver Cromwell and the English Revolution* (1970); and *Milton and the English Revolution* (1977). See also, however, C. Russell (ed.), *The Origins of the English Civil War* (1975); L. Stone (ed.), *Social Change and Revolution in England, 1540–1640* (1965), a guide to a protracted if outdated controversy about the gentry; J. G. A. Pocock (ed.), *Three British Revolutions, 1641, 1688 and 1776*; E. W. Ives (ed.), *The English Revolution, 1600–1660* (1975); M. G. Finlayson, *Historians, Puritanism and the English Revolution* (1983); R. Ashton, *The English Civil War, 1603–1649* (1978); and I. Roots, *The Great Rebellion* (1966). For later seventeenth-century history see J. R. Jones, *County and Court, 1658–1714* (1978). This should be supplemented by J. H. Plumb's important book, *The Growth of Political Stability, 1675–1725* (1967).

D. C. Coleman's *The Economy of England, 1450–1750* (1977), cited earlier, is an indispensable introduction to economic history; so also is his *Industry in Tudor and Stuart England* (1975). Charles Wilson's *England's Apprenticeship, 1603–1763* (1965) is an equally indispensable follow-through. See also B. E. Supple, *Commercial Crisis and Change in England, 1600–1642* (1959) and A. Plummer, *The London Weavers' Company, 1600–1970* (1972). J. Thirsk and J. P. Cooper (eds.), *Seventeenth-Century Economic Documents* (1972) is a valuable source book and J. Thirsk, *Economic Policy and Projects: The Development of a Consumer Society* (1978) an interesting interpretation. For the European scene see C. M. Cipolla, *Before the Industrial Revolution* (1976).

The social history of the seventeenth century figures prominently in general histories; there are relatively few more specialized monographs. See, however, G. E. Aylmer, *The King's Servants: The Civil Service of Charles I* (1961); R. H. Tawney, *Business and Politics under James I* (1958); A. M. Everitt, *The Community of Kent and the Great Rebellion* (1966); I. Roots, *The Great Rebellion* (1966); V. Pearl, *London and the Outbreak of the Puritan Revolution* (1961); A. L. Morton, the *World of the Ranters*

(1977); H. N. Brailsford, *The Levellers and the English Revolution* (1961); D. Pennington and K. Thomas (eds), *Puritans and Revolutionaries, Essays in Seventeenth Century History Presented to Christopher Hill* (1978); A. Woolrych, *Battles of the English Civil War* (1961); M. P. Ashley, *Financial and Commercial Policy under the Cromwellian Protectorate* (1934); J. Miller, *Papery and Politics in England, 1660–1688* (1973); J. P. Kenyon, *The Papist Plot* (1972); and M. Ashley, *The Glorious Revolution of 1688* (1966).

There are local studies in addition to those cited in the booklist for the last chapter. As examples see J. T. Cliffe, *The Yorkshire Gentry from the Reformation to the Civil War* (1969); B. G. Blackwood, *The Lancastrian Gentry and the Great Rebellion* (1978); A. Fletcher, *A Country Community in Peace and War: Sussex 1600–1660* (1975); and J. S. Morrill, *Cheshire 1630–1660: County Government and Society under the 'English Revolution'* (1974). *The History of Myddle* by Richard Gough is a unique contemporary study of a village, explored by D. G. Hey in *An English Rural Community: Myddle under the Tudors and Stuarts* (1974). See also A. Macfarlane (ed.), *The Diary of Ralph Josselin, 1616–1683* (1976).

For taxation see W. R. Ward, *The English Land Tax in the Eighteenth Century* (1953); E. Hughes, *Studies in Administration and Finance* (1934); L. Kennedy, *British Taxation 1640–1799* (1913); and above all, for the later period, C. D. Chandaman, *The English Public Revenue, 1660–1702* (1975).

On religion, society and politics see, *inter alia*, C. Hill, *Economic Problems of the Church* (1956); M. R. O'Day and F. Heal (eds), *Continuity and Change, Personnel and Administration of the Church in England* (1976); A. S. Woodhouse (ed.), *Puritanism and Liberty: Being the Army Debates* (1950 edn); H. Haller and G. Davis (eds), *The Leveller Tracts, 1647–1653* (1964); G. R. Cragg, *The Church and the Age of Reason, 1648–1789* (1960); R. S. Bosher, *The Making of the Restoration Settlement* (1951); W. C. Braithwaite, *The Beginnings of Quakerism* (1982); J. Marlowe, *The Puritan Tradition in English Life* (1956); A. C. Underwood, *A History of the English Baptists* (1947); R. W. Dale, *A History of English Congregationalism* (1907); and W. K. Jordan, *The Development of Religious Toleration in England* (4 vols., 1936–40). See also U. S. Henriques, *The Return of the Jews to England* (1905).

For the role of women see W. Notestein, 'The English Woman, 1580–1660', in J. Plumb (ed.), *Studies in Social History* (1955); A. Clark, *The Working Life of Women in the Seventeenth Century* (1919); G. E. and K. R. Fussell, *The English Countryman: A Farmhouse Social History* (1953); and B. Thompson, *Women in Stuart England and America: A Comparative Study* (1974). The most recent general study is by Antonia Fraser, *The Weaker Vessel* (1984). On children see L. de Mause (ed.), *History of*

Childhood (1974) and I. Pinchbeck and M. Hewitt, *Children in English Society*, Vol. I (1969). C. L. Powell's *English Domestic Relations, 1487–1653* (1917) is a fascinating story of 'conduct books'. See also L. L. Schucking, *The Puritan Family, a Social Study, from Literary Sources* (1969) and P. Coveney, *The Image of Childhood: The Individual in Society. A Theme in English Literature* (1967).

For the alehouse see P. Clark, *The English Ale House, 1200–1830* (1983) and for the coffee house see A. Ellis, *The Penny Universities: A History of the Coffee House* (1956). For other aspects of leisure see D. Brailsford, *Sport and Society: Elizabeth to Anne* (1969) and E. and S. Yeio (eds.), *Popular Culture and Class Conflict, 1590–1914* (1981). For crime and 'rebellion' see J. A. Sharpe, *Crime in Seventeenth-Century England: A County Study* (1983) and P. Slack (ed.), *Rebellion, Popular Protest and Social Order in Early Modern England* (1984).

On higher education see M. H. Curtis, *Oxford and Cambridge in Transition, 1558–1642* (1959) and W. R. Prest, *The Inns of Court* (1972).

For science and technology see H. Butterfield, *The Origins of Modern Science* (1949); A. R. Hall, *The Scientific Revolution, 1500–1800* (1954) and *From Galileo to Newton* (1963); G. N. Clark, *Science and Social Welfare in the Age of Newton* (1949); C. Hill, *The Intellectual Origins of the English Revolution* (1965); H. F. Kearney (ed.), *Origins of the Scientific Revolution* (1964); L. M. Marsak (ed.), *The Rise of Science in Relation to Society* (1964); R. S. Westfall, *Science and Religion in Seventeenth-Century England* (1958); A. G. Smith, *Science and Society in the Sixteenth and Seventeenth Centuries* (1972); and R. Briggs, *The Scientific Revolution of the Seventeenth Century* (1965). There are stimulating alternative views in all the remarkable books of Frances Yates. See also J. V. Nef, *Cultural Foundations of Industrial Civilisation* (1958); A. O. Lovejoy, *The Great Chain of Being* (1936); and H. Hartley (ed.), *The Royal Society, Its Origins and Founders* (1960).

For the arts see J. Harris, S. Orgel and R. Strong, *The King's Arcadia: Inigo Jones and the Stuart Court* (1973); O. Miller, *The Art of Charles I: Painting in England, 1628–1649* (1972); B. Little, *Sir Christopher Wren* (1975); M. Ede, *Arts and Society in England under William and Mary* (1979); and J. Summerson, *Art in Britain, 1530–1840* (1955). B. A. Reay (ed.), in his *Popular Culture in Seventeenth Century England* (1985), breaks much new ground. See also D. Brailsford, *Sport and Society from Elizabeth to Anne* (1969).

Essential contemporary texts include Francis Bacon's *Essays*; John Milton's poems and his defence of free speech, *Areopagitica* (1644); Lord Clarendon's six-volume *History of the Great Rebellion* (first published

1702–4); and John Bunyan's *The Pilgrim's Progress* (1678). There are other claimants including John Aubrey's *Brief Lives* (1898 edn), Donne's poems, Lucy Hutchinson's *Memories of the Life of Colonel Hutchinson* (1976 edn), the Puritan Richard Baxter's memoirs and any good collection of Restoration plays.

CHAPTER 7

THE QUEST FOR WEALTH, POWER AND PLEASURE

Roy Porter's *English Society in the Eighteenth Century* (1982) is the best of the volumes in the useful Pelican Social History of Britain: it reflects recent research and has a valuable bibliography. D. Marshall, *English People in the Eighteenth Century* (1956) and *Eighteenth-Century England* (1962) are older well-informed books. So also is M. D. George, *England in Transition* (1953). They make points not made elsewhere. See also W. A. Speck, *Stability and Strife: England, 1714–1760* (1977) and M. Reed, *The Georgian Triumph, 1700–1830* (1983). T. S. Ashton's *An Economic History of England: The Eighteenth Century* (1955) is still useful.

For contemporary comment see A. Briggs, *How They Lived, 1700 –1815* (1969). Daniel Defoe's *Tour Through the Whole Island of Great Britain* (1724) should be compared with William Cobbett's *Rural Rides* (1820 –30). Likewise, for foreign views, H. Misson's *Memoirs* (1719) should be compared with Pastor Wendeborn's *A View of England* (1791). See also D. Jarrett, *England in the Age of Hogarth* (1974).

For wealth derived from abroad see for the early period J. H. Parry, *The Age of Reconnaissance* (1963); J. A. Williamson, *Maritime Enterprise, 1485–1558* (1913) and *The Age of Drake* (1938); K. R. Andrews, *Elizabethan Privateering* (1964); and, above all, R. Davis, *English Overseas Trade, 1500–1700* (1973).

For the eighteenth century see L. A. Harper, *The English Navigation Laws* (1939); R. L. Schuyler, *The Fall of the Old Colonial System* (1945); K. E. Knorr, *British Colonial Theories, 1750–1850* (1944); R. S. Dunn, *Sugar and Slaves* (1973); R. Pares, *War and Trade in the West Indies* (1936) and *A West Indian Fortune* (1968); T. G. P. Spear, *The Nabobs* (1932); L. S. Sutherland, *The East India Company in Eighteenth-Century Politics* (1952); C. S. Phillips, *The East India Company, 1784–1834* (1940); D. Boorstin, *The Americans: The Colonial Experience* (1973); C. M. H. Clarke, *A History of Australia*, Vol. I (1962); and P. Woodruff, *The Men Who Ruled India*, Vol. I (1953). Interesting questions for this period and later are posed – and interesting information is given – in S. Jones, *Two Centuries of Overseas Trading* (1986). See also P. J. Griffiths, *The British Impact on India* (1952).

For slavery and the anti-slavery movement see J. Walvin (ed.), *Slavery and British Society, 1776–1848* (1982), which places in perspective old and new controversies, beginning with that between R. Coupland, author of *The British Anti-Slavery Movement* (1933) and Eric Williams, author of *Capitalism and Slavery* (1944). See also C. Lloyd, *The Navy and the Slave Trade* (1949).

For the general picture see D. K. Fieldhouse, *The Colonial Empires* (1965) and A. Calder, *Revolutionary Empire* (1981). P. Mackesey deals with *The War for America, 1775–1783* (1964).

For landed wealth, books mentioned in previous chapters are relevant also to this one. In addition, for landed society see G. E. Mingay, *English Landed Society in the Eighteenth Century* (1963) and *The Gentry* (1976); an essay by H. Habbakkuk in A. Goodwin (ed.), *The European Nobility in the Eighteenth Century* (1953); M. Girouard, *Life in the English Country House* (1979); R. A. C. Parker, *Coke of Norfolk* (1975); and, most lively, recent and provocative, L. Stone and J. C. Fawtier Stone, *An Open Élite? England 1540–1880* (1984); which includes an indispensable bibliography.

For early industrialists see T. S. Ashton, *Peter Stubs of Warrington, 1756–1806* (1939); G. Unwin, A. Hulme and G. Taylor, *Samuel Oldknow and the Arkwrights* (1924); R. S. Fitton and A. P. Wadsworth, *The Strutts and the Arkwrights* (1958); H. W. Dickinson, *Matthew Boulton* (1937); E. Roll, *An Early Experiment in Industrial Organisation* (1968); W. G. Rimmer, *Marshalls of Leeds* (1966); and B. and H. Wedgwood, *The Wedgwood Circle, 1730–1897* (1980). See also L. T. C. Rolt, *Thomas Newcomen* (1963); J. Tann, *The Development of the Factory* (1971); M. W. Flynn, *The Origins of the Industrial Revolution* (1973); and P. Deane, *The First Industrial Revolution* (1965).

On 'middling men' see for this and later chapters M. J. Reader, *Professional Men* (1966), a wide-ranging survey, and R. B. Westerfield, *Middlemen in English Business, 1600–1760*. On 'common people' see J. L. and B. Hammond, *The Town Labourer* (1917), *The Village Labourer, 1760–1832* (1919) and *The Skilled Labourer* (1919), still readable books which cover the period from 1760 to 1832. J. J. Hecht, *The Domestic Servant Class in Eighteenth-Century England* (1956) deals with an important and numerous group. See also D. Marshall, *The English Domestic Servant in History* (1969).

For the poor see D. Marshall, *The English Poor in the Eighteenth Century* (1926) and G. Taylor, *The Problem of Poverty, 1660–1834* (1969). For the poor law see J. R. Poynter, *Society and Pauperism* (1960); M. E. Rose, *The English Poor Law, 1760–1830* (1971); and U. S. Henriques, *Before the*

Welfare State (1979). F. M. Eden's *The State of the Poor* (1794) is a classic text to be studied critically. D. Owen, *English Philanthropy, 1660–1960* (1965) is relevant for this and later chapters. See also B. Rodgers, *Cloak of Charity: Studies in Eighteenth Century Philanthropy* (1949).

For the economic history of the period see, in addition to books mentioned in relation to earlier chapters, P. Mantoux, *The Industrial Revolution in the Eighteenth Century* (1928) and P. Deane and W. A. Cole, *British Economic Growth, 1688–1959* (1967). For particular industries see P. Mathias, *The Brewing Industry in England 1700–1830* (1959); T. S. Ashton, *Iron and Steel in the Industrial Revolution* (1924); S. J. Chapman, *The Lancashire Cotton Industry* (1904); and W. B. Honey, *English Pottery and Porcelain* (1933). For wages see W. E. Minchinton (ed.), *Wage Regulation in Pre-Industrial England* (1972).

W. H. B. Court, *The Rise of the Midland Industries, 1600–1838* (1938); J. D. Chambers, *The Vale of Trent, 1660–1800* (1957); and E. Hughes, *North Country Life in the Eighteenth Century* (2 vols., 1952, 1965) deal with particular areas.

On towns and cities see C. W. Chawklin, *The Provincial Towns of Georgian England* (1974); M. D. Gray, *London Life in the Eighteenth Century* (1929); J. Lindsay, *The Monster City: Defoe's London* (1978); G. Rudé, *Hanoverian London* (1971); and P. J. Corfield, *The Impact of English Towns, 1700–1800* (1981).

For the relations of town and country see R. Williams, *The Country and the City* (1973); for the provinces see D. Read, *The English Provinces, 1700–1900* (1964); and for economic and social conflicts in the countryside see W. E. Tate, *The English Village Community and the Enclosure Movements* (1967) and M. Turner, *English Parliamentary Enclosure* (1980). See also J. Stevenson, *Popular Disturbances in England, 1700–1870* (1979). The industrial setting is considered in J. Rule, *The Experience of Labour in Eighteenth-Century Industry* (1981) and C. R. Dobson, *Masters and Journeymen: A Prehistory of Industrial Relations, 1717–1800* (1982).

For urban violence see G. Rudé, *The Crowd in History* (1964) and *Paris and London in the Eighteenth Century* (1952); J. Brewer and J. Styles (eds.), *An Ungovernable People* (1980); and J. Castro, *The Gordon Riots* (1926).

Law is dealt with monumentally in L. Radzinowicz's *A History of English Criminal Law* (1948). For recent interpretations of aspects of the law as seen 'from below', turn to E. P. Thompson, *Whigs and Hunters* (1975) and D. Hay *et al.*, *Albion's Fatal Tree* (1975). See also G. Rudé, *Wilkes and Liberty* (1962). W. K. Manchester, *Legal History, 1750–1950* (1970) is useful for this and later chapters.

On religion see N. Sykes, *Church and State in the Eighteenth Century*

(1934); S. C. Carpenter, *Eighteenth Century Church and People* (1959); G. R. Cragg, *The Church and the Age of Reason* (1962); W. R. Ward, *Religion and Society in England, 1790–1850* (1972); S. Andrews, *Methodism and Society* (1970); M. Edwards, *John Wesley and the Eighteenth Century* (1955); R. F. Wearmouth, *Methodism and the Common People of the Eighteenth Century* (1945); M. R. Watts, *The Dissenters* (1978); A Lincoln, *Some Political and Social Ideas of English Dissent, 1763–1800* (1938); B. L. Manning, *The Protestant Dissenting Deputies* (1952); C. G. Bolan *et al.*, *The English Presbyterians* (1968); and J. Bossy, *The English Catholic Community* (1975). The social impact of Quakerism is studied in I. Grubb, *Quakerism and Industry Before 1800* (1930); R. Vann, *The Social Development of English Quakerism, 1655–1750* (1969); and A. Raistrick, *Quakers in Science and Industry* (1950). See also E. D. Bebb, *Nonconformity and Social Economic Life, 1660–1800* (1935).

There is a general survey of education, covering this and other periods by J. Lawson and H. Silver, *A Social History of Education in England* (1973). See also M. G. Jones, *The Charity School Movement* (1938); R. S. Tomson, *Classics or Charity? The Dilemma of the Eighteenth Century Grammar Schools* (1971); and B. Simon, *Studies in the History of Education*, Vol. I (1960).

On the origins of the 'consumer society' see J. H. Plumb, *The Commercialisation of Leisure in Eighteenth-Century England* (1973) and N. McKendrick *et al.*, *The Birth of a Consumer Society* (1982). On leisure within that society see R. Malcolmson, *Popular Recreations in English Society 1700–1850* (1975) and R. Cunningham, *Leisure in the Industrial Revolution* (1980).

For the finance of government see J. H. Clapham, *History of the Bank of England* (2 vols., 1946). J. Carswell, *The South Sea Bubble* (1960) and P. G. M. Dickson, *The Financial Revolution in England 1688–1756* (1967) are both illuminating. For country banking see L. S. Pressnell, *Country Banking in the Industrial Revolution* (1956).

For the place of women in eighteenth-century society see B. Kanner (ed.), *The Women of England* (1980). Sexuality is discussed in P. G. Boucé, *Sexuality in Eighteenth-Century England* (1982). Immorality is discussed in M. J. Quinlan, *Victorian Prelude* (1941); M. Jaeger, *Before Victoria* (1956); and E. J. Bristow, *Vice and Vigilance* (1977). See also P. Fryer, *Mrs. Grundy* (1963).

For the novel see I. Watt, *The Rise of the Novel* (1957), which should be read alongside the Victorian study by D. Musson, *British Novelists and Their Styles* (1859). See also D. Monaghan, *Jane Austen in a Social Context* (1981) and M. Butler, *Jane Austen and the War of Ideas* (1975). Other complementary studies include E. F. Carritt, *A Calendar of British Taste from 1600–1800* (1948); J. Gross, *The Rise and Fall of the Man of Letters* (1969), which covers later chapters also; P. Rogers, *Grub Street* (1972); J. Bronowski, *William Blake and the Age of Revolution* (1972); H. Ashcroft, *English Art and English Society* (1936); M. Whinney and O. Millar, *A History of English Art*, Vol. (1957); L. Lipkin, *The Ordering of the Arts in Eighteenth Century England* (1970); B. Sprague Allen, *Tides of Taste, 1619–1800* (1945); M. Foss, *The Age of Patronage: The Arts in Society 1660–1750* (1972); J. Barrell, *The Idea of Landscape and the Sense of Place* (1972) and *The Dark Side of the Landscape* (1980); T. Fawcett, *The Rise of English Provincial Art* (1974); D. Stroud, *Capability Brown* (1975); and B. Denvir, *The Eighteenth Century, Art, Design and Society, 1689–1789* (1983).

For the lead into the nineteenth century see A. Briggs, *The Age of Improvement*; C. Ensley, *British Society and the French Wars, 1793–1815* (1979); Élie Halévy, *The Growth of Philosophic Radicalism* (1928); J. Roach, *Social Reform in England, 1780–1870* (1978); A Goodwin, *The Friends of Liberty* (1979); and M. Butler, *Peacock Displayed* (1979).

CHAPTER 8
THE EXPERIENCE OF INDUSTRIALIZATION

The two volumes edited by R. Floud and D. McCloskey, *The Economic History of Britain since 1700* (1981) introduce recent research with a healthy quantitative approach. They are less readable, however, than P. Mathias, *The First Industrial Nation* (1970) and the older brief study by T. S. Ashton, *The Industrial Revolution, 1760–1830* (1948). They should be compared with the excellent, more general study by D. S. Landes, *The Unbound Prometheus: Technological Changes and Industrial Development in Western Europe from 1750 to the Present* (1969). J. H. Clapham's monumental three-volume *An Economic History of Modern Britain* (1926 –38) is far more readable than it appears at first sight: it is packed with interesting detail.

S. G. Checkland's *The Rise of Industrial Society in England, 1815–1885* (1964) does not supersede older studies like W. H. Bowden, *Industrial Society in England Toward the End of the Eighteenth Century* (1925) and G. D. H. Cole, *A Short History of the Working Class Movement* (1937). For contemporary comment see E. Royston Pike, *Human Documents of the Industrial Revolution in Britain* (1966), one of several useful anthologies by the same author.

For later phases in industrial history see E. J. Hobsbawm, *Industry and*

Empire (1968); S. B. Saul, *The Myth of the Great Depression* (1972 edn); A. L. Levine, *Industrial Retardation in Britain, 1880–1914* (1967); and L. Rostas, *Comparative Productivity in British and American Industry* (1948). For the general context see E. J. Hobsbawm's brilliant volumes *The Age of Revolution* (1962) and *The Age of Capital* (1965).

Two other more recent books which have attracted much attention, some of it critical, are K. Middlemas, *Politics in Industrial Society: The Experience of the British System Since 1911* (1979) and M. J. Wiener, *English Culture and the Decline of the Industrial Spirit* (1981).

For the statistics B. R. Mitchell and P. Deane's *Abstract of British Historical Statistics* (1962) is indispensable. See also P. Deane and W. A. Cole, *British Economic Growth, 1688–1955* (1967) and R. C. P. Matthew, C. H. Feinstein and J. C. Odling Smee, *British Economic Growth, 1855–1973* (1982). For fluctuations in the economy and their role in social history see W. W. Rostow, *The British Economy of the Nineteenth Century* (1948); a more detailed approach to the problems it identifies can be found in A. D. Gayer, W. W. Rostow and A. Schwartz, *Growth and Fluctuations of the British Economy, 1780–1850* (1953). See also for the international setting A. T. Imlah, *Economic Elements in the Pax Britannica* (1958).

For the even more controversial effects of industrialization on standards of life, including the quality of life, the best brief introduction is A. J. Taylor (ed.), *The Standard of Living in Britain in the Industrial Revolution* (1975). This should be followed through with R. M. Hartwell, *The Industrial Revolution and Economic Growth* (1971); B. Inglis, *Poverty and the Industrial Revolution* (1971); and G. Himmelfarb and J. Burnett, *Plenty and Want: A Social History of Diet from 1875 to the Present Day* (1966). Burnett's useful studies, *inter alia*, introduce the reader to the Phelps Brown/Hopkins cost of living index referred to at several points in my book. It was first set out in E. H. Phelps Brown and S. V. Hopkins, 'Seven Centuries of Building Wages' in *Economica* (1955) and 'Seven Centuries of the Prices of Consumables, Compared with Builders' Wage Rates' in the same journal (1956).

See also Sir William Beveridge *et al.*, *Prices and Wages in England*, Vol. I (1939); W. T. Layton and G. Crowther, *An Introduction to the Study of Prices* (1940); and the classic study by J. E. Thorold Rogers, *Six Centuries of Work and Wages* (1884). E. H. Hunt, *Regional Wage Variations in Britain, 1850–1914* (1973) is useful. See also C. W. Gilboy, *Wages in Eighteenth Century England* (1936). W. Rowe, *Cornwall in the Age of the Industrial Revolution* (1953) is an early regional study.

For industrialization and social class, E. P. Thompson's immensely influential *The Making of the English Working Class* (1963) should be compared with H. J. Perkin, *Origins of Modern English Society, 1780–1880* (1969). See also among a large number of books on the subject R. J. Morris, *Class and Class Consciousness in the Industrial Revolution* (1979); P. Hollis (ed.), *Class and Conflict in Nineteenth-Century England, 1815–1850* (1973); J. Foster, *Class Struggle and the Early Industrial Revolution: Early Industrial Capitalism in Three English Towns* (1974); G. Stedman Jones, *Languages of Class* (1983); and J. F. C. Harrison, *The Common People* (1984), which is subtitled 'A history from the Norman Conquest to the Present'. For a detailed sociological study see G. Crossick, *An Artisan Élite in Victorian Society 1840–1880* (1978).

On other aspects of labour history, which has boomed since the 1950s, see M. J. Thomis, *The Luddites* (1970) and *The Town Labourer and the Industrial Revolution* (1974); D. Bythell, *The Handloom Weavers* (1965); I. J. Prothero, *Artisans and Politics in Early Nineteenth Century London* (1979); E. Hobsbawm, *Laboring Men* (1964); R. Price, *Masters, Union and Men* (1980); and P. Joyce, *Work, Society and Politics* (1982), which deals with local as well as with class differences.

K. D. Brown, *The English Labour Movement 1700–1951* (1982) has a useful bibliography covering an extensive literature. H. Pelling, *History of British Trade Unionism* (1963) sets out the facts. See also A. E. Musson, *British Trade Unions, 1800–1875* (1972) and my introductory chapter to the first edition of A. Flanders and H. A. Clegg (eds.), *The System of Industrial Relations in Great Britain* (1954). For relevant documents see G. D. H. Cole and A. F. Filson (eds.), *British Working Class Movements: Select Documents, 1788–1875* (1965). For friendly societies see P. H. J. H. Gosden, *Self Help: Voluntary Associations in the Nineteenth Century* (1973). For Chartism see A. Briggs (ed.), *Chartist Studies* (1959); J. T. Ward, *Chartism* (1977); D. Jones, *Chartism and the Chartists* (1975); and D. Thompson, *The Chartists* (1984).

For agriculture and the countryside in an age of transformation see W. Howitt, *The Rural Life of England* (1844), a classic study; P. Horn, *The Rural World, 1780–1850* (1980); G. E. Mingay, *The Agricultural Revolution* (1966) and *Land, Labour and Population in the Industrial Revolution* (1974); E. Hobsbawm and G. Rudé, *Capital Swing* (1973); and J. P. Dunbabin (ed.), *Rural Discontent in Nineteenth Century Britain* (1974).

For the art of the industrial revolution and the impact of industry on the imagination see F. D. Klingender, *Art and the Industrial Revolution* (1947); H. L. Sussman, *Victorians and the Machine* (1968); and A. Briggs, *The Power of Steam* (1982). See also J. Warburg, (ed.), *The Industrial Muse* (1958) and the book by M. Vicinus with the same title (1958).

K. Hudson's *Industrial Archaeology* (1962) remains the best introduction to this popular subject.

Technology is covered in Vols. IV and V of the Oxford History of Technology (1958). See also from a long list of books N. Rosenberg's *Perspectives on Technology* (1976); A. E. Musson and E. Robinson, *Science and Technology in the Industrial Revolution* (1969); R. Hills, *Power in the Industrial Revolution* (1970); W. H. G. Armytage, *A Social History of Engineering* (1961); L. T. C. Rolt, *Victorian Engineering* (1970); M. Williams, *Steam Power in Agriculture* (1977); and, a classic earlier work, S. Smiles, *Lives of the Engineers* (1904 edn). A. Ure, *The Philosophy of Manufactures* (1835) should be compared with K. Marx's *Capital* (1867). For electricity see H. I. Sharlin, *The Making of the Electrical Age* (1963). See also A. and N. L. Clow, *The Chemical Revolution* (1952).

Other studies include T. C. Barker (ed.), *The Long March of Everyman, 1815–1960* (1978), based on an outstanding BBC series; S. Pollard, *The Genesis of Modern Management* (1948); L. Robbins, *The Theory of Economic Policy* (1952); N. J. Smelser, *Social Change in the Industrial Revolution* (1959); I. Pinchbeck, *Women Workers and the Industrial Revolution, 1750 –1850* (1969); M. Hewitt, *Wives and Mothers in Victorian Industry* (1958); and D. E. C. Eversley, *Social Theories of Fertility and the Malthusian Debate* (1959).

CHAPTER 9
WEBS OF COMMUNICATION

For early communications history see J. Crofts, *Packhorse, Waggon and Post: Land Carriage and Communications under the Tudors and Stuarts* (1967) and T. S. Willan, *River Navigation in England, 1600–1750* (1938), *The Inland Trade* (1970) and *The English Coasting Trade, 1600–1750* (1938). J. A. Chartres, *Internal Trade in England, 1500–1700* (1977) deals also with aspects of the subject. Later communications history is covered in P. S. Bagwell, *The Transport Revolution from 1770*; W. T. Jackman, *The Development of Transportation in Modern England* (1962 edn); and C. E. R. Sherrington, *A Hundred Years of Inland Transport, 1830–1933* (1969 edn).

On turnpike roads see W. Albert, *The Turnpike Road System in England 1663–1840* (1972); E. Pawson, *Transport and the Economy: The Turnpike Roads of Britain* (1977); and D. Hey, *Packmen, Carriers and Packhorse Roads* (1980). The later history of roads is dealt with in J. Copeland, *Roads and Their Traffic, 1750–1850* (1968). See also W. Outram–Tristram, *Coaching Days and Coaching Ways* (1893).

On canals see C. Hadfield, *British Canals* (1968 edn) and *The Canal Age*

(1968); L. T. C. Rolt, *The Inland Waterways of England* (1950); A. Burton, *The Canal Builders* (1972); and H. Malet, *The Canal Duke* (1969). Early travellers' accounts are printed in W. Mavor, *The British Tourists* (6 vols. 1809) and J. Pinkerton, *A General Collection of the Best and Most Interesting Voyages* (1808). For an example of an early account of a canal see J. Hassell, *Tour of the Grand Junction* (1812). J. Phillips, *General History of Inland Navigation* (1794) is an invaluable general survey.

M. Robbins, *The Railway Age* (1965) provides a good general account of the importance of railways to the economy and to society. So also do H. Ellis, *British Railway History* (1954) and H. Perkin, *The Age of the Railway* (1970). For earlier accounts see H. J. Lewin, *Early British Railways* (1928) and *The Railway Mania and its Aftermath, 1845–1852* (1936); R. S. Lambert, *The Railway King* (1964); L. T. C. Rolt, *George and Robert Stephenson* (1960) and *I. K. Brunel* (1957); and E. Cleveland-Stevens, *English Railways: Their Development and Relation to the State* (1915).

There are many histories of particular railways, for example, C. J. Allen, *The Great Eastern Railway* (4th edn, 1967). G. Ottley has listed them in his *Bibliography of British Railway History* (1965). For a railway town see W. H. Chaloner, *The Social and Economic Development of Crewe, 1780–1923* (1950) and for the general effects of railways on cities see J. R. Kellett's illuminating *The Impact of Railways on Victorian Cities* (1969).

On steamboats see H. P. Spratt, *The Birth of the Steam Boat* (1898); G.C. Jackson, *The Ship Under Steam* (1928); R. T. Rowland, *Steam at Sea* (1971); and A. W. Kirkaldy, *British Shipping, Its History, Organisation and Importance* (1914).

For bicycles see J. Woodford, *The Story of the Bicycle* (1970) and for bicycle cultures see, *inter alia*, H. O. Duncan, *The World on Wheels* (1927).

On the motor car see St J. C. Nixon, *The Invention of the Automobile* (1936); H. Perkin, *The Age of the Automobile* (1976); W. Plowden, *The Motor Car and Politics, 1890–1970* (1971); and K. Richardson, *The British Motor Industry, 1896–1939* (1977).

The second volume of the two-volume work by T. C. Barker and M. Robbins, *A History of London Transport* (1974) brings out most of the significant detail. Their first volume (1963) deals with the nineteenth century.

On the telegraph see J. L. Kieve, *The Electric Telegraph* (1973) and on the telephone F. G. C. Baldwin, *The History of the Telephone in the United Kingdom* (1925). For the wireless see L. Reale, *Marconi and the Discovery of Wireless* (1963); R. N. Vyvyan, *Marconi and Wireless* (1974) and A. Constable, *Early Wireless* (1980). For broadcasting in this and later chapters see A. Briggs, *The BBC, The First Fifty Years* (1985), which includes a full bibliography; M. Gorham, *Broadcasting and Television Since 1900* (1952); and M. Pegg, *Broadcasting and Society, 1918–1939* (1983).

For the Post Office see H. Robinson, *Britain's Post Office: A History of Development from the Beginnings to the Present Day* (1953) and M. J. Daunton, *Royal Mail, the Post Office Since 1840* (1985).

For newspapers see G. A. Cranfield, *The Development of the Provincial Newspaper, 1700–1760* (1962); A. J. Lee, *The Origins of the Popular Press, 1855–1914* (1976); S. Koss, *The Rise and Fall of the Popular Press in Britain* (2 vols., 1981, 1984); and L. Brown, *Victorian News and Newspapers* (1985). See also L. James, *Print and the People, 1819–1851* (1976). For the news agencies see G. Storey, *Reuters Century* (1951). See also R. K. Webb, *The British Working Class Reader, 1780–1848* (1955); A. Cruse, *The Englishman and His Books in the Early Nineteenth Century* (1930); R. D. Altick, *The English Common Reader* (1963); and R. Williams, *The Long Revolution* (1961).

CHAPTER 10
VICTORIANISM: PRELUDE, EXPRESSION, AFTERMATH

The classic account of the period, still stimulating, is presented in G. M. Young's *Victorian England, Portrait of an Age* (1957 edn), which can be read with profit at different levels. See also J. F. C. Harrison, *The Early Victorians, 1832–1851* (1971); G. Best, *Mid-Victorian Britain, 1851–1875* (1971); and my own books *Victorian People* (1954) and *Victorian Cities* (1963), part of a trilogy which I hope will soon be completed by *Victorian Things*. See also G. Kitson Clark, *The Making of Victorian England* (1962); R. K. Webb, *Modern England from the Eighteenth Century to the Present* (1968), a rewarding survey; and G. M. Young and W. D. Handcock (eds.), *English Historical Documents, 1833–1874* (2 vols., 1956). The best general history of nineteenth-century England was written by a Frenchman, Élie Halévy: his *History of the English People in the Nineteenth Century* (tr. 1928–52) includes four volumes which deal with this period. The best recent social history for the period since 1851 is also by a Frenchman – F. Bédarida, *A Social History of England, 1851–1975* (1979 edn). See also R. Williams, *Culture and Society* (1958).

There is such a wealth of contemporary reading that it is almost impossible to offer a brief selection. E. D. H. Johnson (ed.), *The World of the Victorians* (1964) is a useful anthology of poetry and prose. See also for background W. E. Houghton, *The Victorian Frame of Mind* (1957). There is good anthology edited by P. Keating, *The Victorian Prophets: A*

Reader From Carlyle to Wells (1981). See also J. Aitken (ed.), *English Letters of the Nineteenth Century* (1946). For William Morris see my Pelican Anthology (1962). There is also an interesting selection of pieces from Oscar Wilde to Max Beerbohm, D. Stanford (ed.), *Writing of the Nineties* (1971). The latter should be read in conjunction with D. Holbrook Jackson, *The Eighteen Nineties* (1976 edn).

Individual Victorian books still to be read are countless, but they should include as much as possible of the writings of the great novelists, particularly Dickens, Eliot, Trollope, Hardy and Gissing, a strong dose of Carlyle, Ruskin and Morris, and Blue Books, key documents of the nineteenth century. See also, in particular, Edwin Chadwick, *Report on the Sanitary Condition of the Labouring Population of Great Britain* (1965 edn); E. Bulwer Lytton, *England and the English* (1970 reprint); J. S. Mill, *Political Economy* (1848); H. C. G. Matthew's superb edition of the Gladstone *Diaries*, the last volume of which appeared in 1986; H. Taine, *Notes on England* (1872); W. Bagehot, *The English Constitution* (1867) and *Lombard Street* (1873); Matthew Arnold, *Culture and Anarchy* (1869); Lewis Carroll, *Alice in Wonderland* (1865); Kilvert's *Diary* (3 vols., 1938); Gilbert and Sullivan, *Savoy Operas* (1881–5); T. H. S. Escott, *England, Its People, Polity and Pursuits* (1885 edn); Mark Rutherford, *The Revolution in Tanner's Lane* (1887); Andrew Mearns, *The Bitter Cry of Outcast London* (1883); B. Webb, *Our Partnership* (1948); and R. Kipling's early poems. The title of W. Lovett's *The Life and Struggles of William Lovett in his Pursuit of Bread, Knowledge and Freedom* (1876) speaks for itself. So too do Thomas Hughes's *Tom Brown's Schooldays* (1857) and Edward Lear's *The Complete Nonsense* (1947 edn).

For guidelines – and there are many – see J. L. Althotz, *Victorian England, a Bibliographical Handbook* (1970); Q. D. Leavis, *Fiction and the Reading Public* (1932); K. Tillotson, *Novels of the Eighteen-Forties* (1954); A. Brightfield, *Victorian England in its Novels* (1948); B. Willey, *Nineteenth Century Studies* (1949) and *More Nineteenth Century Studies* (1956); J. E. Baker (ed.), *The Reinterpretation of Victorian Literature* (1850); and R. Chapman, *The Victorian Debate* (1968), which has a full bibliography, although many important books have been published since, among them J. R. Willison, *Victorian Prose: A Guide to Research* (1973). The Oxford History by R. C. K. Ensor, *England, 1870–1914* almost has the status of a contemporary document. Students wishing to explore on their own should read R. Storey and L. Madden, *Primary Sources for Victorian Studies* (1977).

Biographies with an obvious social content include S. E. Finer, *The Life and Times of Sir Edwin Chadwick* (1952); E. Hodder, *The Life and*

Work of the Seventh Earl of Shaftesbury (3 vols., 1886); J. Morley, *The Life of William Ewart Gladstone* (2 vols., 1908); R. Blake, *Disraeli* (1966); K. Robbins, *John Bright* (1979); and D. Judd, *Radical Joe* (1977), one of several biographies of Joseph Chamberlain.

For selected aspects of politics see C. R. Fay, *The Corn Laws and Social England* (1932); P. O'Gorman, *The Emergence of the Two Party System* (1982); N. Gash, *Politics in the Age of Peel* (1977 edn); W. L. Burn, *The Age of Equipoise* (1964), which deals with far more than politics; J. F. Tholfsen, *Working Class Radicalism in Mid-Victorian England* (1976); J. Vincent, *The Formation of the British Liberal Party* (1976); J. Butt and I. F. Clarke (eds.), *The Victorians and Social Protest* (1973); H. M. Lynd, *England in the Eighteen-Eighties* (1945); M. Richter, *The Politics of Conscience* (1964), an absorbing study of T. H. Green and his times; D. Read, *England, 1868–1914* (1979); and H. Pelling, *Popular Politics and Society in Late Victorian Britain* (1968).

For government and society see K. B. Smellie, *A Hundred Years of British Government* (1951 edn); P. Stansky (ed.), *The Victorian Revolution: Government and Society in Victoria's Britain* (1973); and V. Cromwell, *Revolution or Evolution: British Government in the Nineteenth Century* (1977), which sums up a long historical debate about the mainsprings of governmental action. On public finance and taxation see S. C. Buxton, *Finance and Politics, 1783–1885* (1888).

On the civil service see E. W. Cohen, *The Growth of the British Civil Service, 1780–1938* (1965) and on the Press see, in addition to works mentioned in earlier chapters, P. Hollis, *The Pauper Press* (1970). A link between them is A. V. Dicey, *Lectures on the Relationship Between Law and Public Opinion in England During the Nineteenth Century* (2nd edn, 1914). See also for the first twenty years of *Punch*, A. Briggs and S. Briggs, *Cap and Bell* (1972), with copious illustrations.

For Queen Victoria see Elizabeth Longford, *Victoria R I* (1964) and C. Woodham-Smith's two-volume life, the first volume of which appeared in 1972. See also A. Hardy, *Queen Victoria was Amused* (1976). For Albert see R. Rhodes James, *Albert, Prince Consort* (1983), which should be supplemented by Hermione Hobhouse, *Prince Albert, His Life and Work* (1983). See also W. Ames, *Prince Albert and Victorian Taste* (1967).

For the country see the two-volume work edited by G. E. Mingay, *The Victorian Countryside* (1981); F. M. L. Thompson, *English Landed Society in the Nineteenth Century* (1963); D. Spring, *The English Landed Estate in the Nineteenth Century* (1963); M. Girouard, *The Victorian Country House* (1971); and F. Horn, *Labouring Life in the Victorian Countryside* (1976). C. Chevenix Trench, *The Poacher and the Squire* (1967) and R. Carr, *English Foxhunting: A History* (1976) are relevant for this and earlier chapters, as is D. Clifford, *A History of Garden Design* (1962). For a contrast in approach see D. C. Itzowitz, *Peculiar Privilege: A Social History of English Foxhunting, 1753–1885* (1977) and R. Samuel (ed.), *Village Life and Labour* (1975).

See also G. E. and K. R. Fussell, *The English Countryman, 1500–1900* (1955); R. Jeffries, *Hodge and His Masters* (1880); M. K. Ashby, *Joseph Ashby of Tysoe* (1961); B. Copper, *A Song for Every Season* (1971); and R. Longrigge, *The History of Horse Racing* (1979). For a contemporary account of rural England at the end of Victoria's reign see R. Haggard, *Rural England* (1902). For the imaginative response to nature see U. C. Knoepflmacher and G. B. Tennyson, *Nature and the Victorian Imagination* (1977).

For towns and cities see A. Briggs, *Victorian Cities* (1968 edn); H. J. Dyos and M. Wolff (eds.), *The Victorian City* (2 vols., 1973); P. J. Waller, *Town, City and Nation, 1850–1914* (1983); J. Walvin, *English Urban Life 1776–1851* (1984); D. Fraser, *Urban Politics in Victorian England* (1976); E. P. Hennock, *Fit and Proper Persons* (1973); R. Dennis, *English Industrial Cities of the Nineteenth Century* (1984), an admirable study by a geographer; D. Cannadine, *Lords and Landlords: The Aristocracy and the Towns* (1980); and G. Stedman Jones, *Outcast London* (1971 edn).

On poverty see, in addition to books cited in the list for the next chapter, J. H. Treble, *Urban Poverty in Britain, 1830–1914* (1979); A. Brundage, *The Making of the New Poor Law* (1978); G. Slater, *Poverty and the State* (1930); N. Longmate, *The Workhouse* (1974); and M. E. Rose (ed.), *The Poor and the City: The English Poor Law in its Urban Context, 1834–1914* (1985). C. L. Mowat, *The Charity Organisation Society, 1869 –1913* (1961) explores basic attitudes and actions. It should be read in conjunction with A. F. Young and E. T. Ashton, *British Social Work in the Nineteenth Century* (1956); K. Woodroofe, *From Charity to Social Work* (1962); and B. Kirkman Grey, *Philanthropy and the State* (1908). Fact and fiction are related in P. Keating, *The Working Class in Victorian Fiction* (1970). For a brilliant local study see M. B. Simey, *Charitable Effort in Liverpool in the Nineteenth Century* (1951). See also *Toynbee Hall, The First Hundred Years* (1984), a study which I wrote with Anne Macartney.

J. K. Walton deals with *The English Seaside Resort 1750–1914* (1985), as does J. Walvin in *Beside the Seaside* (1971). See also Walvin's *Leisure and Society, 1830–1950* (1978); P. Bailey, *Leisure and Class in Victorian England* (1978); J. A. R. Pimlott, *The Englishman's Holiday* (1947); and J. Lowerson and J. Myerscough, *Time to Spare in Victorian England* (1977). H. E. Mellor, *Leisure and the Changing City, 1870–1914* (1976) is concerned with

Nottingham. See also R. Mander and J. Mitcheson, *British Music Hall* (1974) and T. Mason, *Association Football and English Society, 1815–1914* (1980).

Town and city planning during the periods covered in this and later chapters is examined in W. Ashworth, *The Genesis of Modern British Planning* (1954); A. Sutcliffe (ed.), *The Rise of Modern Urban Planning, 1800–1914* (1980) and *The Evolution of British Town Planning* (1974); and G. E. Cherry, *Urban Change and Planning: A History of Urban Development in Britain Since 1950* (1972).

For housing see A. S. Wohl, *The Eternal Slum: Housing and Social Policy in Victorian London* (1979); E. Gauldie, *Cruel Habitations* (1974); J. Burnett, *A Social History of Housing, 1815–1970* (1978); S. D. Chapman, *The History of Working Class Housing: A Symposium* (1971); and J. N. Tarn, *Five Per Cent Philanthropy* (1973).

On religion see R. Currie, A. D. Gilbert and H. Horsley, *Churches and Churchgoers: Patterns of Church Attendance in the British Isles since 1700* (1977); W. O. Chadwick, *The Victorian Church,* Vol. I (1966); P. T. Marsh, *The Victorian Church in Decline* (1969); A. D. Gilbert, *Religion and Society in Victorian England: Church, Chapel and Social Change, 1840–1914* (1976); K. Inglis, *Churches and the Working Classes in Victorian England* (1963); K. Heasman, *Evangelicals in Action* (1962); E. R. Fairweather (ed.), *The Oxford Movement* (1964); P. T. Phillips (ed.), *The View from the Pulpit: Victorian Ministers and Society* (1978); H. McLeod, *Class and Religion in the Late Victorian City* (1974); G. Kitson Clark, *Churchmen and the Condition of England, 1832–1855* (1973); I. Sellers, *Nineteenth Century Nonconformity* (1977); R. V. Holt, *The Victorian Contribution to Social Progress in England* (1952); and E. Isikei, *Victorian Quakers* (1970).

V. D. Lipman's *Social History of the Jews in England, 1850–1950* (1954) should be read in conjunction with L. P. Gartner, *The Jewish Immigrant in England, 1870–1914* (1960) and C. Holmes, *Anti-Semitism in British Society, 1876–1939* (1979). See also C. A. Roth, *A History of the Jews in England* (1978 edn).

Religion and science are examined in G. C. Gillespie, *Genesis and Geology* (1951). See also W. Irvine, *Apes, Angels and Victorians* (1955); H. C. Bibby, *T. H. Huxley, Scientist, Humanist and Educator* (1959); and J. Burrow, *Evolution and Society* (1966). D. H. Newsome, *Godliness and Good Learning* (1961) is sensitive and illuminating. So also is T. W. Lacqueur, *Religion and Respectability: Sunday Schools and Working Class Culture* (1975).

On education see J. W. Adamson, *English Education, 1709–1902* (1930); J. Lawson and N. Silver, *A Social History of Education in England* (1973);

A. Digby and P. Searby, *Children, School and Schooling in Nineteenth Century England* (1981); E. C. Mack, *Public Schools and British Opinion since 1860* (1941); J. F. C. Harrison, *Learning and Living, 1790–1860: A Study in the History of the English Adult Education Movement, 1760–1960* (1961); M. Tylecote, *The Mechanics Institutes* (1957); M. Sturt, *The Education of the People* (1967); J. R. de S. Honey, *Tom Brown's Universe* (1977); J. Chandos, *Boys Together* (1984); E. G. Roe, *The Victorian Child* (1959); J. Pinchbeck and M. Hall, *Children in English Society*, Vol. II (1973); W. J. G. Armytage, *Civic Universities* (1954); W. R. Ward, *Victorian Oxford* (1965); and R. Rotblatt, *The Revolution of the Dons* (1968). See also J. Burnett, *Useful Toil* (1974).

On crime and punishment see I. J. Tobias, *Crime and Industrial Society in the Nineteenth Century* (1972); M. Ignatieff, *A Just Measure of Pain; The Penitentiary in the Industrial Revolution* (1978); F. C. Mather, *Public Order in the Age of the Chartists* (1959); G. Moose (ed.), *Police Forces in History* (1985); and V. Bailey (ed.), *Policing and Punishment in Nineteenth Century Britain* (1981).

On morality – fact and myth – see S. Marcus, *The Other Victorians* (1966); R. Pearsall, *Public Purity, Private Shame* (1976); E. Trudgill, *Madonnas and Magdalens* (1976); Judith Walkawitz, *Prostitution and Victorian Society* (1980); A. S. G. Butler, *Portrait of Josephine Butler* (1954); F. K. Prochaska, *Women and Philanthropy in Nineteenth Century England* (1980); I. Clehorne, *Towards Sex Freedom* (1936); and A. McLaren, *Birth Control in Nineteenth Century England* (1978).

The pioneering study by J. A. Banks, *Prosperity and Parenthood* (1954) may be studied within the context of N. Tranter's *Population Since the Industrial Revolution: The Case of England and Wales* (1973); and J. Weeks, *Sex, Politics and Society* (1981). See also J. A. Jackson, *The Irish in Britain* (1963) and L. Lees, *Exiles of Erin* (1979).

On Edwardian England see J. Nowell Smith (ed.), *Edwardian England* (1964); D. Read, *Edwardian England* (1972); and S. L. Hynes, *The Edwardian Turn of Mind* (1968). E. H. Phelps Brown's excellent *The Growth of British Industrial Relations* (1959) is far more wide-ranging than its title suggests: G. R. Searle, *The Quest for National Efficiency, 1899–1914* (1971) is illuminating. Graham Wallas's *Human Nature in Politics* (1908) and C. F. G. Masterman's *The Condition of England* (1909) are essential contemporary reading. So too is M. Pember Reeves, *Round About a Pound a Week* (1913). Paul Thompson's *The Edwardians* (1973) is a pioneering study based on oral history; Henry Pelling's *Social Geography of British Elections 1885–1910* (1967) is a revealing study of the political map; G. Dangerfield, *The Strange Death of Liberal England* (1935) is a brilliant narrative account, though open to criticism for its interpretation; 'Plutocracy', a favourite theme (see Arnold Bennett, Shaw and Galsworthy) is discussed in J. Camplin, *The Rise of the Plutocrats* (1978) and W. D. Rubenstein, *Men of Property* (1980), while poverty, an equally favourite Edwardian theme, is examined in S. Meacham, *A Life Apart: The English Working Class, 1890–1914* (1977). W. J. Braithwaite's *Lloyd George's Ambulance Waggon* (1959) offers fascinating memoirs.

For the Edwardian countryside see M. F. Davies, *Life in an English Village* (1909); G. Bourne, *Change in the Village* (1912); Lord Ernle, *English Farming Past and Present* (1912); F. E. Green, *The Tyranny of the Countryside* (1913); Flora Thompson's classic *Lark Rise to Candleford* (1954 edn); and E. Jones, *An Edwardian Youth* (1956). For towns and cities then and later see A. Briggs, *A History of Birmingham,* Vol. II (1952); H. J. Dyos, *Victorian Suburb: A Study of the Growth of Camberwell* (1961); H. Finer, *Municipal Trading* (1941); H. Laski, W. Ivor Jennings and W. A. Robson (eds.), *A Century of Municipal Progress* (1937); and T. W. Freeman, *The Conurbations of Great Britain* (1959 edn).

E. Cadbury *et al., Women's Work and Wages* (1906) is an interesting contemporary study, as is C. Hamilton, *Marriage as a Trade* (1909). See also Lady Bell, *At The Works* (1909); S. Rowbotham, *Women, Resistance and Revolution* (1972); and M. Vicinus (ed.), *Suffer and Be Still* (1972). The Suffragettes are studied in R. Fulford, *Votes for Women* (1959) and the Anti-Suffragists in B. Harrison, *Separate Spheres* (1978). See also A. Kraditor, *The Ideas of the Women's Suffrage Movement, 1890–1920* (1971). E. Pankhurst, *My Own Story* (1914) deals with the making of a militant and her subsequent actions. D. Gittins, *Fair Sex: Family Size and Structure, 1900–1939* (1982) links this and other chapters.

For the Victorian and Edwardian Empire see, *inter alia,* V. T. Harlow, *The Founding of the Second British Empire* (2 vols., 1952); C. J. Bartlett (ed.), *Britain Pre-eminent* (1969); C. A. G. Bodelson, *Studies in Mid-Victorian Imperialism* (1960); R. Robinson, J. Gallagher and A. Denny, *Africa and the Victorians* (1961); A. P. Thornton, *The Imperial Idea and its Enemies* (1959); J. E. Flint and G. Williams (eds.), *Perspectives of Empire* (1970); P. J. Cain, *Economic Foundations of British Overseas Trade, 1815–1914* (1980); E. J. Hobsbawm, *Industry and Empire* (1970); B. Semmel, *Imperialism and Social Reform* (1960); and R. Shannon, *The Crisis of Imperialism, 1865–1915* (1976). M. Hechter, *Internal Colonialism: The Celtic Fringe in British National Development, 1536–1966* (1975) is stimulating on home perspectives. So too is G. Blainey, *The Tyranny of Distance* (1968) on distant perspectives – the early nineteenth-century view from Australia. J.

Morris, *Pax Britannica* (1968) is a highly readable account, supplemented by her *Farewell the Trumpets* (1976).

CHAPTER II
THE DIVIDES OF WAR

For J. R. Green, Victorian social historian, there was too much military history. In recent years, however, the gap between the work of military historians and social historians has appreciably narrowed. There are some good anthologies covering several centuries, like T. Gilby, *Britain at Arms: A Scrapbook from Queen Anne to the Present Day* (1953); D. Winter, *Death's Men: Soldiers of the Great War* (1978); and C. Lloyd (ed.), *The Englishman and the Sea* (1946). And there are fascinating accounts based on personal experience, like T. Gowing's *A Soldier's Experience* (1900), written at the beginning of what has been described as 'a century of total war', *Private 19022* (Frederic Manning), *Her Privates We* (1930) and S. Leech, *A Voice from the Main Deck* (1944). See also J. C. F. Fuller, *The Conduct of War, 1789–1961* (1961).

For the links between the nineteenth and the twentieth centuries see A. Briggs (ed.), *The Nineteenth Century* (1970); B. Bond, *Victorian Military Campaigns* (1967), which deals with 'little wars'; O. Anderson, *A Liberal State at War* (1967), which deals with the Crimean War; and T. Pakenham, *The Boer War* (1979). I. F. Clarke's *Voices Prophesying War, 1763–1984* (1966) is a stimulating study of war and the imagination.

See also, for specific studies within a general context, B. Bond and I. Roy (eds.), *War and Society* (1975) and J. M. Winter (ed.), *War and Economic Development* (1975).

For the twentieth century see A. J. P. Taylor, *English History, 1914–1945* (1965) and A. Marwick, *Britain in a Century of Total War* (1968). The literature on the two World Wars is immense. Good introductions are C. Falls, *The First World War* (1960); A. J. P. Taylor, *The First World War* (1963); and B. Collier, *A Short History of the Second World War* (1967). See also H. Pelling, *Britain and the Second World War* (1979). Two broadly sweeping views of the war from above, each in six volumes, are presented by D. Lloyd George, *War Memoirs* (1933–6) and W. S. Churchill, *The Second World War* (1948–53). See also, for the politics, Lord Beaverbrook, *Politicians and the War, 1914–1916* (1928) and P. Addison, *The Road to 1945* (1975).

The social history of the First World War is explored in A. Marwick, *The Deluge* (1965), which has a full bibliography. An older study of value is C. E. Playne, *Society at War 1914–1916* (1931), which she followed through in *Britain Holds On 1917, 1918* (1937). See also, for a very particular view, E. Sylvia Pankhurst, *The Home Front: A Mirror to Life* (1932). C. S. Peel's *How We Lived Then, 1914–1918* (1929) is illuminating. J. Williams has more recently dealt with *The Home Fronts, Britain, France and Germany, 1914–1918* (1972); this too includes a bibliography. See also J. Terraine, *Impacts of War, 1914 and 1918* (1970) and K. Burk (ed.), *War and the State* (1982).

M. Moynihan (ed.), *People at War, 1914–1918* (1973) includes interesting contemporary accounts. It should be set alongside some of the better known books like Robert Graves's *Goodbye to All That* (1929); Siegfried Sassoon's *Memoirs of an Infantry Officer* (1930); and Richard Aldington's *Death of a Hero* (1929). Compare H. S. Clapham, *Mud and Khaki* (1929), which conveys a very different impression. Recent books include E. Hiscock, *The Bells of Hell Go Ting-a-Ling-a-Ling* (1976) and J. Campbell, *Into the Cannon's Mouth* (1979).

There is an early local account by H. K. Moore and B. Sayers, *Croydon and the Great War* (1920) and a recent one by a contemporary in J. Munson (ed.), *Echoes of the Great War, the Diary of The Reverend Andrew Clark, 1914–1919* (1985), to which I have written a foreword. See also A. Wilkinson, *The Church of England and the World War* (1980).

For the changing role of women in war (and earlier) see M. J. Fawcett, *The Women's Victory and After* (1920); A. Marwick, *Women at War, 1914–1918* (1977); R. Davies, *Women and Work* (1975) and G. Braybon, *Women Workers in the First World War* (1981).

The influence of the war on attitudes to social policy making is covered in P. B. Johnson, *Land Fit for Heroes* (1968); C. F. G. Masterman, *After the War* (1923); M. Swenarton, *Homes For Heroes: Politics and the Architecture of Early State Housing in Britain* (1981).

For the inter-war years see C. L. Mowat, *Britain Between the Wars* (1955), an excellent survey; R. Graves and A. Hodge, *The Long Week End* (1940); S. Glynn and J. Oxborook, *Inter-War Britain: A Social and Economic History* (1976); and A. J. P. Taylor, *English History, 1914–1945* (1965). See also the Oxford History by J. Stevenson, *British Society, 1914–1945* (1984); J. Stevenson and C. Cook, *The Slump* (1979); J. Raymond (ed.), *The Baldwin Age* (1960); R. Skidelsky, *Politicians and the Slump* (1970); and N. K. Buxton and D. H. Aldcroft (eds.), *British Industry Between the Wars* (1979). There are many books on the general strike, including J. Symon, *The General Strike* (1957); P. Renshaw, *The General Strike* (1975); M. Morris, *The General Strike* (1976); and S. Skelley (ed.), *The General Strike, 1926* (1976). See also R. Charles, *The*

Development of Industrial Relations in Britain, 1911–1939 (1973) and E. Wigham, *Strikes and the Government 1893–1974* (1976).

Contemporary works of interest include W. Greenwood, *Love on the Dole* (1933); J. B. Priestley, *English Journey* (1934); W. Hannington, *Unemployed Struggles* (1936); G. Orwell, *The Road to Wigan Pier* (1937); Pilgrim Trust, *Men Without Work* (1938); E. Wilkinson, *The Town that was Murdered* (1939); and J. Hilton, *Rich Man, Poor Man* (1944). See also M. Muggeridge, *The Thirties* (1940). R. Rhodes James (ed.), *Chips, The Diaries of Sir Henry Channon* (1967) presents a different picture. S. Hynes deals sensitively with *The Auden Generation* (1976). See also F. Gloversmith (ed.), *Class, Culture and Social Class in Britain: A New View of the 1930s* (1980).

The social history of the Second World War is well covered in A. Calder, *The People's War, 1939–45* (1974). See also T. Harrison, *Living Through the Blitz* (1976); N. Longmate, *How We Lived Then* (1971); J. Ellis, *The Sharp End of War* (1982); and the huge anthology edited by D. Flower and J. Reeves, *The War, 1939–1945* (1960). I. McLaine, *Ministry of Morale* (1979) deals with propaganda, explicit and implicit. See also. I. Hamilton (ed.), *The Poetry of War, 1939–1945* (1950). One of the best diaries by a foreigner is M. Panter Downs, *London War Notes, 1939–1945* (1971). S. Briggs, *Smiling Through* (1975), with excellent illustrations, should be supplemented by A. Marwick's *The Home Front* (1976). For a different side of the coin see F. Smillies, *Crime in War Time* (1982).

The Oxford Institute of Statistics, *Studies in War Economy* (1946) is a revealing contemporary book; so also is Mass-Observation, *People in Production* (1942). P. H. J. Gosden, *Education in the Second World War* (1976) is one of a number of retrospective official histories.

C. Barnett's *The Audit of War* (1980) is the most important recent book on the Second World War; link reading between this and Chapters 12 and 13 of this book. The same author also wrote *The Sword Bearers* (1964) and *The Collapse of British Power* (1972). See also, however, A. S. Milward, *The Economic Effects of Two World Wars on Britain* (1977); W. K. Hancock and M. M. Gowing, *British War Economy* (1953); M. M. Gowing, *Britain and Atomic Energy* (1964); and R. M. Titmus, *Birth, Poverty and Wealth* (1943) and *Problems of Social Policy* (1951). Lord Woolton's *Memoirs* (1959) and W. Beveridge, *Power and Influence* (1953) are revealing. So too is Jose Harris's biography, *William Beveridge* (1977) and Beveridge's own *Full Employment in a Free Society* (1944).

CHAPTER 12
POVERTY AND PROGRESS

Perhaps the best lead into this chapter is to read successive books by Seebohm Rowntree, *Poverty, A Study of Town Life* (1901), *Poverty and Progress, A Second Social Survey of York* (1941) and, with G. R. Lavers, *Poverty and the Welfare State* (1951). The last of these dealt only with economic questions; other questions were covered in S. Rowntree and G. R. Lavers, *English Life and Leisure* (1951). The evolution of Rowntree's thought and methodology – and its limitations – are considered in my book, *A Study of the Work of Seebohm Rowntree* (1961), which, in the light of voluminous recent writing on poverty, social surveys and twentieth-century political history, must be supplemented for every chapter: in particular see R. Atkinson's *Poverty and Progress* (1973), with the same title as this chapter; P. Townsend's massive *Poverty in the United Kingdom* (1979); W. G. Runciman's theoretical but highly relevant *Relative Deprivation and Social Justice* (1966); D. Donnison, *The Politics of Poverty* (1982); and P. Barker (ed.), *Founders of the Welfare State* (1984), a series of essays on individuals which considers their social leanings and influences. S. Pollard, *The Development of the British Economy, 1914–1950* (1960) is useful.

Before Rowntree, Charles Booth's seventeen-volume *Life and Labour of the People in London*, which appeared between 1889 and 1903, is examined critically in T. S. and M. B. Simey, *Charles Booth, Social Scientist* (1960). See also H. Llewellyn Smith (ed.), *New Survey of London Life and Labour* (1932). For later surveys see amongst many works M. Abrams, *Social Surveys and Social Action* (1951); A. M. Carr-Saunders and D. Caradog Jones, *A Survey of the Social Structure of England and Wales* (1927; revised edn, 1937); M. Abrams, *The Condition of the British People* (1945); A. M. Carr-Saunders and C. A. Moser, *A Survey of Social Conditions in England and Wales* (1958); G. D. H. Cole, *The Post-War Condition of Britain* (1956), which should be compared with his earlier book, written with his wife, *The Condition of Britain* (1937); and D. C. Marsh, *The Changing Structure of England and Wales* (1965).

See also for the statistics A. R. Prest, *National Income of the United Kingdom, 1870–1946* (1948); A. H. Halsey, *Trends in British Society Since 1900* (1972) and, for his interpretation of them as a sociologist, *Change in British Society* (2nd edn, 1981). See also, for the intellectual and social context, M. Ginsberg (ed.), *Law and Opinion in England in the Twentieth Century* (1959); W. L. Guttsman, *The British Political Élite* (1968); H. Thomas (ed.), *The Establishment* (1959); P. Stanworth and A. Giddens, *Élites and Power in British Society* (1974); and R. T. McKenzie and A. Silver, *Angels in Marble* (1968), a study of working-class conservatism.

For social needs and contingencies see J. Harris, *Unemployment and Politics: A Study in English Social Policy, 1886–1914* (1972); B. S. Rowntree, A. A. Bowley *et al.*, *The Third Winter of Unemployment* (1922); J. Jewkes and A. Winterbottom, *Juvenile Unemployment* (1933); S. Constantine, *Unemployment in Britain Between the Wars* (1980); K. Hawkins, *Unemployment* (3rd edn, 1987); and A. Wilson and J. Mackay, *Old Age Pensions* (1941). Compare J. Boyd Orr, *Food, Health and Income* (1936) with Sir George Godber, *Medical Care: The Changing Needs and Pattern* (1970). See also PEP, *Britain's Health* (1939) and G. C. M. McGonigle and J. Kirby, *Poverty and Public Health* (1936). For housing see, in addition to books cited for other chapters, R. Roberts, *The Classic Slum* (1971); E. D. Simon, *How To Abolish the Slums* (1929); and E. D. Simon and J. Inman, *Rebuilding of Manchester* (1935). The history of building societies is covered in E. J. Cleary, *The Building Society Movement* (1965). F. Allaun, *No Place Like Home* (1972) is a vivid relatively recent statement.

For social mobility the classic study is D. V. Glass (ed.), *Social Mobility in Britain* (1954). See also A. P. Heath, *Social Mobility* (1981).

For social security see W. A. Robson (ed.), *Social Security* (1943) and M. P. Hall, *The Social Services of Modern England* (1952). H. L. Wilenski, *The Welfare State and Equality* (1975) provides useful comparative material, as does G. Rimlinger, *Welfare Policy and Industrialisation* (1971).

For the 'origins' of the 'welfare state' – both terms need examination – see D. Roberts, *Victorian Origins of the Welfare State* (1960) and P. Thane (ed.), *The Origins of British Social Policy* (1978). For later developments in social policy see C. W. Pipkin's neglected *Social Politics and Modern Democracies* (2 vols., 1931); T. H. Marshall's influential *Citizenship and Social Class* (1949) and his *Social Policy* (1965); and R. M. Titmuss's searching *Essays on the Welfare State* (1958). See also Titmuss's *The Irresponsible Society* (1932).

I set out to define the term and chart its history in an essay on 'The Welfare State in Historical Perspective', published in my *Collected Essays*, Vol. II (1985); it has often been reprinted, but the perspectives it presents now look out of date. Attempts have been made to plot the evolution of the welfare state at greater length – they look even more out of date – by M. Bruce, *The Coming of the Welfare State* (1966) and by D. Fraser, *The Evolution of the British Welfare State* (1973). R. C. Birch, *The Making of the Welfare State* (1974) is a useful introductory summary. B. B. Gilbert's *The Evolution of National Insurance in Great Britain: Origins of the Welfare*

State (1966) and his *British Social Policy, 1914–1939* (1970) use primary sources to good effect. A more recent study is W. J. Mommsen (ed.), *The Emergence of the Welfare State in Britain and Germany* (1981). See also J. R. Hay (ed.), *The Development of the British Welfare State 1860–1975* (1978), a collection of documents. For a force in the background see also J. Pinder (ed.), *Fifty Years of Political and Economic Planning* (1981). A Peacock and J. Wiseman, *The Growth of Public Expenditure in the United Kingdom* (1961) is valuable in the light of what came after. See also J. F. Sleeman, *The Welfare State: Its Aims, Benefits and Costs* (1973).

For unplanned developments affecting poverty and progress and their assessment see, *inter alia*, R. Stone, *Measurement of Consumers' Expenditure and Behaviour in the United Kingdom, 1920–1938* (1954); M. and N. Ward, *Home in the Twenties and Thirties* (1978); *The Public and the Pools* (1938); J. and D. Langley Moore, *The Pleasure of Your Company* (1936); C. Willet Cunningham, *Englishwomen's Clothing in the Present Century* (1952); J. B. Jefferys, *Retail Trading in Britain 1850–1950* (1954); P. Mathias, *Retailing Revolution* (1967); H. Pasarmadjian, *The Departmental Store* (1954); A. Adburgham, *Shops and Shopping, 1800–1914* (1964); G. Rees, *St Michael, A History of Marks and Spencer* (1973 edn); and A. Briggs, *Friends of the People* (1956) and *Wine for Sale* (1986). The Advertising Association's annual statistics of advertising expenditure are invaluable.

See also K. Roberts, *Leisure* (1970); J. Minihan, *The Nationalisation of Culture* (1977); R. Low, *The History of the British Cinema, 1929–1939* (1979); R. Armes, *A Cultural History of the British Cinema* (1978); D. Sharp, *The Picture Palace and Other Buildings for the Masses* (1969); M. C. H. Smith, *Paper Voices: the Popular Press and Social Change 1935–1965* (1975); and R. Hughes, *The Shock of the New* (1980).

The valuable Derby survey of local leisure activity by T. Cauter and J. C. Downham bears the somewhat daunting (and misleading) subtitle *The Communication of Ideas* (1954). See also W. H. Beveridge, *Voluntary Action* (1948); R. Hadley and S. Hatch, *Social Welfare and the Failure of the State* (1981); Mass-Observation, *The Pub and the People* (1943); J. Walvin, *The People's Game, A Social History of English Football* (1971); and P E P, *The British Film Industry* (1952).

M. Angeloglou, *Looking Back at Holidays, 1901–1939* (1975) has excellent illustrations with more than a touch of nostalgia. Compare *Mr. Punch and his Travels* (1932).

On religion, B. Wilson's *Contemporary Transformations of Religion* (1976) is important. So also is his *Religion in a Secular Society* (1964). See also G. S. Spinks, *Religion in Britain Since 1900* (1962) and S. Yeo, *Religion and Voluntary Organisations in Crisis* (1976).

CHAPTER 13
ENDS AND BEGINNINGS

In relation to this most recent period of English social history it is most
sensible to build up a personal archive of pieces from newspapers and
magazines: the ephemera count. (I would include in my own file as an
example of a relevant newspaper the whole number of *The Guardian* for
22 May 1986). There is one textbook by A. Marwick, *British Society Since
1945* (1982), which has a useful bibliography. See also J. Ryder and H.
Silver, *Modern English Society* (1970); H. Hopkins's highly readable *The
New Look* (1964); P. Calvocoressi, *The British Experience, 1945–1975*
(1978); and S. Beer, *Modern British Politics* (2nd edn, 1969), which is
concerned with more than politics. See also D. Butler and S. Stokes,
Political Change in Britain (1974) and D. Butler and A. Sloman, *British
Political Facts, 1900–1976* (1980). For one view of the Civil Service see P.
Kellner and Lord Crowther-Hunt, *The Civil Service* (1980). See also P.
Ziegler, *Crown and People* (1979). *Social Trends*, an official publication,
has appeared since 1970; the weekly *New Society* has appeared since 1963.
See also T. Noble, *Modern Britain: Structure and Change* (1975).

For the march of time compare M. Sisson and P. French (eds), *The Age
of Austerity, 1941–1951* (1963) with V. Bogdanor and R. Skidelsky (eds.),
The Age of Affluence (1970); A. Sampson's perceptive *Anatomy of Britain*
(1962) with his 1965 version and his *New Anatomy* (1971); and the brilliant
personal interpretations of the 1960s, C. Booker's *The Necrophiliacs*
(1969) with B. Levin's *Pendulum Years* (1970). For the 1970s, out of a huge
but largely unrewarding literature, see C. Davies, *Permissive Britain*
(1975) and N. Shrapnel, *The Seventies: Britain's Inward March* (1980). See
also the *Guardian* inquiry into *The Permissive Society* (1969) and also
K. Leach, *A Practical Guide to the Drugs Scene* (2nd edn, 1974).

For demographic change and its social impact see R. M. Williams,
British Population (2nd edn, 1978); R. Leite, *Changing Patterns of Family
Formation and Dissolution in England and Wales, 1964–76* (1979); G. Gorer,
Sex and Marriage in England Today (1971); R. Fletcher, *The Family and
Marriage* (1962); C. Rosser and C. G. Harris, *The Family and Social
Change* (1965); M. Young, *Leisure and the Family Life Cycle* (1975) and
Dual Families Reexamined (1976); R. Willmott, *The Symmetrical Family*
(1973); and D. Bull (ed.), *Family Poverty* (1971 edn). There is fascinating
primary material in R. Hall's collection of letters written to Marie Stopes,
Dear Dr Stopes (1978). See also R. and R. N. Rapaport and Z. Strelitz,
Fathers, Mothers and Others (1977). Compare the widely read *The Uses of
Literacy* (1957) by Richard Hoggart with P. Wilmot and M. Young,

Family and Kinship in East London (1957) and *Family and Class in a London Suburb* (1960).

On immigration see, out of a still inadequate literature, S. K. Ruck (ed.), *The West Indian Comes to England* (1960); S. Patterson, *Immigration and Race Relations in Britain, 1960–67* (1969); N. Deakin, *Colour, Citizenship and British Society* (1970); three PEP/PSI surveys in 1966, 1974 and 1984, the last of which, edited by C. Brown, was called *Black and White Britain: The Third PSI Survey*; E. J. B. Rowe, *Colour and Citizenship: A Report on British Race Relations* (1969); the Scarman Report on the Brixton disorders (1982); T. J. Cottle, *Black Testimony* (1978); and P. Mohanti's sensitive *Through Brown Eyes* (1985).

For towns and cities see R. E. Pahl, *Patterns of Urban Life* (1970), *Whose City?* (1970) and *Urbs in Rure* (1965); W. D. C. Wright and D. H. Steward (eds.), *The Exploding City* (1972); B. T. Robson, *Urban Growth* (1973); and A. A. Jackson's *Semi-Detached London* (1973). R. Blythe's *Akenfield* (1969) deals with a Suffolk village; P. Jennings, *The Living Village* (1968) is based on village scrapbooks. See also, amongst many studies of particular villages, I. Littlejohn, *The Sociology of a Cheviot Parish* (1963). P. Ambrose has dealt with social change from 1871 to 1971 in a Sussex village in *The Quiet Revolution* (1974). Compare R. Body, *Agriculture: The Triumph and the Shame* (1983) with M. Shoard, *The Theft of Countryside* (1980).

For the economy see G. Worswick and P. Ady (eds.), *The British Economy, 1945–50* (1952); M. Shanks, *The Stagnant Society* (1961); J. G. R. Dow, *The Management of the British Economy, 1946–1960* (1964); and the two volumes of J. L. Burn, *The Structure of Industry* (1979). Useful case studies include D. Heal, *The Steel Industry in Post-War Britain* (1974), now out of date, and the last volume of Charles Wilson's *History of Unilever, Challenge and Response, 1945–1965* (1968). See also D. H. Aldcraft, *British Transport Since 1914* (1975); R. Kelf-Cohen, *British Nationalisation, 1945–1973* (1973); R. Edwards and H. Townsend, *Business Enterprise* (1958); and G. Turner, *Business in Britain* (1969).

For work and attitudes to work see G. Routh, *Occupation and Pay in Great Britain, 1906–1979* (1980); C. Saunders *et al.*, *Winners and Losers, Pay Patterns in the 1970s* (1977); R. Fraser (ed.), *Work, Twenty Personal Accounts* (1969) and *Work II* (1969); and D. Weir (ed.), *Men and Work in Modern Britain* (1973).

See also K. G. T. C. Knowles's neglected *Strikes* (1952); M. Moran, *The Politics of Industrial Relations* (1977); and R. Benewick and T. Smith (eds.), *Direct Action and Democratic Politics* (1972).

Books on socio-psychology, approached in different ways, include F.

Zweig, *The Worker in an Affluent Society* (1962); G. Gorer, *Exploring English Character* (1960); and T. Harrisson, *Britain Revisited* (1962).

For law and order compare K. Mannheim, *Aspects of Crime in England Between the Wars* (1940) and F. M. McLintock and N. H. Avison, *Crime in England and Wales* (1968). See also B. Whittaker, *The Police in Society* (1979); R. Stevens, *Lawyers and the Courts* (1960); and R. Samuel, *East End Underworld* (1981). L. Radzinowicz and J. King, *The Growth of Crime* (1977) puts English experience in international perspective.

For television and the media see A. Briggs, *Sound and Vision* (1979); L. A. Belsen, *The Impact of Television* (1967); A. Davis, *Television, the First Forty Years* (1976); H. Wheldon's stimulating lecture, *The British Experience in Television* (1976); P. Black, *The Biggest Aspidistra in the World* (1972) and *The Mirror in the Corner* (1972); and A. Smith, *The Shadow in the Cave* (1973).

For older media see J. Sutherland, *Fiction and the British Film Industry* (1957); R. Durgnat, *The Mirror for England: British Movies from Austerity to Affluence* (1970). See also R. Gellatt, *The Fabulous Phonograph* (1965); R. Middleton, *Pop Music and the Blues* (1972); G. Petrie (ed.), *Rock Life* (1974); G. Melly, *Revolt into Style, The Pop Arts in Britain* (1970); L. Ayres, *The Proms* (1968); P. Kidson, P. Murray and P. Thompson, *A History of English Architecture* (1975); R. Hughes, *The Shock of the New* (1980); and F. MacCarthy, *A History of British Design, 1830–1979* (1979). See also M. Biddis, *The Age of the Masses* (1977).

For youth and education see G. A. N. Lowndes, *The Silent Social Revolution* (1937); T. Musgrove, *Youth and the Social Order* (1964); B. Simon, *The Politics of Educational Reform, 1920–1940* (1974); K. Lindsey, *Social Progress and Educational Waste* (1926), an interesting contemporary essay; O. Banks, *The Sociology of Education* (1968); M. Young, *The Rise of the Meritocracy* (1958); J. R. Gillis, *Youth and History* (1974); J. Springhall, *Youth, Empire and Society: British Youth Movements, 1889–1939* (1981); S. Humphries, *Hooligans and Rebels: An Oral History of Working-Class Childhood and Youth* (1981); B. Jackson and S. Marsden, *Education and the Working Class* (1962); G. Mungham, *Working Class Youth Culture* (1976); J. Seabrook, *Working Class Childhood* (1982); J. Kamm, *Hope Deferred, Girls' Education in English History* (1965); J. Gathorne-Hardy, *The Public School Phenomenon* (1977); J. Nuttall, *Bomb Culture* (1968); K. Leech, *Youthquake: The Growth of a Counter Culture* (1973); and R. W. Connell, *Ruling Class, Ruling Culture* (1977).

For 'class' see, above all, I. Reid, *Social Class Differences in Britain* (2nd edn, 1981). Contrast the approaches in T. B. Bottomore, *Classes in Modern Society* (1965); J. Westergaard and H. Reske, *Class in a Capitalist*

Society (1975); J. H. Goldthorpe, D. Lockwood *et al.*, *The Affluent Worker* (3 vols., 1967–9); D. Lockwood, *The Blackcoated Worker* (1958); and F. Field, *Unequal Britain* (1974). J. H. Goldthorpe, *Social Mobility and Class Structure in Modern Britain* (1980) combines empirical and theoretical methods. See also A. Marwick, *Class: Image and Reality in Britain since 1930* (1980); B. Jackson, *Working Class Community* (1968); A. H. Halsey and J. M. Ridge, *Origins and Destinations: Family, Class and Education in Modern Britain* (1980); and D. Wedderburn (ed.), *Poverty, Inequality and Class Structure* (1974). Compare S. Meacham's *A Life Apart*, cited earlier, with T. Blackwell and J. Seabrook, *A World Still to Win: The Reconstruction of the Post-War Working Class* (1985). See also B. Campbell, *Wigan Pier Revisited* (1984).

For recent impressions of England, local and national, see R. Dahrendorf, *The English* (1982); P. Theroux, *The Island by the Sea* (1983); and B. Bainbridge, *English Journey* (1984).

New elements in late-twentieth-century Britain figure prominently if often hazily in P. E. Cleator, *The Robot Era* (1955); E. J. Mishan, *The Costs of Economic Growth* (1969); E. F. Schumacher, *Small is Beautiful* (1974); D. Gabor, *Inventing the Future* (1964); H. Hopkins, *The Numbers Game* (1973); T. Forester (ed.), *The Microelectronics Revolution* (1980); P. Large, *The Microrevolution* (1980); C. Lasch, *The Culture of Narcissism* (1980); Barry Jones, *Sleepers Awake, Technology and the Future of Work* (1982); and D. Howell, *Blind Victory: A Study in Income, Wealth and Power* (1986).

INDEX

FOR THE BEST IN PAPERBACKS, LOOK FOR THE

In every corner of the world, on every subject under the sun, Penguin represents quality and variety – the very best in publishing today.

For complete information about books available from Penguin – including Pelicans, Puffins, Peregrines and Penguin Classics – and how to order them, write to us at the appropriate address below. Please note that for copyright reasons the selection of books varies from country to country.

In the United Kingdom: Please write to *Dept E.P., Penguin Books Ltd, Harmondsworth, Middlesex, UB7 0DA*

In the United States: Please write to *Dept BA, Penguin, 299 Murray Hill Parkway, East Rutherford, New Jersey 07073*

In Canada: Please write to *Penguin Books Canada Ltd, 2801 John Street, Markham, Ontario L3R 1B4*

In Australia: Please write to the *Marketing Department, Penguin Books Australia Ltd, P.O. Box 257, Ringwood, Victoria 3134*

In New Zealand: Please write to the *Marketing Department, Penguin Books (NZ) Ltd, Private Bag, Takapuna, Auckland 9*

In India: Please write to *Penguin Overseas Ltd, 706 Eros Apartments, 56 Nehru Place, New Delhi, 110019*

In Holland: Please write to *Penguin Books Nederland B.V., Postbus 195, NL–1380AD Weesp, Netherlands*

In Germany: Please write to *Penguin Books Ltd, Friedrichstrasse 10–12, D–6000 Frankfurt Main 1, Federal Republic of Germany*

In Spain: Please write to *Longman Penguin España, Calle San Nicolas 15, E–28013 Madrid, Spain*

In France: Please write to *Penguin Books Ltd, 39 Rue de Montmorency, F-75003, Paris, France*

In Japan: Please write to *Longman Penguin Japan Co Ltd, Yamaguchi Building, 2–12–9 Kanda Jimbocho, Chiyoda-Ku, Tokyo 101, Japan*

A CHOICE OF PENGUINS AND PELICANS

The Second World War (6 volumes)   Winston S. Churchill

The definitive history of the cataclysm which swept the world for the second time in thirty years.

1917: The Russian Revolutions and the Origins of Present-Day Communism
Leonard Schapiro

A superb narrative history of one of the greatest episodes in modern history by one of our greatest historians.

Imperial Spain 1496–1716   J. H. Elliot

A brilliant modern study of the sudden rise of a barren and isolated country to be the greatest power on earth, and of its equally sudden decline. 'Outstandingly good' – *Daily Telegraph*

Joan of Arc: The Image of Female Heroism   Marina Warner

'A profound book, about human history in general and the place of women in it' – Christopher Hill

Man and the Natural World: Changing Attitudes in England 1500–1800
Keith Thomas

'A delight to read and a pleasure to own' – Auberon Waugh in the *Sunday Telegraph*

The Making of the English Working Class   E. P. Thompson

Probably the most imaginative – and the most famous – post-war work of English social history.